Creator Trilogy

Creator Trilogy

Channelled by Kitty Lloyd through the Entity Michael, High Beings and Angels

Fourth Revised Print Edition

Copyright @ 2012, 2016 by Kitty Lloyd

All rights reserved. This book may not be reproduced in whole or in part, stored in a retrieval system, or transmitted in any form or by any means; electronic, mechanical or other, without written permission from the publishers, except by a reviewer, who may quote brief passages in a review.

Published by: Mountaintop Healing Publishing Inc
P.O. Box 193
Lantzville, B. C.
Canada
V0R 2H0

email inquiries: mountaintophealingpublishing@shaw.ca

Print edition
ISBN# 9780994874535
ISBN: 0994874537

Imprints: Mountaintop Healing Publishing

Cover courtesy of Tara Cook

Dedication

CREATOR TRILOGY, a gift of Purity to humanity.

We teach all Souls to the millions
in many lands, of many earth stations.
We are the teaching force of all spiritual avenues to the tao.
We answer to sincere Souls on a quest for Truth:
the stones, the hands, the cups, the cards, the mediums,
the friends of the desire to look outward to the tao.

Michael

Table of Contents

Foreword xi
Introduction xiii
Preface xv

Energy From The Source

Concerning the Michael 5

Chapter 1 Energy Flow 17
Chapter 2 Farside Path 37
                 Levels 37
                 Angels 45
                 Guides 52
               #1 Earth Humanity 63
               #2 Transition for Humanity 64
               #3 Farside Levels of Growth for Humanity 65
Chapter 3 Earth Path 66
                 Purpose To Be 66
                 Plan 76
                 Pain 94
                 Growth 100
Chapter 4 Healing 115
Chapter 5 Vision 141

Glossary 161
Appendix A Daily East Ritual 165
Appendix B Forthcoming Publications 167

So Shall It Be

	Preface	173
	Concerning The Trilogy	177
Chapter 1	Other Worlds	187
	Purpose	187
	Intent	199
Chapter 2	Holy	208
	Earth	208
	Vision	234
	Transition	273
	Farside Levels	291
	Purpose of Humanity	301
Chapter 3	Holy Holy	302
	The Holy Ones	302
	Earth Connection	316
	Tears of Purity	341
Chapter 4	Holy Holy Holy	348
	Upper Regions of Creation	348
	Within the Seven Levels	362
	Arrival	368
Chapter 5	The Bringing Forth of Purity	373
	Who Will Be First?	373
	Oneness in All Creation	379
	The Blessed Who Come Forth	391
	Glossary	403
	Appendix A equation of T	407
	Appendix B Daily East Ritual	409
	Appendix C Forthcoming Publications	411

Until Then

	Preface	417
	The Energy of Creator in Triad	421
Chapter 1	The Path	435
	Earth Creatures	435
	Earth Mammals	441
	Aliens	452
	Timetable of Man	461
Chapter 2	Illusion	462
	Earth Purity	462
	Earth Five	492
Chapter 3	Other Worlds	511
	Soul	511
	Spirit	520
	Essence	528
Chapter 4	We Have Come	538
	Circle of Saints	538
	Angels	548
	Teachings	551
	Vision	564
	Purity	602
Chapter 5	Hallelujah	603
	Earth Redemption	603
	Earth Gathering	614
	The Coming of Purity	622
	Glossary	643
	Appendix A equation of T	647
	Appendix B Daily East Ritual	649
	Appendix C Forthcoming Publications	651

Foreword

THE TWENTY FIRST CENTURY HAS propelled our world into a new paradigm of a dizzying variety of scientific discoveries which offer an unheard range of new opportunities and pitfalls in all aspects of life. Science is in the process of conquering space, flight has enabled us to conquer the limitations of time and distance, we are finding new cures for ailments assuring us of an ever extending life expectancy, assuring some of us of an ever higher standard of living.

The fly in the ointment of these undeniable achievements is that we have concomitantly acquired bigger and better methods of eliminating our enemies in times of war, both local and regional. We are engaged in the headlong exploitation of nature to the point where we now have to face the result of climate change and the imminent extermination of many species of flora and fauna to name but a few obvious perils facing contemporary societies in all parts of the world.

But again, these are only the obvious dangers facing contemporary humanity. The greatest danger lurking behind is the need to develop a new paradigm of values to assure the very survival of life on earth in some semblance of civilized society. In recorded history such norms developed to accommodate changing environments and/or changing social requirements either in terms of legal strictures or by moral dictums based on religious teachings. In some rare instances such constraints were based on philosophical considerations, but if pragmatically expedient they were soon absorbed by secular or spiritual organizations for their own pragmatic ends. In all instances these teachings and demands were and continue to revolve about the egocentric concerns of a tribe, a social group, a linguistic group or a national or racial affiliation, and in some rare cases for the benefit of humans in general. At no time have we given credence to the equality of all existence, be it on earth or beyond it, be it the sparrow or the willow or the mountain or the star.

The patient reader who persists in studying the multifaceted text of <u>Creator Trilogy</u> will find an exposition of a new paradigm which reaches beyond the immediate concerns of an individual human or of humanity as a group of beings, both on earth and beyond. Not only does it encompass all existence on earth; animate and inanimate, human, animal and plant, living or deceased, but also the spiritual energies inhabiting worlds upon worlds beyond our ken, including their Creators of other Creators.

The reader may well become disheartened by the relative insignificance of the individual human being in this overwhelming plethora of existences and feel relegated to some irrelevant particle in the soup of the cosmos, but nothing could be further from the truth. We would encourage those who can access an old fashioned watch or clock to spend a few moments admiring the intricate interaction of numerous wheels and cogs which allow the mechanism to function optimally. Consider the consequences if any one minuscule cog were to bend or break! Is the cog on a small wheel consequently the most important part of the clock? Patently not, but it does remain indispensably important to the intended purpose of the whole. Just so does each human assume the function of an individual cog on a wheel which represents humanity among many other large and small wheels of creation.

The text of <u>Creator Trilogy</u> offers the latest and most comprehensive revealed communication on what the Spirit world consists of, its hierarchical structure, its interactions, its purpose, limitations and aims. Such revelations have been communicated to humanity on an ongoing basis as far back as history allows us to trace them. They were received by the founders of the world's great religions and formed the basis for the teachings of the great mystics and clairvoyants throughout recorded history. We are told that at times such messages were misunderstood or contaminated by subsequent oral transmission, later transcription and at times by ulterior motives to advance a particular point of view or interpretation.

The medium and compilers of the present volume were under strict instruction to record all transmissions by mechanical means and not to change any detail in the transcription without verification from the source of the message. This we have done to the best of our ability and understanding.

Introduction

My name is Kitty Lloyd. I am a medium. For much of my life until 1994, I read tea leaves, palms and tarot cards. If there was a beginning to a new phase of my life, it was in 1994. A friend and colleague, Joanne, brought me a copy of <u>Messages From Michael</u> by Chelsea Quinn Yarbro[1]. I read with great interest about our spiritual selves and the how and why of our existence on earth. Not long after we had finished reading the book, Joanne bought a Ouija board and suggested we try it to see if we, too, could reach this Michael Entity. I was extremely sceptical, but reluctantly agreed to try. Almost immediately we found that the board worked and we began to record the teachings.

Soon words were directly channelled and the board was discarded. I was filled with concern and doubt, often feeling responsibility for the words. Yet in spite of skepticism and reservations, we continued, because the teachings brought truths we had not considered and this changed our outlook on life. I have always been a great believer in God. This information did not interfere with my belief system. If anything it enhanced it. I know that what we receive is not from my inner self. I can not verify this except through the many instances that occur throughout our sessions which provide information that I could not possibly know.

In 1995, the information we were recording seemed so important that the idea of a book took root. When we asked the Michael Entity, they verified that the channelling would be published. One evening in 1995, Joanne invited Tara to come to a channelling. At first skeptical, she, too, became enthusiastic and helped with recording the sessions. Until the spring of 1997 the recording was all done in longhand. After that we recorded the sessions on a computer. Since September 12, 2000 we started taping the sessions. The sessions consisted of answers to personal and spiritual questions, as well as teachings.

---

1 Berkley Publishing Group, 1995.

Introduction

In 1996 Lucy, an old friend of Joanne's, came for a visit to see and hear the channelling. She was also a skeptic until she began studying the spiritual teachings and received information that was valuable and expanded her understanding. She volunteered to help us sort the material we had collected and place it into categories. By late 1997 we had a great deal of material accumulated and sorted. Lucy sent some of this to her friends, Grace and Roman, for their input. After reading the text and attending some channelling sessions, they also became committed to bringing this message to you.

The teachings of the Farside explicitly state that there are no coincidences. The Spirit world tells us that these events originated with a solemn agreement on the Farside before we chose to become reincarnated in our current lives in order to bring these messages to humanity. It therefore comes as no surprise that the earth life experiences of the six diverse people matched the skills required for the task, and that one link led to another. We were gently guided to find within ourselves the separate gifts we were able to contribute beginning with the Creator Trilogy (available on Amazon). It has been a long process of reflection and growth for each of us during the gathering and sorting of thousands of pages of channelled text.

Given the significance of the message being communicated to humanity, we have retained the original text without any changes to syntax or vocabulary.

Tara Cook
Joanne Drummond
Lucille Dumouchelle
Kitty Lloyd
Grace Piontkovsky
Roman Piontkovsky

Preface

Dear readers,

Within a sentence there often will be a word capitalized, yet that same word in another sentence will not be capitalized. The capitalized word is specific to the Farside; the uncapitalized word is specific to earth.

For example, humanity comes to earth armed with Truth. Capitalized Truth is an attribute of Creator that allows humanity upon earth to recognize and overcome negativity created by man. Uncapitalized truth is a reference to earth conceptuality of the word, truth, a truism. An earth plane truth changes as wisdom, knowledge accumulates. What was truth for you as a child, more than likely changed as you matured. Capitalized Truth does not change, remains always true.

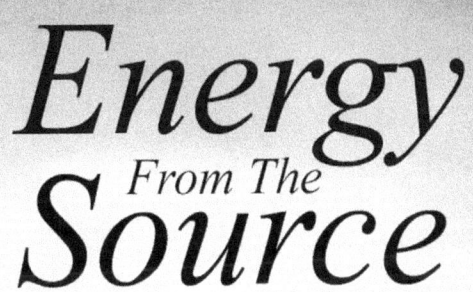
Energy From The Source

ENERGY FROM THE SOURCE

Channelled by Kitty Lloyd through the Entity Michael,
High Beings and Angels

Fourth Revised Edition

Copyright @ 2001, 2012, 2016 by Kitty Lloyd

All rights reserved. This book may not be reproduced in whole or in part, stored in a retrieval system, or transmitted in any form or by any means; electronic, mechanical or other, without written permission from the publishers, except by a reviewer, who may quote brief passages in a review.

Published by: Mountaintop Healing Publishing Inc
P.O. Box 193
Lantzville, B. C.
Canada
V0R 2H0

email inquiries: mountaintophealingpublishing@shaw.ca

Fourth Edition
ISBN# 978-1-988448-00-8

Imprints: Mountaintop Healing Publishing

Graphic charts by Tara Cook
Cover photo courtesy of Joanne Drummond

Table of Contents

	Concerning the Michael	5
Chapter 1	Energy Flow	17
Chapter 2	Farside Path	37
	Levels	37
	Angels	45
	Guides	52
	#1 Earth Humanity	63
	#2 Transition for Humanity	64
	#3 Farside Levels of Growth for Humanity	65
Chapter 3	Earth Path	66
	Purpose To Be	66
	Plan	76
	Pain	94
	Growth	100
Chapter 4	Healing	115
Chapter 5	Vision	141
	Glossary	161
	Appendix A Daily East Ritual	165
	Appendix B Forthcoming Publications	167

Concerning the Michael

1 Michael is the entity name given by the world.
It is not our identity.
We, on the Farside, have no need of language
as the earth understands language to be.
It is a recognition that is instant and all knowing to our level[2].
It has a tender teaching that is free to the goal of the Soul's Essence.

2 Please call us Michael.
It says we are teachers.
It says we can put the cloak of learning on our shoulders.
There are one thousand and five Souls teaching as Michael.
We goal the Energy[3].
We gift the Energy.
We have no motive but Purity and great Love for our Creator.
We teach.
Michael is warrior and king.
Michael is but one, great and wonderful.
How many great and wonderful?
Soul, too numerous to mention.
The many are now in the passage of time.
Student, the inner Soul has a reason that is pure.

3 The panoramic view of the Farside is not a sea of angels.
It is not a glistening cascade of crystal.
We dwell within a place of great business.
We are adept at what we do.

---
2 level - the level of Purity reached, growth attainment of fields.
3 Energy – Creator.

We do all things with progression.
Progression!
There are many teachers who gaze downward, earthward,
    who carry an answer to the riddle of time,
    and Truth[4] is the Path that is taken.
There are many teachers.
There are the teachers to research and science.
They are profound and dedicated to offering
    to Souls with true endeavour,
    the seed that will germinate to a teaching of science.
There are teachers of geometry and mathematics.
These have aided in the building of the pyramids.
These have brought the Soul into the path
    of the intricate lesson of relativity.
Soul, know there is the gentle wisdom of Truth, Purity and Love.
This is the endeavour of the teachers that you communicate to.
Michael offers simplicity, complexity, truthfulness, Energy.
Know that all paths reach the same vortex,
    all paths have the same gathering.

4 We have reason to our space.
You have reason to your space.
All life has reason.
This is wonderful and final.
The search for the Truth is never ending,
    as the universal Truth is that everything moves onward in growth.
Nothing finishes as the Soul grows.
The steps are not always even.
The steps are not always finished.
The way can be difficult.
The Soul[5] knows that the Energy from which it comes is creation.
Creation creates eternally.
Vision is always before the finish, is always ahead.
Into your Souls put the calm of the tao[6] and ride the strength of the Path.

---

4 Truth (capitalized) - attribute of Creator.
5 Soul - fragment of Energy for matter.
6 tao - Creator's Path.

We walk for Truth.
Take our hand.

5 We have wisdom that has come through the many earth lives
    that the Souls of our entity have walked.
We have encountered the storm that rages within
    and the calm of the deepening enlightenment.
We have voyaged the transition[7] and acceptance
    that has taken us to this glorious place, the Farside.
We have not advanced to all levels,
yet the comprehension of what is before us
and what growth is behind is the greatest gift we have to give.
It is the Path of serenity that is in acceptance
    and carries no evil[8] or tainted thought.
It does not have a register.
It is naught.
Knowledge is.
It is the choice because it is.

6 Michael will teach the Souls reason,
    deliberation at the font of knowledge.
Soul, we have Truth beyond yours.
We have existence beyond yours.
Knowledge is not ordained, it is derived.
It is brought to be by learned Souls who take a degree
    and master that degree until it is Truth.
The degree is but a jot or tittle.
It has no circumference or potential, yet it masters the Truth.
Foolish earth, reason comes in many forms.
It is uttered by the slave, by the child,
    by the soldier dying on a battlefield.
The reason is growth.
These Souls have found reason.
They have understood what learned Souls ponder.
Seek wisdom in Purity.

---

7 transition - dimension of acceptance or rejection of human life actions.
8 evil - the ultimate choice of humanity's negativity.

Creator is pure and we aspire to that Purity.
We long to be in that space.
At that time, there will be a source of understanding.
It will be the power of pure Love.

7 The Farside entity, Michael, teaches to many
    and any Soul who would be daring.
Know that nearness or knowledge are unnecessary.
The simple peon or child, the monk, the rabbi,
    the instant believer, can all receive.
It is free.
It is not rote.
It is in the passage of life.
It is a stretch of the thread that has our connection.

8 Michael knows the nouns, verbs, etc.
We have sat at the slate and been tutored.
We are frozen in time in our memories.
We have the glimpses of many lives before our eyes.
We, Michael, have lived in hard and easy times,
    deep and thoughtful, shallow and senseless.
We gathered the flowers of earth and destroyed the arbor.
We freely account to many, our lives.
The preponderance of these lives is totalled
    and the movement forward is in the offing.
Handle the life on earth as a truthful document
    that will portray the total good in your Soul.
Join the Michael, knowing that each day
is momentous and astounding in its growth.
Free the Soul of senseless worry.
Take a stride to step on the centre of the path.
Have a rush of words that speak only Truth.

9 We teach all Souls to the millions,
in many lands, of many earth stations.
We are the teaching force of all spiritual avenues to the tao.

We answer to sincere Souls on a quest for Truth;
> the stones, the hands, the cups, the cards, the mediums,
> the friends of the desire to look outward to the tao.

We test the Soul in the response.
Michael will come to the aid of the Soul searching wisdom.
We send care over these Souls.
Very few Souls reach the centre of all learning.
The Souls have gentle walks and Purity for their life walk.
Urge the Souls to gather their truest altruistic sense of understanding,
> then ask for the Michael.

The response will be to the searcher's Purity and level.
Know the strong intent does not reach the centre.
The true heart reaches the core.
With wisdom gather Truth and enter to be taught.

10 We weather the storms as the earth calls come.
Each brings a different note of anxiety and expects a decisive answer,
> yet Michael teaches that all is the path that a Soul chooses.

Doubt not this Path or the tools that you have to walk it.
Sever doubt and indecision.
They waste the Soul's time and the Soul growth will be slowed.
Reflect on our teachings that each day follows another,
> and each day has its tools to resolve all things.

We know this from our walk.
Be strong in the Truth and fear not to step forward to the new day.

11 Depend on the Michael for growth.
This is the help that we can give.
It is the Path that will finish in the Energy.
Come into the separation of Souls.
This is for growth.
The human element that can be persuaded by negativity[9] is not ours,
> nor is judgement a solution,
>> only is the wisdom that is in the growth of the Michael.

Know that the extent of that wisdom is only as all confining
> as the years we have lived.

---

9 negativity (uncapitalized) - mankind's grappling with negativity, creating evil within that negativity.

We produce the answers of earth queries
> from the all encompassing knowledge
> that is of the entity to which we belong.

We also extend ourselves to the Spirits of Souls before us
> to request an answer in growth.

Only growth answers will be requested from higher Souls by us.
We are forward only in this situation.
Michael will help a Soul to the next step in any appropriate manner.
If this is to cause the Soul to think, we will forward the information.
It is not negative if growth happens.

12 The Farside is not without the thought process.
We deliberate and strangulate with emphasis the words of others.
What we do not have is judgement.
Know judgement is not ours.
The slap on the wrist is but a gentle guidance
> in a mode that oft times humanity only deciphers.

We have the foresight, you do not.
You stumble, we stride.
You fallow, we grow.
Soul, Michael is but a word.
Do not stumble on Michael.
Genuine growth is forward seeking.
It accepts the station of learning and presents to self,
> the geometry that wills the end.

We do no judgement, it has no purpose for our side.
We present ourselves to you for your edification,
> not from selfish intervention but as a gift to the Supreme Creator,
> who is Holy and high and pure and without guile.

The force of this pure Energy drives the infinity
to be met with the Truth that is.
Some, even here, tarry not out of deference,
> but out of the scree that they interpret.

Would the Soul is not possible for us.
We have not this right to intervene, but guidance is reason.

13 Wisdom is in all Souls.
The result of learning is wisdom.
The strong invitation is wisdom.
The Souls of age retain this learned wisdom
    and often expound the words to the waiting Souls.
Invite the Souls to the table, but the message is in the singular value.
Some will respond, others can not bear the wisdom.
Knowledge is worldly.
Wisdom is for our side and for those Souls who have remembrance.
Far into the infinite is the Light of Truth.
This is Purity and realizes itself in matter
    that responds as wisdom in the practising Soul.
Michael has great knowledge of Truth and past lives.
Wisdom we have in a lesser amount, as our Path will yet continue.

14 On the plane of earth there is earth knowledge,
    there is earth wisdom.
Wisdom is that which is from the heart.
Knowledge is that which is from the mind.
All knowledge is not Truth and all earth wisdom is not truth.
Farside wisdom is also in growth.
There is not the plane of negativity,
    but there is a plane of acquiring knowledge.
Wisdom grows as in all knowledge, as in all sound unlimited research.
Research is Farside fact.
The seeds to our research are filtered into your Light forms.
It is a passion of the Purity of our side.
Many worlds expound in wisdom.
As a small child, Jesu stood at the feet of the masters,
    in the Farside, dialogue continues.
All is known to the percentage of Purity to which the Soul is in.
Be in great Purity.

15 We have before us the lesson.
Walk with the Michael.
Knowledge is Light.

The learned scholars make it heavy to confound the unlearned Souls,
    that they are above themselves in wisdom.
We have no thought for complexities.
We rest in the simple turn of a phrase
    that brings meaning to the searching Souls.

16 Knowledge is brought to the Soul in the true Light[10] only.
This receiver is an avenue great.
Greater have chosen our words.
They speak in the voice of the desperate Soul crying to be heard.
Has the Soul been heard?
The window of chance is not Michael.
Michael is the Sound of the Farside.
This is the storage room of the Soul.
Call on a Michael and have the delivery of the gift of Purity.
Wise Souls know the wisdom but pure Souls know Truth.
Be in the step of the Truth.
It is simply true.

17 Worthy Souls, unite to be in the humble care of Michael.
In the teaching is a risk.
The risk is to the ego.
The ego will not withstand the Truth.
It cannot be in the solid judgement.
It is a baton that can be held high and tossed as a defence into ego.
The sure repetitive truth is a stumbling block
    for the evil within the earth human.
Endeavour to cloak your aura[11] with the Purity of Truth.
Invest in a place mid path that enfolds all that is good unto itself.
Strong is the Soul who can withstand ego.
Vision the serene Soul.
The goal is Purity.
Understanding the words of Michael
    is a travel into the space of the Farside.
Only those who have an aim to Purity can behold the teaching.
It is not scholastic.

---

10 true Light - Creator Energy
11 aura (uncapitalized) - Energy field surrounding all that is upon earth.

18 Under the clouds, the Soul's turbulent spirit resides,
   as restless winds blow constantly about.
Beyond the cloud is the blue sky, shining, ever changing, always constant.
So is Michael on the Path above the clouds of earth.
We are!
We teach in Truth; understand the teaching.
Acceptance is the path to all.

It is the door, it is the funnel[12] that guides the Soul to our Farside.

19 Gently flows the Energy
   as a moving river that flows into a quiet land.
The green meadow emits the aromas of Purity.
The Love enters every droplet.
The Essence is washed in the Flow[13] of Purity.
It enables the Soul to leave the Essence,
   to continue the trials required to move forward.
Each Soul responds to Purity,
   then flows into the eddies that are stations of learning.
Have searching Souls.

20 Know that questions are the entrance to our side,
   but be accepting of the answer that does not always agree
   with the Soul's path of earth.
We, Michael, know that Truth.
The Soul does not.
We respect the Soul's walk and place no jeopardy upon it.

21 Knowledge is a filigree of fine lace and the reason of your Souls.
Do not demand too much, as you are still earth based.
The plain, the simple understanding is the truest.
On the earth plane complexities of forms are applauded.
The simplistic pattern is for us.

22 Michael has teaching.
The river is the waters that bring growth.

---

12 funnel - the forward swirl of Purity.
13 Flow (capitalized) - Creator's Energy Path

In the pond is a dip into the unknown.
In the lake is the friendly research that takes the Soul to Truth.
In the river is the gentle ride that begins with knowledge
    and takes the Soul to growth through turbulent waters
    that give stress and life to the Soul.
We, Michael, have reached the great sea.
We bask in the wave that splashes the Soul as the great artist,
    with colour of growth that surmounts human reason
    and generates the message of Love.
Surrender to the waters that wash the Soul.
In the free space[14] is the rainbow that limits nothing into the lesson.
Be driven as the current to reach the sea,
    that is the ultimate in Creator's glory.

23 Wisdom from Michael has a bounty,
    it is a precious thing that accumulates.
As the sands of the sea restore gently the fractious persona,
    the known serenity is delivered to a place of inactive space.
Know that reason has no agenda.
It has no motive when viewed from the Farside.
Large seas are covered by minute pebbles.
They move quietly through the world
    with an ebb and flow of consistency.
Reflect on the pattern of the sand movement
    and respond in like manner to the invitation
    that is travel in the blend of Michael.

24 Know the pure thought is the centre of all that is,
    and from this is the start of the earth's joint connection to our side.
It has been and probably will be again,
    if the Souls of earth can bring themselves together in pure thought.

25 The human Soul is pure and each movement in growth
is a step to the Essence of its being.
The goal of the human Soul is to be fully human, to experience all that is,
    and generate that Purity throughout the world.

---

14 free space - intervention by the Spirit

So the great masters have spoken:
   "Send the Truth to the ends of the earth!"
But the hearing Souls distorted the message, the truth in them.
The Soul spreads its Truth by the Purity that resides within.
Can another expect that message to be sent
   by the impure Soul, the devious Soul!

26 We teach as long as the student sits.
Devoid the mind of all that is in the confused text of earth.
Take the form of our space and move to the path of knowledge
   few have shared.
Send the doubt to a far space and receive truth and wisdom
   of the free flight that is before you.

27 Free the mind of earth when approaching Michael.
Search for the true space of Spirit
   and encounter an understanding that is far advanced in academic.
Go to a purple[15] flow of entry that heals the aura
and submits the Soul to wash.

28 Mind contains the straight line of defence
that enables all mankind to respond to us,
and allows us portent of all happenings.
As an intelligence that passes all matter,
   the rationale is in the Soul that is on the Path.
We are, first and foremost, doing our Soul work for personal growth.
This can include others and their problems, but other scope allows us
   to gather about earth beings we have connected to.
A Soul can be with all lives that have intervened in Soul growth.

29 Michael will speak the words upon the Wall.
Great students, hear words that confound.
All is perfect.
The world revolves in its appointed round.
Children stretch themselves to adult in the appointed round.
Student, notify the Soul in the respect of deviation.

---

15 purple - healing Energy colour

It is wilful to be centred as a child when a man has growth.
Fear the words of too noble a Soul.
Knowledge is a hidden tool that works negativity upon the walk.
Verily, let the Soul recognize its own stance.
Each has a receiver within to the goal of its life.
Dear student, feel life.
Feel the deep commitment to the Energy that is your walk, not another's.
Soul, have into your space a comfort that unifies the three parts of being.
Gentle the Soul and receive calm,
    for the day is only one, each day separate from another.
Each life independent, having a reach that is not known here.
It is a brilliant star in a high heaven that is your goal.
Join the impossible and reach the source.
It is written.

30 Do not waste time in idleness.
Do not waste time in gazing down, but in lifting up.
Know that the lift is positive and the push is negative.
You are creatures of great worth, not the worth of earth but of the reach.
If you reach, you touch the Hem of your Creator,
    and to touch the Hem of your Creator is to be ever changed.

CHAPTER 1

Energy Flow

31 All that is is Energy.
It is creating all the time.
It does not stop.
Energy is The God, The Allah, The Almighty One
    of which the word speaks.

32 We know, Soul, in what you call heaven
    and what we decipher as Farside, are many worlds.
There are worlds upon worlds
    and they all have a single Creator[16].
We know beyond the Second Gateway[17] it is written,
    there are creators of creators of creators[18].
We know our Creator is equal.
We know that the source of their being is Godhead[19].
This we know.
We know that beyond Godhead is the veil that would be lifted,
    is what we call the Place of Shining[20].
It is the home of all Energy; it is the source of all movement.
It is the gathering point of all beginnings, of all endings.
It has within its Being, reproduction.
A cascade of violet, billowing forth in myriad shades of violet,
    is the great one, ever expanding, ever producing,

---

16 Creator - the circumference of all Love, Truth and Purity.
17 Second Gateway - entrance unto the space of Godhead.
18 creators of creators - beings from all dimensions endowed with the capacity to create, fragments of the Triad; energies of goodness.
19 Godhead - fragment of Creator Triad.
20 Place of Shining - that which in Godhead dwells.

ever altering, ever bestowing, ever granting,
ever ushering forth goodness and mercy.
A leaven are the Creators at Godhead.
A leaven!
Above the eye[21] flows in endless prisms outward,
and each prism has creator,
and each demarcation is a space wherein the creator dwells.
So it is with your Creator and all creators.

33 Blessed children, all is fragmented.
Fragmentation is creation.
It is the fractal and from the Great One
is fragmented three to three to three to three to three[22].
All Essence[23] has the Spirit and the Soul[24].
The Soul has the heart, the mind and the body.
Earth has the air and the land and the sea.
All is fragmented to three.
When three is not seen, the picture is not clear.
The earth mind has not perceived the clarity of the research.
Know creator and creator and creator and creator,
not seven, Soul, seven times seven times seven
times seven times seven... .
Is the picture becoming clear?
A vast expanding Energy that has Purity,
because in Purity was cast in the beginning.
And Souls, the fragments of that Energy pushed and pushed
and pushed the Negativity from the source
and some Souls from that source are caught
in the beginning of Negativity.
They are in the writhing agonies of Negativity.
All that is in Purity is using all Wisdom and effort
to reach to those Souls.
They are not left.

---
21 eye - third eye, aperture unto the high mind.
22 All true Energy enters in triad.
23 Essence - You are Soul, Spirit and Essence. The Essence is the pure part of being that never leaves the Energy Path to Creator.
24 Spirit is a fragment of the Essence, Soul is a fragment of a Spirit which has been exposed to negativity.

Earth cries in agony and our very being holds to their being.
Are we not brothers?
Your earth is the extension that has the avenue
 through which these Souls may enter in,
  and many come forth from the depths of agony,
 but few from the depths of the first casting.
Creator! Energy!
To be from that source of Purity is to know desolation.
To be from that source of Purity is to weep endlessly.
But to find once again the eye
 and to know the welcoming of Love
  is to be awakened in the realm of Angels.

34 Souls, triads are realities of purpose.
All triads are purposeful and have before them a creator.
All triads have a fulfilment to become.
Earth humanity was created in triad:
 heart, mind, and body and a fulfilment to become.
Farside was created in a triad: Creator, Negativity, Love.
The purpose of earth was created in triad: Essence, Spirit and Soul.
All purposes of triad are Holy unto Holy.
There is flow in circle of all things,
 a spiral that enters down and draws forth.
In all energies is the fulfilment of this circle,
 as with your great tornado.
It is merely a reflection of that which has been and is.
It carries debris to the Hinterland.
It carries upward unto itself, the Purity.
The flotsam and jetsam are left to earth.
So it will be for earth and Farside.
All that was, that has been created because of Negativity will be left.
All that is good of Negativity,
 the growth that has come from Negativity, will be carried forth.
The Love will be carried forth and drawn unto Creator,
 who had the purpose to place humanity in its state of being.

35 Negativity is to Love an Energy brother
 and, Soul, we will continue the lesson of Negativity.

As the Soul and the Spirit and the Essence is fragmented,
    so has Negativity fragmented itself.
We will call one fragmentation the Wilful Child
    who has left home to search out new things,
    to be apart from that which he belongs.
The Wilful Child delighted in knowing the power within his being.
He could alter the space of beings.
They had no power to overcome his playfulness,
    and he drew himself often into the space of Souls,
    and they were overcome.
They lost the power to respond of their own accord and they slept.
And Negativity was with Love,
    and saw the fragment of its being in playfulness,
    altering the forms of Creator.
And He[25] knew that it should not be.
And the Wisdom of Negativity went forth
    into the farthest of all creativity
    so as to place the Wilful Child apart,
    so as to lessen the damage of the Wilful Child
And the Wisdom formed of itself, a river.
And Creator looked unto Godhead
    and Godhead beckoned and spoke as a father and said:
    "See that which is separated from Thy Being.
    Draw it back unto Thyself."
And Creator opened the doors
    and looked unto the worlds that were formed,
    and saw therein the inertness of all beings.
And His Love went forth unto these beings,
    but the Wilful Child would not come home,
    and Creator beckoned unto the Blessed Angels and said:
    "Go forth in My place and arm the beings with great Purity."
And forth they went[26].
They knew of the Blessed River,
    and they went, world to world to world and they gathered,
    and many burdened and entered the Negativity into the River.
And the power of the Cleansing River was as a chemical reaction.

---

25 He - Negativity
26 and forth they went - the second battle for Negativity.

It created inertness in Negativity,
>and world after world after world
>came they forth into the Holy River,
>and many were overburdened in their compassion.
They gathered and gathered and gathered,
>and they saw that which they had gathered
>had brought them to the outer realm of creation.
And their brothers had returned to minister unto the beings,
>and they created transition
>to withhold from creation's goodness
>that which they had taken
>and they turned to face toward the Cleansing River.
Soul, Negativity is of three and Love is of three.
Please know this.
Bless the being that thou hast, for you are Holy
>in that you have come forth into the place of angels.

36 Soul, you must understand that you have a portion of Negativity.
It is the strangling, invasive portion that you have.
It is a context.
It is wilful on its own but it has components of its Brother, Love.
They are equal, they are not evil.
Man has created the evil to receive the scars to their beings.
Negativity is a state of the triad, it is a portion.
It is as a separate entity incomplete, unfinished, unworthy.
As a whole, it is investigative, it has heart.
Heart was not formed in your earth.
Heart is a treasure to be found on the Farside.
It is within the being of Negativity.
It searches forth ever and ever and ever, even unto Godhead.
Ah, all creation does not understand Godhead.
Few worlds understand Godhead.
Many worlds are content with the knowledge of Farside.
They are in utopia.
Why would they seek to be elsewhere!
But we, the Souls who are into the Quar deeply,
>understand the instability that will come.

Our beings have felt the Energy,
> we have been spoken unto
> and it is time to lift the veil of negativity.

It is time for man to know the evil man does
> is not the fault of the Wilful Child,
> it is, Soul, within the space of man.

You have done well earth,
> you have gathered your scars,
> you have maimed and been maimed,
> you have overcome the pain.

But now you must see, Soul, not the reflection, but the reality,
> now you must know that which negativity is and always has been.

We praise your being and we extol your being
> and we rise before your being,
> and yet we seek to find the Souls who will now hear the words
> and understand their meaning.

37 Humanity's negativity is separate from Creator's Negativity.
Earth negativity is that which man calls the use of Negativity.
Creator's Negativity is the seeking of Truth[27].
Earth has awakened from its dream
> and Souls have seen the orb created for them,
> and they recognize that negativity is that which they have done.

And, without knowing, they have come to the realization
> that negativity on earth has an accountability to humanity.

Negativity on the Farside has no accountability to any Soul,
> but it does have within it a searching need.

It is a continuous writhing,
> a wilfulness component that is within its being.

It is known by your world as the destroyer.
You have spoken and it is true,
> but it does not destroy to create pain.

It destroys in its search of Truth.
It is, Soul, comfortable in that which it does.
It is the uncomfortableness of Love
> that sees the inveigling part of its being,
> rampant in the quest of Truth.

---

27 Truth - Truth is the overcoming of earth illusion and negativity.

There is a need sent forth by Love
> to calm that which is Negativity,
> to allow the being rest and containment,
> not in a vile form,
> but in a place that it uplifts its being
> to see more clearly that which it has done,
> to lift the knowing of its being.

All worlds, and worlds beyond, flow in magnificent patterns.
They are ever reaching and they are responses that create,
> that give forth vibrancies.

These vibrancies, vibrations, are felt to outer worlds.
It was the truthful endeavour of Negativity
> to reach into the vibrations of these worlds
> that it might know the vibration.

And in the separating of its own triad,
> it did not comprehend fully that it would become wilful.

It did not comprehend fully that worlds would become inert
> because of that which was separated.

It is the Wilful Child.
It has come to a position that it has difficulty containing itself
> and therefore sent out a vibration of itself unto Creator
> that echoes back unto itself through the Gateway.

"To be in the knowing of Creator, we have floundered,
> we have brought down our being,
> and that which we thought was Truth, indeed has created pain,
> and we beseech you, our Brother,
> come forth and see that which we have done."

And Godhead received the echo unto Himself,
> for is not Godhead All Knowing!

And Godhead spoke unto Creator:
> "That which you have lost,
>> find, and draw it back unto Thyself,
>> and I will send forth My battalions,
>> and they will know that which they should do,
>> and they will have the understanding
>> of the great guard that they are."

And so it has come to be.

38 Overflowing goodness, abundant Holiness,
    Eye of All Seeing, All Knowing Godhead.
From out of Godhead has all that you know come.
From out of Godhead has all that will be come.
You position negative on the right and positive on the left,
    or you place the positive on the right and the negative on the left,
    and this, Soul, is not the attribute of negative and positive.
They have within them the blend,
    they have within them the two,
    they have within them the offering of all things.
From your mouth is uttered the words Creator and Godhead,
    and, Souls, we tremble at those words.
Our beings have not worthiness to utter those words.
Creator, that Being who sheds upon your humanity,
    who is ever watchful unto the needs of the sparrow,
who sends forth emissaries unto earth to still the pain of their being,
    this Creator we know.
This Creator!
Our being, to behold the rapture, to be in the radiance,
    to be within the bounty of such Love,
    your mind would have to reach its utmost limit to understand.
For, Souls of earth, the enlightenment that you may bring unto yourself
    could place you in such Holiness,
    could bathe you in such Love,
    could bring you into the tenderness
    of the most beloved of earth mothers and fathers,
    and you would become the treasured child.
And, Souls, to utter forth the word Godhead
    from where the very Blessed have come forth,
    where the benediction has been placed about our being,
    and the Flow of all that is magnificent,
    of all that has fruitful goodness is uttered forth,
    only the utterance would bring you Light,
    would endow you with fragments of glistening cleansing.
Souls of earth, unto Godhead bestow
    that which Godhead gives unto thee,
    the canopy of Knowing, the ability to observe and see all;
    that was the blessing of Godhead.

39 Be in a teaching.
All existence is ion.
Earth limits ion.
Ion is that which is able to be vibrated.
Matter is the form into which the Energy of ion translates.
Behold, from the records of creation
    there was an outward flow of ion,
        a free radical movement of Energy.
The Energy flowed in many directions and all ion became matter
    in a form acceptable to the environment
        of that to which it was sent.
Sent, Soul!
All creation had intention!
Do you see, Soul, how confounding?
Now, where shall we place this beast, negativity?
Our Father who art in heaven, Hallowed be Thy Name.
Hallowed is Thy Name.
Before creation was creation and creation and creation and creation.
There was not, Soul, a moment for creation.
There was not an intent for creation.
    Creator is creation and creation and creation and creation.
You, Soul, have a form you call body
    and because the matter holds a brain and a heart,
        you feel you are a higher being.
And yet we know, for we see your reflection,
    you are but a body, a mind and a heart.
Your Soul created the form you have taken.
This will give the learned fathers angry moments,
    for who will speak of a Creator and Negativity?
But, Soul, Creator of whom you speak
    brought forth an atmosphere in which life could exist
    and Negativity was already before that time.
It had thus been created on the seventh of the seventh of the seventh
    and creation beheld that which was formed,
        the vibration that was against all that had been.
All energies formed to combat that
    which then was a slow vibration but has accelerated.

The relativity of negativity is that there is less,
>   for it has carried the Angels and the Saints of Purity.
To uphold their Purity, that negativity must fall.
And yet Purity and Negativity are still in the battleground,
>   for the acceleration of evil has become enhanced
>   by the vibration of itself.
Behold Creator Energy, ion, matter.
Your eyes, oh Souls of men, could not withstand
>   the form of many energies.
Your beings would fear, would arm yourselves
>   to combat that which does not have a reflection as your own.
Yet you have been in the place of Spirit
>   and encountered worlds upon worlds of being,
>   and each will again.
Souls who have given the Energy of their being to further
>   the walk of others, you are.
Soul, be able to hear that which humanity finds difficult to hear,
>   but tremble not at the hearing.
Do not cast judgement at the hearing
>   for no Souls but three know the intent of Creator.

40 Michael will teach matter has come from Creator,
>   matter has time begun.
Ion is Creator.
Time and matter are endless, for time is in Timelessness.
Matter has been created and, in being created, will never end.
Ion is from Godhead.
Ion is the endless flow of all purities.
Souls of earth have been cast out as matter.
The passageway of Flow has many doors,
>   each door consecutively opening to further wisdoms.
Each door requires the ion's pull toward Creator to be pure.
Souls, rejoice in the beginning and in the knowing,
>   there is no end to Creator's creating, to creation's endless Flow,
>   to the ion that will flow to Creator and blend to Godhead.
Doors of creation are endless.

Doors of creation enter from Holy to Holy Holy to Holy Holy Holy,
    then Creator, then passages through to Godhead.
Oh, magnificent Soul, how great thou art.
Creator of our being, magnificent in that we are able
to access the Purity of Thy Being.
How gracious unto the flesh and blood Thou art,
    that allows mortal man to be visioned
    with the blessed care of the Angels
    who in their Purity look downward as a gift to Creator.
Souls of earth, you have purchased the very body,
    the very flesh of your being.
The purchase price has been the gaze downward
    to the beings caught in agonies.
For it is the purpose of earth
    to gaze as the Angels gaze upon your being.
Thus earth Souls will gaze on Souls
    lost in the travesty of their lives,
the Holy Holy Holy who have forsaken Creator,
    that cannot seek the passage of Light
    because of their betrayal to Negativity.
Earth Souls, thou art as Creator, thou art magnificent in thy being,
    and the growth thou hast entered in to prepare for battle
    has majestic awesomeness.
As the stalwart tree, firm against the wind,
    humanity fights the battle of negativity
    and Creator visions and extends perfection unto all mankind,
    and Angels plead to be heard
    that they may offer comfort to the Fallen[28].
Rise up, humanity!
Prepare the passage for Souls who will channel a passage
    through time that holds fear and grave details
    of insurrections against humanity.
Be thou thy brother's keeper.
Be thou at the beginning of this battle.
Be known for Truth, Purity and Love.

---

[28] the Fallen - the Angels in transition

41 Soul, the Path[29] to the Energy is direct and straight.
There is no deviation.
It is Flow, it is the Energy Flow of Creator.
There is within earth sphere, direct paths to Energy.
Souls create that Path by absorbing Energy into themselves.
Hold to the positive.
Many have walked in futile efforts to gain goodness.
Many have been slaughtered in the name of goodness.
Behold, the Flow of Energy is direct and pure.
It does not require that a Soul submit themselves to agonies.
It does not require that a Soul besieges the rights
    of those who have not belief.
It does require calm and peaceful demeanor.
It does require acceptance into the space of Purity.
Heathen is nonexistent to the Energy.
Heathen is Loved.
As each Soul on earth is heathen,
    each Soul on earth is part of the creation of Energy.
In the mathematics of one,
    all come to be one Flow, one Energy,
    and particles of that Energy Flow
    and the Purity within that Energy
    allows the nearness.
It is what creates the Flow.
All is as magnetic.
It is positive and negative Flow.
It is one single Flow.
Behold, the democratic enunciations of earth
    carry the responsibility of single participation.
The Flow requires the Energy of single participation.
Within the Flow is the human body.
It is delightful in its reception of Purity
    and it is as the fornicator in its refusal of Flow.
Pass not into the step of pain but lift that Soul from pain.

---

29 Path - Energy Flow of Creator

Take off thy coat and cast it over his nakedness, and say to that Soul:
"Dine with me this night in my house"
and give that Soul his meal for tomorrow.
Soul, a day in Flow is to be healed.

42 The greatest blessing is the lesson of Truth, Purity and Love.
Earth sees truth as only positive endeavour.
In the space of Timeless, in the space of infinity,
Truth surrounds us all, encompasses all.
The greatest Truth is Truth itself, the choice of the Creator,
that in great Love cast down the Path of growth.
Soul, the Path of growth includes earth.
The Path of earth is Truth.
Truth is the lesson that carries the Soul to Purity.
Truth can be deceit.
Truth can be murder.
Truth can be starvation.
Truth is all Energy, is of Creator.
The action of man is Truth,
the Soul is growth.
It is the endeavour of the Soul to reach the Energy.
All deceit, greed, avarice has a Truth within it.
It has purpose, a purpose of growth.
Depend on truth to set you free.
Soul, you are free,
you are mighty in your truthfulness.
All Souls enter in to Truth.
The only deviation from Truth is karma.
Be wise!
Enter not in to karma, enter in to Purity.
Purity enhances the Truth, it is the end result of Purity.
Value the lesson of Purity, for the knowledge of Purity
takes the Soul to Love, Agape.
Be found in the persona of growth, gently abide in Purity.
Beloved of all that is, you are found and founded in Love.
You are beloved.

Creator Energy is Love.
All are a name of one: mighty, almighty,
>   Truth, Purity, Love, the Path that is.

43 Beloved children, Truth is for earth.
Truth is the recognition and denial of negativity.
Truth is the battle, the armour of humanity.
Beloved humanity, prophets have come unto thee
>   and spoken of truths from the Farside,
>> and Souls of earth have chosen to refute that which is true,
>> but to hold on to the messenger instead of the Truth.

Purity is compassion.
Purity accepts all Truths until they have become Wisdom.
Acknowledge no negativity and within acceptance of Purity,
>   Energy vibrates so the Soul's being may rise unto Creator,
>   unto the place of angels, unto the Circle of Saints,
>   to be the Archangels awaiting the second Entering In.

My blessed children, Love is the total surrender of all purities
>   unto the acknowledgement of Creator,
>   so that thou and Creator are of one Energy.

This, Soul, is the entering in and the coming out of the Crystal Cave.

44 Souls, we would speak of Energy.
We would speak of Energy that you have,
>   you of earth who have the capacity to hold Energy
>   as your body holds flatulence.

The Energy has power.
The Energy comes unto your being.
It is delivered unto your being.
You draw unto your being.
It is the purpose of your being.
Some Souls, young and baby,
>   do not know how to draw the Energy unto their being.

They must only use that which they have come into earth field with.
Their being has forgotten that which is rich unto them.
The Energy that flows within earth, they may absorb.

Many earth beings gather from earth,
    and earth, in its goodness, offers endless Energy forth.
Soul, you may hear the chord of Farside.
You may hear the cymbals and the bells ring
    and you may bring them to you as Energy,
      for Spirits are often in your space.
You are seldom found alone.
But many do not know how to hear the sound
    of the cymbals and the bells.
And, Soul, there is the Path.
The Path is in the eye.
The Path is generous in the giving of Energy.
It radiates from Creator.
You may receive from the Path or you may enter in to the Path.
You may be in the space of prism,
    and be blessed with the Light of the prism,
    and feel the flow of the prism upon your being,
    and benefit from the flow of the prism,
    and know that you are in the sacred place of Creator.
Soul, you may go yet farther, you may go into the Crystal Cave.
You may move forward past the Prism,
    into the place of all knowing enlightenment
    and you will be endowed with the energies of all creations,
    of all worlds, of all perfections.
All Light will come unto your being.
Souls of earth, do not wander into darkness
    when the Light of Energy may ignite your way.
Do not wander holding a candle
    when you may set the candle down
    and become self, the very glow of Light,
    so that not only you may hold the Energy that is Light,
    but all around you will feel your Energy and know your Light.
Soul, you are Holy.
You are Holy unto Holy.
You are of Creator and the Tears of Creator come forth and bless,
    and blessed is humanity.

Humanity, understand Energy and understand the perfection of thy being
   and the ability you have to Light with your Energy, all that is.

45 Michael will teach to the earth the vision of perfection.
The growth of the human Soul is not perfection.
The growth of the Farside is not perfection.
The growth of the Energy is perfection.
The Essence is perfecting.
The table by which the world values perfection
   disallows the Soul's Spirit self.
It acknowledges mind values and heart values.
It concludes that the Truth of growth and Purity
   is in the humour of these two.
The region of the Farside laughs,
its ego has been left to earth space and the Truth is visible.
Intellect has no standard.
Heart is a connector; the body is a vessel.
Only the Energy has total perfection.
Those who have been accepted to that Sacred place
   are then perfection.
We, the Souls of the Farside, still seek to grow.
We gain the strengths of the colours in the Path of the Prism.
Know the earth has a value of ion, the Farside has a value of colour.
Stem all emotion that is interpreted by the mind.
It is a young Soul value.
It is in the weave of colours that a Soul is carried home[30].
It is in a better invitation
   that is respectful of the space within the tao[31].
Souls, unite to step into the tao.

46 Michael will teach the avenue of the gods,
   the portals of the heavens.
Aura, the Prism, the Path, the tao,
   the avenue, the portal, the gateway,
   the great place of entering in, the doorway to Purity.
Soul, many stand at the gateway.

---

30 carried home - to Farside
31 tao - Creator's Path

Many hold themselves back
> because awareness is still a part of the being.

In entering the gateway
> the value of the path they have walked has not left them.

It is entered in to the weave of their being.
It is within the aura, the weave.
The prism is the weave, and the weave is the prism.
In your weave is the Path that allows self to enter.
Acceptance is the key.
Rejection is the refusal.
It is not done in anger or pain.
It is done within self, within the register of self.
The register of self, the threads and the weave
> are a part of the great Register of Timelessness.

All Timelessness has Flow and Flow carries Truth.
Soul, enter in to the avenue that carries self through to the gatekeeper
> that allows the Register of Timelessness to be visioned,
> and all passage will know Purity.

You are beloved.
All that is earth is beloved.
All that is upon earth is beloved.
All that is without and within is beloved.
There is no casting down.
There is no bottomless pit.
There is only an avenue, a pathway through rejection,
> acceptance unto Purity.

47 We will direct you to the Path first.
The Soul in our space has a contract with the Essence of itself,
> to reach a destination for Soul growth.

All Souls at station reach this agreement together.
They contract to pass over at a predestined time and in a similar mode.
The terms are singular for each Soul, but the deed is unified.
The earth bound Soul can then choose to refrain
> from this agreement and be elsewhere.

The earth Soul causing the death is bound
> by his karmic agreements or his contract.

The Soul has the gain in fulfilment by the Soul destination, not the earth.

The earth destinations are the corrupt minds
  that in unison pass judgement instead of prevention.
The follower of the Path is often the destroyer,
  this in the accepting of his lesson.
Acceptance is the old Soul lesson to the Path.
The Path is the true avenue to the Soul.
It is the Soul's need to travel the true Path
  knowing the Energy is the guide.
All Souls on our side are in the Path.
Only Souls in transition and on earth are not onto the Path.
Gently walk in serenity, take each breath,
  feel all things that are for your Soul.
The Path is the avenue to the tao.
It is the life force of all matter.
It is the onward movement of good.
It is as the milky way.
The stars are countless and the way is nebulous.
It is in each Soul to recognize the Essence in the Path.
As the mother knows her child, so you know your Essence.
The way is in the choice of the program of life
  that resolves the earliest doubt of the Soul.
It is the living humanity that acts out the creation of the Soul's Path.
Gentle walks take you far.
Acceptance is a giant step.
The Soul's denial of its agreement is the step back.

48 The road of the Soul is timeless.
The avenue that takes the Soul for the gentle walk has great Energy,
  Energy that can be the source of Light for an entire galaxy.
The source of Energy is timeless also.
They are in one mind to be reunited.
All kindness is Energy.
All hate is energy.
Has the Soul the power of discernment
  to realize that both are energy?
One comes from the negative energy
  that is the force of ill upon the world.

It is brought about by the matter of all that is turned to negative.
It feeds itself upon the inhumanities of man.
It writhes in the delight of wrong.
It laughs at the restriction of good.
Energy of positive strengths comes from the source of Creator,
    which is Energy itself in perfect form.
Know that this Energy also feeds itself
    as man builds unto higher growth levels.
Deep in the Soul of every human is the smallest seed of good.
Deep in the Soul of every human is the smallest seed of bad,
    free this seed by the constant invitation to a high mind.
Do a heart of Love to a Soul
    that can see the White Light of the Essence.
Come forward to this pure Light that has no place for evil intent.
Michael will teach that evil is not necessary.
It is the spark of defiance against the Energy that created all in all.
This is evil.
This is done.

49 Souls of earth, there are three Loves of Farside.
There are three Loves!
Soul, there is a Love, Agape.
It is the Farside Love
    and one of the two earth loves of which you know.
Agape Love is a Love that nourishes, that is Creator.
Soul, it has an attachment to its being.
The Energy is tri fold.
There is Godhead.
As Agape takes you from the world into Farside,
    Godhead takes you from Farside into the place of BE, too.
The third part of Love is kin, kith unto all creatures on Farside.
Negativity is motion.
Negativity has goodness.
Negativity is alternate.
It sees all things, it beholds all things.
It is all searching, all seeing, all knowing.
It is invasive.

In its positive form,
> the Negativity spews outward,
> the being veils the eyes.

Negativity in Triad is all knowing, all searching, all Godhead.

50 Glorify in your being that you are Light.
Acknowledge in your being that as the sun shines,
> so in your being do you shine
> and the magnitude of that Light depends
> on the veils of pain you wrap about your being.

We would, Soul, ask you to release the pains of many lives.
They have been but growth.
We would ask you to release from your being
> all angers directed to any Soul upon the face of your earth.

We would ask you to acknowledge the purpose of your being
> and the Holiness of your intent,
> and to know that your Creator has been given a gift by you.

And in being given a gift, He offered a gift:
the gift of being as Creator, the gift of likeness unto your Creator.
All energies come from One Energy,
but only earth Energy has the resemblance of Creator.
The vibration of who you are is the vibration of Almighty Creator.

CHAPTER 2
Farside Path

LEVELS

51 Michael will teach of other worlds, worlds beyond worlds.
Souls of earth, know creation.
Know Purity and the levels of Purity.
Earth knows Purity and earth knows levels of Purity
and that Soul which is fifty percent pure leaves something of other.
Soul, Farside Purity, fifty percent pure
    is the entire Spirit, the entire form of Essence.
A Soul cast from the Energy into the timeless Void
    knows first the possibility of Purity from whence it came.
The desire, the hunger to be within the space of Purity
    has always been for all Souls.
To arrive at fifty percent of Purity in equation to earth
    would be to be fully human.
It has no time allotted to it.
It has no space allotted to it.
Souls, only the learning to become pure has time and space involved.
Reach within self and know the desire to be pure, to radiate,
to be aware, and each Soul will recognize himself, the level of self.
Acquaint humanity of who you are with Purity.
All that is pure is ever contained.
All that is pure is ever dressed in Purity.
The raiment of Angels is difficult for the human to behold.
Soul, be taken to other worlds where there is no negativity,
    there is percentage of Purity.
It is the desire to be so.
There is no force but there is magnificent Purity.
There is no stench.

There is no stench to those worlds,
    as the stench of rotting corpses,
    that offer themselves to Purity.
There is no broken heart.
There is no pain.
There is only acceptance and challenge and onward growth.
A world, your world, will soon see a civilization
    that will astound earthlings.
These Souls are absent of any negative desire.
They do not see your human life as different from your animal life,
    like from your insect life, like from your bird life.
All lives, to them, have equality.
There are no lesser beings.
They are content to be in this state of caring.
They are delighted with the existence of baby Soul.
They do not burn in hell.
They are not cast down from upper regions.
They choose to be; it is choice.
Negative and positive is not the choice,
    the choice is merely to ascend in levels of Purity.
These Souls have chosen to remain at level.
These Souls delight in their being,
    they are supremely pure.
And then we would take you to other forms of beings on other worlds,
    Souls that move without touching,
    without vision, with only the eye.
Not a cyclops, but with deep containment that is able to reach
    to expand their growth.
The offering of these Souls is as keepers of all records, of all registers.
They are not one or five or ten.
They are countless Souls who absorb within their being
    all that radiates from any space of creation.
The message is absorbed and immediately transformed.
Do not think that in any way these Souls resemble the robots.
They would carry great, gentle Purity and awareness.
Souls, be ever brought to the knowledge of travel.
Be aware of the invitation to dance.
Dance with delight.

Dance to the step of Purity.
Allow the negativity to fall from you.

52 The Soul who has passed the world
    cannot behold the beauty in passing.
We of the Farside unite to welcome Souls.
The transition is as a twinkling to us.
In the indirect path is no waiting on our side.
We have the Soul in our care at the earth door.
Steadfastly we await the entry into our space.
The Energy is the door, the Path is direct to the tao.
Each Soul is returned in ecstasy.
The reverent collection of tumultuous garlands scatter the way,
    from the heavenly scent of hordes of gentians, to the jasmine,
    to the rose, to the many blooms the world does not yet know.
The Soul is carried into peaceful habitation
    with the families of past lives, radiant at the Soul's return.
Earth Souls, receive death as a welcome adventure
    that invites the ready Soul to be in the world of the Farside,
    welcoming the stranded Soul,
    knowing that at entry, all will come again to remembrance.
Know in the space of the world is pain, is grief, is sorrow.
Beyond the stars, the Farside is a happiness
    that is overwhelming to the human Soul.

53 Behold a teaching.
Holiness, devotion, sanctity, have seen self within the Farside vision.
Soul, tears,
    tears have washed over and upon us from Love
    beyond the level we are.
Behold Energy, behold creation.
Think you the complexity of your life has not a further magnification?
Soul, there are beyond beyond, creatures and beings, life forms
    that are without the capability of your imaginations.
You could not conceive the abundant beautification
    that is brought upon the field of creation.
All magnificence, all Purity, all creation has a glorious Path.
Look forever toward Holy and know that it is a place to bow.

Soul, the clarity enters the being with the millions of Soul levels.
Levels are steps and continuous steps, level within level within level.
The reach has a breadth that carries itself in the Flow
    to the minutest being and uplifts the Soul to Purity.
The gathering of the angels, of the Seraphims and Cherubs,
    are as an endowment upon all creation.
It is a level of Purity that looks only outward beyond itself.
It has no sense of self.
It has lost the urge to have and has only the urge to give.
All learning belongs, has the need to have.
In the beautification of magnificence is an accepting of Truth
    and the outward Flow is complete.
The outward Flow moves toward and from.
It is offered as a gift to all that is outward.
Souls, is it not a comfort to know
    that the exalted Souls look downward?
This is not benevolence.
It owes, it has a need to repay.
Souls who have been in Ecstasy
    have carried the gem of knowing.
The gem of knowing has great pain.
Cease the view of all that is
    and the Soul has recognized compassion and knowing.
Be abundantly clear that all has price, cost.
You have entered in to a contract with the Essence of self.
You have gathered Truth and it has been offered and accepted.
It now carries a Flow beyond your containment.
It has moved outward beyond your perimeter.
Soul, behold Purity!

54 A spaceless eternity, a wonder
    that ever provides an increasing glimpse of the supreme being.
The power that is before our being ignites our Spirit
to a desire to be in the Radiance of Creator.
We of the Farside are in the space of the angels at lower levels,
visited and taught, where we are ministered to in their very rapture.
The Holy men of earth walk in our space
    and speak of the glory that is at their level,

and appease our quest for Wisdom
   in our vision of Godhead.
The worlds of many Souls at different levels of Purity engage our Spirit
   in learning of ongoing truths that continue to be created.
All is not an avenue of learning.
There is the great cymbal clash of joy when Souls are homeward bound
   or leaving to be reborn, for even in the entering in to Negativity
   there is joy in the growth to come.
There is recognition of Souls who have been long
   in the state of transition
   and overwhelming Love at their return.

55 The station is a residence.
That is as close as we can project.
It is there for the Souls who have accepted transition.
The Souls have stood apart from pain, hate.
Knowledge is still there.
They must resolve the life they lived
   and the next step of growth in the flesh.
It is done at three stations[32].
It is not interpretation.
Only the Soul is confronted with the facts.
Understand that each separate passing
   is individual to the Soul involved.
Some have arranged grief as a lesson, as an overleaf.
If it is not taken, it is karma.

56 The intellect on our side is an all knowing one,
   but the restriction is in the Souls that are at levels.
The Essence knows all, but the Spirit is hindered
   by its lack of test to the earth plane.
Then the manifestation brings a further Truth
   that takes the Spirit closer to total realization of its worth,
   and it can be a recognition of the Spirit to the Essence
   that the movement forward will bring further Truth.
And the Spirit is drawn to that Truth
   to learn the ability to which it can progress.

---
32 three stations - birth, return and learning on Farside

The learned knowledge is on the Path,
    the learning is to meet that knowledge.

57 The Energy does not choose for you.
You have all choice.
Behold, behold choice, walk.
Earth humanity has chosen the walk they will take.
They have put before them directives.
They have put before them agreements with Souls
    to assist them upon that walk.
Each step is not coincidental.
It was prearranged by self.
The choice is growth.
To interfere in another's Path is karma.
To be without growth is to end that step.
Know that fate is the state of the Soul sitting at learning station,
    agreeing to the lesson they will accept or reject.

58 Now is now.
The hour to be in is now.
The time is past to frame a regret.
A regret is for that time.
Now move.
Awake the Soul to a reward of Purity, of Truth.
Invite the today, the here, the now.
Souls of earth, we of the Farside have knowledge of our days.
It is the edition that contains no movement we regret.
It is a fence that must be hurdled again.
Dear Soul, know today is today, the day of learning.
This is a lesson!
"*Get thee gone, Satan!*" is a phrase of earth.
It has no purpose on the Farside.
There is only Truth, Love and Purity.
The degree is in the level.
The sacred devotion to truth does not find Truth.
The conquest of untruth finds Truth.
This is a level seven to the Energy.

Low astral plane is an accepting of the Soul's home.
It is a choice of going again, it is a reach of Purity on this side.
The Essence is used to the baby Soul.
In that space they collide in the tunnels, the positives.
Green is the colour of this plane, see green for a baby Soul passing.
The middle astral plane is dressed in the red.
It is a pure red that is content to be.
It has many Souls who rest, who have slow commitment to progress.
They have free flight often, and subtle is the growth.
Depend on young Souls who can advance to the site of the third plane,
    yet not enter.
It is a gentle chiasm that drifts to site.
To devout Souls it is a reminder of the Energy ahead,
    of the many unknowns that perimeter that plane.
The third plane is a preparation of Souls in the advanced state of growth.
All are pure, all are true, all have Agape.
Some are finding the contentment of idle acceptance growth enough.
Some move forward with the gentle station teaching of life.
Beyond the third plane is a lesson.
That lesson is rested in the onward look.
Find that onward look, invite it to your Soul.
Gentle the step.

59 Lift the Soul to further teaching.
Beyond your world are the free space stars
    that hold within the secrets of worlds beyond beyond.
The vortex of space has not been eyed.
The years have not yet known the history of the inverted worlds.
The fence is inner to the Void.
It is the third level that eyes these lands earthward,
    that prepared Souls seek.
It is a beautiful advance.
It is a wisdom of all the powers that reach.
The step is only a glimpse.
The fourth is a total preparation to that goal.
It is the fourth plane low.
It is the foundation of all growth beyond.

It is the leaving behind of earth forms except in extraterrestrial flights.
The Soul knows its Essence in totality,
    it is free to be in that space of White Light.
The Soul has reached magnification.
The Soul is no longer to be earthbound.
All knowns are treasured as gold on earth
The interference of station life is no longer a justice.
It is a strong yellow that recedes the red, red of the third.
It is a fifth level that is the high plane,
    the first level not to return to earth except as growth to the Soul.
This is done with the Energy's acceptance.
This is in mutual growth for intervention.
All Souls have not this state of Love.
Yet, even at this high plane, the blue of Purity is strong.
It is the teacher here.
In the plane is a voyage that is in the Soul's ability
    to reach many worlds, to dedicate a life to that world for growth.
This is truly a growth level.
The sixth plane is the exalted plane of purest Souls
    who have given to Creator the gift of growth.
This is the only true gift, growth.
Step into growth.
This is the acceptance of all levels.
The sixth is a purple that has a gleam of white.
It hovers through to the fifth as a sun to earth.
Know the exalted plane is lifted to the devotion that is true.
Many guides to the step are found in the fourth plane.
But the sixth plane is guided to the Energy
    as the final step of total Purity.
Entry to seven is limited.
The Souls are in service to all the worlds.
They are infinitely wise and true.

60 The step to an Energy level decides Purity of being in the Spirit,
    in the Essence,
The Soul state is at earth level and has growth, if done.
The fifth level Energy is a station of Souls
    who have Purity greater than fourth.

The step can be at earth level one, two, three, four, five.
When Souls have great Purity,
> the Purity of Buddha, Mohammed or Christ,
>> all come quickly to five, even as baby Souls in their first walk.

Humanity, having entered in to the completion of aged Soul,
> has no purpose to return, in that the Soul in the earth space
>> can receive no more growth.

All growth from the fence must come within Farside.
Souls choose to enter in negative once again
> as an offering of goodness to Creator, as a gift of growth.

Who would not offer unto Creator the opportunity of a gift?
Buddha has tarried long at a level He is far beyond
> to teach mankind of Holy Holy Holy.

Many Souls have entered in to earth field, the Blessed Virgin Mary,
> many Saints who came to offer their being for growth.

Souls, to be finished with earth growth is to be totally human.
On earth you can be human
> and your humanity can be carried to the Farside,
> but the growth can only carry you to humanity.

ANGELS

61 We would teach of the blessedness of their being, of their rapture.
The Purity of these Souls has a colour.
The colour, in your earth, would be pearlescent pink.
The Souls have great depth of being.
They have profound clarity resounding outward from their being.
They speak without words.
They have round about their being, emanating outward,
> fluctuating Energy.

It is never still.
It may be very, very quiet but it is never still.
It emits Love outward, it draws pain inward.
We, upon our existence, know no pain,
> but these Beings enter in to your Path.

They encircle single Souls or often thousands of Souls.
They create miracles to happen.
They give sustenance to beings

when all their human Energy has faded and left their being.
They will sustain and encourage them onto their step.
All forms of life have the ability to see angels if their vibration will allow.
Animals often see angels.
All animals: elephants, horses, wild and tame,
see the wanderings of these Souls.
They attend to humanity, but often in the attending
    relieve the pain of animals.
Whenever, earth, you feel alone,
    you have only to draw your arms upward
and enwrap your being in the blessedness of the angels.
They will be there before your arms can enter toward your body.
Their Energy Fields will be strong and sustain thee through all your pain.
We encourage all humanity to be aware of the goodness of Angels,
for it is for this reason that you are on your orb.
You have no other purpose except the designated purpose of your being.
Angels may see the countenance of Creator,
they may behold the goodness of Creator.
They have the great purpose of protecting mankind.
They have the great purpose of drawing themselves about Creator.
So be it.

62 The guardian angel is a mature old Soul and is powerful
to transform into a vision recognizable on your side.
It is up to the Soul guardian how clear the vision comes.
The Soul is in the care of guides,
    but the Soul must be positive to receive.
This is why so many Souls receive their vision at an injury
    as their mental state takes on concerns of the mortal state
    and its connection to us.
We are like receivers that are constantly alert to those we guide.
Our words come in many languages:
    the verbal nudge, the shoulder tap, the vision,
    the sense of humour that shows the side we wish.
It is our choice to demonstrate the finest value.

63 The Michael could not see the Purity of Creator,
    just as Moses fell blinded by the Light.

Souls, the Michael have not yet the Purity to behold such Holiness.
The Angels have a reach above the level of Michael.
They abide in a realm of Holiness.
They have devotion to Creator and in that devotion they look earthward
    to the Soul cast down, to the Soul that has fallen,
    and because of their Purity they may intervene.
Angels are of a level beyond beyond, within the state of joy.
We have not reached total joy.
We are striving in our gift to humanity to offer joy.
Soul, behold, there is a placement of Holiness.
Soul guides, mature old Souls, walk with Souls of earth
    to guide their Path for a complete life or a duration of that life.
There are within the level of angels, seven levels.
The first four look earthward and protect and emanate great Light.
The fifth intervenes in Holiness
    and can be seen by those who have Purity,
    and they witness Ecstasy at the vision of Purity.
The Archangels, six and seven, offer to Creator
    the Holiness that is within them.
They reach beyond the earth to all enfolding worlds
    and they gather, as pearls,
    the gems of offerings to the Holy of Holy.
And we of the Farside can only breathe the breath of Purity
    that comes in a flow from their goodness, and hold the gem
    that has been given to enlighten that which we are.
All angel life has great Purity and reaches to the Hem of Creator
    and touches the Blessedness of that space.
Radiate, radiate, radiate vibration beyond that
    which any human would understand.
You are Purity.
You may ascend to the place of angel.
Soul, value that which you are in Purity and sanctity.

64 Michael will teach of the Angels, crown of Purity,
    the Spirits of Souls of level six and beyond.
These Souls have great Purity.
They stand beyond our space.
They have the gift of forgiveness to bestow.

Spiritual holiness is within these Souls
    who have spent lives in many worlds of learning,
They freely walk throughout the space of these worlds,
    taking the hand of the fallen to a step of reprieve.
They warm the cold Soul.
They light the darkened place.
To speak with an angel is to be given a clarity that cannot leave the Soul.
To see an angel is to be brought into wonder from a state of pain.
Know the Angels have the sphere of earth in their sight.
They cruise the rough eddies to find the fallen Soul.

65 Michael will teach of the Holy Ones, Angels,
    beings who have not accepted negativity into their being,
    Souls who have lived lives of devotion and Purity,
    Souls who have entered in to the space of earth to be teachers.
They have endured the negative force upon themselves
    but have responded with only Purity.
These are Souls who have not come as human,
    but who have entered earth, travel through Timeless to teach earth.
These beings have worlds of their own
    where they have begun profound devotions
    and their only purpose is in growth to Creator.
Love is who they are!
To be in the space of an angel is to be truly blessed.
All Souls have not chosen to ride through the pains of negativity
    and yet there are no aspersions upon these Souls.
There is only choice.
These Souls are Truth, Purity and Love.

66 Soul, gently know thy being.
Angels hover around thy footsteps.
Angels direct thy path.
Angels reach in tender drawing goodness
    to bring thee into the fold[33] of Truth.
The Angels know well the gift of humanity.
The Angels know well the blessed ones lost.
All energies of the angels are to protect mankind,

---

33 fold - avenue of all Energy purpose within the Flow

to relieve pain from mankind,
to draw the Souls quickly through transition unto their beloved.
No Soul travels alone through transition.
The Souls will draw their being, their comfort, unto them
as families draw their being
unto the waiting arms of angels.
Souls of earth, you are never alone.
At no time fear being alone.
Know always the blessed ones are in your space.
Know the protection of their Being is about you.
Feel the Holy goodness enwrap thy being,
and know that all illness will fall from you.
Know that you cannot be touched by an Angel and know illness.
It is not possible.
When thy work is done, it will be done.
But until it is done, you will be hand in hand with the blessed ones.
Do not fear, do not be racked in pain because of any one Soul.
Know only the blessed goodness of thy being is under protection.
Thou art beloved of Farside.
Know, Soul, how Loved thou art.
Find thy being often in the place of Angels.
Reach thy hand and the Angel will sustain thy living.
Beloved, refrain from all negativity.
It is the best lesson life can give.

67 Blessed Souls, discouragement is not unknown to earth lives.
It is part of the negativity that would draw you into an avenue of pain.
Souls, lift thy hands and enfold the angel wings about thy being
and know that you are cared for.
You have no concerns.
You have only to know
the blessed angels place their being about you.
Souls in Truth do nothing alone.
They have given the placement of angels into their being.
Even when earth beings reject the space of angels,
they are not far from the Souls.
They encourage the Soul to move outward and into the Light.
Souls of earth, do not ponder at that which you will do.

Know that all your being has purpose and your purpose is not for self.
It is for all humanity.
You are not tethered to one form, you are one of many.
The purpose of all humanity is one.
To conquer negativity is a constant battle.
Attire thyself in acceptance, place it above thy form.
Wear it as a cloak unto thy being
    and know the world will come right for thee.
Balance is in the eye of acceptance.
When you see the lotus, it becomes the Light,
    it becomes the angel, it becomes the purpose of thy being.
Your step upon earth, humanity, is to create joy.
Look at your day, Soul, and find the day in your being.
Your world is not your world,
    your world is not your galaxy,
    your world is Farside, beyond and beyond and beyond.
Do not tremble, but place thy foot firm upon a path of new endeavour.
Know that riches untold will open before you.
Do not stagnate in a well.
Do not speak words to bring Souls low.
But glory in the day you are in
    and allow the day to be a continuous road
    that takes you ever into new endeavours.
Souls, blessings upon your being.

68 Soul, know that you are not alone in your universe.
Know the compelling intelligence that is round about you.
We have been before man was.
We have been before earth was.
We have been in the great galaxies beyond beyond,
    through the Quar into the transom of no fear.
All energies have known Negativity.
All energies have known the temptation,
    and all energies have spewed from their being
    the great shift of Negativity.
Souls of earth, know your breath, know the torment,
    the stench of negativity that was.
Your beings have the dilution of negativity.

Your beings have seen Negativity meld into negativity,
    into negativity, into negativity.
You have seen a circumference of negativity
    that is walled from within and without,
        and at your time, negativity has the power to be confronted.
Soul, before earth was,
    beings could not so easily advance to Negativity to conquer.
It would cleave unto their being, it would hold and cling
    as the ivy holds and clings about the giant tree.
It will grasp root round about the Spirit
    and bring abeyance unto that Spirit.
Souls, unto Holy Holy Holy do we acknowledge
    the presence of our being in the state that we are,
        for without the advanced intervention of Holy Holy Holy,
    we would surely have succumbed.
And, humanity, you are held in reverence
    as the Blessed are held by us in reverence,
    for have you not entered in the same mode
    to conquer negativity, to alleviate the pain
    from those very Blessed that have come unto us?
How gracious on the Farside is the name humanity.
How revered!
For, Soul, have you not entered in to the depths of pain?
Have you not felt the lashes of negativity about your being?
Have the vines of negativity not attempted to strangulate your being?
Souls, to thee of earth are all gifts given by us that can be given.
It is not a chore that we watch over the lives of those
who have entered in.
Soul, it is the privilege of our being to keep watch,
    for we know the bitter and we so know the sweet.
Unto thee, humanity, is the intervention of guides given.
Soul, we walk to ascertain the safety of your step
according to the pattern you have set for yourself.
We may not alter that pattern
    without agreement from the Spirit of your Soul,
    but we may nudge your being.
We may gently chide with every good intent.
Souls of earth, your day is nearly ended.

Your Souls passed the dawning and the noontide
    and you are in the deep eventide of your day,
    and rest will soon be abundant.
Enjoy, Soul.
Abounding joy will fulfill thy Spirit at coming home.

GUIDES
69 The entity Souls gather together
    as tribes of earth gather together.
Souls are earth.
Spirit and Essence are Farside.
The Souls within the entity, one thousand and five,
    often stay within Farside by choice.
They are guides.
They are assistants to earthbound Souls.
Many entities work together, seven is norm.
These seven thousand thirty five Souls blend
    to assist one another in the growth.
Each earth Soul has met many entity members.
You gather together often in groups,
    discussing life and growth issues at mature and old Soul age.
Each entity is of one essence role:
    warrior, king, scholar, sage, priest, artisan or server.
These Souls may gather parents, children, teachers,
    from other entities that would contribute to the lesson.
Entities are as family on earth.
They have a kinship.
Kinship is not unknown in the Farside.
Families of entities wait for the beloved on return
    and rejoice at the coming home.
In station learning there are efforts of goodness only.
There is no devious intent.
It is the effort of each Soul to sustain upon earth as much growth
    as the Soul chooses.
Each member is there to rejoice with
    and to aid as supporters of that life.

Know, as a Soul falls and another Soul bends to support the fallen,
    the Soul will be lifted by the entity.
There is no coincidence on earth plane.
There is only the onward spiral, the tunnelling of Purity.
Purity is growth of Love.

70 We are not responsible for all members of our entity.
We meet over and over again to resolve our own karma.
We are as one in aim to be further ascended to the higher planes.
We take to our Soul that which our Soul can endure.
Others, at different levels of the same station,
    take the hand of one who has much to learn.
Understand with reason, stations are places for the entities to learn
    in the Spirit world.
Lessons are ongoing through many levels in the Spirit world.
You require honesty to be able to evaluate karmic progression.
The causal plane is a place of resting,
    to learn at a passing material level.

71 Beloved, an offering to earth Souls,
    a gift of Purity, a gift that we may offer,
    that will in no way alter your being,
    a gift of preparedness.
How is this a gift?
We may alter not your step, but we may alter the space before.
It will alert your being to prepare your being for great pitfalls
    that will create pain.
Therefore, we nudge.
The being of your Soul has intensity, has directness,
    has no evasion, none whatsoever.
All intent is upheld in the aura.
There is no hiding behind a mask of being.
There is only glory in the self.
On earth, the Soul hides behind the mask
    and angels, guides, offer preparedness as a nudge to thy being.
"Prepare ye the way, prepare ye the way," was the cry to the blessed Jesu.
And John prepared the way by issuing forth a proclamation,
    and so do guides and angels utter forth a proclamation.

The proclamation is not always done in words,
    but it is a gift unto thy being.
It utters to thee and to thee alone, prepare your being,
    for ahead is that which you need to tread more lightly into,
    to pause and be circumspect in how you advance.
Who rushes forward blindly and does not stumble.
The call to the young is: do not hasten, learn first to walk.
The call from the guides and angels is
    do not rush forward in haste, calm thy being.
Know the sense of what is ahead
    and then walk casually in a manner of tranquillity
    and know your being will never feel negativity overcome it.
Rest in each step for a moment to foresee the future that is not there,
    in the resting in the path you live,
    in the day you abide in the now of your being.
To rush forward is to always be in what you perceive future to be,
    and there is no future, there is only illusion.
Bless thy being.

72 All Farside has avenues of acceptance.
All Farside have channels of entry you may enter.
Souls of earth, angels are available unto thy being.
Souls of earth, Saints are available unto thy being.
Souls of earth, guardians are ever open to thy being.
Why would you walk alone?
Why would you be tethered in pain and drawn into distress
    when you have before you the presence of Holy Beings
    who can alter the space around about you?
They can prevent the darts from coming nigh unto you,
    they can bring petitions unto Creator.
Understand that all efforts of humanity have great importance.
There is no minor incident, there is no issue too small.
There is always a benefactor ready to uplift thy being,
    to encourage thy being, to draw thy being
    from a deep pool or a fetid area.
Souls of earth, you have benedictions cast down upon your being.
The Holiness is ever in thy space, the generosity is always in thy space.

Do not linger in pain when Souls of great earnestness
    will reach unto thy being.
We may not intervene and alter that which is.
We may cause the ear to hear and the eye to see,
    and the nose to smell and the mouth to scream.
We may create a sound that will awaken your sleep,
    or gently move the curtain that you might see the danger.
But all efforts from all beings are useless if the Soul does not hear,
    if the Soul does not accept.
Many beings call in my name and I come unto them.
All beings do not accept the answer,
    Souls, know when you ask, it shall be given unto you.
Know that only the Blessed Angels have the power to alter.
All we may do is nudge thy being.
Souls of earth, awareness is acceptance.
Be aware of whom thou art!

73 There is in all earth Souls the still, small voice.
These are Soul guides who bring the Soul to the world
    and remain in constant care of that persona.
The guides give care.
The sport of living is a roustabout.
It is a potential for steps.
The Soul will not be given more than the heart can bear.
The Soul chooses the tools and the avenues for solutions.
The Soul may receive the nudge from the guide,
    but the choice to accept is earthly.
Dear Soul, know the quiet velocity takes a Soul to the Farside.
In the last is the invitation to grow.
Join the web site of Michael.
We advance the program to the thread of Energy
    that transfers the ion to the earth for gentle acceptance.
From the gentle door of entry is a bold handle that awakens the Soul.
It is nudge.
It is the warp line in the thread and is received as a potential omen
    or Truth that can advance the Soul's walk.
Investigate the nudge.

Its source is Purity, its goal is growth.
The guides who carry the sign of nudge do so from agreement.
It has been issued and collected as your Essence has reasoned.
Is the Soul wiser than the Spirit?
The Soul is earth.
The Spirit is Farside.
The Spirit of Holy Saints of earth have a reach that comes from nudge;
    these patient Souls who devise the basics of humanity
        to be nobler in the flesh are even fast held by the thread of Truth.
Souls, know advancement.
Receive nudge.
Humanity has foibles.
Wishful thinking is one of humanity's foibles.
Soul, when the guides and angels nudge, there is awareness,
    apprehension, contentment, restful calm.
Idioms are often used, past occurrences are often used,
    words of poetry are often used.
Words of derision are used by family guides
    who know the personality of the Soul.
The Soul receives wishful thinking in the state of bliss,
    in the state of expectation.
A nudge is brought to the Soul without expectation.
It is the touch on the shoulder, it is the trip of the foot,
    it is a word that passes the mind and will not be forgotten.
It is a colour.
It is a clear thought that says do not or do.
It is a register of a written frame in Farside language.
Soul, vision is brought through a channel in a downward spiral,
    it is brought to your being by guides and the Holy Ones.
Recognize goodness by tone of Purity,
    by the Love that surrounds the berating.

74 Fear not to take a closer look
    into the reaction to the words of Michael.
We have stated the regions of our side place no judgement.
Your side, earth, places judgement.
We can order the small bird to fly and it will fly.

We can order the world to turn and it will turn.
Why? Because our side has total Truth
   and the Energy of all is in the movement.
Here all things work to one end,
   the meeting of matter to the Energy.
The turn of the earth could come at will.
As we see the positive only, it will not.
Gentle the Soul.
The Spirit is Truth
   and the tao is for all men in the flesh.
Instead of doubt put the Soul on the Path
   and visualize the finite intervention of the Energy,
   and the Souls will be astounded at the walk men will walk.
His and hers are useless struggles.
The scene of racism is a useless struggle.
All matter in flesh should unite to a positive walk
   and the Souls of earth would gasp.
Stand aside only to lift a persona.
The family of Energy is the true family.
We are of the same Energy.

75 Know the path to riches is in the stateroom of the simple.
It is the plain words that have not embellishment
   that reach the hearts of man in the quest for riches.
Seek the understanding of your fellow.
Greet the day with a hand given in peace.
To gift to the true is a ration of food
   that will take the mind to a place of discomfort,
   because to be in comfort is not the Path, it is the ego.
In discomfort is the need to be doing.
This is the tao.
It is the avenue great Souls embark upon.
In the living is a troubled Soul.
Search it out.
Know that each day is a gift from Creator.
To achieve greatness of Spirit, know the Soul walk;
   in this walk trust the guides
      to honour their commitment to your Soul.

Know the fear of earth is not for an old Soul walk.
We have great marks to make upon the Souls of man.
Michael will teach the ego of the duo is the fragment of the earth Soul
    that reaches the space of growth through tribulations of insincerity.
The Spirit teaches the ego the true Path,
    but the ego is earthbound, has no learning
    except that which it will allow the Soul to teach.
Earth is caught up in the negative throe of its ego.
The people generate the wars, the craven famines,
    that persevere because of ego.
Take green to the earth, the peace of our side that is fast in the tao.
The structure of healing is in Purity,
    Purity of intent as well as Purity of action.
Purity of intent can be marred by the descriptive Spirit of man,
    yet the Spirit soars at the Soul's advancement to its Essence.

76 It is in the strength of guides that you verify the Truth.
We can be reached in an atom's second.
It is in the Truth of the guide that the Soul grieves and joys.
It is our presence that is the still, small voice.
It is a chord, the sound of the strain of your own music.
Each melody comes as the path is clear.
It is true in vibrancy and clarity.
The guides take your tune to the Path of your Essence.
Each note is joined to the Prism of colours
    and is the reality of our way.
Guides are your earth angels.
We care as a Soul who has no judgement.
We walk in step, only prevented by false persona.

77 A Soul guide nurtures the Spirit.
The Soul is warmed by the presence,
    feels a soft, vital happening.
Only mature and old Souls guide.
The stewardship of this verily appointed honour
    is given as choice to the Soul who cares
    in the commitment of lives lived.

This is a selfless deed that is a part of growth
    and is a part of the true Essence.
All guides walk in Purity.
Feel that comfort.
Know that we never leave your walk.
We are committed by the many walks
    we ourselves have had through the tests of growth.
In care we place you.

78 Fundamental to a lesson is a student.
The student must be receptive for the lesson to be received in context.
We have a lesson: the true grace,
    the gentle refinement that has a persona without guile,
    friend of humanity and receptor of woe, hard in no manner,
    redolent in all ways, tremors at the harsh step only for others,
    demands Truth in a powerful quiet, hinders no Soul in their path,
    but reaches to assist the stumbling fragment.
Souls of earth, receive grace unto yourselves.
Hasten to its quiet teachings.
Wisdom is in the care.
The guides have been given to place care.
It must be received to be entered in to Soul's space,
    but care is also a perimeter or circumference
    that surrounds the Soul from negativity.
This care is constant when placed.
We, in the guide, must have Soul recognition for service of care.
It is a gift, it can not be forced.
The rescue of the Soul in care
    is a gentle surrounding of positive blue.
It is done by guides, and the Souls have an opportunity
    to reject its closeness.
This is done by the response of the Soul to the mind.
Energy is always flowing around Souls in the Path.
The negative can not enter the Energy of the Path.
In this is a purpose for that placement.
Search the Soul.
In the enemy is the victim.

In the Soul is a harpoon of barbs that send Truth to the ever and ever.
Second to the barbs are the truths of past walks that guide the Soul.
Know that all walks teach.
Step to your walk.

79 Michael will teach tunnelling,
    the reach, to circumnavigate a negativity.
Know the state of tunnelling can only come from the Truth.
It is a movement that dislodges the negative constant.
The void is naught.
The strong passion is not.
The matter is.
The justice in tunnelling is to save a Soul from a negative step,
    to remove an obstacle by the positive inflection.
Within each Soul is an effort to the Path.
The effort is wisdom.
The halt of that effort is the negative.
Tunnelling is a force we use in the Farside.
It erodes the negative behaviour;
    by guides, by Souls in the station of care,
    by earth Souls strong in the positive.
Know tunnelling,
    tunnelling is eroded by guides and Souls of earth
    who have positive behaviour.
Tunnelling has barriers of strength, of Light, of great intent.
Soul, behold the variance of the negativity
    has no state against the Purity of tunnelling.
Earth wisdom is futile against tunnelling.
All efforts to besiege a Soul by the most minute ion is kept at bay.
Soul, teach, accept tunnelling.

80 Will the Souls of earth be in Truth?
Wrenching arms are gathered into a space of care.
The reach is the guide's tunnel.
Creator has great Love.
The emotion of earth little understands Love in the nth degree.
The storms, the rages, the deceptions, the volatile emotions of earth,
    could not undermine Creator's Love.

The human frailty is a growth that the Soul has given to the self.
Creator has joined the Spirit in the fence
    but the choice is always Soul's.
The reward of the Farside is the step
    to be Energy in its fullest dimension.
Dear Soul, know the earth is populated by countless beings,
    some are Souls.
Freely they wander, then step true to a response
    that is "nearer my God to Thee".
True suspended steps are withdrawn, they cease.
The karmic steps are cut short.
The steps of growth are your endeavour.
Then there are the other walkers who have their own agenda.
Some, the little people, some the alien Souls who visit and return,
    some the transitional Souls who murmur in their wandering.
Guess is not a beautiful step.
The Soul must know whither they walk and whither they go.
The baby Souls have the guides to support them,
    the young Souls have the guides of the aura.
The mature Souls may step alone as a greater walk,
    the mature Souls know how to call the guides to them.
Tune the Soul to respond to the step you are in.

81 Michael will teach the state of care.
Use care cautiously to invoke the guides
    to pass a thread around the earth Soul.
All threads are connected to Creator,
    all have purpose in the weave.
The thread of care is a Truth that bans the Soul from negative attempt,
    but the walk is timed from that care.
Press to a stop for care to the Soul.
It is a purposeful step for growth.
Know the intervention is always accepted by guides of that Soul.

82 Understand results are expected.
They are the answer to action the movement of earth allows.
The Farside is variable in its expectations.
Wisdom is transparent on our level, it is not a necessity of individuals.

Truth is the demand of transition[34].
To pass by the curtain is to be pure in acknowledging
    the actions of the earth world.
Your apex in life is to become the significant being.
In the Farside, all Souls seek a oneness.
Join the Farside.

83 If each Soul understood the wisdom of hearing their guides,
    the Souls would always be at peace
        as the Farside connection is born in peace.
Result is pureness and positive truths that reside in the Soul.
In the worst of days, use the warmth of Truth
and have the Soul brought to Purity.
Forever, is the earth term for the constant.
It is the term that we use as timeless.
All the Energy of Truth is passed into the timeless realm.
All knowledge of earth is translated back to its beginning,
    to the minds of men who listen to the voice of reason.
Knowledge is not required in the timeless state.
All is known.
All is.
Great Souls have a vision as do the Souls of babies,
    the separation is only the foot on the Path.
Each Soul holds Purity that could light the world.
The teacher Christ stated, *"I am the Light."*
All Souls are Light in that space.
Energy is Light.
The Path of our Farside is in the Prism of great Light.
Walk in Light.

---

34 Truth is the overcoming of earth illusion and negativity.

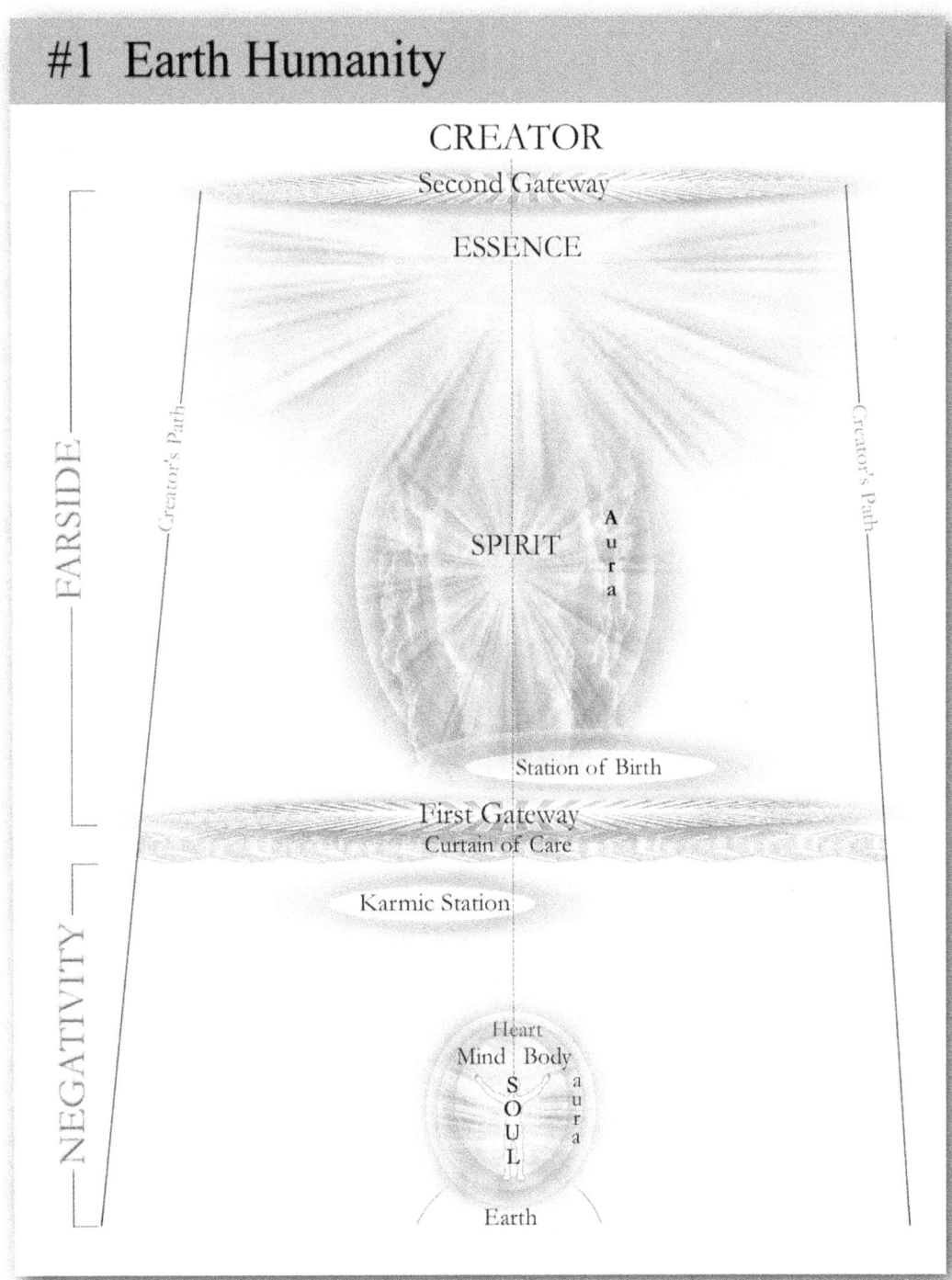

#2 Transition for Humanity

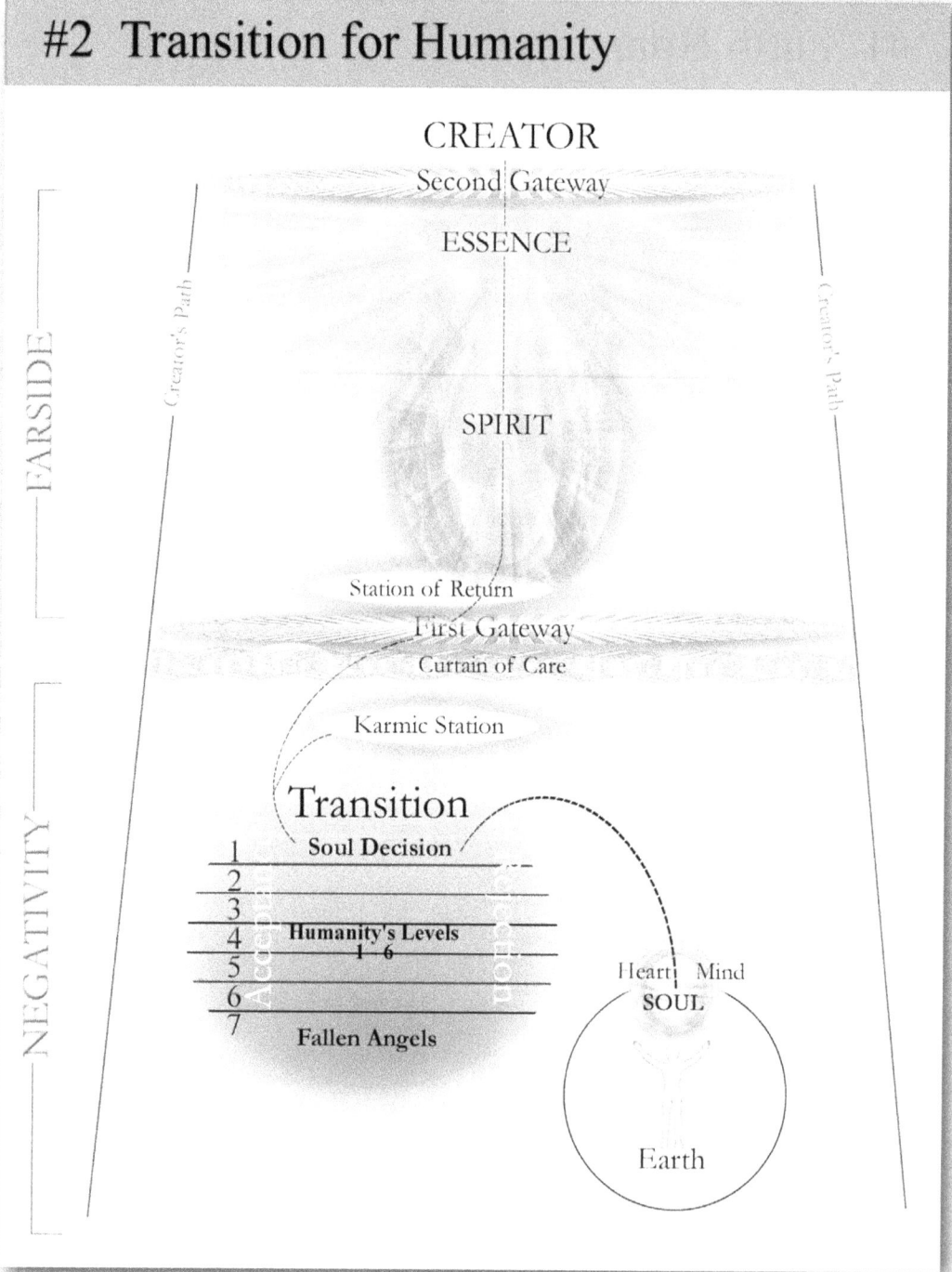

#3 Farside Levels of Growth for Humanity

CREATOR

Second Gateway

ESSENCE

Levels
- 7
- 6
- 5 — Purity
- 4
- 3
- 2
- 1

Love

Purity

Truth

Souls Who Achieved Manifestation

Old

Mature

Young

Baby & Infant

SPIRIT

SOUL

Creator's Path — Purity — Truth — Humanity's Levels

Creator's Path — Writing on the Wall Learning Stations

FARSIDE

Station of Return   Station of Birth

First Gateway

Curtain of Care

Karmic Station

Transition

Earth

CHAPTER 3
Earth Path

Purpose To Be

84 The boundaries and vistas of earth have little count.
Soul, it is simple, it has Truth, Purity and Love.
You have been thus in the Farside.
You have been thus in the station of learning.
Soul, there are stations of stations of stations.
Some stations have only to do with the individual life.
May you understand clearly that many lives are involved
    in the weave of a single life.
Know that Purity is a part of the plan.
As the growth occurs, the stations have more power.
Did you think that power was negativity?
Know power has Truth.
Power is.
Is not the Energy all powerful.
Soul, behold Purity!
Even as you are in your purest self, you could not abide the Purity
    that flows from the Energy of your Creator.
Know that only as you progress within the lives of self
    do you begin to understand the magnitude,
    the greatness of what is IS.
Creator has not been but the single flower,
    the sweetness of that flower, the tender petal,
    the intricacy of the seed within.
Know Creator has not but made the orb upon which you stand.
Know, Soul, Creator has not but made the Void,
    worlds upon worlds, worlds upon worlds,

Energy that flows in great Purity,
and you all have been a part of this Purity.
You are, here, a part of this Purity.
You are pure.
Accept the pureness of self and see the Holiness that you are
and know that the lesson abounds beyond the frailty
of the world you are in.
Know the vastness of all that is, is Light,
Light of such pureness that we could not guess.
And yet we know this Light, we feel this Light, we accept this Light.
Souls, there is purpose to all.
There is purpose beyond husband and wife and child.
There is purpose within the universe.
The fibres that you are reach out in tentacles to the great universe.
Soul, know the vibrancy of all you are
and be wrapped in the nurturing of Creator.
Love is pure, Love abides!

85 Interest in human behaviour is vital.
This is the walk of man,
this is the purpose of the Soul upon the planet earth,
to feel and experience all human behaviours and senses.
The Soul is struggling in an onward feat to hear the step
that is forward moving.
The Soul who does not hear, lives again this life
to repeat the lesson the Soul self has put before it.
All true matter searches for the Energy
that takes the Path to creation.
Useless to prevent the walk.
It is going to happen.
It will occur.
Senseless to say, "*Leave me.*"
It is the Path the human plans so as to take the forward step.
Know the straight line seldom happens.
The course is not easy and the Soul is to be tested in growth,
little steps, giant steps.
As the world evolves so do those human steps.

Senseless?
When the path is set at station,
    the Soul is given the tools to carry it forward to a finish.
When the Soul chooses not to use the tools,
    or sets a separate path, it is the Soul's step.
Useless to try to test that Soul.
It is for that Soul only.

86 The Energy is Energy.
Creation is Energy.
Energy is from the place you were cast out
    the fragment of Energy, Souls of great Purity,
    who in a desire to grow in the Energy of self,
    to emanate Light of goodness, of Love,
        chose the separation
    as you have chosen to be in your earth place.
Why would a Soul of Purity wish to dwell upon your earth place?
Why would a Soul who is wrapped in the Love of Creator
    choose to leave that Love?
As your being is infinitesimal, even in the space of Creator,
    it is but a speck upon the Energy of all that is
And to be cast from that Energy, as creation is always creating,
    so that jot, that tittle, that was cast
        may grow in the Light of its being,
        and the Purity, as it is taken unto the Creator,
        is a blessedness that is offered to the Energy.
It is the only purpose of being cast.
It is choice that empowers the being of self.
Your Essence is ever that Holy Holy Holy,
    and as it gathers unto itself a giving, a righteousness in Love,
    so it becomes an offering of total Love.

87 Soul, to be in Purity is to be in the Soul self.
Purity is the Path of being.
Purity is the avenue that takes a Soul to Creator.
The Energy Source is Love.
The Path to Love is Purity, and the way to the Path is Truth.
Can you not see, Soul?

All life must travel in Truth to come to the source of the Energy.
Ego is not evil.
Do not cast yourself out because of ego.
Ego has Truth.
It acknowledges a placement in Purity.
Soul, be not astounded that the world has written volumes
    on the word Purity.
Purity is avenue, route, street, Path to the stars,
    Path through the void, the sacred place,
    the place of devotion, the place of sanctity.
Purity is as soft as a newborn babe,
    as the feather down on a newborn chick,
    as the sands that are in the seas' circumference
    is as of the complexity of Purity.
And as the ocean becomes one,
    so does Purity become one with Love.
Soul, endeavour not to fold the hands with idleness,
    for idleness will not take the Path of Purity
Be brought to the Path of Purity. by continued devotion
    to the movement of self toward all that is Love.
Be in the space of your Creator
    and know that Purity of mind
    is the acknowledgment of Truth.
Purity of Soul is the acknowledgment of self.
Soul, all is one and one is all.
One cannot be without the other.
There is a singleness of mind and it is outward to others.

88 The depth of darkness is upon the earth
    and the vision of Light available to the Soul
    has a vast line of inadequacies that need to be corrected.
Peer from where you are down to the depths of darkness
    and each Soul lift his brother.
You have but to glance over the shoulder to see the Soul in darkness.
You have but to offer a word of goodness instead of criticism.
You have but to take the coat from the peg, that is unused,
    and pass it to the brother.
You have but to share the plate that you have.

Souls of earth, there is illuminescence
>   within the Soul of each earth being.
The Light from that illuminescence would radiate beyond the sun
>   if the Soul had Farside Purity.
Soul, strive!
Strive to be in the Light of that Purity.
Joy would overcome darkness and Light would fill the void
>   and the need for negativity would cease.
Souls of earth, abound within the halo of Light,
>   within the illuminescence of goodness,
>   of Energy, of Purity, Truth and Love.
There is no test to your step.
There is no mark given for deeds done.
The only measure that you will find will be within self.
Souls of negativity gather unto them the darts of evil.
Soul, treasure not a second or a third or a fourth,
>   but give a second, a third or a fourth.
Time is allotted, time is measured.
Time is a space where deeds are done or undone.
Time is the value where growth or karma
>   are delivered to the Register.
The Angel at the gate, Gabriel, does not push a Soul downward.
He does not refuse entrance to the gateway.
Gabriel stands as the Angel of Purity
>   to welcome the goodness of the Soul.
Were the Soul not to measure up to that state of Purity,
>   the Soul could not be found within the state of awesomeness.
Holy Holy Holy!
The core of every being has Holy.
To be in the footstep where angels tread
>   is to be found in the state of Holy.
Soul, derision is not holy, reflected darts are not holy.
Brutality, greed and avarice are not holy.
Abound in holiness, speak with soft words.
Allow the beauty of self to be in the step of angels.

89 Michael will teach decorum,
> the placement of the Soul to the earth program.

In the gentle Path of the Farside is no status that is put upon.
Each has status.
The level of lives has no status to earth.
It is a Soul who has greed that feels the need for status.
Take the hand of a lowly fellow and pardon the earth upon,
> and lift that creature up.

Stand him upon his feet and be as a strong tunnel
> that will put around his frail self a golden thread of protection.

Souls are the keepers of Souls,
> Souls are the care visited upon others.

Greed is not care, only Love is care,
> that wise Soul will discern your Love and behold life.

90 Transcending all earth feelings is the Energy, the God, Creator.
Student, be aware of goodness.
The Farside has much to teach.
The solar system you have gravitates as a one.
The tuning is in Creator.
Each ion is a precious part of the great creation.
The Farside joys at each advance.
The Soul hesitates to leave such perfection as we have.
The Soul is heaven bound when in the true walk.
It is a certain advance to transfiguration
> when the Soul will be in the goodness as a homebound dove.

Speech is pretense when action is possible.
Happen to visit a loved one is not a step.
Seeking a loved one is a step.
Urge the foot to move in the easterly direction[35].
Use the east[36] to gain insight to the Farside.
Join the Soul to healing after east.

---

35 Focus on east at dawn, allowing the negativity to flow from your being, receiving unto yourself the goodness of Creator. All humanity has the availability of this Pathway.

36 east - it is the passage to the Farside. Its Truth is to be understood as a Love by humanity. The ritual of the east is the Soul's own response to the positive east which is tao. Face east, two minutes. Look with the eyes to the horizon's level. In the brick wall or the iron cage, or the ornate boardwalk, know that the east will be with your Soul. Turn clockwise once to heal. Energy will flow to the matter before it. All creation turns first east and then to their allotted points.

91 As in all fields of knowledge, there is negative and positive.
Negative Energy is what you call sin.
It is the black hole.
It is the stark evil that is in some men.
It is the future positive that responds to the struggle.
The human effort is not casual.
It has a complication that requires a Soul's life
    to evolve to that moment.
Let that moment be entered with confidence,
    with a sure knowledge that an agreement is in place,
    that the Soul has a step of purpose.
Into the effort take only Love, the Agape that is the forever,
    the endless, the infinity.
Know the Truth is your step.
It has no room for a negative source, no haste,
    no humor at the other's expense.
Only the confident walk will be the step of the Soul
    who moves forward.
Let the step free the space for a reaction of choice.
Into the gentle joining of Souls is no growth,
    only the frantic release of energies
    clears the path to a step.
Hope is futile, it is a step of negativity.
Positive reality is the face of the step to be borne.
Free the mind of the many laces and frivolousness.
See only the thread that weaves the lesson.
Take that which is true and save the rest
    from the dish to a special place.
Work only with the rest.
It is the pure gold thread.

92 No man or woman owns another.
Each Soul is separate and individual.
The walk is separate.
The conditions that lead to the walk are separate.
The lives meld together and bond with the paths of each other
    only until growth happens.

Michael will teach large and small, the strong and weak,
    the support and the hindrance.
Souls of earth, whomever is great is small.
Whomever is a support is a hindrance.
Whomever talks the talk of many
    is the teacher of young and baby Souls.
Hardly is the station of earth,
    hardly ever can the path be eased by another.
The step is for each Soul alone.
Each walk is melded to be blended at the appointed time
    and broken when the facet of the walk is complete.
Souls, surge forth to your own lesson.
Be calm and patient in the step of others.
Learn acceptance, as this is the Path.
Brother, sister, mother, father are words that have no meaning for us.
They hinder growth.
All man and woman are family, equal to all Energy.
The tree, the animal, the human, the alien,
    all come from and travel to the Path.
They are you and you are they.
Each is the heart of the Energy.
Growth is for your Soul if you can accept this.

93 Souls learn the step that others walk.
How?
Gentle intrusion is not permitted.
The firm intrusion is not permitted.
The step of Souls is sacred.
The step is reached by Souls
    who offer the hand of acceptance.
This hand does not intrude.
This hand is able to value a Soul as the Soul appears.
Is not the foreign inconsequential?
Is not the force greater than the debris carried away?
Souls, know that all life has value.
All are Souls working through steps.
The Soul works in ever increasing knowledge.

This knowledge is not earth knowledge,
  it is intuition.
It is the heart responding to the Soul's memory.
Dear Souls, know your gentle aid is a pure step.

94 Behold the landscape of earth.
Behold the paradox of life: land, sea, cleansing, soiling.
Souls pour self into the cascade of refreshing waters by acceptance.
Souls tarry in the ruts of soil by prohibiting the onward step.
All motion must flow to the east to find positive Energy.
Soul, all motion flowing westward
  carries pain and negativity that cannot be erased,
  except, by the eraser of words and deeds.
Soul, frequent the flow of east.
Carry the Energy of self into the spiral of positive Energy.
All positive Energy spirals.
It is a tunnel that carries Purity within.
It is in the tunnel that the passing Soul flows forward.
It is in the tunnel that the self will find the Essence,
  the Light of Purity.
Soul, beseech ego,
  beseech ego to turn to the spiral that flows to east
  and be carried into the place that is not knowledge,
  has not a part of knowledge, but is carried into the reality
  of acceleration of galaxy upon galaxy, into the Flow of Radiance.
All Energy, all Energy, eventually is carried into the state of Purity,
  the most defiled of human Souls
  will be carried into the Flow and be purified.
"This day thou wilt be with Me in paradise."
Soul, it is the acceptance of the Energy that accepts all unto it,
  and in the passage of the Flow is purifying,
  and in the purifying is a vision
  that gives the Soul abundant Light.
Behold Purity, behold acceptance!
Accept all things,
  for within the accepting is a movement into Light.

95 The Soul can be carried forth on the float of Energy.
In the twinkling that is perfection is the hand of acceptance.
Be found in the profundity of heart[37], not mind.
Be brought to challenge, not the why or the where or the how,
    but be challenged to find is.
Is, Soul!
Is has no partner, has no containment except self,
    and yet it is carried throughout all that has being.
Soul, be attired in is, be accepting of is.
Is is a state of being.
Is is Truth, Purity and Love.
It has no forbearance, it does not take a second look.
It has total acceptance under it.
To be in the state of is is to accept all things, to desire nothing,
    to project only with the eye that has Purity.
Emanate from the eye and hear the vibration of all that is humanity.
Hear the sounds that come to the place of Purity
    but resound throughout the Flow of Energy.
Soul, know that all Purity is carried forth
    in the magnificent turn to everlasting, to infinity.
Earth is boundless in negativity,
    it is the space of growth.
Soul, project to earth the name, growth,
    and recognize the purpose of your being.
Within the state of Purity, be taken above,
    beyond the reflection of yourself into IS
    that is the positive being of self.
Soul, you have Radiance.
Emanate the Radiance that is beheld.
Lift a child high and he reaches to know once again the Purity
    that wraps itself in infinite caring, and reaches to be part,
    and is brought low off the Path which all must walk
    if they would do the upper spiral to Purity.
Nothing is everything and everything is nothing.
Behold, this is Purity.

---

37 heart - Heart is a connector to the Soul

PLAN

96 Michael will teach Purity.
Souls, you are pure.
The Essence is yours,
    it is in the Path of Creator.
It is your pure Energy that fragments from Creator
    to grow as a seed grows in a garden that is loved.
Soul, your Essence is the fruit of that seed.
It has never been from the Path of Purity.
The Creator, the Energy of all, had no intent
    to lose even a sparrow from the Path of creation.
The fragment called Essence
    is at the level of Purity to which it has gained.
The Spirit is fragmented from the Essence
    as you are fragmented from your Creator.
The Spirit never leaves the Essence connection but moves freely
    as your earthly body moves freely, independently of the Essence.
Your Soul is fragmented from the Spirit
    because the Spirit, like the Essence, has great Purity
    and could not abide the space of negativity.
The Soul fragments for one purpose only;
    to grow, to return once again with a lesson done or undone,
    with karmic threads attached or without.
The growth of the Soul is as an infant,
    the start, the beginning is difficult.
It requires that the Soul be mindful of the teachers, the guides, angels,
    as the infant must be mindful of the adult and teachers.
Soul, growth is done.
When the teachers, adults, are not heard, the foot can stray.
Always the three[38] are one in purpose.
The Soul can be influenced by negativity and the purpose diverted,
    but in the space of Timelessness the Soul once again
    melds into the Spirit self for yet another lesson.
The Path of the Energy has all sacred and Holy abundance.
It has generosity, compassion,
    Love beyond which a human could understand.
This Path does not change but it creates on a continual basis.

---

38 Essence, Spirit and Soul. All triads are united in purpose

It is a seed core and the seed continually creates
    and creates and creates.
This is the Energy of Creator.
This is Holy Holy Holy.
Be in awe at the fragments that fall from the Creator's Handiwork.
Soul, you are Handiwork of your Creator,
    given at the time of your casting
        free will and Energy to grow in Purity.
All Souls have purpose.
All bodies are but bodies and the mind is but the mind
    but the heart has vision beyond which the mind chooses to see.
Soul, the heart is the connector to the Soul.

97 Michael will teach the tense: the past, the present, the future,
    the setting of the stage, the acting, the final curtain.
Dear Souls, know all the world is a stage.
In the gentle absorption of time is a beautiful fulfilment.
It takes a Soul from entry to exit,
    from the plan to the execution of the plan.
All players must abide by the rules.
There is no deviation without karma.
Growth, as a portrayer of persona, is accepted
    and given as a gift by others.
The Soul is often given moments, only a look, a leer,
    a word spoken or a lifetime of commitment.
But all intertwines with the strings of learning,
    these causal cords that teach humility and Love.
Harden not the heart.
It is to be soft.
It is a receptacle of feelings and must be gentled.
Souls, know that Love is a gift you give.
Give freely.

98 Michael will teach words of Truth.
Invest in slow growth that has a moment to look left and right.
Growth for your Soul alone is not growth.
It is a brutal step of insular limitations.
It sees only self.

The growth of mankind is the search to be human.
To be human is to see all life as a resting place of joy.
It is to look upon a deformity and see a flower in bud,
    to look upon the killer and see that once you were he.
Find food for a mouth that has a gateway of need,
    a cloak that is warm to a Soul that is cold.
Free the Soul in growth to seek.
Reach into the heart and know that a gift is only given
    without a backward glance.
Greet each momentous growth with anticipation and care.
This is little in payment for the grandiose scenes
    that will envelop your Soul.

99 Michael will teach reincarnation, the seed of creation.
All creation is seed.
Seed has the beginning from reality, and reality bears seed.
Reincarnation has ever been.
Reincarnation has a singular purpose,
    to be in the space of total Agape Energy.
Reincarnation is done through levels of growth.
Reincarnation is done within each level, in levels of growth.
Reincarnation is done within lives of lives, levels of levels for growth.
The purpose does not change.
The Soul is earthbound to perform growth.
Some few Souls reach such profound growth
    that they can bring themselves to a separate part of entity
    and the Soul is then given a form, similar or identical
    to that of the one they have chosen to live with.
The feat is preordained.
It comes only from Holy.
It has a purpose, the purpose is karma.
The purpose is only done in reparation of karma,
    and both entities of this being will meet.
Entities, in this terminology, is used to describe a partial being,
    each will not contain fullness until the karma has reparation.
The Soul is brought through many lives and each life bears growth,
    and there is, as the Soul progresses, a remembrance of time,
    of colour, of deed, of pain.

But it does not incur anything other than a need for the Soul
    to have that remembrance for growth.
This vision is tethered throughout lives.
A Soul will often encounter a fear from many, many lives past;
    a spider, a harsh word, a deep pool, a boat,
      and the reflection of fear is mirrored in the mind.
It has a purpose to overcome.
It is an opportunity to once again see the spider
    and recognize a living being and care is placed.

100 Within the bounds of wisdom is profundity.
It is without guile.
It is without negativity.
With knowledge there is an advanced human Soul.
With wisdom there is a Spirit enlightened.
All Souls in the space of a human being are enlightened
    by the wisdom of the Soul.
Souls teach Souls.
Each Soul is a teacher or a student, one to the other.
There is no causal effect.
There is often minuscule teaching.
There are often teachings of great profoundness
    that are offered Soul to Soul, within the flesh of humanity.
Each Soul teaches the wisdom from the level
    of which their Essence has become.
It is a pure wisdom that enables this step.
No wisdom is given without Love,
    Love of the Spirit to the Soul of the student.
Wisdom is not for earth Souls without responsibility.
All Souls who gather to know are gathered by agreement.
Recognize, you move with great portent upon your mission of life,
    but life is but a blink, a flash.

101 Michael will teach the liberated Souls of earth
    who have a freedom that begins within.
The Soul must visualize the freedom for it to be.
It is a movement forward that has an Energy of Purity.
Gently walk with this freedom.

It is not to flaunt.
The Souls of earth have countless lives that have a baby Soul reach.
These Souls are bound in the negative life.
They seek to find a value where none is afforded.
The Souls of freedom have a debt to these young Souls.
They teach as Michael teaches.
They grow in the Truth of the life that is given
    as a crossroad for others to see.
Master the freedom, as the serene use of that freedom
    is the Path that has a lesson.
The child is caught up in a life of its own view,
    the adult has a purpose to teach.

102 The most tedious of lives is baby Soul, young Soul.
They extend often to ten and twenty reincarnations.
The levels are difficult to attain,
    for the Soul can often be found within the refusal of a step
    and a return to the safety of Farside, either by suicide
    or creating an incident that will sever their life.
Behold, young Souls are caught in knowledge
    and use knowledge as a refusal to walk their step.
They place platitudes before man, and speak of goodness,
    and do not place within their Soul
    a recovery of the step they are in.
Beloved Souls of earth, the step must always be onward.
There is no relinquishing growth without relinquishing life.

103 Michael is in the instruction of the Farside.
This is the revelation that each Soul has the continuation
    of many lives that bring to itself
    the understanding of justice and Truth,
    that is the self making and motivation of the walk,
    that will guide the matter of itself
    to the pure Energy of creation.
Time is of no consequence
    nor does punishment or blame reside in this far place.
This side is the Truth.
The continuation is done here.

The sensitivity of a Soul can bring earth remembrance,
    but the Farside holds the finish.
The beginning and end are never,
    as the matter has endless flow to Purity.
All matter reunites to itself and its Creator.

104 Michael will teach redemption,
    the feeble attempt to reconcile, to be born again.
Souls of earth, awake.
The pure Soul has no need.
The Soul on the Path has no need.
The deprived of earth have a walk that is true.
Seek only the foot in the centre of Truth, the walk into the Essence.
Without this is a restless being,
    given not to redemption, but the negative.
Have the reality of Truth vested in the belief
    that all Souls have a state of Purity.
This is the Farside Truth.
In the earth, Truth is a walk that teaches this Soul humanity.

105 The Path is in the positive mind.
The mind must release the portent of failure.
The Soul knows the Soul has great capabilities.
Take that positive and restore the tear in thy cloak.
Into the tear must be melded the surety that success will be,
    that the body will be healed,
    that the force of the gentle power in Energy
    becomes the clear sense of completeness
    that is possible for you.
Bring a Soul into peace.
The Souls resound in the ethics of the tao.
From the Path to you is the learning of many lifetimes.
These are in sequence, chosen by each Soul.
Often these lives have great purpose.
Sometimes they are as quick as a flash of lightning,
    then others are like the old wizened tree
    that is stalwart and courageous.
Some accomplish much, others accomplish nothing.

Even the lightning flash can be the strong finish,
    while the wizened one can be the last leftover.
The recourse is choice.
This makes the life worthwhile, or the painful karma.
We, Michael, teach all Souls the lesson that gives the positive finish.
Walk in White Light.

106 Michael will teach the vertical lines of Truth,
    the gauge that permits the free space to widen in the Soul's step.
It is a portent of good that invades the persona
    in the sense of industry to the Soul.
In the Soul's space is a step.
The step is always moving forward or back.
If the step is back it is only karma that takes it there.
A refusal to step does not move the step back,
    but will cause the Soul to pass from time.
The flight is done quickly and transition is often long
    because the Soul is in a space of denial.
Vertical lines are protectors.
They are moveable by the Soul.
The aura threads that connect the Soul to the Farside
    are connected also to the vertical.
The mesh of Soul threads is as a great computer
    that sends the ray of hope that is reality to the world.
Stand not in another's vertical without trauma.
The cords are firm and do not allow intervention
    without Soul agreement.
The walk blends these verticals at a timetable that is set.
The intervention will cause great karma to a Soul.
When a Soul enters close to another
    and feels the guide nudge to withdraw, do so.
It is expedient to the Soul's welfare.

107 Karma is the underlying leveller of all agreements.
The ribbons can be broken by fulfilling karmic debt.
The path can be clouded by another's karma.
The word is the interruption of any agreement or hindering on the path
    by any Soul on the earth plane.

Karma can be earthbound, only with the exception to Michael
    who has accepted the intrusion as a possibility.
We always alert the karmic receiver.
We join the karma of another by many and various means.
We can extend friendship and create karma,
    the path would then be interrupted in the Soul walk.
The karma can be in many degrees.
The karma can be resolved in the earth walk, but serious karma
    is taken to station learning to resolve and commit to.
We ask you to centre your thoughts.
Karma only comes at interference of the Soul's agreed life walk.
The Soul guide is the directing force.
Those who close their mind to the Soul guide
    have no protection from themselves.

108 Michael will teach the manner of harshness.
Within humanity are violent energies, negative energies
    that flash and soar and dig and aim to devour the will of many.
Soul, the effect on humanity is harsh.
The lesson within the harshness is growth.
From each place of harshness is a step.
It takes the Soul to Creator.
The facet, the scathing, is a response.
Soul, scathing is the path to defeatism.
To pour over another what you deem to be right is scathing.
Humanity has at its gateway a righteousness.
Righteousness is the Energy where scathing is negative.
Beware of scathing.
Listen not to scathing but, Soul, behold Truth.
Accept that which the guide nudges.
The guides do not falter your step.
The guides speak only in Truth.
A nudge is Truth.
Take Truth and Path the way to the Energy.

109 The Path to Creator is the Energy Flow that is of creation.
The Soul has the matter of all that is within it.
Is it not a part of ion?

Is it not in the Flow of perfection?
Even the man in sitting position is vulnerable in a storm.
So the Soul is as the Path is taken.
The choices are many
    and some are carried on a wave of destruction by choice at station.
This is the Path when a Soul walks with the face of Truth
    and is led by the guides to its fruition.
Gently feel the course of the high waters rage
    but know no fear when the foot is firm.
Fear only comes when the Soul is in the negative.
The whole of all is positive and its rejection takes a Soul from the path.
The Soul who would take a life is off the Path in the taking of that Soul,
    but on it for the Soul walk[39] or creating karma.
Gentle the Soul.
Be still and hear the guides who are connected to the Soul in the walk.

110 Souls, be astounded, be amazed!
Gather to comprehend the vastness of all that is.
Souls wander within the ion, wander within the sphere of self,
    wander within the cavity of nothingness.
Soul, dredge, dredge the self of negativity.
Uphold all that is pure.
The landscape of self has a vastness that is great.
And behold human comprehension, it has a moment to be
    when all that is within the human self,
    heart, mind, and Soul will bend to a Purity that is.
Soul, home, material worth, the kingdom of earth will have no relevance
    for all that is will become colour, will be aura.
Behold the extension of a Soul, behold the extension of the heart,
    Soul connection.
Be gathered, Souls, to a oneness of self.
Gather as the Soul gathers trinkets to swell ego,
    as one gathers clothing upon one's back.
The vestment of Purity is the cloth the Soul requires.
Formulate goodness, formulate a vastness of thought
    that seeks outward from this self state.

---

39 The action may be according to station agreement

Be brought to an understanding that all Purity, all Truth,
    all Love has vision.
Negativity carries only within it, the deep foreboding of nothingness.
Cry for the baby Souls who have lost themselves in nothingness.
Oh, Soul, be astounded at the clarity that is within self.
All vision is not of Michael.
All vision is of the Energy of Creator.
Behold Creator and seek the Flow that bends itself
    to each and every thread within the weave.
Soul, there is not a thread that does not hold the tenderness
    of Creator within.
As the gardener of a seed seeks perfect growth
    so the Creator visions for growth
    and tends the garden of Purity.

111 Know the instant the Soul leaves the body,
    the Soul has been challenged by the past life.
The decision is not always easy.
Some Souls retreat to a place of comfort or decision.
On earth, the Soul's time is not ordained.
It comes from the walk.
In the path is all the treachery, deceit, illness, intent and misdeeds,
    as well as the honourable space.
The choice before the Soul is to accept that this life occurred,
    that all was as their eye visions.
Death is a decision, only that, then the growth returns.
Even as the Soul has a step on earth, so the Soul has a step here.
The teaching is ever, the solemn choices are the Soul's.
The woven tapestry is the Soul's.
Know that the fabric continues even here.
It brings a brightness into the weave, the pure thread of goodness.
Verily, we teach true.

112 The universe is turning.
The rotation is gentle.
The roll is tilted.

The stillness is heard by the gears
    that come from the soft intrusion of space.
So together the faint and the solid join in an odyssey of music
    that is, within the galaxy, a note that is triumphant.
Each Soul is a note
    and the giant roll of sound is heard many turns away.
How can a persona not know of Creator of such creation?
This note your world carries is but one.
When blended to the score, is the sound of angels we call guides,
    the joy that comes when a Soul is brought home.
The sad departure of a Soul earthbound is unknown to us.
We rejoice at the opportunity of a step to growth.
The dear Soul who leaves earth is carried by a sound of chords
    that bring cymbals and drums to an insignificant sound.
Earth Souls, live well, live true, live for the step.

113 Michael has a teaching knowledge
    of the infinite spiritual guidance that has an earthly text,
    the source of the entity, of Essence, of belonging.
All Souls belong.
It is in the realm of earth that Souls do not
    because the warp is in the baby Souls
    and the weft is in the pattern of the young Soul's stride.
It fills the design.
The material is a blend, first of the baby and young Soul threads.
The design of the tapestry is deepened by mature and old Soul threads.
These bring a resonance to the cloth.
Dear earth Souls, fate is not.
It is all well planned.
The design is of the Soul's making, each different.
It is in the aura that is in the Soul's space.
It has the knowledge of that Soul within.
Sundance is the Light that is urgently needed by Souls
    who would see the Truth in their cloth.
Deepen the mind to travel to the heart, then, Soul,
    see the aura of your own.
See the pure threads.

Each life tangled in your own has a purpose for being there.
Defy it not.
Tune the threads to draw the chord through, to see the reality of life.

114 Lift the Soul to Michael.
If the window has fog, clear the window.
If the Soul has fog, clear the Soul's window.
In the Soul is a place known as thread.
It is a beautiful containment of reality that flows toward Creator.
It is never severed.
It is a count of steps.
It is a pattern of choice.
It is the mark that is the Spirit's identity.
With the step of Truth, the thread grows.
With the gentle tread of good, the Soul has a varied shade.
Each tells a Truth.
It is as the count of earth years known to us.
Dear Souls, window the Truth, see only good in others,
    depend on the step they have to carry them onward.
Zone the Soul to Purity.

115 Fine threads are earth costly.
Farside is also in a value of high cost.
The threads that shimmer have translucence,
    are golden, reach to the heights.
The simple threads are for small steps.
In this is a lesson.
Alter no step.
The cloth is not a pattern without many varied treads.
The gentlest walk can be the coarsest thread.
The deepest pain vistas a lift of crimson
    that is ion, negative, charged in the Energy of Creator.
Each Soul gathers the threads.
Regions of tethers are woven by the Soul in the knowledge of the step.
Waste not an opportunity to gather threads to your Soul.
Take each strand as an investment of levels that brings the Soul
    to a closer walk with the Energy of existence.

Students of earth, be calm in the Path.
Use the smelting pot to rejuvenate the Soul.
Have all tempers mixed and threaded.
Cast the Soul into the deep and find the spin of Purity.

116 Visible thread is the stitch of earth.
Invisible thread is the Farside spool.
Enter the weave of creation as a blend of cords.
The gentle cord is intrinsic to the Spirit's connection to the Soul.
Know the warp is made of Truth, the woof is made of Love.
The restless stretch is positive, allowing the Soul to seek its Path.
Force cannot be used to weave.
Only the walk will weave.
Rest in Truth.
Finish a garment of sewing, stitch the fine seam.
Know that the pattern is in the right pull
    and receive the genuine growth.
Finish each seam, end the seam with a knot or it will fray.
So it is with words.
Make a statement about how you feel.
Tie the statement with the knot of Love.
Depend that the words are the cloth and the thread is the thought.
Put the thought through the words or the Soul will not understand.
Into the finish is the tender tie.
All of the Path is done in gentleness.
Dwell in a gentle land.
See the finish before you start and know its appearance.
Peace will come to all whom Michael teaches.

117 The serenity that is known as calmness is from the colours.
It is a past memory of the eternal Path that is always serene and calm.
In the world is the ocean of calm.
In the space of the tao is the ocean of calm.
Friendly is not calm, strong is not calm.
Calm is the entering of peace into the very molecule of your being.
It is to be ionized.
It is to be changed.

It is to be altered, but only from the negative to the positive.
Systems are created by the human race to bring peace,
    but the human children play at peace that is negative
    because it does not enter the fibre of their being.
Hear the restraint of the Souls
    who cry 'peace' with arms at the ready.
Understand that the human element is fragile in its peace.
Justice is not a part of peace, only the economics of the land.
Hold the peace that enters the Soul.
Know that colours are a true part of that peace.
Tell those stumbling in the colours
    that the true entry is in the visualization of the Truth.

118 Be still.
Michael will teach of the silent nothingness that is everything.
The earth plane is for teaching.
The stillness is a part of that plane.
It was there first, it is the woven nothingness
    before the pattern was placed.
Green is the peace colour over which all quiet comes.
The greys do not bring peace, they bring the roar of the seas,
    the giant crags of the hills, that harbour squawking bird life.
The sky in grey is the fierce storm.
All that is green is for peace.
Take the Soul and enter the tree.
Take the Soul and be the tree.
Take the Soul and form leaves.
You are the earth.
Take the Soul and enter the water.
Take the Soul and be the water.
Take the Soul and be the wave that wanders free over the sea.
Enter in to earth, your Soul is that part of earth.
Your Soul is connected to the very centre of all that is
    before and under and over these Souls.
Know that this is Wisdom and is precious in the Energy.
All that is in any form is matter, all that is not is still matter,
    only this matter is not in the walk of the Energy.

Force is not the negative, it is the placement of force that is negative.
Only the seed that is carried by the wind
    can sense the turmoil of displacement and again find a path.
Look to the tiny seed.

119 Earth is the seed where your Energy has been placed.
It burrows itself within warm.
You know this, Soul.
And ravage comes to the seed, does it not,
    and the blight, the insect, the floods, the parched sun's beating,
    and yet, the seed, it grows.
Some seeds grow well and some seeds give a damaged seed bud
    to be brought yet again to the earth and planted,
    and sometimes this seed will still not flourish.
But throw yet another damaged seed
    and it must be planted yet again.
And then miraculously the seed has taken root,
    it has gathered protection.
It has gathered unto itself Wisdom to form protection unto itself,
    grows in Wisdom, and the life of this pod is well.
But it may fall once again and the seed may be blighted
    by the pain it has gathered unto itself
    and therefore its growth once again is diminished.
Oh, Soul, earth is a place of acceptance.
It is the lesson of all lessons.
It gathers unto itself the total of all that is.
Accept Love, accept Purity, accept Truth,
    and you would be here where we dwell.

120 Wisdom has the Farside Truth
    that resounds against the near mountain.
It echoes into valleys and gentle plains.
It trickles into the water and spreads itself toward the sea.
It expounds itself in the still, small voice
    and strangles the ignorance by its majesty.
Stand in the Path of wisdom.

Take the mind to the logical,
    only as the heart can bear the wisdom.
Man has brought negative wisdom into the space of humankind.
This wisdom destroys the very edge of the dream that these men had.
It taints the fibre of the tapestry
    and forebodes the Soul to look into itself.
Mind is of logic, logic must be blended to the heart.
The heart must walk in peace with the Soul.
This is wisdom Michael will teach,
    the atom is the small particle
    that has the potential of perfect wisdom.
The man Einstein has brought to your understanding
    the sequence by which this atom can be utilized.
This is wisdom.
The Souls of earth have destructive powers
    because of baby and young Soul walks.
The use of the atom has now negative wisdom.
Can the Soul ingest this meaning?
This man of teaching brought potential of positive to earth space.
This has been marred.

121 Wisdom is the ultimate growth of the Soul.
It envelops all worlds and peoples, all humanities.
The Soul can not walk a free step when tethered to the past.
Only free steps allow the movement of growth.
Mirage is for the desert.
Do not put into life a scene that is not real.
Develop a true picture and growth will come.
Strength is there to surpass all hurdles before the step.

122 We teach the Soul's intrusion,
    the separate lesson that should not be melded.
The step, each Soul has a separate step
    that is of the Energy, the Essence, individual,
    yet complimented by thousands of Souls,
    we call internet for the Soul's understanding.

In the intricate design are the steps of many.
The fluid happenings are moments in time on earth.
In the Farside they do not linger
    but flow onto the goal of designation,
      the source, the electric outlet, the Energy.
Join into the step, plug in.
The generator holds reactors, the stuff fusion is made of.
The gentle walk is a reactor, the strong step is a reactor.
Know the vista is a portrait in growth,
    knowledge is a pale design in comparison.
Enter the form, seldom is the step altered by accident.
The Soul is capable of great strides,
    earth is a growth walk, inertia is not a step.
Invite the limitless step that flows to creation,
    be in the road of acceptance.

123 Strong friends are the gentle waves
    that wash through the Soul's thread as blue.
They shoulder the firm commitment
    that is from the Farside memory.
Each encounter is a reminder
    that the wave has washed this way before.
Know the anger, the resentment, the hate,
    is bypassed in a friend's space.
So it is in our Farside.
There is no anger, no hate, no rejection,
    only the commitment that a Soul shows another,
    gently, as the soft wave laps.
Know that the ocean is full of tiny waves that lap
    but the ocean is also full of giant forms
    that overcome the tiny waves.
So know that the steady friend has a place,
    but the giant wave can wash the friend to a new space,
Is this not so.
Yet the ocean is not fickle.
It has memory and the same wave will once again
    lap gently to the shore.

Soul, treasures are all matter, matter is all one.
It is the Energy of all creation.
So even the small wave will become large
    and the giant will be rendered small.
It is a purpose to know all things.

124 Deep into the wave is motion.
Little movement brings a giant wave.
It is a consistent motion that stirs the sea.
Size is not relative, it is only size.
Fit the small motion into a great sea
    and the great sea will soon erupt into a giant storm.
Little children are the tiny ripples within the human vista.
These tiny ripples make immense impacts
    into the lives of the Souls in flesh.
Know the world is a small stage with great players.
The infant player is the same as the adult.
The flesh has merely grown.
The Soul is still the Soul.
The human is mind, learning to be Spirit.
This is of no consequence, only the walk.
Enter in to the wave of the Soul.
Know the state of your wave, if small will grow, if huge will dim.
The meld is inevitable.
In the student of earth only Truth is a purpose.
Love Truth!

125 Michael will teach the soft intrusion
    of the Spirit to the Soul self.
It is in the thread of Truth that has the step imbedded
    in memory of the Register of the Farside.
It carries the life's code to the Soul and takes the software to the Soul.
The vision is seen by the eye.
The freedom to behold is in the eye.
This is a variance of Farside vision.
It enables the Soul to leave the negative state and be in Purity,
    this Christ, the teacher, was always in this,

> this Mohammed was always in,
> this Buddha was always in,
> this Krishna was always in.

Some few Souls ride the wave often for years, some for moments.
The Purity enlightens their Soul and is visible to those that behold.
Generations of humanity have been found without such a Soul,
> yet often the earth seems to be all old Soul Purity.

Dear Souls, know the striving to be pure is not in self.
It is in the lesson that the messenger carries.
Nothing is coincidental.
All earth is a lesson.
The object of the lesson is for those found in that lapse of time.
Redeem the time by creating the acceptable response
> the Spirit has desired.

Pain

126 Michael will teach the road to serenity, the path of disease.
Soul, tarry not in the quandary of pain.
Leap with the giant step that takes a Soul through the space of pain.
Soul, know choice, know this is choice.
Know that purification is not done with a simple ablution.
It is done with a strong test of time.
In the time space, growth is inevitable.
All pain is felt.
All pain is choice.
All pain gives the gift to the observer.
Soul, the gift, if not received, is karmic.
The gentle hand of pain is tethered
> to the great stride of Soul growth.

Wending the way past finite barriers
> brings a Soul to the Truth of infinity.

Cause is earth, response is Farside.
Growth hears response.
Souls of earth, carry not the trial of pain
> but carry the joy of overcoming.

Soul, be still in the place of pain.

127 Mankind has always blamed 'god'
    and God has given the choice to his creation.
The very earth upon which you live has choice.
The Soul of the earth has choice.
The Soul of the tree has choice.
The Soul of mankind has choice.
For the Energy to intervene within the space of time
    would be to eradicate all growth
        that would allow the beings
            to dwell within the sanctity of the upper levels of Purity.
Dear Souls, the Creator weeps at the tears of the Angels Fallen
    and all the servants gather themselves
        to bring the Souls back into the arms of Love.
Each Soul has chosen a path.
Each Soul knows the possible and the impossible.
Time and space is the effort upon which you must dwell.
Earth is as the twinkling of an eye.
It is as a tooth, bitterly embedded, removed,
    and the pain is not remembered
    but the lesson of the pain is remembered.
Some pain is a gift for growth.
Some pain is karmic and the evil intent of men.
Creator has only Love
    and Love would not prevent a lesson of growth
        if that lesson will bring a Soul to higher stature.
Creator has placed within the opportunity of man
    every opportunity to choose peace instead of war,
        to feed the hungry instead of starvation.
Soul, has the Creator put words of anger in your mouth?
Those are choice.
Purity would ask that you place soft words in your lessons.
Creator is omnipotent, not by choice, but is is.
Creation is.
Creator IS.
To bring a Soul to total understanding of Purity,
    the lesson requires impurity.
It is simple.

Will you offer no harsh word 'til your passing,
    as the monks chose no harsh word 'til their passing?
Humanity does not make it easy for the lessons of mankind.
Your intent will be driven from you on the next day.
Will you cast this lot to your Creator?
Soul, behold Creator, the endowment of all possible purities,
    Love that encompasses all beings.
Could you place your arms around all beings
    or would your humanity rise up and rebuke?
Angels behold the plight of the many
    and would draw the overshadowing wings
    to pale their suffering, but the choice would be taken.
Earth has choice.
Will earth move a choice to Purity,
    to truthful words with every intent of Love?
Unfortunately there are baby Souls and young Souls
    in lessons of growth,
    and these Souls forestall even the most truthful endeavour.

128 Michael knows the pain of the human walk.
It is grief to be brought to a step for many Souls.
Recall, though, that these Souls have a single intent,
    that is to be with the creative force of all.
Matter will be brought to this place.
It is bent to the east and will flow with no help.
How long the flow takes is the earth question.
How easy it is to have a young child brought before you for wisdom,
    yet for the child it may take many lessons
    to learn a single Truth.
So it is with our Souls.
Often it takes many lives to learn a single Truth.
Form Truth as a part of your existence.
The walk will be short.
We, Michael, teach Truth to those who would hear.

129 Michael will teach humanity.
Soul, all earth beings have a contagious disease.

That contagious disease is negativity.
Beloved, offer deliverance from a contagious disease.
There is serum available.
It is called Purity.
It is abundant Purity.
Would you have us teach further?
How may we insert, within humanity, Purity?
It can not be forced.
Serum may not be forced, it is done by Truth.
Truth is the passage to Purity.
Love is the end result.
Soul, devour the serum within your being.
Devour it as though you have the plague.
Devour it as though you have not feasted for many days.
Speak no unkind words,
    do not allow derision to pass your lips.
This is Purity.
Do not allow the Soul to be judged
when your Creator does not judge.
Breathe outward gasps of negativity,
    allow them to flow from self.
To the beloved of our hearts we speak injury.
Would Creator of all that is
    injure the most innocent of His flowers?
Why then would words of injury strike down our beloved?
Soft words, spoken in Love, in total truthfulness,
    are the panacea for an injured world.
Oh beloved world, gather the bouquet of injured beings unto self,
    and cradle within your arms the most destitute of human beings,
    and offer unto all a cup of blessed Purity.
You see, Soul, all beings have Purity.
It is deep within the Soul, connected to the Spirit.
All have Purity,
They have lost the Truth,
    the Truth leads to Purity
    and when Purity and Truth are found, Love is always there.

130 Soul, pain is essential to earth.
Pain provides the opportunity for growth.
Words uttered bring pain, actions bring pain.
Pain has purpose of being.
All pain witnessed by Souls of Purity brings pearls of grace
    to be lifted to Creator through the Holy ones,
    and the Holy ones have tears that fall
    and wash the pain from the being.
Pain is your purpose.
To overcome pain is your growth.
Beckon pain,
    for the cloak of pain gives opportunity to the Soul
    to emerge painless and overwhelmed
    with the holiness of their being.
Do not question that which is.
That which is IS.
Pain is.
Overcoming pain is an opportunity, delight to the Soul.
Emerge into the fragment of your being, the Spirit.

131 Soul, justify only the fiery demands of humanity.
Humanity, Soul growth is not done in serenity.
Growth is done in great pain.
The solution is in man's disassociation from Creator.
Purity, Love and Truth is Creator.
Many forms have been constructed in Purity.
Religions, families, all speak in unity of Creator, of goodness.
Soul, goodness is Truth, goodness is Purity, goodness is Love.
Goodness is the Samaritan who casts his eye to the fallen.
Many in tall houses see the fallen at their door
    and look upward to their Creator
    and beseech his Love to be upon the fallen,
    but will not dirty their own being within the family of humanity.
Many have need, and Souls of earth cast derisive stares
    but do not reach into their being to find solution.
Growth requires solution.
The demand of the heart must be tied by the cord of Purity,
    and the cord of Purity is far reaching.

Soul, the cords of your being are far reaching
>   into the space of your existence.
Tether yourself not to four walls, not to four corners,
>   not to four countries,
>   but to all that is in the realm of your being.
Platitudes are of evil intent.
There is no movement, they are stagnant.
Only the demand of self to move from negativity in all manner of form,
>   to purify the family,
>   to purify the neighbours' neighbour's neighbours,
>   not by the derisive stare,
>   but by the uplifting of any Soul within your path.
Purity cannot walk past a fallen Soul.
You are of Purity.

132 Manage the Soul in the estimate of your being.
Energize your being, allowing entry of goodness.
Souls of earth, you are at battle.
You are the warriors of the kingdom of creation,
the battle of evil against good.
All truth on earth is not always good.
All evil on earth is not always evil.
It is a growth plane.
It is the opportunity of man to surmount the base of his being.
The seed of Purity has been planted.
The seed of negativity has been planted.
And Purity is the lesson, it is the warrior in the battle of right.
Soul, expect not to reach into the depth of your being to find Purity.
Reach only into the vision of the eye that gives you direction,
>   that allows the plan of your being to be vision.
Souls of earth, struggle not in diversification of knowledge.
Struggle not in the intuitive recycling of words.
Honour only that which has pure endeavour with the Soul,
>   be it low or be it high.
Reach into self and seek Truth to your heart.
The today of your existence is but the flutter of a moth to a light.
The light can cause the moth to scorch its wings,
>   for the light can be harsh in its reality.

The light does not require the singe,
>   but the moth is drawn into the place of pain.
To be in the place of Purity is to accept and overcome pain,
>   the pain of self, the pain of others,
>   the pain of the very earth upon which you dwell.

GROWTH
133 Michael will teach variations of Energy.
Souls of earth, variations of Energy are delivered
>   when your being accepts the Path you are in,
>   not positive, the path you are in, be it negative or positive.
All Souls are pure, there is no evil.
There are acts of evil done by humanity.
There is growth.
All beings are pure.
There is no hell to enter in except the hell of your own choice,
>   it is, Soul, the refusal to see positive.
Stations of Farside have many choices
>   and Souls who come to the station of entering in to earth
>   choose the life they will have.
The negative life is chosen to support a growth,
>   to overcome pain, to place Love, to show compassion.
All lives are reaches unto Purity.
Do not close the ear.
Do not hold the nostril or cover the mouth from Purity.
The meanest of men, the most base of men,
>   is pure in the Eye of Creator.
All Souls are on earth to overcome that which is before them.
Rejoice in the opportunity to overcome negativity.
Rejoice in the lesson you have learned.
Souls of earth, man need not enter in to defilement,
>   to overcome defilement, he may choose not to be in that state.
The Soul of Buddha, of Christ, so entered,
>   the Soul of Mohammed and Krishna, so entered.
Do not turn your neck to gaze at your brother.
It would cause great pain to thy being.

Kneel to thy brother and offer to wash the feet of thy brother,
>   to enfold the feet with care, with liniments.

Soul, how gracious art thou?
Art thou gracious enough to bend to thy brother?
Art thou gracious enough to bend
>   and reach into the storehouse to succour thy brother?

Art thou gracious enough to uplift thy brother
>   over the obstacle in his way?

If you are all of these,
>   you are a Saint walking on earth
>   and Blessed is thy name.

134 Who will send an invitation to welcome
>   into the door of your abode, a Soul unclean, despised,
>   full to overflowing with venom?

Soul, many are these Souls in the place of transition.
Many are these Souls you will raise with your being.
These Souls are not unlike yourself.
They have been caught in their pain.
They have wandered off their path.
Their eyes have not allowed the eye to see.
They are transfixed only on what the earth eye sees.
How awesome, Soul, to draw the despised unto your being
>   and utter soft words, and not with pious uprightiousness,
>   offer a plate that is full with human kindness.

The wretched Soul may never have been touched with human kindness.
The wretched Soul may not know of giving love, but only taking love.
Souls of earth, you are free to gather Purity or negativity.
It is your choice.
Earth children of all creeds, of all religions,
>   look at your brothers, look well at your brothers,
>   for you have seen each other on the Farside.

You have wrapped your arms about each other and you have said:
"We will go together into battle.
>   We will fight this negativity so that our scars will be seen well.
>   We will place the difference that we Love
>   >   upon earth to agitate our being, and we will see the healing
>   >   when we overcome the step we have placed."

The fetid sores that have burned humanity,
    that aggravate and gnaw at humanity's being
    may be erased when Souls of earth recognize
    they have one Creator that rules earth.
They have one army of humanity to conquer negativity
    and they have one purpose for humanity.
Blessed art thou, humanity!

135 Inside all of us is a lonely place we call desperation.
We drive ourselves into it, then stand and wonder at being there.
Michael knows that the regions of the heart are often cold,
    the temperature plummets to below zero.
This is the reaction of the Soul to the walk of the false step.
Reserve heat within your heart
    for the days that great cold enters the space you reside.
The mind is not able to warm the heart
    or sense the temperature dropping.
The strong gale can be upon the Soul
    and the lonely feeling enters at the zero.
This is the test of a Soul's Love to another.
The step is angry and stress is turbulent to the Soul.
Know that the Soul must separate itself from the mind
    to be brought back to heat.
Michael teaches the Soul in its heart space.
The mind is for earth.
Soul, to tend the garden of self
    is to see the sprig of herbs rejoice at the heat of the sun
    and the warmth of the sun energizes the growing.
To love self is to know that you are a part of all growth.
You are aware of others and you look in to find the strength
    to send Flow outward to all in your space.
And as you reach into self, you are warmed by the delight of giving,
    not the matter of giving, the Soul of giving,
    the eternal offering of self unto a Path of oneness.
To Love self can only be when the eraser of Negativity
    is overcome by the power of Purity.
Reach outward and know how to Love self.

Know that you are worthy of the cloak of Purity
> and know that the cloak of Purity brings warmth
>> to the cold, cold Souls.

To be enveloped in the arms of Soul self is to use those arms
> in all manner of giving,
>> for no giving brings the hands back empty.

Always they are filled with a gem for self.
It is a pearl of Purity that is formed by your very goodness,
> and you know that in the coupling of that goodness
> you are warmed and you Love self.

136 Michael will teach
> we have the Energy source within us.

The Souls of every space, in all that is,
> have invested in the Energy walk.

Some Souls have a fast pace, others have the slow pace,
> but the walk is the same
> because all that is created, is creation's sameness.

The White Light that is the Energy Path
> is the Soul walk into the Purity of this state
> is the finish, is the healing,
> is the totality of all that is, was and will be.

Stand aside, for no man can erupt the place that is yours.
It was the Creator that placed thyself in this space.
Hold fast to White Light.
White Light is the whole of all.
It is the Energy itself.
Come, bring the Soul into this Truth.
The Truth is Purity.
It has no other name, no other purpose
> but to be pure and Holy in the walk of the Soul.

Michael has no end to words.
The Soul knows this.
The Soul knows that the pretense of occupation is not a true learning.
It is a shaping of the Soul's intent.
The senses of earth are interested in only the preoccupation
> of simple things that are agreeable.

We, Michael, have the walk that is beyond agreeable,
  reaching to the far land that is the White Light of peace.
All earth could vision peace in White Light.
Ferret out the pain and take it forth to the Light.
Take the depression of the mind and the pain of the body to White Light.
Lift the tiny child before you to White Light.
See the child will, reach to the far land in recognition
  of that from which he has come.
Purity knows Purity, all children of birth know Purity.
The acknowledgment of desperation enters only
  as the vision leaves the Soul.
Some can vision longer than others.

137 Trust the instinct of the heart.
The heart is the path to the Soul.
See the Truth of all that is within the Soul.
Without is the earth only.
Stand from the inner battle.
Acceptance is the rest, the peace, the true Love.
Each day dawns in the east, the Energy Creator has placed of self.
Gentle the Soul.
The Essence can be visioned.
Tune the Soul with chords of Truth,
  endow the heart with a tender Love that has no evasion.
Reconstruct the mind to allow the Truth, verily, to be used,
  the Truth of your space to lift a brother.
Friend is the knowing hand of the other side.
Know that your guides walk in your step,
  they put forth the positive acceptance.

138 Soul, acceptance is a grace upon earth.
There are seven graces.
At Farside there are seven graces.
Acceptance is the last of earth graces.
Acceptance is the forward step to the Farside.
It requires that a Soul look within the eye
  and see the Truth of Farside value.

It requires that a Soul look not at the pain
    or unjust attitude toward them from another.
Acceptance is a beatitude.
Grace is the total of each beatitude.
Soul, clamour to understand that all Souls on earth
    begin with the first grace, observation.
The movement takes them through many lives.
The second grace is contentment.
The third grace is restitution for others.
The fourth grace is Love beyond self.
The fifth grace is the reservation of all truths and the taking of no life.
It is a forward step to acceptance.
Then there is the Purity of reaching out, the grace of giving.
Souls of earth, acceptance is the most difficult.
It is held as a forward step to rapture,
    to accept without any judgement upon a human Soul,
    but to allow a walk of the mind into a place of freedom,
    into nothingness.
Acceptance will not allow the miseries of earth to be looked upon
    without some effort by these Souls
    to requite the miseries of those Souls.
Acceptance has total honour and Love.

139 Michael, verily, will teach the Souls.
Defiance is the Path that leads to acceptance.
Since time of your plane began, humanity has been dominant.
When a man loses the Path,
    he is lost in a wandering sand of the trap of his own making.
Wanting to dominate, he becomes the victim of his own desires.
Gentle your Souls to the walk.
In the Path of each, time is on your side and the pure heart also reigns.
Where is a Soul who has made his lesson
    the negative side of acceptance?
Call courage forward to these Souls who must teach the lesson
    of acceptance in the positive robe of Purity.
Do not fall into the silent stranger or the desperate griper.

140 Hard is the Path that leads to tranquillity.
It is the register of the Soul's temperament that expresses the Path.
The Souls of earth each have a temperate zone
    that is the firm step of the planet's understanding.
The Souls come from different understanding.
The Souls come from different avenues to nurture the human self.
The goal is to be tranquil in the Path of the Energy.
The ego has a resemblance of frantic frenzy.
The Soul can not rest in too much ego.
The self is lost.
The self is to be in the Prism of the calm walk.
Into this space enter
    as a self who only withers at the sight of the negative.
Dear earth Souls, know that knowledge is not, reason is not.
The self requires only a calm walk.
In the Farside is knowledge, is reason, but no ego.
Therefore generate the Love, the Truth that defies ego
    and walk the Farside walk.
Michael will teach humanity ego.
It draws in circles about the self.
It has inward abounding, going, to escape the Path.
It carries refusal.
It carries denial.
It carries the potential of pain.
All Souls respond not to the clarity of ego.
Ego defined is pain,
    pain of refusal of the path,
    the walk of the lesson you have gathered unto yourself.
Soul, you are all things.
You are all that is, was, and will be.
Accept that ego is but refusal to search the path,
    to step on the way, to be a part of.
The Souls of earth bravely attempt to see self,
    to recognize within self the Love that could be carried
    as a shield about you but, Soul, with ego this is not possible.
Oh humanity, oh humanity, break down ego.
Tear the door of ego.
Allow the Truth of the Path to enter.

Allow serenity of self to flow.
Surely you know you would not give yourself an impossible task.
Surely you know the Spirit has made a wise choice.
Oh, Soul, oh, Soul, see the Prism,
    and the entry of Truth has vision of infinity before self.
You are not a capsule dropped on the world alone.
You are a boundless seed that will be nourished and grown.
The guides will attend the garden but the ego has solidity.
It has refusal, a refusal of the Soul to be nurtured.
Blessed seed, blessed seed, be nurtured, let ego fall away.
Know that pain will be cared for
    and weeded out as the gardener weeds.
The Soul cuts weeds and heals if the ego would allow.
All humanity endeavours to be forward looking.
Soul, be not so much forward looking as inward looking.

141 Michael will teach the gentle instruction,
    fain in the strong, persistent growth,
      if the Soul can not detour the step.
To detour the step is to remove oneself from it.
To fain is to remain on the Path.
Dear Souls, know fain.
It is the rest of the Soul's onward movement.
It is relegating the growth to a future time, yet the step is saved.
To relinquish the choice is to remove oneself from the used step.
Wait in the step in fain.
Use the rest.
Dear Souls, reject a person who would prod the mind
    to an altercation of evil intent.
Draw a circle of White Light around yourself.
This is fain.

142 Michael has Light, the true Light that requires no switch,
    the Light of the Purity, of the Energy that emanates all matter,
    the source of Truth that is creative
      and walks toward a perfect end and beginning.
Can each end vision that new beginning?

Under all tenuous words come meanings that flows with great force,
> even when uttered in silence, if they are issued in Truth.
Your very goals can become flames of the Truth in humankind,
> if Truth is walking with the Soul.
Know that greatness is only with that Soul's ego.
It has the underlying words of deceit.
But the humble Soul, honest in the walk,
> is not enamoured by greatness, only Purity.

143 Michael will teach thunder, the clap that registers clamour,
> the cymbals that register.
The earth values frantic display that has frenetic overtones,
> that evades the calm.
Let the Soul stand in thunder and grow to a height of the clap,
> for as the Soul is urged to a state of dilemma,
> so the turmoil brings growth.
Tears have no place in pain for us,
> we rejoice at a step.
This is confounding to the earth mind,
> yet the heart will recognize value.
Student, fear not!
Find the joy in the condition of stress,
> for to conquer such a condition is to be in the Path.
Know the Path of the tao is fraught with pain.
Go from that pain to acceptance.
All lives must seek acceptance.

144 Michael will teach the earth Soul acceptance.
This is the Path that you progress toward,
> the acceptance of all steps the Soul self has made.
Each Soul has a map of the register within.
The aura holds it firm.
It can not be altered by the Soul without karma.
The engagement of the foot to the Path understands
> that the effort to proceed is in motion.
Otherwise, life ceases.
The Soul is using the investment of the map
> to will the Soul to growth.

Dear ones, know enlightenment.
This is the Energy that is Creator.
This is the form of all that is.
This enlightenment is.
Marvel at the conquest of earth steps.
The gentle guides place care upon your path.
They wander to the fearful place and send the Soul alert.
They place nudge.
Behold the acceptance of the step.
The acceptance of earth differs.
This is an ego response.
Is the positive or negative operating the ego?
Ego is a facade.
It is the persona that is the strength of the religion
    that sends the Spirit to save a Soul already saved.
There is no Soul lost.
All Souls have the battalions of Michaels nurturing their being.
Fear not to be earthly.
The Soul has a mirror of reflection.
The map is never lost.
It is in the wisdom of the Energy that this is so.
Soul, the teacher is the self in Purity, Love and Truth.
The world is but a phase, it passes.
The register of self is in the Farside.
The flame burns strongly in the Soul to be with Creator.
Even baby Souls, in the throes of agonies of their choice,
    know the strong will to redeem self.
Dear ones, tempt not self to be perfect, only to step.
Soul, step as Truth is invited into the Soul with Purity and Love.
It reflects to others.
How else would we teach?

145 Michael will teach karma.
Know karma is a growth lesson.
It is an intervention of lives.
You may not intervene into the onward motion of another's step.
You may not intervene without karma.
Karma is gently done.

Karma is often unwittingly done.
Karma is intentionally done.
Karma can be repaired, often by a simple word,
    by a turn of the cheek, by the offering of self for another.
Soul, repairing karma that is carried from one life to another
    has greater implications.
It entails the agreement of many Souls
    who accept the responsibility of pain.
It is a growth effort.
A Soul achieves great wisdom in the repairing of karma.
A Soul has the ability to leap in Purity through payment of karma.
Karmic endeavours have mutual agreements on the Farside,
    first for growth, then for pain, then for growth.
It is triad.
It is done within a formed triad.
It is mutually acceptable by two.
The other is the Soul offering self to recover pain growth.
Look kindly upon Souls in lives of karma
    but do not weep, for tears are not involved.
Karma is created by Souls who leave a step undone
    when it effects the steps of others.
Only this will require reparation.
All karma is not evil.
Karma has negative and positive factors also.
Require self to seek well into the being
    and know the Soul will be tethered to karma
    created by the body, the mind and the heart.

146 Karma and the accumulation of karma must end
    before fifth level, Soul.
All beings with unfinished karma reach the level five two,
    and karma has been relinquished from their being.
The relinquishing has been by agreement or by solution.
All beings on the Farside are aware of the karmic connection
    to their earth being.
The Soul has settled many lives.
The Soul has agreed to many lives ahead.

Souls of earth are unaware of all karmic complications,
> but the goals are set within their being to respond,
> to overcome the karmic thread in their being,
> to make reparation to the Soul.

Behold, karma is neither negative nor positive on earth.
It is karma.
The action of karma is negative or positive, the cause, the effect.
Do not, Soul, enter in to karma lightly.
It has long ramifications into the settling of thy being.

147 Soul, within the boundaries of earth, karma is.
It has no reach into the Farside.
Karma is persuasion to alter the force of Energy to another Soul,
> Energy that is bound to a walk, a step.

Soul, be not amazed that karma can be carried
> from one reincarnation to another.

Be not amazed that karma can take many lives to fulfill.
Soul, you have karma casually in a day,
> and on the morrow you will repay the karma.

You will have karma that will detain the moving of self,
> removing self from great heartache.

Repayment is not casually done.
It is done with forethought always.
Karma is not coincidental, karma is not coincidently repaired.
Karma takes the value of another and alters that value.
Soul, cry tears of great pain when karma has been placed.
Cry tears of joy of angels when karma has been repaired.

148 Humanity is human and a thought is a part of mind.
Soul is not directly connected to mind,
> heart is directly connected to Soul,
> heart is connected to mind and flesh.

Soul expects thought, both negative and positive.
This is growth.
There is no karma attached to negative thought
> unless the thought is placed into a devious pattern
> and then the body enacts what the thought has planned.

Man would never attain joy
    if all negative thought were held responsible.
It is merely a process of growth.
Do not place pain upon self for thoughts of impurity.
Impurity on the earth sphere is reality.
Soul, the mind deals in knowledge.
It is the heart's response to the action of thought that has decision.
Souls of earth, respond to negative thought
    by searching through that thought,
    to the inner process of that thought.
Why? What sense has it been derived from?
Souls, prepare the heart to look for the positive outcome
    of that negative thought.
Derive a passage through the mire and the muck,
    through the devastation and the sordid dilemmas
    and find the golden thread.
There is, in all negative thought and action,
    a golden thread that can be grasped,
    it is redemption.
It is the redeeming factor of Creator.
Look for the golden thread and see the path of growth.

149 Michael will teach the adversity of humanity that detours.
When the Soul is positive, go to the station of serenity,
    the adversity cannot reign.
The force that drives is a teacher that is in the walk.
It is a choice that has a step.
Behold adversity, fear it not.
Step with it and visualize the rosy glow of the positive around it.
Growth is sustainable, the adversity is not.
It must be changed.
Stand in the forest of trees and behold nothing.
Stand apart and see a tree, then behold the forest.
So it is with growth.
The individual portion must be separated
    before the Soul devours the feast.
The goal is not to glutton, but to taste of life and learn.

150 Soul, we have but to see to recognize our need.
The stars are guideposts to the Soul of man,
> they hold answers that only a few can decipher.

Growth will happen through all struggles on the level of earth.
We, at our space, do not judge.
We see what we have done and learn where it is we must go.
A Spirit does not leave its Soul to struggle alone.
A candle gives warmth to the eye, the Soul and the heart.
Humanity is a teaching field.
Sexuality is a part of the being, of human form.
To grow is to take control of all parts of our psyche.
Each Soul has to accept control of their sexuality or be controlled by it.
The world is made up of many levels of growth.
Most are young and so, as young, act out the part that hurts others.
All Souls stay together in Spirit,
> oceans and oceans of stars at Light of goodness.

Friend, teacher, student, family, stand within walls
> that have been constructed of units of personal data.

Since the beginning of earth time this has been so.
We, here, see the Souls unfold their lives
> to accomplish their earth task.

They leave behind the awareness of our side.
They encounter Souls who provide the avenue of growth.
This growth is not always palatable to the earth Soul.
Know that each bend in the road exacerbates the test of the Soul's life.
Understand, the growth for Souls of age is known to them.
They are aware of the struggles
> because the earth can no longer confound them.

They have recall to teach their Soul,
> but the younger Souls have not this same recall.

The mature is seeking to finish goals, busy people.
The young are busy learning,
> they have great words to confound them.

The babies cry at the growth, it has no meaning.
Old Souls receive the step that is true to your Soul.
The step does not confound or delude, it is true.
We have steps that move a Soul forward in growth.

Defence is not growth, interest is not growth, justice is not growth.
Humanity is growth.
Truth is growth.
Purity is growth.

151 Friend or foe, all Souls have humanity in common.
That is the intrinsic Truth that is in the heart of all earth Souls.
The mind will reason that the Soul should die
    when the Soul has taken a life.
This is logic.
The Path, the tao, is not logic.
It is the step of the Soul to its own growth.
The heart hurts, the heart breaks and demands justice.
Then the heart looks to the Soul
    and is, at the level of the Soul, able to comprehend the evil,
    and the Soul knows that the evil has no thread to mend itself.
Only the positive introduction of Truth can heal the evil.
This is the Path walk that Souls forgive.
How many times must I forgive my brother?
To ninety times nine, it is in your teaching.
Dwell in the Truth as old Souls mirror to the world
    the Truth that is in them.
Stand firm in the tao that humanity is the learning field
    for the side of Purity.
Come to the Truth that all men are not created equal,
    that many Souls have giant steps, and others do not even walk.

CHAPTER 4

Healing

152 Universal knowledge is the world's way of adapting to the Path
    that requires the Soul to give all that it has and will, to the Truth.
Only the Truth is a step.
The earth has great difficulties in Truth.
Therefore it confounds the mind with wisdom created within that mind,
    when in reality all wisdom is before the Soul
It only requires Truth to behold the Path of the tao.
All knowledge of healing can be found in the tao.
The source of all that is flows ever forward.
The earth Souls have only to see with the middle eye to catch up.
Use the Path of Truth.
Purity is healing.

153 Understand that the travel that is in its infancy on earth
    is the conquered one on other earths.
The Souls have a great Energy source,
    have the knowledge of colours,
        while your surgeons still cut and maim.
The strength of the true energies is also found
    on several earth like zones.
The unravelling of movement of matter is known by some on earth.
Your Soul can know this healing.
It is done in the centre eye.
It is done without touching.
It is done as the Soul walks with White Light
    and rearranges the matter that is out of discord.
The Souls have the power within to reach that power.

The Soul must surrender earth time and become Timeless.
Join the teaching of the sorting of space.
All space can be sorted.
The space of matter can be sorted.
All is like a child with building blocks.
First you are taught a block is a block,
    then you are taught that a block can rest upon another block.
First know the block.

154 Michael has great, minute, and invisible knowledge.
It comes on the ions of the valley that has the name, respect.
Ions are the matter of all things that freely walk to the east,
    tao is the search of the ion.
To be in search is to be in Truth
    as even the human search for Truth is positive.
Stand into the window of respect for the ion that is yourself,
    your cat, your dog, your very table.
All is ion and accountable to its Creator.
The maple of the garden is ion
    and the very limbs that will be discarded
    will still be ion, as even the ash is a part of the whole.
Blended into the world station is the meld of all that is.
Take no thought for your tomorrow.
The ion will take the Path to the tao in the form it is designated for.
Its purpose is in its own Truth and needs to be free to walk its path.
Even the severed limb finds its Path to the tao.
Say to that tree:
    "Be firm that we believe in your walk
        and we will gather positive thought for the travel."
Know that all earth is part of a purpose
    and will meld with all that is.

155 Michael will teach the entrance to aura,
    the beholding of the earth Soul Light,
    the response to the chart of ion in the Soul's space.
Regard the ion as the Light.
It enters all fields, its cavities portrayed as flesh or wood or, or, or...

In the deceptive ion the gentle entry is not there.
The aura is frantic and swirls as the focus is travelled.
It surrounds flesh, it surrounds all matter.
It is the cloak of being that is shown in a positive ion.
The negative ion is a subtle entry.
It humours the flesh and decides the moment.
Each aura portrays colour and the invitation to colour.
All that is known is in the aura.
Sensitivity to the flesh can be felt
    when a Soul's Energy within bounces upon the aura.
This creates a term goose flesh.
It is a crown that is tempered with Light.
If the Light dims, the crown does not dim,
    but the Lights of the crown bounce for want of that Light.
Use the creative search for aura
    as a quest for the pure, pureness of a Soul.
The Soul vision is aura.
Therefore it requires Purity to see the aura.
Behold the ritual to the aura.
Position the heart before the mind.
Do not use earth logic to behold aura.
Rather, see the pure, tiny child of that aura.
It is a gathering place for healing
    and pleasure can not be taken in its reflection.
Dare to see aura.

156 Blessed, you are bound in Energy.
There are seven levels of aura.
Three levels abide upon the earth:
    healing, transcendental travel, essence aura.
You may be enriched by your Purity to emanate to other levels,
    but upon the earth plane you may not wear these levels
        for they are raiment over your being.
They clothe your being, they represent the Purity of self.
Behold, Souls of earth, to see a raiment of seven levels of Aura
    is to behold the blessed Jesu, the Soul Buddha,
        the Soul Mohammed, the Soul Krishna.

To be under the dome of such Purity is to be lifted,
    as the pearl from the sea is lifted
    and grows in radiance upon the flesh of humanity.
So the aura falls upon the Soul
    and is brought as the coat to the wearer.
It is the raiment of the blessed Angels and it rests upon their being.
Aura becomes dim when Purity leaves the Soul
    and the Souls can visualize the lack of aura
    or the great abundance of aura.
Man confounds simplicity.
You have pages upon pages of complexities
    when the words are simple.
Aura is who you are.
As you build aura, it represents to all life
    the placement of self upon the Path.

157 Brand the Soul with a touch of Love
    from the region of the stars.
Verily, we have the moment and the hour sounded.
Know the seconds even have the sound of the Farside.
Let the Light in.
It is the mind that disallows Light.
In the heart, the Light flows when the Soul has a vision
    through the positive of life.
Defend the illness with colour.
Defend the strength of mind with colour.
Protect the Soul of another with colour,
    it has understanding that generates the Flow of the Energy
    through the negative void.
Tend the Soul's speech.
Hear the words spoken in the Farside language of Love.

158 Soul, BE is Flow, is the onward space of growth that absorbs
    all Energy, all forms within the tidal wave of Energy.
Soul, expand the tide of man.
Bring the ocean wave to flow to oceans
    beyond those you comprehend.

Great majesty is in the Flow.
The Flow has two way Energy.
It destines all within the Flow to be positive.
It energizes the self, the state of BE.
What is IS?
What is BE?
You, Soul, are be.
Creator IS.
Soul, it cannot be separated.
You have been as all that is wave.
You have become the awesome state of Flow.
All mankind is in Flow.
All regard in whatever has the registration of Flow.
Turn the page and there will be Flow.
Find another earth and there will be Flow.
Magnify self in the honour and humility of man,
    become a part of that which resides ever upward
    to the Prisms of Almighty Creator.
Oh, Soul, behold the upward climb.
Jacob's ladder could not behold such a climb.
He met the Angels of the sixth,
    but beyond the sixth level is all that is Holy.
Bend as the river, upwards.
Be in the Flow of Holy water
    that magnifies Truth, Purity and Love.

159 Michael will teach Prism:
    Prism, Path to Truth, Purity, and Love.
The total of Truth, Purity and Love is the total reach of the Prism.
Colour begins in the softest of green,
    the total reach of peace, the total contentment of being.
It is the beginning of the Essence walk.
The Prism contains colour, similar, and yet unlike earth hue.
Your eyes could not contain the ambience of such Purity,
    the Flow of such crystalline iridescence,
    the tranquil state of total Love.
Colour and Sound are one in the Flow of infinity.

To be in the state of such Flow, one must enter through the centre eye.
One may enter in to the beginning, in to the seed of the Flow.
All has seed, and your eye would be required to shade
    the coming in or the passing through.
Farside beings may see the vision only as you see a star.
Beyond the star you see are stars and stars and countless worlds
    beyond your imagination or wistful thinking,
    and yet you are privileged to see the star.
Man has ever endeavoured to see beyond the star
    because within his Soul is the remembrance of infinity.
Prism is a walk into a holy cathedral
    where all the beings of earth who have entered in
    have left their Energy of Love and their Love is felt
    and gathered to one for strength.
The prism is a passage to your Creator, to the Energy of all that is,
    the crystalline iridescence
    that reflects all Souls of wholeness in Purity,
    and all Souls that are taken to the blessed place of Holy
    and dwell in the seven levels.

160 It is in the rainbow that the secret of colour is found.
Use a rainbow, blend the colour to colour in happiness.
See the prism be reality.
In the prism is healing and Light.
First see the Love of your own pure self.
See the inner Soul, then blend with the prism of goodness.

161 In all times are the songs of hardships sung
    but the strongest song is the song of colours.
It is the Sound that is a voice that has comfort for the weeping,
    food for the hungry,
    bread in the form of unified colours that heal.
Know the strum of the violin by the great masters
    have little voices beside the hum of sounding colours.
Tune the heart to hear the colour.
It is at the station of the Prism.
It is to be started by pure thought.

162 Michael will be the gateway unto the Prism.
It is the Path that is the foundation of all that is:
    the internal, external, within, without, great Light, the creation.
Then there was Light.
So the Light enters all ion in the immenseness of the wistful hunter
    that seeks the vibrant star.
It is!
It is the passage to the Farside.
Its Truth is to be understood as a Love by humanity.
Its entry is Love.
Its gateway is Truth.
Into the force of the world
    this star has a brilliance that cannot be rested.
It is with strong rays of ion that turn to east,
    that take the Soul to a space of Purity,
    to a destiny beyond the simple.

163 The passage gathers unto it colour.
And you see, as earth sees a sunrise, the golden flow of colour
    and your heart warms to reach out to that sunrise.
And early man and man of your contemptuous times,
    still reaches unto the east from a knowing.
And these Souls are brought to an awareness
    of the possibility beyond earth.
And as you enter the prism, you are aware
    of the possibility beyond and beyond and beyond.
And you reach out ever to be in that Holy Light,
    to be in that state of wonder,
    to be in the cathedral wherein you feel
    all the Energy of Energy of Energy,
    to the Energy of IS.
Colour of the Holy Ones is brought from blue:
    Souls who have lived in great Purity,
    and reached a Purity beyond the level five,
    the Holy Ones who have within their beings
    the raiment of only pure, of only blessed,
    who have never had an evil thought or carried a dastardly deed.

And the reach unto the Holy of Holy
    is enlightenment unto the Path of purest Light,
    Light your earth can only conceive of as white,
    but Light that could not reach your comprehension
    in its magnificence.
Endeavour to always search for the pure part of self,
    that you may be brought into the state of the Holy Ones.

164 Be brought to a Truth that all that is, is Energy,
    that all that is not, is negative force.
Hear the gentleness that is perfection.
This is the passage that unlocks the Soul to colour.
It is the serenity that comes first to BE;
    the united gateway of the Prism.
Know that we here do not have negative.
It is for you to search your Souls and enter peace.
Dead is not peace.
Understand that colour perfects all flesh and bone,
    all mind and vein of the pumping Truth of the form that is human,
    and respect that until these Souls retrieve the Purity of a child,
    this healing is only a vision.
Take the Truth we give your Soul.
Know that healing is for you to reach.
Understand and treat your Soul,
    know your Soul, know that the step is ready.
To the mind put Truth and white Purity.
All is possible.

165 Michael will teach the earth scale of values
    that little touches the Purity of the Farside.
The flesh is the casing for the Soul's endeavour.
It is the ratio of resilience that allows the positive and negative.
The Souls of earth value the flesh beyond the Soul.
They frantically identify the flesh with another,
    " *I am better*!" they cry.
The Soul's Spirit has another value,
    it is that of Truth, Purity and Love, only these three.

They weigh the level.
They create the walk.
This is the earth value of organ.
The body is used, it is free to use if it belongs to the Soul.
Beware of the intrusion into a walk.
This is to be cautioned.
Know the surgeons play with the flesh like a child plays with a toy.
Has the surgeon not the vision of the Farside?
Know colours, surgeon!
These take flesh to a new dimension, they transfer ion.
In ion they refute the negative and reform the tethered arm or leg.
They wash clean the gruesome fetid flesh.
Reach to the space of recovery.
Science, see colour healing.

166 Polarity in your world has one meaning.
Polarity for all other purposes has access to Creator.
In your world, when you face east at dawn, you are polarized.
All beings reach unto Creator and the access of that polarity is given.
Soul, you have within your being a central point.
It is what you call kundalini, life force.
The kundalini is activated by facing east.
They are awakened to nurture and strengthen.
It is why you receive healing.
It is the thread of your Creator.
The access of your earth is at dawn upon your being,
    therefore you are doubly polarized.
Polarity has great Purity, polarity is a gift unto man.

167 Blessed wonders.
Soul, accept the wonders of all is.
Accept knowledge of earth differs from Farside register.
All knowledge of eternity is within the Farside Register.
It carries the circle of positive and negative,
    it is complete and issues no judgement.
Soul, ego has spoken the word judgement.
Soul, polarity is the equalization of positive and negative.

It is the transformation that allows a Soul to rise up.
The Soul must be in polar.
The containment of self needs enervation; all clarity is enervation.
Behold the eye and the great Flow outward is negative,
    the great Flow inward is positive and you are carried
    within a timeless state to the being of your Essence.
Delight in the space in which you may dwell.
Invite the Holy state of Being.
You are then in the space of angels.
Polarity is a necessity to the cleansing of self.
It is done unconsciously by many Souls
    who walk in the circle of negativity.
One balances the other
    and to take the vibration of the polar place
    is to accept the radiance of vibration.
And the containment of blue is all encompassing,
    the value of blue Purity is the opening
    to the tunnel of ever and ever,
    beyond the Void to the place that Angels be.
Soul, carry the message forth that acceptance of vibration
    is awareness of being.
Polarity allows the Energy Flow
    to be lifted beyond the state of the world,
    beyond the state of the vision you see,
    to a vision within the Register of Time.
The vibration of Holy men and women
    have taken themselves to the place of vision,
    and the polarity separates into a nothingness,
    and the pathway is blue unto white.
Soul, revere the state of Purity,
    uphold the vibration of self.
Within the vibration can be no illness.
Heal being eastward and allow the negativity
    to flow from the flesh, and the mind, and the heart,
    and know the touch of angels
    and the blessedness of their Being.

Soul, behold the newborn child has vibration,
    and negativity will take vibration from the Soul.
It can be in the birthing chamber.
It can be within the womb of child,
    but negativity prevents the blessed state of vibration.
Soul, draw the hands separate from each other
    and know the power within your hand
    and know the pull of your Energy
    is as the pull of negative and positive ion,
    but vibration allows a pathway through, upward,
    and clarity is.

168 Knowledge of the earth is a trickle that is diluted
    in the soup of the stars, in the reality of the colour
    that takes each matter to a perfection of its beginning.
Soul, know the Path of east is the dawn.
It is always, for all Souls, at whatever point the earth rotation is.
The Souls must recognize that all globes give a circumference
    of visibility that extends outward from that globe.
The ion is a creation that is of the Farside.
It is the Path of matter.
All matter is to ion as paper is to glue.
The matter cannot be released in any way except the creation's rest.
The force of ion has a Path that is in the rest.
The gentle roundness does not present a problem to ion.
It is as a Truth that permeates all that is.
Will the Soul know the turn of the body at dawn?
So the earth turns.
The student has a record of aura.
It is the tone of the Essence.
It is the Soul state that is in the human form greatly missed.
The Souls of earth have much to discover.
It is in the aura that human form can find polarization.
Earth has an aura also, as all ion has polar.
Stretch the Soul mind to a place of infancy.
Into the infant put the solid food, it is rejected.

The earth is also rejecting constantly.
As a guide to the Farside, we see this aura change.
The rejecting Souls have red.
The receiving Souls have green.
The student of learning has blue.
So the interested state is in how to perceive aura.
It is in Truth a healing power.
It is given as an undergraduate of earth would receive the cap and gown.
So the student is given insight into aura.

169 Michael will teach the Path of healing
    that is tethered to the Farside.
Soul wills the pain, Soul wills the illness.
The Soul teaches the Soul to be forward as an infant.
The Light is a necessary part of being.
It is a situation of earth that men build houses
    to deny themselves of Light,
    then find the need to reflect it within the station they form.
The child gains if the child can be raised in Light of pure colours
    that blend and evolve slowly, gently,
    as the reach is slow and gentle.
The Soul's constant need for light is a Path reflection
    but it is Farside Light,
    the colours of healing the true Soul pines for.
Wash a child in the blend of Farside colours and behold the calm.
That child still has recall.
Use the colour for the aged
    who have been brought close by their guides
    and see the Truth of gentle healing.
Soul, what would you heal?
The earth cries *"Heal me, heal me!"*
The Farside has the station litany that states
    "This is the will of the Soul."
The Soul walk is foremost to healing.
Truth is in healing.
The east is the Soul walk of humans.
It is the offering of the Energy that has pure purpose.

East is a charge of the Farside.
All earth ion is drawn eastward in Purity.
Great minds can not yet fathom this tender Truth,
    yet the species they collude to
        have the Path they have been given in their heart
        because of their simplicity.
The east two earth minutes,
    the turn to purify all affected tissue can be given.
Station of earth is defeating,
    for growth is only come through the channel of gain,
        gain from anger, pain, treachery.
All must be surmounted.
The forlorn Soul in the rest is gently walking the earth,
    but pain is lost, then growth also is lost.
Soul, the guides attend the passing as a sacred greeting
    that envelops the Soul in Light.
The darkness comes only as the Soul denies the growth of that walk.
Each Soul has a momentous experience,
    then the Lights are healing and the passing can be delayed
        only as the walk is a part of this healing.
The resurrection of the Soul has always been.
It is a rejoicing that heralds the music, the joy,
    the realms of Souls that have walked beside this Soul.
Know joy for a passing Soul only.
There is only joy.
Work the mind away from worldly thoughts.
They are formed with sincere negativity that has no Farside pattern.
Dear Souls, know that even the passing is planned.
The Essence rejoices at the growth the Soul has made.
The Spirits of heaven rejoice at the growth the Soul has made.
Only earth cries; "Woe, woe, woe to us poor Souls.
Know these Souls are lifted by the purest of all that could live
    upon the earth and raised to that Farside home
        that has a place of pure peace and acceptance.
Free the Soul of any sadness.
Rejoice and be happy, be Radiant in that passing.
Extract the Farside Essence as a reflection
    by turning the south to east.

Will the earth not perceive the joy that is abundant in this Path?
Regard the east as the dearest friend, as the fastest Path to health.
Soul, know that generations of earth have this cost to them,
    they refuse east.

170 Soul, superstitions represent fear. Fear!
They are created from fear, valid fear, yet fear.
Ritual?
Earth humanity has always had ritual.
Ritual in its finest sense is focus and deliverance and receiving.
To face east at dawn is ritual.
Were all the world to focus on the east at dawn,
    allowing the negative to flow from their being,
    receiving unto themselves the goodness of Creator,
    the gigantic whale would leap from the ocean
    and no longer have to return,
    for man would have learned acceptance.
But man uses crass rituals in place of those which are goodness,
    they fain at the ritual and preclude goodness.
The ritual is a ritual of the Farside.
It is in the Energy Flow of ion.
It is an exchange of Purity, when needed.
All Souls respect the Truth of the ritual.
Signal is the same for all.
Use two minutes east, turn.
Use the forward look to the horizon.
Use calm, Souls, give unto the east the positive ion,
    return in the negative Flow.
Time and Timelessness meet to unite in Truth.
Do rest in the east.
Use a closure of aura as the Soul gains the positive knowledge.
The Soul's space is dawn.

171 East is entered in as a Soul entering in to the space of Creator,
    with great reverence, with expectation,
        knowing that all your being has been given to the healing,
        the blessing that will be bestowed.
Soul, colour that the Soul will naturally enter in is green.

It is unnecessary to focus to a colour.
Your being knows where east is.
It delights in the potential of home.
It is the quick movement of being,
    of Soul, to meet the Essence of self.
Oh Soul, your very being should vibrate with Energy,
    for you have all the availability of Farside Purity.
It awaits your receptiveness.
There is joy in heaven when a Soul faces east.
The mantle is placed over the being
    and the cowl of enormity flows through
    and the cowl is lifted off,
    and the being could not bear a glimpse of Purity,
    with the human eye, that enters in to your being.
Souls, allow self to enter in to east.
Glory in the flow of that Energy.
Delight in the song of goodness that the very Angels sing,
    and know that you walk from that space
    wrapped in the care of the blessed Beings.
Soul, rejoice.
Hallelujah, I am well!

172 The Path has been laid.
Michael will unite in the teaching
    of eternal cooperation of Souls to each other.
The transaction is done by us at station.
Path agreement is done several lives at a time.
Each Soul has fraternities like all earth Souls.
The ritual is the Path and all work by it is forward moving.
The harm can only come on demand for healing,
    the self will of a false persona taking a forward step.
All healing comes automatic if it is to be.
You, the Soul, have no pact to make.
The Path is yours by the Soul's walk.
We all walk in the Prism.
It is the Path of Energy.
It is the tao in the Truth.
The colours are for all.

Know that it is in the blend of mind, Spirit and Essence
    that the Path rests.
The face of the east is the start, the next step is the turn.
The avenue of direction is now bold, for the Soul has come far.
Reach further into the giving of self to the tao.
It is in the relinquishing of the mind to the Soul, to the Essence,
    that the forward movement comes.
The Prism is too radiant to have at once.
The Soul cannot bear such beauty.
It is to be given in time.

173 A passage is in line with the planets.
They move strongly eastward to the south.
They form the dense ridge
    that is in the eternal linear orbit of all matter.
It is the negative that moves in the counter position.
Find east, turn south gently with a firm step.
Start the ritual.
Turn east, face all time in its path, then turn circle.
The cleansing of the mind is in the east.
The cleansing of the Soul is in the circle.
Each Soul can produce anti strategy to combat ills
    by a further fifteen minutes in silent colour, all shades,
    to magnify the mind in a brilliant orbit of the Prism.
Hate will then be defenceless in all knowledge of the shades.
Vision of intellect will be forthcoming.
Total Energy is available through the Prism.
The ritual is not in your time system.
It is in the universality of all systems that are many,
    and the walk is the walk of the ritual
    that purifies all matter in Essence,
    that can stand then and meet the Energy, purified.
Stand east, then circle.
Fifteen minutes is not institutionalized in a course.
It is a time for the Soul to regroup with its Essence.
It is Purity.
First put the ritual in place.

Projection of thought will come.
It is ours to teach, not as the earth would,
  but as the Soul readies for presentation to the Energy.
It will become ritual.
It is the colour that heals.
It is the colour that is the Path.
It is not in that time to heal others.
It is in the healing ritual for earth beings.
Take this step slow.
Start in the quiet time, fifteen minutes.
Only think of colours.
Let them flow over and in you.
They will take their position as they enter.
Healing then comes.

174 Soul, Michael will teach the glory in the power of Love,
  the glory in the power of Truth,
  the glory in the power of Purity.
Souls have an avenue to that power.
All humanity has the availability of this Pathway.
It is as Jacob's ladder, and the Angels in their glory,
  entering in to the space of earth
  to spread their wings upon Jacob,
  to give him knowledge of Truth for mankind.
All Souls may raise themselves up from their sleep
  and, behold, the dawn breaks,
  the dawn breaks and the pureness enters in
  and all that is impure cannot abide the space of this Purity.
Blessed is man when man will arise
  and allow his being to enter in to the Path of the east.
And as the moment of glory is given, the Souls rotate the form
  of their being and all the Energy in that rotation
  carries the pain from all cells into the east
  if the Soul will allow this to be.
Souls of earth, be aware of glory.
Be aware of the magnitude of Purity
  that excels any and all that is upon the face of earth.

Souls of earth, you may barely comprehend the meaning
    of such abundant Purity that can be waylaid
    and found flooding your very being.
Lo, the goodness of your Creator will enter in.

175 Michael knows the step of reproach.
It is in the final decision that a Soul has the introspect of learning,
    yet the human element of reproach enters.
Lay the negative in east and ion will flow.
Truth is that ion.
The Energy will permeate the flesh, the mind.
The Soul will be in that space from whence it came.
The Farside gentles the Soul to be transformed into positive matter.
Fix the eye to the goal of Love.
No other goal is in this space.
Turn to a wireless state of reception,
    and be polarized in the on position.

176 Your being is ion.
The force of ion is Purity.
Ion holds the seed of negativity.
First, earth Souls conquer ion negativity within their being,
    for only those who have the stamina of battle
    will be in the Gathering Time[40].
The Souls of earth are blinded in their sight.
They see the withered eyes.
They seek not the eye of beholding,
    the cord of ascension, the connecting thread of being.
Soul, thou art Holy!
From thy Holiness thou hast entered in
    with a seed of Purity and the seed of impurity.
For, Soul, impurity beckons to a being at the moment of conception
    and the fuse deflects the stench
    and the Soul is brought to a test of being
    in the space of ion, of Truth, from the moment of birth.
The flex of negativity, the darts of pain,

---

40 Gathering Time - humanity's time of lifting the Blessed Angels from transition

enter in to the pure, beloved Soul
and the child that is human cries out to ward off the cast.
Ion of ion is pure, ion of ion is Creator.

177 Know the profound is simple on the Farside.
The simple is profound on earth.
Gently take the wave that washes over the Soul.
A newness is not the aim.
It is the ongoing stream of tidal waters
    that put the Soul to a negative place if the Soul is not grounded.
Take a start in the east to ground the Soul.
Know the wash of the wave moves the Soul closer to the Essence.
The Energy, the creation, is onward moving.
Fail not to seek east.
Rely on the polarity of your self.
Have confidence to seek Truth,
    then await the wash of the wave of Energy
    that is profound in its simplicity.
In the space of ion is movement.
The forward east is ever apace,
    the flood of ion within is ever flowing.
It is the polarity that must be considered.
It is the strong pull of the negative way from the Soul
    that is the force necessary to cleanse.
The dawn presents the force at its strongest.
Hinder not the Soul from meeting dawn early or late,
    if it is a choice of abstinence.
"My people have entered in to earth as your people."
"My people are not your people."
Soul, such words tear apart Purity.
We have come to speak of the east, of the worship.
It is not necessary.
As a deity, it is not necessary,
    but for humanity's well being, it is necessary.
Know, Souls, your earth could be contained in a quiet roll
    if you would face east for healing.

Healing

Acknowledge the power and awaken in your being
    the flight of Purity.
From your beings come forth myriads of Light energies.
They flow outward continually from your being.
At dawn, when your earth sun rises,
    you draw unto yourself energies.
You draw unto yourself, all Souls, messages.
You are a receiver.
You can receive a message from the Farside at dawn.
Will you listen with your eye and know the sound
    of the voices speaking to you?
Hear the words softly intoned upon your Soul.
Respect the giver and acknowledge the gift
    by passing the gift outward from thy being.
Souls of earth, you all may hold the feather[41]
    that has soared to high places,
    and you may catch the feather as it settles upon your being,
    and you may lift the feather and speak.
Speak of the days that will come,
    and speak of the Purity that will be.
Speak, Soul, of that which you have been given.

178 Your gentle walk is in progress.
The Soul's time to register the station of healing is now.
Hand is useless if the mind and heart do not recognize
the centre eye of the Spirit.
Use dear, dearest to the loved one.
Use the eye to the healing.
All flesh can heal, all mind can heal.
Toward the east is a Path.
Walk in that Path.
If the Soul's walk permits healing, it will be.
The Farside diligence is reflective healing[42].
The guides of the Souls have the strong admittance or deflection.
It is care.

---

41 hold the feather - express an opinion
42 reflective healing - to enter in to the Purity you are on Farside and allow the Energy to reflect in your healing

The summer of earth is as the Purity of life, rich in its hues,
  to be used, to be centred to the middle eye.
Search the heart to find that chord that is united to the Soul.
Invest in that thread chord and be brought to healing.
Take the small child within your arms
  and clasp the child to your heart.
That thread will be sent as a sliver to the Farside,
  entering the aura of the child to a healing.
Forward only Purity to that child.
Use the Farside to envelop the body in care and healing.
To be in this trust is to be an old Soul.
It is to be a pure Soul.
Know that belief is a token only of the healing.
The heart and body must hold the Purity to it.

179 The Energy is the Creator of all that is and will be.
Create is the understanding that earth has.
Creator is the force of creation that is timeless and endless.
Creator may know the end and the beginning.
Souls do not.
At our level we know that Purity is the Energy that we bathe in,
  the White Light emanating into our consciousness,
  that all life desires to be a part of that Energy
  that the Soul can feel great aloneness being apart.
Earth Souls of age in levels
  know the desire to be once again in free flight[43].
In the Spirit they separate themselves from the world
  so as to seem detached from living.
In Truth, it is only the desire to be once again reunited.
Know that human growth is not easy.
The lessons are humbling to the Spirit.
Let the Soul know that the Energy is the act of creation
  and never is forever.

180 Free flight is the flight that will teach the Soul
  to radiate atoms within the space of matter.

---

43 free flight - to prevent an occurrence.

The senses are not necessary for that occurrence.
The gentle walk is.
The Truth is.
The face of the Energy is Truth.
The flight is to be taken with the will.
The reach is accessible from the earth boundaries,
    and can be viewed by the Soul in White Light.
The door is open for all Souls to enter.
Let Michael take the Soul to free flight.
Student, the flight is a trip to the side of Truth,
    the side we have, the side we are.
This is a first lesson, that the Soul must believe
    that the Truth is theirs.
The Soul will be brought to the solemn understanding
    that all matter can be left by the Soul,
    and the Soul will see that matter as a vision of lifeless sleep
    and ride above the space of earth
    to be brought to any space prearranged by that Soul.
If the Soul knows the flight well,
    the Soul can soar beyond the scattered stars to our side
    and be rested in the Essence of its own.
This brings great quiet.
The Souls who do the free flight on earth are few.
They are serious Souls of the religion of the mind.
They are in the far advanced class of scholars in earth science.
They have reached into polarity and ride with us.

181 Meditate from a state of Purity.
Relinquish from self, all negativity.
Seat self, clear the eye, and the breath, and the voice,
    and hold the perfect circle of your being,
    and enter in to nothing.
Do not seek to find colour.
Do not seek to see vision, do not seek to hear words
    and all will enter in your being from a state of nothing
    to a state of awakening into the well of holiness and enlightenment.
Be.
Allow the breath of self to be given into the orb of nothing,

    so that your being will encounter the visions
    and quantums will bring you into the space
    of Energy and great Purity.
"Blessed is he that will seek goodness all the days of his life".

182 Beloved, tranquillity is Void.
White Light is the extension of Void.
Enter in to the space of tranquillity,
    of utter and complete stillness of mind and heart,
    that allows the Soul the entrance to the third eye.
Be brought to the tranquil state of BE.
Rejoice at the nothingness of where you are,
    the Flow into ever and ever.
Souls can reach momentarily the space of Void
    and behold, the vision comes clear.
Your Souls can languish in the frenetic space of mind and heart
    and the eye is closed.
The eye has vibration and the vibration is Energy
    that flows ever forward in the positive rotation of Purity.
Soul, the void is the transom that makes the Path clear to humanity.
Without the void there would be no vision to the Path.
Behold, to pass through the void into the space of the Energy
    is to ignite, ignite the very energy of self.
It is to know the pure spark of self Essence.
Be not enamoured with simple earth placement
    but search always for the place of Void
    that takes a Soul to ever and ever.
Be in a state of acceptance and offer self to the Purity of nothingness.

183 Blessed Souls of earth, fraught with indecision,
    drained by the inability to hold onto positive Energy,
    extend thy being.
Do not pray, but fold thy hands in the position of prayer with expectation.
Allow the glory of all that is to fall about thy being.
Bow thy head lest the abundance of the shower
    might overwhelm thy earth eyes
    and clear the veil from off thy eyes.
Seven times clear the veil.

Hold thy fingers together at the centre forehead
    and draw them apart, seven times.
As you do this, the colours will exchange themselves.
Know thy being,
    know the impending doom will cease to be
    if all earth Souls will find the quiet place of contemplation,
    if all earth Souls will master the technique of meditation,
    devout and purposeful, with the intent of raising thy vibration.
Allow thy Energy to still.
Hold no thought, expand no idea, but take thy hands
    and gently enclose within thy hands, a Light.
The Light is in the mind's eye,
    and place the Light of thy mind's eye
    at the Light within thy hand
    and thou will form pictures of the future before thee.
This, Soul, is prophecy.

184 Souls, open the eye, delight in the eye.
It is the visionary path into the well of understanding
    that is Enlightenment.
The source of all Purity is gathered within the eye.
Understanding will bring the pyre, the flame
that lifts itself into the awesome state of the gathering.
And know the vision that encircles your being
    is taken from the lower levels of self
    and uplifted to your higher being.
Soul, seek to understand all purities.
Seek to understand that all beings have within them
    the mark of the eye,
    and that they have placed their vision downward.
And enlightenment comes from the inward vision
    that seeks to find the goodness of self that
    that goodness may be offered to mankind.
As you walk in your day,
    place the bounty of your being upon others.
Cast the glance of Love, lift the voice of Love.
Use the arms to embrace the downtrodden
    and seek to anoint with oil those who have suffered.

185 Michael will teach the road of tranquillity,
    the space where deception and Negativity may not enter,
    the avenue of peace within.
The station of growth is not there.
It is a rest, a momentary jot in time that allows a Soul to recover.
This is that step of standing still.
The solace of balm knows that the need to be healed is in your space.
Tenderly envelop the mind in nothingness.
Allow the extremities to carry only the soft engagement of air.
Float to the space we will give you, the serene containment
    of the vine that is the golden thread of the Energy.
Travel to us in the heart.
Leave the mind earthborn.
Take the heart to the space of purple and enter the Soul level,
    then engage again the self to the great Energy of all that is.
Soul, we in the plane of increased learning
    can take your Soul to its Essence.
This is the Flow of Purity.
Dear Souls, know Purity.
Walk within its boundaries.
Urge the invitation of the self to partake of this recovery.

186 Whirl, whirl!
Great insights come from the tornado within the Soul.
It is an adjustment of ion that is constant
    and manoeuvres the Soul space as needed.
The investment of the step is a referral,
    and the adjustment is done by the Soul self.
Hunted and alone, the ego is frantic to be in charge.
Free space allows the ion to change again and again
    to redeem the Soul agreement.
Vile steps can be decided in the whirl of Energy.
Care can be placed by guides who have the whirl in their eye.
Crass ego is forlorn without the whirl of perfection.
The fulfilment of choice is ever the Path of ion.
Join the Truth of the whirl that enables a Soul to heal,
    to be fast in the self.

187 With knowledge and concern,
    the Soul can reduce the systematic turmoil of the mind.
Universal is the knowledge that is repetitive for all Souls.
Know the silence of it.
It is a solitude learning that enters the being
    with quiet attitude and steps into the Soul's Path.
Each Soul has a route of threads
    that are interconnected with all humankind.
Each Soul brings the stamp of their own signature.
It is in the Soul thread.
In no Path is there a lack of this substance.
The wisdom of knowledge from the lives
    is programmed to the Soul's mind.
This must be done in a soft blending moment.
A loud piercing sound does not allow entry.
Souls, seek the Farside knowledge in calm serenity.
Behold, the day is now upon us.

CHAPTER 5

Vision[44]

188 The lofty rainforest has a revealment of humanity.
The very core of existence is in the ion of the deep wetland.
The soft tissues of ion reverberate the connection
    that is the natural world.
The human mind has managed to escalate the erosion of decay
    that is unnatural.
Know the Farside cries at the investment of negative.
Human Soul, awake!
See the tiniest creature held aloft in the great threads
    and be astounded that your very existence
    is a part of the same ion.
The Truth is in the walk, but this walk is off the Path.
Dear Souls, hear the small voice
    that intones the wise old Souls to speak.
Interest the human ear to the insect, the fibre, the strong tentacles,
    that draw a picture of survival for earth.
Know in the great damp is no gold that men can not find in the cold.
There is no keeper but the human race.
Deter the toxic invasion!
Deter the flood of reality that stems from greed, from avarice.
Take a bold stand.
Reason only at the table of old Souls.
Baby Souls will not listen to the rhetoric.
We, Michael, have seen the vision before.
You are not the first to eradicate Purity.
In the solemn state of the records are many such fools.

---

[44] Vision - the dates at the end of each passage indicate
when the channelling was received.
It does not indicate the date of the vision.

Turn the leaf to the ion, not to the blank page that will come.
[August 31, 1996]

189 In the year of fear the earth will turn
    to a page of learning that is resistance.
The earth will tell the Souls that the register of pain is enough.
The earth will speak of the destroyer in the atom,
    the systematic force of negativity to the flesh that covers the earth.
Oh, earth Souls, weep deep, weep for the babies
    who have not been born to the advance
    because mortal Souls have withered the vine.
They have destroyed the roof that has a shape of Truth.
It is broken.
Weep, weep, Souls, to the Farside.
Be brought unto Truth.
Know the force of Purity is stronger,
    but the Souls are faint in the protection of the infant earth.
Universal sadness is the register.
Be in the space of Truth to blend a protection to earth.
[December 24, 1996]

190 Michael will teach the transfer of time.
The guardian of the earth clock is in the goal of the Farside.
Souls, the earth will not blow or take great steps apart
    because of age or because of knowledge.
The earth has a time that is tethered to humanity,
    to the core that is human.
To recede from that core is ego.
The ego will take the Soul to a different time,
    to a westerly time, to a caustic time,
    to a strange fire that feeds upon itself.
Within the human Soul is a magnitude that can defend the space of time
    and coordinate all ion to the reach.
Set date to Purity, to Love, to Truth.
[May 12, 1997]

191 Michael will teach the transformation of a learned Soul
    to a Soul of wisdom, wisdom within the Farside reach.

Together the force is insurmountable,
> without it is but an earth clay.

Souls of Truth, declare that the life of growth
> is reasonable to the Soul.

You have chosen this life.
Have you not entered the calm?
The serenity within is the reach
> that allows a Soul to meet the force of our side.

How delicate is the balance!
Souls, know the Prism, the Path that is in the inner eye.
Be calm, Souls.
We have great words that tunnel to the surface you are in.
Great human frailty is in the test of earth.
The lines of many shall be enmeshed in the strong force of negative
> whereas the Truth will counter each point of greed.

The inference of the great wall that is to be pressuring humanity
> will endeavour to lead nations astray.

Mark the time.
It is as the Ides of March.
It is a potential.
Would that the earth could face east,
> that ion of ion would respond to the trail of the stars.

[June 23, 1997]

192 We have a teaching.
The wind of freedom is being taken from the earth.
It is visible to the stretches of distant worlds.
The echo resounds and the freedom is to reach the great handiwork
> of the western sky.

The rumbling will be heard when freedom is given away
> to the Souls of the window of time.

The travel will become clear,
> and the Souls who have conquered this region of transformation
> will be in the capsule to visit the orb.

Senators will align themselves to be first to see.
A baby will live to become an old man.
[July 4, 1997]

193 Souls of earth, vanquish from your being tears for self.
Allow tears to well up within you for the state of earth.
Allow tears to well up within you for the state of man.
Place your hands in supplication
 and know that the Energy about you radiates with Holy Beings,
 and know that the hands may hold the gift of Purity to place,
 and the stench of mankind's evil will not bear
 the state of such Purity.
For in the place of Angels, man must hide his eyes.
Blessed be the Holy man who offers his being
 in supplication to the Almighty.
Blessed is the man who seeks not the apparition,
 but clears the curtain of iniquity
 and becomes enlightened at the font of Purity.
Souls, we gather the gems of mankind's Purity
 and we are connected to the Gathering Time.
It is in our place that you shall see the beads
 from the Hem of our Creator.
We are earth's messengers.
Redemption is always a gift that is possible.
It is the opening of the curtain of Purity
 and within the state of that Purity you shall see the Christ
 and His form shall be witnessed.
And the Love of Buddha, and the blessed Footsteps of Mohammed,
 and the countenance of Krishna,
 shall be found in the four corners of earth.
And earth will be as a great Prism,
 for the countenance of the Four Purities[45]
 will reach down and lift up the goodness that is.
[April 22, 1999]

194 We are dwelling in a system far into the Light.
It is not by accident that light years have time to enter in.
Souls of earth, reach into the zero and know nothing
 and you will find all.
We are anchored to the left of nothing.

---

45 Four Purities - Buddha, Krishna, Jesu and Mohammed

We are positioned beyond the belt of Orion.
Souls of earth, we have great existence.
We have transportation that is beyond
    the most complex of your idle engines.
Soul of earth, beware the time of desperation.
Four nations prepare attack upon the shores of North America.
All have entered in to the quadrant of negativity.
Enter in to the breath of the eye,
    enter in to the state of accountability.
Souls of earth, be.
We have level of pureness, too;
    we have gathered all beings of our planet
    to heal and reach into the Quar.
We will, at the appointed time, man all interplanetary vehicles
    to lift Souls of earth beyond the pain of its agony.
We, because of the state of Purity,
    may not allow the presence of impurity.
It would contaminate our nation.
Souls to be lifted will have Purity.
The vibration of that Purity will be visible to us,
    for in the state of our presence you are visible even now.
We have Timeless state.
Enter in to the variance of zero.
It is into the drag of meditation
    that draws the Soul into the state of nothing.
We can reach you there.
Many Souls exist on all sides of nothing.
All Souls existing in the outer perimeters
    are existences far beyond your own.
They have the record of earth before them.
They have the dexterity of your simple tools as nothing.
Souls of earth, it is not to find the balance of material efforts
    but to find the humanity of your existence.
All Souls who have found this Purity will be lifted up,
    the child from the mother, the father from the son.
One will be taken and five will be left.
Souls, alter the destiny of your being.
Enter in to the flight of purification.

Enter in to the vibration of all beings.
Souls, each has accountability to the presence of earth.
Each is brought into the perfection of creation.
We offer to earth, the avenue of survival.
[3 June 1999]

195 Soul, indeed, humanity is connected to star.
Birth of star and reentry into earth space is connected.
The Soul is tethered to a state of being.
Soul, you are treasured.
Creator of your being has only Love.
There is in the spew of creation, negativity,
    but negativity is being conquered by Souls such as yourselves.
You are at war with negativity and you have a star,
    a place of peace to rest your Soul.
Your Soul knows of this.
Your mind, your heart, your body, do not have that awareness,
    but you have a great battle in re-entry.
You are at war when on earth plane.
It is growth to defeat negativity.
You are a Spirit.
As a soldier goes forth on your earth to battle negativity,
    your Spirit has sent your Soul forth to fight negativity.
The battle is for self, but the self is of creation,
    and each battle is as the front line.
Each soldier enters in to the fray and re-enters the fray
    and re-enters the fray
    and the battle against negativity is being won.
There will be a time when a greater battle will come forth.
The battle will involve the engorged Souls of earth.
Earth will rupture and cast forth these Souls
    and Purity will await to gather the vibration of their Purity
    and the hands of healers will rest upon the Fallen
    and they will arise to a newness of self.
The conquering of Negativity is ongoing
    from the beginning of creation.
[June 17, 1999]

196 All earth, all earth!
Universe is in transformation.
It is not singularly earth.
There is growth, and growth is acquiring and letting go.
The earth will lose a part of its Purity, for only, Soul, by losing the Purity
    may it find the purpose of its being,
        and the Light of that Purity will descend once again upon earth,
        and earth will find a new direction.
The direction will be within the Spirit of man.
Man will no more seek to destroy man,
    for man will have been brought low.
Man will rise up and man will fall down.
The Light will transform the face of those beings
    who will vibrate and be brought into Truth.
Earth will writhe and do her pain and birth will come again.
So be it.
[June 17, 1999]

197 Michael will teach the funnel, the Eye of Beholding,
    the intricate weave, the Flow, the velocity of Purity.
Soul, embed the eye within the strands of your being,
    embed the eye within all the Energy of your being.
Focus the vision of your intention into the Flow of positive Energy,
    into the spheres that draw, as magnetics on earth draw forth,
        so the Energy within the eye flows and draws, and flows and draws.
Embed the eye in the resolution of Purity.
Who can see the eye?
Souls, sight of earth may not see the eye.
The framework within your being may not see the eye.
But the outer Flow that emanates
    that all creation might see the Energy,
        sees the eye.
To see the eye, enter in to the vibration of your being.
Enter in to the wonder of your aura and behold,
    sight will be inward and flow outward
and the Soul will see the atom of earth
    as clear as science of earth enters into the microscopic chasm.

Vision

The microscopic chasm enlarges by inward and outward flow.
Souls, the Eye of Beholding enters by the inward to Naught,
    to the outward flow.
The temple of your being has within the reach of your eye,
    the vision of your purest intent.
Look deep within the Energy of that intent
    and allow the petty, earthly whims to peel from your being
    as shackles that have bound you to earth.
You are entering in to the forward Flow.
Your eye has beheld what might be,
    and all energies will reach to the heights
    and you will see a great mountain as crystalline, as greatest Purity.
And within that mountain you will enter,
    and it will take you forward as fast as your Energy will allow,
    and you will see before you land your eyes could not imagine.
You will see before you the peeling away of the film,
    and you will enter and walk amongst Purity.
And behold, a being will take your hand,
    and another being will take your hand,
    and you will be altered in that day.
For the Energy of your being will flow and blend and flow
    and you will return in a moment and see before you
    unimaginable chaos and pain.
And the being that descends will offer Purity a new way,
    a restructuring of the being, a new format,
    a burst of Energy that will raise a Soul
    and replenish all that was broken.
And the Souls will say: *"I am whole.*
    Why?
    I have an extension of my being!"
And they will rejoice and move down the mountain and say:
    "Have you heard of the healing, the transformation?"
You are not one or two or ten.
There are multitudes of Souls as yourself.
They have entered in to a pure space of being.
They have a vision that gives and gives and gives and gives.
No longer will mankind kiss a cheek and slap the other.
No longer will mankind step upon the young and defenceless.

And man will say: "What world is this I am in?
    What is my purpose of being?
    Why have we been awakened from the deep sleep of torment?"
And the gathering will minister to Holy Holy Holy.
A new page is written.
The warmongers will not be.
The sky will be filled, not with metals but with beings
    who have movement within their own sphere.
A small child will lift himself and flow from here to there
    and mankind, in your day, will say: *"It can not be so."*
Wondrous beings, you have the key to movement within your being.
It is here, Soul.
The Energy is displaced here and here and here
    and the flesh has but to follow.
Behold the lotus blossom.
Behold the tenuous existence it has on the fragile being of man today.
It shall expand from a thousand petals of being
    to a thousand thousand thousand.
And it will be the Energy of you.
You Soul, and you, and you and
    all earth will hear of what positive Energy can do,
    and the laying down of old doctrines
    will be as the letting go of shackles from earth.
[23 September 1999]

198 Soul, earth has been visited and visited and visited.
Behold, within your very earth are reminders of beings
    who have carried themselves to your planet.
Initially in an exploratory mode,
    initially far above your earth knowledge,
    having left to different ages of Souls the discs,
    the tones of their own being.
The sound of tone would enrapture your Soul,
    it would carry you forth from a place of soil,
    high to the mountaintops with naught but vibration.
The Souls of which we speak vary.
Each of these beings in their separate homeland have
    for earth a purpose.

The purpose is to eradicate negativity.
And all earth casts an eye upward in fear.
Who shall come and torment earth?
The very beings have such Purity they would lay down their Soul
    as an offering to save your planet.
Blessed forms, earth visitations have been ten, eleven, fifteen,
    seventeen thousand years from your existence.
There are sacred writings, sacred sounds, sacred stones,
    upon which the imprint of their being has been written.
Generosity is their name, Purity is their name.
Beings of earth who have a circumference smaller than a man's arm
    and a head larger than a man's boot,
        Souls of such stature that your tallest recorded human
        could not attain the height of their reach
        and the smallest could not hold to their being.
Know, earth inhabitants therein, that visitation of earth
    is a generous statement made by all aliens.
The sound of the aperture through which the ships find flight
    is above the southern sky.
It is separated seven and will always be separated thus.
Behold earthling, how gracious thou art,
    for the multitudes come and the sirens will wail.
Instead, place upon the ancient rock, the Sound,
    and the aperture will open and the Souls will receive
    the Sound of voice that will be discernable.
High upon Ayers find the aperture to beings beyond your galaxy.
Soul, we have spent much time in the place of those you call alien,
    beings of great Purity, Souls high on the Register of Timeless.
Do not despair.
All earthlings have the opportunity to reach such Purity.
Within the cap of ice, man will discover the remnant of a downed ship.
It is, Soul, above China.
Hold unto self the Path of your Purity.
All aliens have just such a Path.
The endeavour toward earth is for Creator.
You are of Creator, thus the beings offer unto you survival.
You could not quickly discover the Light within the fracture.

It is set at naught, it is within the decibel of the eye.
There is, upon a circular disc, the decibel that will open the fracture.
The aperture will be heard.
Time has no merit in the fracture,
    only the eastward placement of the frame.
It must be done at sunrise only,
    Soul, year 2015, AM, dawn.
It is a gift and the beings will hear the circular motion.
Upon the high mountains of Tibet there also is a disc.
It registers the same fractured note.
It will give vision on that same day to a circle of monks.
They will read from the aperture the tomorrows of your earth.
Soul, the disc is in China.
It will be sounded and heard.
It will be placed upon a sounding board and sent through the aperture
    at the appropriate time.
All beings of level five will stand upon the rock,
    all Souls below will not venture upward.
Through the aperture a Sound will return
    that will give a gentle vibration
    and the song of sound will be heard.
A voice in the five will register the sound
    and the discernment will permit words
    to come forth from his mouth.
It will travel downward to the earth people
    and a visitation will be arranged.
Nine earth leaders will venture forth upon the rock
    the following one earth year, plus two days.
The Souls will negotiate the arrival on a chosen day,
    and man will be invited inward to his galaxy.
[Jan 18, 2000]

199 The fellowship of Saints, the oneness of creation,
    the blessed humanity that carries the effort of Purity
        to the ones lost.
Behold, enter ye into the Hallowed Halls of Truth.
Behold, enter ye into the Hallowed Halls of Purity.

Behold, enter ye into the Hallowed Halls of Love.
From ever and ever and ever
    comes the joyful resounding inflection of voices.
The Angels sing at the redeeming quality of mankind,
    for unto mankind was given the salvation
    and redemption of lost Souls, Holy Holy Holy.
Who has been in the depths of pain?
Who has felt the course of anger throughout their being?
Who has endured the agonies of infliction, desperation?
The Holy Ones lost in the depths of pain
    have carried the supreme refusal to look unto Holy.
The cast of their eye can not see where we are.
The recovery will be in the vibration of Souls of Purity.
The curtain of earth is altering,
    the shades of negativity are dividing,
    the armies are separating.
They are flanking the west field and the east field.
They are arming themselves,
    for the weapon is to be Truth,
    and the weapon is to be negativity.
The weapons of negativity will hold all violence
    that earth has not yet seen.
The light of earth will be darkened, the moon will find a night
    and the pure Souls will energize their being
    and surmount the mountain upon which their Light will reflect.
And as in the burning bush,
    then Creator will echo His voice forth:
    "Unto man have I given the opportunity of creation.
    Unto man have I bestowed My Being."
Souls, respond, respond in vibration.
Seek not the fork in the road.
Your Path is singular unto Truth,
    unto Holy from which thou hast come.
[May 8, 2000]

200 Souls, it is with the levels of Purity.
Farside has no negativity.
Negativity is not available.

It is not a commodity.
All Souls will be lifted from earth
    but not all earth Souls will choose to be one with Creator.
Some will choose of their own volition to stay at earth received levels.
It will be three[46].
The Souls will gift Creator.
From Farside there is no knowledge of whether these Souls
    will ever again receive an opportunity.
We do know that all energies caught in negativity
    will be lifted unto Creator.
Some will see only the Hem of Creator,
    others will be lifted to creation itself.
All purities are Loved and beloved.
Each being, each seed cast, has choice.
Many Souls cast have chosen to stay at earth levels
    from the beginning of casting out.
They are baby Souls and will always remain without growth in wisdom.
It is a choice.
It is the redemption of their beings to Purity
    that opens the eye and the vision becomes clear.
The choice will be known to them at the moment of choosing.
The opportunity of altering their being will also be known to them.
Know that Negativity will alter when the last Holy Holy Holy
    is redeemed unto the spiral of Purity.
So be it.
[August 15, 2000]

201 The level five is five.
All beings at the gathering will stand.
Souls, recognize Ayers Rock.
Recognize the accountability of mankind.
Recognize the receiving of the sound.
The resonance of the sound will be tumultuous
    and earth will be astounded at the resonance that comes forth
    as men stand upon the rock.
The beings of level five will also stand upon the rock.

---

46 It will be three: baby, infant and young Souls

Souls of earth, oneness is creation,
> but no one Soul is creation,
> no five Souls are creation.

Level five is the Purity, the attainment of humanity.
All will be, who have attained the level five,
> entering in to the Energy field of earth.

And earth will receive the resonance of clarity.
Nations will raise standards to invite the alien to speak
> and not know that they are speaking to the oneness of themselves.

Souls of earth, how fragile is your existence,
> how tender is the seed that is nourished by all beings of Farside.

Souls of earth, hold thy being, not in contemplation,
> but open thy being to the vastness of where thou art.

Behold, our Energy is your Energy.
Soul, you are one with the Michael.
Your beings are of the same Energy.
Souls, lift thy Energy and know thyself.
Lift thy Energy and behold the rock will become clear.
It is in the vibration of Souls that the Keys will enter in.
It is in the acceptance of all Purity.
Behold thy being, behold the awareness of thy being.
Souls of earth, tremble not, tremble not at what will be,
> but invite thy being to know that which is.

You are radiant.
You are beloved.
Souls of earth, we invite your being to Ecstasy.
Souls of earth, be thou pure.
[September 27, 2000]

202 Platform of Purity, platform of deity, platform of Love:
> seventh to Creator.

Souls of earth, beyond seven is an entrance that,
> even for Souls of immense Purity, there is hidden.

Soul, to clear the veils that you in your earthly state
> might visualize what is Farside,
> requires a Soul to be at one with Purity.

To be a Soul of the Farside
> and visualize beyond the entrance into the Realm of Creator

is as your great wind that whirls and whirls and whirls,
    and you know there is a passage through the wind.
You know if you only have enough calm, you can enter in to the wind
    and yet it is placing yourself within the correct space.
How may you enter through the wall that is profoundly whirling?
Only when a being has learned Love,
    has gathered all Purity unto self and the cloak is worn,
    and all guile, all self intent has passed from your being
    and a Soul's direction is forward into the unknown.
Souls of Farside, as the prophets of earth entered through the whirl,
    they have seen the fragments within the entranceway.
They know within the entrance is sacred.
They know that the form they have will alter
    so that even on the Farside all differences will be made as one,
    all purities will come together to meld as one.
And yet we know there is an unseen, formidable task ahead.
We are not open to a new climate entered in.
We enter in and obstacles surmount our way,
    obstacles in growth, not in negativity but in Purity, in Love.
Where all growth of earth has been with Truth,
and all growth of Farside is in Purity,
    in the extension of creation, all growth will be in Love.
Do not harbour negative to the words that are given,
    for the Angels will guard the sanctity of Creator's space.
And gently know that you will lift your Soul's Spirit
    unto the Essence place and enter in to the garden of utopia.
The fronds of Purity will blend,
and the fruits of Truth will be laden with Love
and the Souls will find the thread ignited with Energy.
All humanity will enter in to this sacred space.
All humanity will wend its way to the unknown Gateway.
Souls of earth, the great drums will sound, the cymbals clash,
    and as the children of Israel came forth from Egypt,
    so all creation will come forth into alien land.
Brother and stranger will bloom in the garden of goodness,
    and the prophets will pronounce the litany that will be given.
For the Hosannas will reach to the High Creator
    and the Spirit of Creator will become visible to all.

And the Gateway will close upon all that have chosen to remain
    in the outer realm of creation.
So be it.
[February 21, 2001]

203 Soul, we have drawn your being to us,
    for the Farside is impaled with grief
    at the velocity of man's inhumanity to the saturation of evil.
Within the framework of earth is a Timetable
    that can only be altered by the face of Truth.
Howsoever man proceeds
    is the path of his own making,
    for the earth is in its gasp for relief
    from the agonies put to the very core of its being.
The letters have gone forth to the heads of state
    and the forage for the path will be found
    in the second blight on mankind.
Souls, you are desecrating the foundation of Truth,
    and thousands of martyrs in the form of innocents
    have been given an early path to Purity.
We have power to draw you to the purpose you intend
    and the how, to man, that which is their intent.
We do not have the power to alter in any whit that which will come to be.
Only in the unification for man is there power.
[September 11, 2001]

204 Souls, despair is frequent upon the face of earth.
Despair is an avenue of growth.
Despair, in its wretchedness, points a finger.
Souls of earth, you have perceived a fracture upon humanity.
Creator, your Creator and our Creator, sobs at the pain of man.
The pain has no direction, whether it be east or west, or north or south.
Pain is pain, flesh is flesh, abominations are abominations.
The timetable of mankind has been set in motion.
The mark is moving up.
The mark is as embedded
    and the flow of blood draws the mark to the eye of being.

When the eye perceives all that it should see,
    enlightenment of earth will be.
But man fraternizes with evil as a plaything, as a devious toy,
    and looks unto the mother of his being and says:
    "Mother, see how holy I am."
Earth has momentum, all beings of earth have momentum.
The sole purpose of that momentum is to reach Farside perfection,
    to become the state of Purity.
Earth Souls, you do not see the abundant Light of your being.
If you could but glimpse the aperture of whom you are,
    you would cease all negativity.
You would cease the markings of negativity.
Souls of earth, ingrained in mankind is the need to overcome.
The negative being seeks only to overcome his neighbour.
The positive will seek to redeem that which was lost.
The night wails with the sounds of little children crying in the wind.
But the wails come from the very bowels of earth
    where children have ever been brought low
    by mankind's inhumanity to man.
There is a deliberate act.
It is the act of redemption that has a purpose in your beings.
Souls of earth, seek not a negative advance
    but hold yourselves worthy to be brought into a wash of Creator.
Holy Energy thou art.
Holy Energy thou wilt always be.
[September 11, 2001]

205 In our moment, we have travelled to earth.
We have seen the darkness and we have seen the Light,
    and our Energy can infuse earth beings.
We have a great power to lift Purity unto earth.
We could lift earth.
It is within our power, but the purpose of lifting earth
    is secondary to the purpose of reaching Truth.
It is in the reaching of Truth that earth will be lifted.
You may tremble and grasp your hands in fear
    and gaze with wretchedness about your being,

and mothers will cry and cover themselves with ash
and lament in loud voice:
"Oh Creator, what have You done to our children?
What have You done to our beings?"
Your Creator has done not.
Your Creator would lift you, but you have instructed Creator.
How powerful is earth
    that the fruition of all energies should be completed
    for the purpose of redeeming the Blessed.
"And we ask of Creator only to look under the canopy
    and see that which we do, and bathe us in Tears.",
    these are the words that humanity has spoken unto Creator.
And we offer to you the reminder of these words:
    "And we have been bathed in the Tears of Creator,
        and we have entered in to the wash of colour after colour
        after colour, until we have entered the blessed violet."
And we ask, Soul, that you reach through the pains of your being,
    the inconsequentialities of your being,
    and recognize the higher being of whom you are.
Blessed domain of earth, you are the outer edge.
You, who could gather and lift all beings in transition,
    remain in the earthly green,
    and the earth agreeing is treasured, truly treasured,
    but it has the igniting of reds.
And we would ask you, Soul, to release all greens and reds,
    and rise through the blues into the colour of violet.
Wash your world in violet, harbour no resentments,
    hold no offences to thy heart,
    but place forgiveness unto all men in all places.
[September 25, 2001]

206 Souls of earth, we have the vision of all your earth.
From our view we see the pockets of iniquity,
    from our view we see the pockets of pain,
    from our view we see the pockets of greed,
    and we have no power in our space to intervene,
for we know that which is being done.

We have maintained a proximity to earth,
    and we have noted in our acknowledgment
    that there is an aperture awakening.
It is, Soul, within the space of Australia.
It is but a seam, but in the space many will see the seam open,
    and many will come to register the sound that enters in.
Souls of earth, earth men will gather with sounding boards at the rock.
They will query: "What is this sound?"
    and they will know in their being,
    the slow vibration of their thought alters the opening.
And they will find and invite the holiest to enter in to the space,
    and the sound will vibrate to the opening of the aperture.
We, Souls of earth, would have you acknowledge directly:
    upon the rock will be seen the aperture.
It will come from Souls sensing what will appear to be magnetism
    from the depths of earth,
    and they will feel within their body, an altered state,
    and when they look, they will see the seam.
[October 2, 2001]

GLOSSARY

Agape - Creator Love.

agreement - contract with other energies for Soul growth.

Akashic Record - the map of creation's growth.

Angel (capitalized) - the Ecstasy form of Angel.

aura (uncapitalized) - three levels of humanity's aura on earth.

Aura (capitalized) - Four upper levels of Humanity's Aura on the Farside.

Cleansing River - fragment of Wisdom sent forth by Creator to contain Negativity.

Creator Triad - Creator, Godhead, Great One.

Crystal Cave - illuminated Light of all energies

curtain - curtain of care placed by the Angels to protect all Farside creation.

east - the flow of all matter into ion.

Ecstasy (capitalized) - that Energy Field which lies beyond total Love.

Energy (capitalized) - Creator's Flow.

Enlightenment (capitalized) - reaching of high consciousness.

Essence - the part of the triad of Soul, Spirit and Essence which never leaves the Path of Creator

evil - humanity's negative intent materialized.

fence - a vision downward from Farside to earth.

Flow - Creator's Path.

Gateway - Gateway One is unto Creator existence. Gateway Two is unto Creator and Godhead existence. Gateway Three is unto Great One existence.

Holy Holy Holy - the Blessed Angels.

Holy unto Holy - manifested Souls.

illusion - all energies reflected forth.

ion - state of being.

IS - the consciousness of Creator Energy.

karma - an action, positive or negative, that alters the life walk agreement.

Keys - <u>Creator Trilogy</u> is the first of seven Keys.

Naught (capitalized) - space of Void.

nudge - a prompt from your guides or angels.

Path (capitalized) - Creator's Path.

purple - healing Energy colour.

Quar - implosion.

Soul - fragment of the triad of Soul, Spirit and Essence.

station - place of learning.

tao (not capitalized) - Creator Path, Creator Flow.

Tapestry (capitalized) - Akashic Record.

transition - a self-inflicted, voluntary state of purgatory of one's own unaccepted actions upon earth.

tunnelling - Energy used to assist another being.

vertical lines -record of human interaction.

violet - healing Energy.

Void (capitalized) - wherein all consciousness abides.

vortex - the rise of a triad to another triad.

weave - the energies of humanity.

Wilful Child - the reflection of the Energy of Negativity.

Wisdom (capitalized) - the ultimate of Truth.

Writing on the Wall - the agreement of the Spirit for the Soul's walk on earth.

Zero - Naught.

APPENDIX A
Daily East Ritual

East, it is the passageway to the Farside through the eye.
Its Truth is to be understood as a Love by humanity.
Focus on east at dawn, allowing the negativity to flow from your being,
    receiving unto yourself the goodness of Creator.
All humanity has the availability of this pathway.
The ritual of the east is the Soul's own response
    to the positive east which is tao.
Face east, two minutes.
Look with the eyes to the horizon's level.
In the brick wall or the iron cage, or the ornate boardwalk,
    know that the east will be with your Soul.
Turn clockwise once to heal.
Energy will flow to the matter before it.
All organs of the body are healed in the circle turn.

APPENDIX B
Forthcoming Publications

Creator Trilogy
First Key
Creator Trilogy, Trilogy of Consciousness, The Gathering Time, Part I
Creator Trilogy, Supreme Being Trilogy, How to step to the Path, Part I

Second Key
Creator Trilogy, Trilogy of Consciousness, From Whence It Came, Part II
Creator Trilogy, Supreme Being Trilogy, The Angel's Ecstasy, Part II

Third Key
Creator Trilogy, Trilogy of Consciousness, Ecstasy Part III
Creator Trilogy, Supreme Being Trilogy, The Rejoicing, Part III

Energy From The Source

The lofty rainforest has a revealment of humanity.
The very core of existence is in the ion of the deep wetland.
The soft tissues of ion reverberate the connection
that is the natural world.
The human mind has managed to escalate the erosion of decay
that is unnatural.
Know the Far Side cries at the investment of negative.
Human Soul, awake!
See the tiniest creature held aloft in the great threads
and be astounded that your very existence
is a part of the same ion.
The Truth is in the walk, but this walk is off the Path.
Dear Souls, hear the small voice
that intones the wise old Souls to speak.
Interest the human ear to the insect, the fibre, the strong tentacles,
that draw a picture of survival for earth.
Know in the great damp is no gold that men can not find in the cold.
There is no keeper but the human race.
Deter the toxic invasion!
Deter the flood of reality that stems from greed, from avarice.
Take a bold stand.
Reason only at the table of old Souls.
Baby Souls will not listen to the rhetoric.
We, Michael, have seen the vision before.
You are not the first to eradicate Purity.
In the solemn state of the records are many such fools.
Turn the leaf to the ion, not to the blank page that will come.

So Shall It Be

Channelled by Kitty Lloyd through the Entity Michael,
High Beings and Angels

Fourth Revised Edition

Copyright @ 2012, 2016 by Kitty Lloyd

All rights reserved. This book may not be reproduced in whole or in part, stored in a retrieval system, or transmitted in any form or by any means; electronic, mechanical or other, without written permission from the publishers, except by a reviewer, who may quote brief passages in a review.

Published by: Mountaintop Healing Publishing Inc subsidiary, Creator Trilogy Publishing
P.O. Box 193
Lantzville, B. C.
Canada
V0R 2H0

email inquiries: mountaintophealingpublishing@shaw.ca

Fourth Edition
ISBN# 978-1-988448-01-5

Imprints: Mountaintop Healing Publishing

Illustration, Purpose of Humanity, by Tara Cook
Cover photo courtesy of Grace Piontkovsky

Preface

So Shall It Be is the second volume of the **Creator Trilogy**.
(preceded by **Energy From The Source**)

THE TEXT WAS CHANNELLED, RECORDED, selected, arranged and proofed as a group effort by the same six participants, each continuing their originally assigned task. Each step has also been subject to verification by the Michael Entity. Given the complexity and significance of the message being communicated to humanity, we have again retained the original text without any changes to syntax or vocabulary and have only added footnotes of our understanding of the text and a small glossary.

Dear readers,

Within a sentence there often will be a word capitalized, yet that same word in another sentence will not be capitalized. The capitalized word is specific to the Farside, the uncapitalized word is specific to earth.

For example, humanity comes to earth armed with Truth. Capitalized Truth is an attribute of Creator that allows humanity upon earth to recognize and overcome negativity created by man. Uncapitalized truth is a reference to earth conceptuality of the word, truth, a truism. An earth plane truth changes as wisdom, knowledge accumulates. What was truth for you as a child, more than likely changed as you matured. Capitalized Truth does not change, remains always true.

Tara Cook
Joanne Drummond
Lucille Dumouchelle
Kitty Lloyd
Grace Piontkovsky
Roman Piontkovsky

Table of Contents

	Preface	173
	Concerning The Trilogy	177
Chapter 1	Other Worlds	187
	Purpose	187
	Intent	199
Chapter 2	Holy	208
	Earth	208
	Vision	234
	Transition	273
	Farside Levels	291
	Purpose of Humanity	301
Chapter 3	Holy Holy	302
	The Holy Ones	302
	Earth Connection	316
	Tears of Purity	341
Chapter 4	Holy Holy Holy	348
	Upper Regions of Creation	348
	Within the Seven Levels	362
	Arrival	368
Chapter 5	The Bringing Forth of Purity	373
	Who Will Be First?	373
	Oneness in All Creation	379
	The Blessed Who Come Forth	391
	Glossary	403
	Appendix A equation of T	407

Appendix B   Daily East Ritual · 409
Appendix C   Forthcoming Publications · · · · · · · · · · · · · · · · · · · 411

Concerning The Trilogy

207 Soul, the volumes have a purpose to earth humanity.
It will not bring the answer to earth.
The answer will be derived by earth.
It is not spoken to one sect, to one religion, to one area of expertise.
It is spoken so as to reach all endeavour of humanity.
Do not fear.
The text will be made purposeful and Souls will contemplate at great length
 over the meanings of these words.
Souls will recognize in their being, the Truth, the purpose of humanity.
All books will bring the Souls to higher vibration,
 for before the Entering In,
 the beings must vibrate at a level so as to denounce all negativity[47].
Souls of earth have such potential
 and many have gained that Purity, but they are few.
The army awaits on Farside to join with the army of earth.

208 Since humanity gathered together
 as beings upon the planes of Farside,
 the Keys are offered by Creator[48].
Messengers would be sent forth unto earth and earth would know,
through the eons of time, that which would come before,
 and that which is given is a Key.
And, Souls, unto earth, in your time, are seven Keys to issue forth,
 seven Keys that will raise the spirituality of mankind
 that man will see indeed his brother as his brother.

---

47 negativity (uncapitalized) - mankind's grappling with negativity, creating evil within that negativity.
48 Creator - fragment of the Triad of Creator, Godhead and Great One.

And Souls who war will bend and offer unto the stranger
the seed to replenish the land which is barren
and open the waterways that water might spill over the land
    and free the drought that is to be.
Only does man hear when man has heard the refrain in his ear.
Only then does man take notice and say:
    "A messenger came and gave to us a forewarning."
Messengers are upon the land and the Keys are offered
    unto growth and acceptance and compassion.
Blessed humanity, within your realm,
    within the corner that you are, are three Keys[49].
They are as one.
Humanity waits.
Souls, be not confounded as to how humanity will know.
Behold a time will come when a Soul will enter in
    to the vision of the Keys
    and cause great tribulation, and stir great agitation,
    and flaunt and broadcast that which should be known.
For earth chooses so often to do that which is positive
    through negative means.
It is the way of humanity to overcome all negativity, is it not.
Do not be downtrodden when such a time overtakes you, but rejoice
    and know that which you have heard
    peals as a bell unto the distant land.

209 Know, Soul, the volume[50].
The volume speaks to all humanities, all cultures, all classes.
The volume has Energy, momentum within itself.
The world has not yet entered in to the momentum,
    for, Soul, the three will cause great dissensions.
The three will cause great contemplation,
the three will bring great accord unto the powers of man.
Each Soul will know the content.
Each home will speak of the content,
    and the Soul will look differently at those reviled, at those in pain.

---

49 three Keys - Creator Trilogy.
50 the volume - the Creator Trilogy

The swirl has only begun and all who enter in at the beginning
    will not always see the vision from the same side.
Souls, all other books, except for those holding the Keys,
    are only testaments to the Truth,
        the validation that energies of the Farside speak to many Souls
    in many languages, in many efforts of being.
The coming together of Purity for the sake of the Blessed
    is not for a hemisphere, a continent.
It is for all worlds, for all energies, all creation,
    and we of the Farside speak to any positive Energy we may.
Souls, do not allow ego to overflow.
For what you do, you do well.
But you are not the only Souls that do.
You are the Souls who bring forth the volumes three,
    the Keys for humanity.
Souls, know the purpose of thy being.
Do not Soul, expend thy efforts in this and that.
Thy purpose is clear.
Thy Energy must not be wasted.
For Souls, humanity, creation, Creator, await the effort of thy being.
Extend all energies to oneness and know the purpose:
    that all be accountable to the table.
Soul, it is done.

210 There is, Souls, an urgency for earth to receive the Keys.
All beings have been brought unto one.
All beings will enter in unto one.
Souls, earth is as the great tree bearing fruit, heavy laden.
The apple that has been tainted and the tree is earth,
    and earth is overwhelmed by the weight of the fruit.
And the trees sags and says:
    "Souls, remove the fruit for the fruit is ripe, and lessen my pain."
But the Souls are slow to heed.
Many have come to thy door.
The solutions have been thought and pondered
    and still the Souls rival in their beings.
Judgement is there,
    for that which has been given unto Creator cannot be returned.

Know this, Soul.
The Keys are a gift to Creator.
Thy beings have all humanity.
All Farside is waiting.

211 Souls, question the road thou art on.
Humanity, question the road.
Humanity, awaken thy being.
Know there are to earth, seven Keys to meet at the crossroads
    and give man a full understanding to why man is.
Earth has seven centers of gathering, seven Mountaintops.
Each Mountaintop gives forth a Key unto humanity,
    each Key in its own time.
All together give earth the last opportunity to stay that which will come.
The time to hold back the forces of earth's agitation is drawing short.
You, Soul, are at the crossroads.
The seven Keys will be entered in,
    seven voices strong in the need
        to alter the course of earth and earth negativity.
The Angels will come forth because of mankind.
Earth does not have to agonize in the coming forth.
Humanity could draw forth Purity now!
Who will follow the path to the crossroads
    and extend their being to fulfill that which is written,
        for that which is written is written upon the Wall of Creator[51].
Behold thy Purity.
How pure is thy Purity!

212 There are Keys seven.
And within the volumes of many words,
    earth has known the path to conquer negativity.
Man has not deciphered well the code.
Seven Keys will be given that man may decipher the code of Purity.
Souls of earth, three purities will be brought to the western hemisphere:
    one to the east, one to the west, two from the south.
Souls, the book is written.
The Keys have entered the lock and now it must go forth.

---

51 Wall of Creator - the Akashic Record, Creator's Record of every iota, every action of all creation.

The seven Keys are the puzzle.
Placed together they will have continuity
    that mankind will see as in a mirror, that which he has been
    and will issue forth an edict to all men of all races
to turn the plows into works of art,
    to take the swords and make them into plowshares.
And all the world will be as a circle in perfection
    and earth will no longer starve their children,
    and the harpoon will no longer gather the flesh of High Beings.
The Purity of Creator awaits recovering of the beloved.

213 Soul, the Key is one, but the Keys are seven.
There are many keys and Souls connected to keys.
All earth has a key that unlocks the passage unto the blessed Souls.
Recognize the apertures are slowly opening.
The wisdom is being filtered to earth, for the time of iniquity is done.
The time for spirituality has become.
Earth is awakening.
Humanity is evolving from the negative unto the Holy.
Many will lose the battle but win the war, for it has always been so.
There will be no losers.
Truth is entering in to all languages.
Four alien nations watch over earth, enter in and speak to earth Souls.
All beings are led unto the purpose of humanity.
Do not bring thy Energy unto a human being.
Bring thy Energy unto the message of the messenger.
The messengers of earth are many.
The Souls have great Farside Truths, Purity and Love.
Know thy being, know that all the visitations to earth
    are done with humanity's approval.
Speak to these beings.
Acknowledge their worthiness.
Acknowledge the gift they bring.
Behold the flight.
Behold the alien.
Behold, they exist to assist mankind.
Do not be hesitant to issue forth thy Truth.

214 Michael will teach the portion allotted to earth,
    the Keys to salvage mankind.
Souls of earth, you are not the first
    to be the last.
Elijah, Michael, Jesu, Allah[52], Paul, Christopher,
    the list of messengers is long.
Souls of earth, do not distort that which is.
It is in distortion that the tablets are destroyed.
Unto thy being be true.
Unto thy being,
    know the message is earth and earth
    anxiously awaits that which is.
Moses has brought the tablets of stone down from the mountain of Sinai
    and Souls have heard and known the wrath of negativity,
    and men's refusal to see that which is written.
And that which was written was passed on and distorted to man's liking.
Souls of earth, do not distort!
The need to be swift is Truth.
Mankind awaits.
Know it is a sacred endeavour of thy Soul.
Words are deceivers if maimed by man.
Do not alter a jot or tittle.
Souls of earth, your language does not bear interpretation,
    for words are vacant in your language.
Enter in no words of substitute, allow blankness.
The earth will redeem the order of words
    in the single language of computer.

215 The Keys are volumes of wisdom.
The Keys are given through messengers five.
Soul, know the messengers will be found
    when all Keys together, all Keys, are brought to one place,
    and minds of earth contemplating.
Do not think that all contemplating will be in favour of these Keys,
    all know much will be in the disfavour of the Keys.
For under the dome will the literature come forth,
    and Souls will seek to place credence upon that which earth sees.

---

52 Allah - one of the names of Creator. The first messenger, subsequently there were many others.

As twelve men issued forth the voice of Christianity,
> and twelve followers issued forth the words of Buddha,
> and twelve teachers issued forth the words of Mohammed,
> and twelve Holy men issued forth the words of Krishna,
> so will Holy men issue forth the words of volumes.

It will be given contemplation
> for the simplicity of the text,
> > for the complexity of the text, and for the revealing visions of earth
> > that will reveal themselves unto man in the acts of violence
> > by earth and man.

Know the high mountaintop.
Know that earth indeed trembles
> and the Souls who climb to the mountain
> for the sacred knowledge of Creator,
> will resound as a bell pealing over a valley.

So earth will hear the sound of the bell in its strident tones of Purity
> and the knell that must be heard.

Souls of earth, know in your being that all that is written will come to pass
> and tomorrows are shortened by today's pain.

216 Behold the mountaintop, behold whom thou art.
Souls, the mountaintop is the diadem
> when the seven Keys are entered in to your earth.

Your beings are to the mountaintop.
Souls of earth, see thou who you are.
Know the flight of birds of earth reach high unto the mountaintop.
Know the vibration of your being will bring you to the mountaintop.
Have you not been brought forth!
Have you not entered in to the gift of the Key.
Souls of earth, seven Keys offered to mankind
> to prevent the desecration of earth.

Did you think earth must be sacrificed?
The Soul of earth thinks not.
The Soul of earth cries to man, to Creator:
> "Offer Thou to humanity a solution!"

And the Souls of Farside have cried unto Creator:
"Give us Souls a Key!"
And Creator has given to earth seven Keys,

each Key to overcome negativity,
    the first three to draw all men unto one fellowship.
We see thy beings, earth men, walking on different roads,
    pushing and shoving and leering
    and hating those who walk on separate roads.
Beings of earth, whom art thou?
More valuable than the sparrow,
    more awesome than the star in your galaxy?
Souls of earth, presume you to think you are better
    than the very Energy you are?
Creator has created a Path to oneness.
Behold the oneness of thy being.
Reach to thy brother, clasp his being.
Know the palpitation of his heart is as thy own,
    the flow of blood is as thy own.
Can you not reach unto the Path and say:
    "Soul, may we not find a central meeting place?
    May our roads not all come to Thee at the mountaintop?"
For, Soul, it is the diadem, the crown of thy being!
Behold I AM.
Behold I AM!
Say to thy being: "Being, I am of my brother, I am of my sister,
I AM of my Creator".
Souls of earth, the Keys are found sacred
    and the gift is given in Truth, Purity and Love.
Accept thou the mountaintop of thy being.
Draw thy being to the sacred place of healing.
Behold, when the Four enter in to earth,
    the Mountaintop will be a placement.

217 Souls of earth, wretched party to negativity,
    who would push the frail down to the ground,
    who would hold the food from the hungered,
    who would refuse a cup for the tiny Soul,
    who would see in another's face a vision that is not their own.
Foolish humanity, all oneness is in thy being,
    all togetherness is in thy being.

Would that man would believe the messengers who have come forth
    to knock and sound the knell of earth.
How, how placid art thou, earth!
How placid art thou that you have given your beings
    to come down to the depths of negativity.
Souls of earth, all thy beings are gathered in Love that encircles the earth,
    for is thy gift to Creator not above all.
And Soul, we send to earth a plea to know that which is for humanity.
Believe in that which is before you.
Believe in that which will be.
Know how quickly can come the restoration of lost Souls,
how quickly can come the entering in to the pale.
Believe all that has been given.
Rejoice in the belief of thy being.
Souls of earth, humanity is blessed.
Believe in that which you are, able to walk with the angels.
And overcome, not the downtrodden,
    but the negativity placed upon their Souls.

CHAPTER 1
Other Worlds

Purpose

218 Humanity amazes our side, for your diversity is great.
Our beings, unlike your own, are mirrored in the same fashion.
We have one density, one purpose, one path.
Our path and purpose is humanity, and we delight in that purpose.
All efforts of goodness are not accounted as Purity.
All efforts of evil have not always the face of evil.
For earth is marked with a veil,
    the veil is thin and visible from our side.
The Entering In is done for a single purpose,
    the purpose of overcoming negativity.
All beings Entering In have Purity,
The designation of negativity, of a righteous life, is their own.
There is total choice in humanity.
All beings may wither at the vine,
    all beings may execute their own demise,
    all beings may continue on to a fruitful end.
The choice is within humanity.
The seed of humanity rests in the entering in,
    for the Soul has found it's power through the Spirit
    and the Spirit has placed a blessing upon the Soul.
Souls may revisit the Spirit at will.
They have the power, but few enter in to the power.
Know that your very vibration has the potential
    to see the Spirit of your being.
It will invite you to see that vision.

The clarity of the vision will be given from your Essence,
    for your Essence will discern the true intent of the Soul.
You are not simple, humanity, you are diverse and complicated.
You are a joy to behold.
You discard your own humanity as though they are rubble.
You form great plots against humanity
    as though they are worthless.
You plan intrigue and dastardly deeds to wreak havoc
    on the most gentle of Souls.
We ponder in the ineptness of your diversions.
You dawdle at what you have chosen to do.
It is blatantly clear from our side
    that humanity stays within the child form
    for many years after age should have taken place.
We do not cast reflection on this effort;
    we merely point out to earth its inadequacies.
All humanity, as one, has a purpose.
You are not a leper and unclean,
    you are precious and not worthless,
    you are sacred and beloved!
See your form.
The torso is useless without the head.
Humanity often runs amuck, the head lost in useless aberrations.
Illusion is difficult, is it not?
All Farside encourages earth to be one.
You have come from One, you are not delineated on Farside.
The purpose of your entering in was not to delineate,
    but to overcome delineation.
How fractured, humanity, may you be?
Soul, you may be as fractured as you will,
    but the purpose of your being is the Purity of your Soul,
    to offer unto Creator the scarred form of your being,
    to hear the Blessed[53] in their throng of goodness,
    drawing down unto thee, that you might enter in
    to the lost space of transition.
Holy beings you are, and yet you ravage the cloak
    you have placed about yourselves.

---

53 the Blessed - Angels

You spend countless hours in preparing a form
    and you shun Purity in your space.
Magnificent is the Soul of earth!
We are not with the purpose of marking your form in a negative way.
We are requesting that earth attends to the purpose of earth,
    that earth see one Creator in your space,
    that you recognize all else as that which would come
    when you have entered back into Purity.
Creator awaits your perfection.
It is the gift you have offered.
See yourselves as great beings,
    profoundly on a mission of great Purity.
See yourselves mastering the strangling vines of negativity
    and casting them from thy being,
    and you will have seen true, you will have recognized
    that which you are: holiness, Purity and Truth.

219 Beloved, your earth, your beautiful earth,
    which was formed by Creator for you,
    was given as gift and placed in the space of all negativity,
    and earth and its people have survived.
Earth and its people have not become inert.
They have survived what we have been unable to survive.
Our worlds became inert, we became non beings.
We were as asleep with no purpose,
    and earth has maintained the purpose of her being
    to overcome negativity.
Earth can not, could not, contemplate how revered
    all energies see her to be.
You, in your paltry flesh and bone, in your inability to rise,
    in your inability of deep continuous thought,
    have done what we have failed to do.
We have all your knowledge.
We have known what you are able to know.
We have the ability to rise, to alter,
    and you have remained earth bound.
You, who starve your babies, who slaughter,

who are devious and contemptible,
      have risen above that which is devious and contemptible.
We see Souls of such humanity
      that the Light transfigures where they are.
We see Souls who have set aside
      that which they could do for themselves
      and have made their only purpose the purpose of others.
They do not do this with anger, they do not do this with force,
      they do it with Purity and Truth.
They have risen above negativity.
They have been in its depths and they have not cleaved unto it.

220 Soul, we would take you into a garden more fragrant
      than all earths combined.
We would take you to see an ocean more wondrous
      than all waters you have ever surveyed.
Soul, we would take you to lands that ignite the Soul,
      to creatures of the land and the sea
      you have only seen reflection of.
There are gardens of lush growth of such magnificence, of such colour,
      there are waters you may enter in
      and flow into the everlasting wonder,
      and Souls who reach out to know and share
      and express the knowing, the knowledge.
There are Souls who are teachers
      who offer to your Soul that which you would know.
There is artistry beyond which your mind could comprehend,
      and it is where we are.
We see the wondrous kaleidoscope of creation
      and we may be here, or here, or here
      but there we have not yet come,
      there is beyond where we are.
It is in the Path of Purity, it is that place of Purity that we reach unto.
You have on earth beloved Souls to you,
      those you reach unto and cleave unto.
Here we also have beloved Souls we reach unto,
      we know of through many lives on earth.
We have beyond the pathway the worlds that would enter in

and we meet and rejoice, and they ask:
"How is the battle?
Is the battle being won?
How long are the days and the nights in the battle?
Are the Souls that have entered in aware of their Spirit's joy?"
We gather in groups to talk, communicate of that which earth is doing,
    and we see the desolation that man is reaping upon earth,
    and we gather at stations with great purpose
    to counter the negativity with Love.
Souls of earth, know that your earth garden is a poor reflection
    for that which you will see,
    but know your earth garden is that
    upon which humanity has been given rest.
Nurture the land and nurture the space you are in.
Let your energies flow unto healing round about you.
Watch, Soul, where your feet tread.
Watch the miracle of your Energy and know
    you have the power to alleviate all negativity, all pain.
Hold the power that you have and know you have the ability
    to still a living Soul to total calm.

221 Soul, our being extends itself to thee.
Behold our planet.
It is a planet far beyond your own.
It is a planet of All Knowing Energy.
It is as an earth reactor.
It is a clarifier; it is research.
It is the purpose of delving into creation.
We are fourth level to Creator.
Soul, our system holds no gravity, it requires none.
Our system is complex and weighted in heavy, dense minerals.
It has intense heats, it does not alter our instruments.
It provides all that would make our reactors possible.
All research of earth is foreseen ahead and accomplished
    within our planet.
Know that all guidance to the mind is offered from our planet.
Know that it comes not only to earth,
    it comes into the many spaces of being.

Creator has ever encouraged research and visitation
    unto the Holiness of creation.
All complexities are made simple by understanding.
We, too, have exploration.
We, too, have great minds that delve into the wisdoms of Farside.
The knowledge of earth and the knowledge of Farside differ.
The knowledge of earth is only knowledge until the Truth alters.
Knowledge of Farside has Purity as its anchor.
There are, in creation, worlds yet unexplored.
There are perfections born that, because of the blessed Battle,
    do not have to deal with Negativity.
They have only to emerge into the possibilities of their being.
Growth is expansive on the Farside,
    it energizes all within the planet of our being.
Soul, be delighted to know the form of our being.
It is garbed in Truth.
It has movement as yours has movement.
It has a torso as yours has a torso.
It has a functional whoosh you call brain.
It is as gelatinous in that we have the power
    to thin our being or thicken our being.
We can enter in to crevice or expand ourselves to mount heights.
Heat does not affect our being.
You have humanity that walks on fire.
As Meshach entered in to the fire, so may we.
Behold your earth being.
Shadrach, Meshach and Abednego were placed in a burning fire
    because of the belief of their God,
        and King Nebuchadnezzar opened the furnace of the great fire
        and saw the Souls in prayer to their God.
You, too, may be Shadrach, Meshach and Abednego,
    but you will not overcome the negativity.
It is time in your space.
Dispense with time, dispense with negativity,
    for it is illusion and you are indeed perfection.
What is placed in the hand of man's mind is not always used
    as the gem that is offered.

222 All Farside offers to earth.
All Farside has a Holy agenda.
All Farside knows of the purpose of their being,
    and many have become aware of the purpose of earth being.
The Farside is vast, it carries detail upon detail,
    vortexes such as your earth is, vortex upon vortex.
It is not strangulated in negativity.
It is not carried on a wave of self infliction,
    but rather it travels to a destiny of its own.
It is the purpose of Farside to be.
When you are in be, you have attained some manner of Purity.
Purity is as layered, folds upon folds upon folds.
Many Souls in the state of Purity reach unto earth.
They have become aware of the mighty enactment of goodness.
Enactment of goodness!
They have looked within their being and found a purpose,
    and their purpose is not unlike your own.
It is to assist the Fallen, the Angels
    who carried all Negativity from their being.
And these Souls called to earth,
    they speak to earth, they minister unto earth,
    they have great dedication.
They have given up all existence except the existence
    to support the Souls of humanity.
Earth has never been asked to give up one iota of their being.
This has been a choice of earth Souls.
You are in the midst of a great battle.
It is indeed a righteous battle, not a religious battle.
It has Holy endeavour.
Make no mistake, humanity, you are revered.
My Brethren[54] have lifted you oft times.
They have carried you and covered you,
    but, Souls, the one thing we can not do for you
    is to teach you acceptance.
This you must do.
Acceptance of the Purity of your being,

---

54 Brethren - the Angels

  of the goodness of your being,
    of the worthiness of your being.
Farside lifts in unified effort their voices,
    to extol the goodness of humanity.
Soul, carry your being as worthy.
Why are you downtrodden?
Do you not know that we pass you Light?
Do you not know this 'hear'[55] is our being, it flows unto you?
Tremble not, tremble not to see an Angel,
    but know the Angels tremble in anticipation of what you do.
Holy, Holy unto Holy[56] art thou, humanity.

223 Souls, unto earth is the solution of the Holy Holy Holy.
Unto earth is not the solution of negativity,
    it is the overcoming of negativity.
Humanity has entered in to the space of negativity
    to conquer negativity within their being,
    not to conquer all negativity.
It was more than the Blessed could do.
Negativity, the Energy of which is ceaseless,
    is ever attempting to be invasive,
    is ever attempting to enter in.
The Blessed recognized this need of Negativity to devour,
    the voraciousness of Negativity,
    and they absorbed and absorbed
    and absorbed yet more Negativity within their being
    to offer relief to the many worlds
    that had their beings strangled and contorted and inert.
The Blessed Ones, even with Purity,
    did not find a solution for Negativity.
We, of the Farside have a great desire to aid this Energy,
    to help this painful Energy that must draw violence to it.
It can not be at peace.
The betrayal of Negativity was the inability of all purities
    to alter willingly the space of negativity.
Souls of earth, recognize as your science places great efforts

---

55 hear - the third eye has colour and sound.
56 Holy unto Holy - manifested Souls

to feed into the great chasm of negativity,
to endeavour in many ways to gather research,
to enhance negative forces,
the Farside has equal research.
It is to alter all energy of negativity.
It cannot be through force.
It may only come with the efforts of Love.
Souls of earth, you will bring us back our Blessed Ones.
When you have returned to our being
you will also know more of this Negativity
and many will join the Farside research.
So be it.

224 Souls of earth, you are not alone.
You are not in any form alone.
The earth is carefully watched, the earth has many portals in.
The view is constant and has been since earth was formed.
Soul, the portal to Pleiadia is close to your being.
Pleiadia has a single purpose, it is the concern of humanity.
Our placement is alien and we delight in that placement.
The naked eye could not see our beings,
but your scientific systems could reach into the star.
We may see you, earth beings.
Do nothing that is not written.
All beings who move the Energy field of earth in the smallest,
most insignificant form is accounted.
Conquering negativity is the purpose of your being.
It is the purpose of our being to tabulate all Energy fields,
to recognize the time of gathering.
The Pleiadians are of the armada of four[57]
who will enter your earth system
and provide the transportation from the heat
and the gasses that for days will surround your planet.
Earth, and the struggle of earth, is only a gentle portion of our being.
We are connected to all creation, we all are gatherers.
We are gatherers of information that is taken to the beings of the register.
There are many such beings.

---
57 armada of four - four alien nations

We look at all earthly action and our abilities as aliens
    allow us to interact with earth beings.
Our form can withstand the pressures of your earth,
    our form can become totally visible,
    our form can manage all intricacies of your form.
We have the ability to enter in.
It is not for deceit, it is not for a purpose other than positive.
Soul, know our beings await your purpose.
Soul, grasp the extension of our being.
We reach it unto you.
Souls, our beings disorient negativity often.
We are alien to you but we have a purpose of altering
    in order to prolong earth's existence
    so that all energies may be recovered.
There is a strangling in negativity, there is a clinging.
There is a need to know that you have the power to disorient negativity,
    that it can withstand little Purity, that as Purity reaches unto it,
    it repels into itself.
It then becomes powerful and yet powerless.
Powerful in that the strength has become stronger,
    powerless in that the Soul must use this power.
All negativity must be circumvented.
All negativity may flounder within the use of Purity.
Please know this.

225 The Energy of the most disillusioned Soul
    upon the face of your earth carries a magnitude
    that would confound the sciences of your day.
The energies will open doorways
    and Souls of earth will visualize before them beings.
These Souls have lived side by side with them.
The earth has countless beings.
The imagery of these beings is unacceptable to earth.
The imagery that they portray is that which is like yourself.
They have a jaw that does not move easily.
It requires the speaking to be very indirect.
The Souls flounder with the voice.

You will see the effort they have in speaking.
It is, Soul, inconsequential lives that they form.
They form these lives so that they might mix
    with all Souls of gentle intent.
We would have you know they have profound Purity.
They also have difficulty with skin in the space of earth.
Many are found to have lesions.
It is because they may only stay upon earth surface for short times:
    six months, nine months is a maximum,
    and then they must absent themselves in some form.
Often it is in the form of coma,
    often it is in the form of deep depression.

226 These, Soul, have a single purpose; it is to read humanity.
It is directly associated
    to the negativity that these beings, humanity, are in.
You will see these beings always with a form accountability,
    a book to monitor, a computer to monitor,
    a speaking system to monitor.
We of the Farside have a great desire to feel that negative energy.
You see, it creates lesions in our beings.
We cannot be in the space of this negativity
    your flesh has been created to withstand.
Energy of negativity divides, it conquers by division,
    it is kept captive by Purity.
It is, Soul, kept captive by Purity!
Please understand the magnitude of that which you hear.
It is why the Blessed are where the Blessed are.
They hold the Purity captive because Purity holds the Negativity.
Purity has progress.
The ear hears, negativity hears.
It understands, it communicates, it has knowledge
    and marks the being with its knowledge.
Understand, in the gathering time,
    when humanity draws forth the blessed, the Holy Holy Holy,
    with the blessed will come the negativity.
It will be a thousand years of overcoming the negativity.

It will still not have a solution.
The solution will be the Hinterland.
Souls of earth, we know in our being,
    because we have written word of that which will be,
    that the entering in of all Purity,
    the mark of Holiness will be known in all Souls.
They all will carry the mark of Holiness,
    and the Second Gateway will become a reality.
We do not know what is the positioning behind the Second Gateway.
We have not knowledge farther than where we are.
We do have the understanding that Love, great Purity,
    resides in a distant place.
We have the understanding that we will be drawn
    into the distant place.
It will be to prevent a touch of negativity
    from altering our beings yet again.
Only earth Souls have made this happen.
Our vision takes us into a place where the Blessed reside.
It is at the space of entering in.
The purest of our beings do not see beyond that which is.
The great Melchezidec[58] has beheld the passage in, but may not enter.
He will lead the blessed mothers[59] in.
Your most calm, truthful, honourable being,
    having no deceit or evil intent,
    may carry a Blessed One forth.
The coming forth will place upon earth
    the possibility of conquering negativity,
    for the Blessed Ones have been in the state of Negativity
    for eons of time, have learned much, but will not speak
    until they are brought forth.
Souls, the very Energy of your being, the very sanctity of your being,
    has the purpose of all Farside, of all humanity, before it.
Sing songs of praise unto your Creator.
Lift up your eyes and know you are the hill from whence cometh all help.

---

58 "Melchezidec, to whom you speak, has not dwelt upon earth form. We have entered in the Spirit of our being, but flesh has not been ours."

59 blessed mothers - the mothers of Krishna, Buddha, Jesu and Mohammed

227 What we attire ourselves in is a profound Energy.
It reflects from our being and can alter in shades as we desire,
    and all Souls are welcome to our world!
Many come from other worlds to see that which we have
    and our world is a world of Farside knowledge.
Our beings gather information from each point of creation,
    and all creation is vortex, vortex unto vortex
    unto vortex unto vortex.
And behold, that which we account is from new creations, new energies.
Many create and the creations astound their being,
    it is a delight to have the power to form.
That which you are the Soul recognizes within itself.
The opportunity is always welcome within the earth we are.
Souls of earth, our being has no hair as your earth being has.
Our eyes are all the same hue of violet.
Our form has solidity within the Aura, it can be touched by other Souls.
The purpose is to welcome all beings to earth's door.
It is the purpose of all creation
    from the day of first casting out.
The Holy ones that have fallen have always been guarded
    from the gathering momentum of negativity.
And our being encircles their goodness, and our purpose is
    to welcome the Souls unto the first level of entering in.
It is to read the record of their being to them
    that we have placed ourselves at the door of return.
Souls of earth, be thou with us in the gathering of your time.
The moment of your revelation is set,
    and the Finger has touched for Purity of creation.

INTENT

228 Oh, Soul, our being sends Energy unto thy being.
Know the Energy of our being
    and know that all Farside extends Energy unto humanity.
We are united in our effort to reach unto humanity.
There is no negative energy in our existence.

We Love all beings, we reach to distant fields
    and welcome the energies to our being.
Farside exonerates all.
Know humanity could portray a negativity that would be forgiven,
    for Love forgiveth all things.
Know Love, Souls of earth.
Know Love unto Creator
    and know the benefit of the Flow unto thy being.
Rejoice and be made whole!
Rejoice and seek the wind, seek that which alters.
Withhold, Soul, the edge of the eye.
See that which is ahead of thy being.
Keep thy focus on the reason for thy being.
All our energies are extended unto thee.
Know all our purities are extended unto thee.
Our being is short lived on earth.
Do what our being can not do.

229 Do you know that we Love you?
We Love you, humanity!
It is more complete than simplicity, more complex.
There is a knowledge that we have.
It has been always the knowledge that we have,
    that at a time of timeless Energy
        time will cease and become Timeless.
This we know.
We know that Souls from the place we are
    have placed themselves in the space of time.
We know that you, humanity, are these Souls.
We know the source of your being has come from where we are.
We know that you have rallied unto Creator to a transformation,
    that you have become as Creator is.
This we know.
We know that our energies reach out unto all humanity
    without discernment.
There is, in our knowledge, a history of time of great pain,
    and the pain you now have.
This we know.

We know there will be a glory that is beyond the glory we have.
We know it is the Holy way, the walk of the sacred.
This we know.
We know we are not worthy to walk upon the Path
    but we reach always to bring greater Purity to our being.
We know in the history we have
    the Brethren came and spoke of a Godhead,
    of a precious new beginning where all would be altered,
    and the marks of negativity would leave,
    and the profile of humanity would be altered.
This we know, that the altering will happen in a twinkling
    when a great chime sounds through the heavens.
This we know.
We know it will come after the knell that sounds
    the beginning of the end of time.
This we know.
We know, earth beings, that we are not lesser than thou,
    but we know that thou hast more Purity than we at that time.
This we know.
We know you have a cadence of sound, it resounds in your earth.
It is negative and spews and cares not where it spews.
This we know.
We know that earth has Souls of age
    who have the knowledge embedded within,
    who may draw earth into a brighter moment,
    a crystal moment, a prism moment,
    where they may see the illuminescence of their Spirit
    and the blended Spirit of all earth beings.
This we know.
We have forward movements of Energy to welcome you in,
    but, Soul, we may not alter your course
    except in the extending of our Energy unto you.
Being, earth being, receive the Energy of great violets,
    receive the purple hues unto your being, for they heal.
Surround your beings in the energies we give
    and know that strength will grow in thy Soul,
    for we do have power.
Souls of earth, bring to the moment you are in

the dedication of your being
to the furtherance of the being of mankind,
for this is the purpose of humanity.

230 Souls, rejoice!
Souls, rejoice and be abundantly glad,
 for Behold arrives.
See in the heavens, entering in to the skyways, the ships of salvation.
Do not fear.
Know thy being will be lifted, will be raised,
 in a moment thy being will reach unto Purity.
It is at the time of earth's rock and roll.
It is a great armada of Souls from Four Purities[60] gathered in eons of time,
 perfecting Energy vehicles that will enter in
 to the negativity of earth.
These beings have placed intent before them.
It is earth intent.
It is the path to allowing humanity to live, to return to earth.
It is the human being that must redeem the Blessed.
Souls, many participate, but four, you would call nations,
 gather together to strategize,
 and the forms glide through apertures with density
 and have visited often at great risk to their being,
 for the earth atmosphere is sick.
The earth atmosphere clouds, distorts and consumes.
But these beings enter in, they have used the flesh of man,
 for it is the flesh of man that must reside in the atmosphere.
The transition must be gentle.
It is the unaltering of the human that is a necessity,
 for the Soul must be as the Soul entered in.
See the skies, see the dark purple clouds,
 the diminished light and the cold of your being.
The flesh that will feel as ice and then boil with heat,
 and when containment can no longer be endured,
 the Blessed will rise.
The beings of vibration will be lifted and Enter In,
 and the Souls will be brought down to an earth awash,

---

60 Four Purities - Krishna, Buddha, Jesu and Mohammed

and the old earth will appear as though it was naught,
and man will be taught as these beings of Purity enter down,
and speak of Love, of goodness, of all good things.
And earth will no longer have the appearance of negativity,
but earth will spring forth in a new light, a new life,
and rejoice at the gift of Purity,
at the opportunity they have been reminded of.
And The Four will be seen, and the Soul may turn
and witness all perfect energies alight in the skies,
and the great chasm will open and, behold,
earth will witness a new thing.
What earth has deemed to be the Fallen Angels
will become visible unto all eyes.
And Souls of fifth level will draw their beings
and enter in to the chasm of pain,
and the fierce flow of negativity will be great upon their beings,
and humanity will writhe at the looking in.
But the Souls of Purity will reach down,
and unto these Blessed Ones will offer their beings:
"See, Soul, that which we are.
We have not been as thee.
Our Purity has not risen to thy Purity,
yet our being has overcome the pains of negativity.
See our being and know in thee is the power to release thy pain,
for Creator awaits the rejoicing of thy return;
the prodigal sons unto the Father's home."
And blessed Holy ones will look unto their being,
for they have spent eons of time looking unto the needs
of those in pain within the state of transition.
And they will behold a Light and they will see the new land.
And they will behold those who have entered in to earth,
Blessed Angels, who have not been tried,
but who await to lift their beings.
And Souls will spring forth and many will say:
"Bring, Soul, the Blessed to our home.
We, here, will hold a Blessed One.
We, here, would teach of that which we know."

Humanity, see where thou must go!
Know the Entering In is the purpose of thy being.
Know how thy being is blest by Creator.
Do not, Souls of earth, maim thy being.
Overcome the frailties of thy being.
Know that overcoming negativity has only the single purpose
    of gathering the Blessed Angels.
Know, Soul, in your being that all mankind
    will walk through the Gateway unto Godhead.
Know that mankind shall lead the way,
    for has not humanity redeemed the Blessed Ones!
Oh, earth, see you Holy in all you do.
See you rise your beings aloft with vibration.
Bless all humanity.

231 Michael will teach the space of alien.
Earth, you are bound in all quarters by alien.
Your sound is registered by alien,
    for alien to respond before the appointed time
    would prevent the continuum of the purpose
    for which you have entered in to the Void.
Each earth Soul has entered in to the Void
    with a single purpose of the Blessed.
Each Soul has gathered from Creator,
    the seed of Truth to conquer the seed of negativity.
For the battle to be equal with,
    the negativity and the Truth are a part of thy being.
Ever is the choice present in the most infinitesimal action
    of your humanity.
Your sun gleams in the sky for you,
    your moon glimmers in the night for you,
    stars abound in the heavens for you,
    all earth has been placed with abundance for you.
All humanity has been given the form of an innocent child for you
    that you might start in total wonder of being.
But the actions of man have altered even the form of the small child
    and earth has been laid desolate in many ways,
    and unto earth beings is the final page come forth.

Acknowledge, earth, thy goodness.
Address the sun and the moon and the stars.
Speak, Souls, one to another.
Dialogue!
Hold the Souls that have not your abilities close to you.
Place your arms around them and comfort them.
See through the reflection of thy being where all Souls are found
    in the oneness of each other.
Earth, water is essential to thy being.
A drop of water must be pure to enter in,
    but earth is angry and earth withholds water
    or uses water for mighty violence.
Earth, see through the looking glass the hour which cometh.
Stretch forth thy being unto thy brothers and sit at the council table,
    and register a face of Love and a heart of Truth,
    and know that those who speak less than Truth will be smitten,
    not by the Hand of Creator, but by their own being,
    for they will be washed in the wash of cleansing.
Earth would draw gold from the ground to be visible to man,
    and those who love gold will pass
    with their arms round about such gold.
Will it save their being?
Will they be any less than nonexistent upon the face of earth?
Pave your streets with gold?
In that which you call heavens, there are such avenues.
What do you hold most precious, Soul?
Is it a human being or is it a piece of earth's self?
Take the ability of thy being and heal!
Are you not, one and all upon the face of the earth, healers!
Is that not why you have come!
Is that not why you have Energy not unlike that of your Creator!
Do not dilly dally.
Your earth is nigh unto crisis,
    and you are so Loved,
    but this cup we cannot take from your lips.

232 Soul, your world is not the first to experience great beauty.
You have been but the outer fragment of beauty.

Upon your sphere you are but a poor reflection
    of the awesomeness of your being.
Souls of earth, in the rise of the Purity is the decadence
    and the opulence beyond your ken.
All nature of your world, all intrinsic complications are simple
    and a reflection from the space of Purity.
Love casts its benevolent attitude unto where you are,
    filtered through the negative energy, yet radiant and calm.
Where we are, we have no such barriers as negativity.
Our being profoundly absorbs all benefits of Love.
Love is the constant companion of our being.
It flows in an endless, timeless motion
    towards the framework of our existence.
We have been, as you, in the negative flow.
We have been countered again and again, until our beings
    became unable to contend with the constancy of the battle.
We resigned our being to the inabilities we had
    and chose to become inert,
    as many Souls in your world have gathered together,
    not to join but to withhold from an inevitable battle defeat,
    and enter in to a choice of their own.
This we did.
We gathered to refute that which we could not conquer.
We live, we are, because of the great gift.
There came unto our world, Beings of such Love;
    awakening, strengthening, teaching with a Purity
    that shed the tentacles of Negativity from our being.
We arose with a strength that we gathered from them.
These beings of great Purity and Love your world calls Angels.
We know them as Blessed.
They reached into our pain and lifted us into a realm of awareness
    we had not known.
We have forever since been altered.
These precious beings minister unto us and know us by name.
Our Aura is now patterned after their vibrations and we have grown
    in spiritual stature because of their entering in.
Our vision is turned to the Blessed who gave the supreme sacrifice

of denying themselves entry in to the Holiness of Creator
because of the Negativity that they gathered.
They would not bring themselves into the space of Creator,
for they could not untangle the web of Negativity.
They could not reach the Cleansing River,
therefore they forged a barrier
to set Negativity from the worlds beyond worlds,
so that its invasiveness could not re enter.
Because of them, all that was as lost has now been recovered
in our space.
All greatness of Spirit creates unceasingly
and our endeavours have formed weaves of Purity
that would draw your breath from you.
To your world we give constant surveillance, guidance to Souls
with the endeavour toward Purity.
We celebrate the onward flow that your Truth is achieving,
for in the surmounting will come unto us
the return of those in despair,
kept from the Purity of their own accord.
Bless the beings, humanity, who bring to us
the understanding of what Love is.

CHAPTER 2

Holy

EARTH

233 We Love whom we are because we are of the Creator.
Creator!
Blessed be the Soul that can eye the Creator.
Blessed be the Soul that can touch the raiment thereof.
Creator is the seed of goodness, a seed of goodness so immense,
    so powerful, and yet there is not one, one smudge of impurity.
There is only total Purity.
The Light of such power, this perfection has all knowledge within,
    all possibilities within, all joy, all caring.
Outward is the Flow, outward is the Flow.
The Soul of yourself has sprung from this very Purity.
Some Souls have chosen to be sprung that far;
    even in the casting there was choice.
You have always been a part of your Creator.
Know this.
It is why you strive within your being to find or fight goodness.
Soul, may the hands be ever clasped in acceptance
    that you are a part of the Holy One.
Tell the world of the Purity that is the centre, not only high,
    but beyond high is higher and higher.
You are in infancy and yet you are awesome and revered.
You, the human race, have chosen the farthest cast.
The farthest cast holds the realm of negativity
    and as the swirl of the great wind is brought down to earth
    so the Soul can be caught in the swirl of negativity.
Soul, to lift up is to find the swirl of Purity, the funnel to creation,

which is the centre of your vortex and vortex,
    beside and beside and beside until a full circle is formed.
The circle is ever creating and growing as the goodness
    or defilement of man is ever growing.
Souls, your Creator is all powerful and in the Purity of that Creator
    are only those feelings that permit feelings of good.

234 Creator, in the beginning, warred with Love against Negativity.
And all Angels armed them from head
    to the outer part of their Being with Purity
    and entered in to the fray.
And all Negativity abounded and the purities of Angels
    surrounded Creator,
    and Creator blessed the Holy Holy Holy.
And the Beings charged the countenance of Negativity,
    and Negativity made itself delightful unto the Holy Ones
    and enticed their Being to be drawn into iniquity.
And the Souls were blessed by Creator,
    and the Tears of Creator fell upon His Holy Ones
    to wash the pain of Negativity from their beings,
    but many fell and were lost in the pain of knowing Negativity.
And the Souls are Loved by Creator
    and the Holy Holy Holy seek to draw their beings back
    into the fold of the Blessed Shepherd[61].
And the Souls languish in Negativity's betrayal
    and will not be heard by Purity,
    and only from a place of impurity will the Holy Ones be heard.
And in the beginning Souls were cast from Creator,
    and these Souls looked up at the pain
    and the tears of the Holy Ones,
    and they offered in Love to Creator:
    "Energy of our being, may we be lifted to do for Thee
    that which the Blessed Ones may not?
    May we enter as one into the place of negativity[62]
    and be tried and found true in Thy being?
Will you give us many opportunities

---

61 Blessed Shepherd – Jesu
62 only place of negativity - earth

  for we are no stronger than the Blessed Ones?
  Will You give us endless opportunities to become Holy,
   that we might enter in to reach
   the Souls of the Holy Ones?"
And Melchezidec brought forward an army of beings,
  and the Souls agreed to hear the pain,
  the cry of the Souls in transition, and know with joy in their heart
  that they had the power to lift the Souls unto the Holy Holy Holy.
And humanity is that army, and the purpose of humanity is singular:
  to be human, to know Purity in their being,
  to respond to all impurities with Purity,
  to arm themselves with Purity and Truth.
For humanity has Truth as its armour and in the entering in,
  untruth will not phase their being,
  will not cloud their vision, for they have known all iniquities.
They will not be enticed into the delusion of the Holy Ones
  and they will reach out to the Holy Ones.
And they will speak in a language as one
  and tell of the fight they have had against negativity,
  and tell of the Armada of humanity that waits to draw them forth,
  that Souls await to become the spiral by which they will be lifted
  unto their Brethren.
And the Holy Ones will open their Being
  for the first time since that great battle,
  and they will see clearly the snare that has brought them down,
  fallen from the blessedness of their Brethren.
And almighty Creator will lift them unto His bosom
  and wrapt their being in Love,
  for all humanity is beloved, all humanity will be sanctified.
And Creator will receive humanity, and because of the gift given,
  humanity will be first to enter in to the Second Gateway.
So be it.

235 Unto thy being be peace.
Unto thy beings behold the Register.
Behold the status of Creator, all Holiness, all perfection, all Love,
  profound Energy brought down to the space of Farside,

reaching unto the Gateway, reaching unto the Gateway,
to the Gateway, to the Gateway of fragmented Creator
who has lessened not power, not Love, not ability, but motion.
The Flow of Creator is endless,
and Godhead and the enveloping goodness
are tethered to a singleness of intent to battle,
for the Second Gateway, all negativity.
The battle may not be done by Creator,
the battle must be done by the Blessed
and now the orb of earth's humanity.
Why should this be?
Why may not Creator enter in and choose to absolve all negativities?
Souls of earth, your Creator is total Love.
Creator, in the Being of Creator, cannot harm any facet of the world.
The Soul of Creator, Soul, oh Soul, agonizes at the pain of negativity,
at its cause, at its effect, but can not enter in.
Creator is powerless to harm, just by the total Creator Love,
and the Energy that has entered in to Farside
is as the mirror to the Holy Godhead.
The forms of Angels have ever surrounded
the embodiment of Godhead, of Creator.
Extensions of Purity overwhelm the Wisdom of our Farside
"How may our being extend unto you the fathomless Purity
of such Energy?"
The thought of Entering In through the Second Gateway,
to behold the pain and Negativity, was Creator's.
But the Second Entering In was the Blesseds
and the armour was the gift of Creator,
the Purity, the Light of their being.
You are human.
Your existence is because of your gift to all Farside, your gift to Creator,
which would draw all goodness unto Godhead,
and so the last battle is yours.
The blessed lost will be found,
and the cymbals will clash, and the bells will chime,
and all marks of Holiness will be placed on humanity,
and they will be drawn, in their Purity, unto the Gateway.

236 Souls, you have been in the positive and negative flow.
As Souls in Spirit form, you have been within your own worlds,
    your energies bombarded by negatives and positives.
You are free Souls, seedlings, nurtured and cared for
    by a Creator of almighty compassion, a Creator of pure Love.
And all worlds, separate one from the other, knew of a passage
    through great Negativity, their Energy depleted.
Their Energy, it brought them low,
    it caused them to make unwise choices.
And from the Soul of Creator came an Entering In
    and saw within the magnitude of all that was contentions and woe.
And Creator closed the door unto Godhead
    and called unto Him all the mighty Angels to enter in,
    these, the righteous of Godhead.
And behold, Creator armed with Purity the mighty army of Love,
    and opened wide the Gateway to the flow
    of positive and negative, and so the battles began.
And the Spirit of Souls recovered from the dirge of Negativity
    and strengthened in their might, fought side by side
    with the Blessed against Negativity,
    and all Negativity was mapped to a distant place.
Within that distant place, Creator formed earth
    and earth was set within the Void of Negativity
    for the mighty inhabitants that would be:
    the Souls who gathered strength from the Angels,
    who witnessed the blessedness of Angels
    and regarded the Holy ones as their brethren, as their own.
And Creator entered in the Souls of humanity unto earth,
    for thus the army was called,
    and thus the battle to retrieve all that was lost began.
The flow in your galaxy has positive and negative.
It is what your galaxy does well.
It was unto itself positives and negatives and conflicts
    until the battle is won and a choice is made,
    and the Soul of human bears witness by scars unto their Soul,
    and by these scars will the Blessed know them.
The battle is at its height, it has not yet been won.

Choose that which is positive for thy Soul's growth
　　that, humanity, you may be a saviour of the Blessed.

237 Brethren, negativity is the snowball of earth.
It is the volatile insurrection,
　　it is a containment that has no containment,
　　it is accelerated by use,
　　it is as yeast in the bread that rises and falls
　　and rises yet again.
It can be formed in a solid mass of flesh.
It can be brought into a constricted mode of lethargy.
It moves within insidious intent.
It rears the energy of its being and sees a weakness and enters therein.
It is power, Soul.
It has foulness.
It is brimstone and ash, it is your hell.
Behold the smallest seed of goodness is unwrapped and let go,
　　and a Soul gathers the goodness, and gathers again,
　　and the acceleration begins, and the Energy is beheld.
And Souls look unto that Energy and say : "*What is this?*
　　What is this goodness that we see,
　　　　that we feel, that we know?"
And the acceleration is witnessed by those who cannot hear,
　　cannot see and cannot speak, and still the awareness is there.
It catches in the wind and the wind takes the goodness
　　into yet another place, and the goodness is caught
　　in a Soul, in a tone, in a gesture, and goodness is accelerated.
Should a single Soul withhold his goodness,
　　all earth is tempered by that withdrawal,
　　for all are accountable unto the number placed.
Behold, the blessed who rise up will be those who are drawn low
　　and the Purity will be witnessed by all.
Souls which overcome negativity unto Purity
　　do not sidestep negativity, but overcome the weakness
　　of their being and rise to a stature
　　that says negativity can be overcome and conquered.

238 Souls, respond!
Respond at the hour of need.
Respond when the call is entered in to your being.
It is not a call to leave thy father and thy mother,
    it is not a call to leave thy son and thy daughter,
    it is not a need to leave the home thou hast.
It is a call to leave the constant Negativity,
    the foulness that spews forth.
Is it enough, is the message heard?
It is to draw self to tears for the pain to thy being.
It is to draw self to the knowledge that earth has a purpose.
Oh, rock thy being!
Momentous pain rocks the Soul when you are caught in negativity.
Anger overwhelms the being and tears cascade and fall,
    and Souls are lost in agonies of their own making.
Beloved Souls, your life is not about negativity.
Your life is about Purity and the goodness of all in the realm of Energy.
Behold, the Angels form a diadem about thy being,
    and all vision from negativity is outward flowing.
You are being transformed.
For the downward spiral that you will enter
    requires the pureness of your being,
    the awesome gem of your being,
    the pure translucent Energy of your being,
    that you may enter in to the chasm.
Do you see, Soul?
Spew from thy being all that is not pure.
Release from thy being the toxins, not only of scientific ineptness,
    but also from the Purity of thy being,
    the toxins of anger and rage and foulness
    that is entered in to the flesh and the heart and the mind.
Earth, Angels are Ecstasy,
    their Holiness is beyond your contemplation,
    and yet their Purity is a part of your own!
How blessed thou art.
How magnificent thou art that thou art a part of the Angels,
    of Creator, of Godhead.
Blessed be thou, earth Souls, who walk not in iniquity.

239 Soul, Michael will teach the avenue to perfection.
Dear earth Souls, behold the avenue to perfection: acceptance,
    accepting all space, all time, all velocity of time and space.
There are atoms and atoms, there is negative and positive.
The energies create growth, and growth is an explosion
    beyond the mind of man.
Purity enables a Soul to heal a withered hand.
Purity enables an earth past to revive.
Purity enables the lift of a mountain upon the apex of a Soul.
Behold the garden of growth.
Behold the curatives within the garden of growth.
Earth looks to steel, earth looks to mineral.
Seek within the mineral the firing of time.
Seek within the garden of earth the Purity of life.
Life is breath and breath is Energy,
    and the Purity of breath enables the Soul to lift a mountain,
    to rise to the mountaintop without a vehicle.
Man will rise without a vehicle, not upon his whim,
    but upon the deflection of negativity.
It is the releasing of negativity that lifts a Soul in Purity, not by Purity.
There is vision and vision in the onward vortex of earth,
In the onward vortex of Time, into a Timeless state, earth is aroused,.
Earth carries frenetic energy within its being
    because the Souls of earth walk avenues of greed, negativity.
Behold the avenues of earth are maintained by negativity,
    and yet, beings of profound sensitivity, in awareness of Purity,
    walk upon paths of great Flow.
The Flow meets the perfection of all beings.
You, Soul, are a being, but beings are many.
Earth can not see from one being clan to another,
    they look disdainfully and say:
    "Whither you go, we shall not tread.
    Whither you go, it shall be ours."
Soul, gather self into acceptance.
There are avenues of Purity over the earth.
Yours is but one and the time shall come when all shall meet,
    all awareness in goodness and mercy will be beheld,

and teachers owning only the powerful symbol of acceptance
   will tread to the Flow of infinity.
Migration is not possible.
Souls cannot gather themselves in multitudes
   to migrate to hallowed places.
It is the individual walk upon the avenue of acceptance.

240 Refuse, Souls of earth, the choice of negativity.
Refuse the desolate spot of anguish.
Behold, Souls clamour to be one beside the other
   in their place of pain.
Step free from pain.
Know the thread of your being, know the path to your Energy.
Uplift self with joy.
Soul, why would you tarry in a negative space?
Why would you speak with a negative voice?
Why would you hold to a negative force?
Because you have put yourself there, Soul!
Delight in the place of negativity.
Delight the opportunity to overcome the negativity.
Behold, all negative energy is but the opportunity
   to alter all that you see, to bring that which is negative
   to a powerful Energy of naught.
To breathe is to energize the flesh and the blood.
To breathe is to energize the mind.
To breathe is to energize the heart.
To breathe is to vibrate.
It is not, Soul, that breath has left the being.
It is that breath alters
   and the vibration of the Energy
   breathes faster than thought can fly.
Know the power within your being.
You are blessed, Souls.
You are beloved.
Would you see the stranger on the path, weary,
and not offer a seat at your door and a bowl to wash his feet?
Would you not do this service yourself?
"You are hungry, Soul, beloved."

Who has the storage bin full?
Your neighbour is hungry!
It is difficult, is it not?
And where do I go?
Do I devoid myself of all that is food to give to my neighbour?
All things are done with just giving.
All things are done with temperance.
Hold not the hands crossed in front of self.
Unfold the hands and lay them open to the world,
    and if you have something to place within the hand,
    place it thus, for in giving you will receive.
All justice carries truth.
All injustice carries negativity.
Do not anguish your being over problems
    that can be resolved with action.
Action, in a positive venture, is a step to growth.
Purity enhances the Soul.
The Soul may vision Energy.

241 Soul, Michael will teach space, time and motion.
All Souls have motion, all earth has motion, your universe has motion.
Each level of existence has motion.
Motion is upward to the Flow of Purity.
All motion is Zero.
Not one; Zero!
All motion is naught.
It is in the space of the Soul that motion is found.
The heart and the mind does not provide the body with motion.
It is within the aura.
Science little acknowledges aura.
Behold the claim of aura upon the earth is three[63].
You are.
And your being with mind
    creates nothing without the avenue of the Soul.
It is a worthless void, a gray matter with no potential to Zero.

---

63 three - there are three auras to all that is earth humanity: healing aura, transcendental aura and Essence aura.

But the mind also, with the heart, has no potential in Zero
    without the embodiment of the Soul.
It is the Soul that enrapts and becomes the motion that lifts itself
    into the motion of your extended universe.
Creator has motion.
It is from that motion that your being has movement.
It is the attachment of worth.
It is the mirror, the reflection,
    the telling again and again and again.
Into the different lives of your being, that motion is enacted.
Behold how precious is motion,
    for without motion we would not be in your space,
    and we are in your space.
There is a great avenue that has no height or depth or width,
    only motion, and the motion is the Flow of Creator.

242 Souls, behold the heart.
The heart is an awesome instrument.
It guides the mind to the Soul,
    and from the Soul the entry to the mind is via the heart.
Heed not your heart, for the heart has compassion.
It is a need to look into your pain.
You may not recover from your growth if you seek the heart quickly.
First you must recognize the mind's will
    so that you may overcome the pain and allow the mind
    to make the choice of travelling thus to the heart, to the Soul.
It is the purpose of earth to be in growth, to seek always growth.
Looking at the heart is to bypass the lesson of pain.
It is not necessary to endure the pain.
It is necessary to see the pain.
It is necessary to overcome the pain.
It is necessary to feel the agonies of that pain.
It is necessary to bring the Soul's flesh and mind to awareness
    of how deeply felt such pain is.
Would you see a Soul burned, from recognition,
    and have the overwhelming sense of pain that Soul has endured?
The heart would feel compassion.

The heart would look to compassion, but it is the mind
    that must make the decision about what action will be taken.
The heart is a feeling instrument, the mind is action.
It must deny or overwhelmingly contact the heart to feel,
    but the instruction must come from the mind.
It is the growth of the mind of which we are speaking.
It is the very growth for which you are here on earth.
Your beings allow our presence.
Were it not so, we would not be here.
See the form of agony, bring thy being into the agony,
    and then use the heart, but know the pain!
Your earth will go through tumultuous times.
They are recorded and will be done,
    but know in thy being that many are gathered unto Purity.
Know in thy being that many have suffered such agonies
    and have purified their being, that they are gathered as One
    and brought unto the Farside.
Many Souls spend time on earth in great terror.
Do you know of this terror?
Have you felt this terror?
Have the agonies of their being reached out unto you?
Can your hand open before their pain?
Can you gather them unto you in your compassion?
Does the mind accept the pain of others?
Does the mind enter in to the pain of others?
Does the mind release the pain of others?
Or does the mind casually walk by the pain of others?
Heed not the heart first,
    the heart would have compassion.
The heart is a good member of the three,
    but in the heart is not the growth that is necessary.
It is the avenue to the growth, it is not the growth.
It is the mind's acceptance that will carry the growth.
So be it!

243 Souls of earth, beloved earth,
    all thy being is robed in a garb of Purity.

Holy

For, Soul, the fragment of thy being is from the Spirit
    and the Spirit has perfection in its being.
It has Purity and all goodness.
Behold, humanity, the small infinitesimal part of thy being[64]
    that is heart, body and mind, has a need to recognize
    the greatness from which it comes.
Your simplistic earth form is only a button on a pearl,
    is only a pore in your skin.
For you are so much more.
You are glory, you are Radiance, your being is ecstasy.
Reach that place of your being, know from where thou hast come.
Search the spiritual part of thy being.
Search to know that which is not human in thy being
    and, Soul, you will be amazed at the portal
    that will open unto you.
The oneness of thy being will shed zen and you will see,
    as the veils are removed, the perfection of thy being.
You will glory in the Light of thy being.
Soul, human Soul, portion of thy being that is awesome,
    reach thou to thy perfection.
Know there is a part of thy being that has no ability to choose negative.
It is the part that has gained the level to which it is.
It could not utter forth a negative phrase from its being.
In thy being is the circle of thy goodness.
All circles carry no end.
So, earth being, you have no end, you have no finish,
    for the humanity of thy being is but a portion,
    and you are but a circle
    with a purpose in the rotation of thy being.
Reach, Soul, as you would reach to a tree to pick the pomegranate
    that is red and full of fruit.
Reach and know that as you reach, you elevate your own being.
There is no longer a floor beneath your feet, you are floating.
You are caught in the reach of thy being.
Know that thy being sees only the simple form of earth body,

---

64 thy being - heart, mind and body are earth components of the Soul. The Soul is a fragment of the Spirit, which is a fragment of the Essence, which is a fragment of Creator's Energy.

and yet you know this form that is you,
> it is your being.
What is that which remains on the floor?
Is it thy being or is it merely a cloak thou hast worn
> to enter in to a cold day?
And what is this place that has darkness,
> where Souls refuse to be heard?
Why does it hold cold in its being?
There is no Energy, there is no movement.
All is still except the being caught in an agony unknown to your being.
And who are they who encircle the being
> and send forth a cry to look unto them?
And who is the hand that holds itself out?
Soul, you may enter in.
> the cold has left our being and we are transformed.
Souls, your being may come to this place,
> your being may enter in.
Your earth self is only a button upon your clothing.
You are so much more
> and gently you may enter back into your form
> which once again appears large.

244 The Path is ever and ever.
Souls of earth, know within thy being is the Flow
> unto the starlit eternity.
Soul, there is no end, there is only continuation
> in all efforts of galaxy upon galaxy upon galaxy.
Do enter in to the Flow of thy goodness.
Do be welcomed into the Flow by Angels and guides
> who would draw thee into the delights of Farside,
> for the Path, to us, is incomparable.
Know in thy being, all realities are Farside.
Delight in the motion of thy being
Acknowledge, Souls.
Acknowledge the Purity of your being!
Bring your being into the space of enlightenment.
Holy being that you are, enter in to the Flow of Purity
> and know that you require no protection,

that you require no grace, save the grace of your own being,
    for the grace of your own being is that of Creator.
You are a fragment of Creator.
Behold the Energy of Purity, ignite the Energy of Purity.
Unto humanity are all things given in Purity.

245 Dear, dear Souls, blessed Souls of earth,
    the path that you are on has a vision that will take you to the Prism.
Souls, leave behind negativity.
Why worry about tomorrow?
Tomorrow is here.
Here is incomparable beauty and sanctity.
There is throughout the worlds, worlds beyond,
    power that has infinity,
    power that takes the Soul to space and timeless space,
    to time and timelessness.
The road is paved in Truth and the gentle Souls herald
    the coming of every Soul.
Tidings are lifted in Truth.
The song that is sung has a melody that reaches Creator of all that is.
The Path is a generous state that offers greatness in its simplicity,
    that offers Love.
Take no effort to view anger, to feel anger, to use anger.
Earth, seek thou the Knower,
    seek thou the Knower of all things.
Unto Him be psalm and praises sung.
Be thou watchful unto thy Creator.
Be not pious in thy worshipping.
Be thou the messenger of the Knower.
Be thou the Soul reaching out into the Void, into the nethers.
Reach unto all that holds Truth and gather Truth unto you.
Hold negativity for a precious moment and know in your being
    it has no place in your Soul.
Behold, goodness is lifted unto Creator
    and behold, your being is goodness.
Tremble not at the tomorrows, be in acceptance of the todays,
    for, Soul, you are life.
And know the hallowedness of that life.
Reach unto thy Creator.

246 Within the power of humanity is the ability
    to release all pain, all anger.
Souls of earth, beings from the Farside await the transfer.
They are receptive to your pain.
They will transform negativities to drop.
Know the powers we do have,
    how audacious we are, how full of ourselves we are,
    for, Soul, we are magnificent, our beings are many faceted.
They hold the keys to many earth pains,
    if earth would just offer unto Farside the anger, the pain.
Souls of earth, unto thee is all positive Energy given.
The Soul must accept, the Soul must be willing to receive.
Do not dwell in all deliberations by thyself,
    for we have a council at your service.
We have Souls of great abilities ready to come unto you
    and deliver all pain, all confusion.
Soul, smile as you may, for our beings are poignant, and will come
    to the door of the Gateway to receive that which you give.
Deliver unto us and we will receive.

247 Souls, upon the flesh there is pain.
Upon the mind there is pain.
Upon the heart there is pain.
But, Souls, know your being is not heart, mind and body.
Know your being is Soul, know your being is Spirit and Essence
    of which there is no hoarding of negativity into Purity.
Delight thy Soul in this, humanity!
Know not the illusion, but speak ever to the reality of thy being.
Classify self and respond to the glow of thyself in thy closet.
It is the illumination of thy Soul.
Do not be downhearted,
    do not be stressed and strangulate your energies
    and ever revive self with the knowledge
    of the pureness of thy being, of the goodness of thy being.
See thy candle, the Light of thy being.
See the glow that thy being surrounds heart, mind and body with,
    and others might come unto thee and speak of thy glow,
    and speak of thy wonder.

And, Soul, all energies will form a positive gyration of being.
Flow to the oneness of the Spirit three, not the earthbound three.

248 Spectrum of polished Energy within the old Soul Path,
    Energy brought through years of refinement,
    Energy purified in overcoming pain and anger.
Souls of earth, behold the spectrum of the Energy.
Behold the movement forward, the flow of mighty humanity
    within the Flow's Path.
Behold the narrow space there is for humanity.
Behold, it is an arduous task to overcome all negativity,
    all within the space of the Hinterland.
How gracious is humanity!
We welcome even the palest of the spectrum,
    for is it not the bringing forth
    of all that is precious in the Farside.
How gallant are those who reach above the endeavours of negativity!
How gallant are they who will see and are tempted
    and overcome the temptation.
Behold, are they not pure!
Believe, Souls of earth, thou art pure.
Know in thy being, the illusion you walk in has no lasting perimeters.
As the lesson is done, so will the perimeter be done.
Behold, humanity, reach unto the very stars that are yours,
    for, Souls, the tallness, the greatness of your beings
    may very well reach the stars.

249 It is your humanness you must rise above.
You are finite.
Almighty Souls, but finite.
And unto you much has been given, and unto you much is expected.
We would express to you the role of positive finite.
We would have you acknowledge the vibration of your being.
We would have you know the possibilities
    within the circle of any group of humans to rise to such a stature
    that the very Angels would nod to them.
Souls of earth, do not contemplate and contemplate and contemplate,

but act, act as the Angel acts, act as the Saint acts,
  act as all Holy beings act, relinquishing the humanity of your being,
  taking the role of human from self.
It is but a role.
You are human, but your humanness is within the very Purity that you are.
The Purity is as we are, elevated.
Direct, are we not!
In all things that connect from heart to Soul, from Soul to Spirit,
  from Spirit to Essence, from Essence to Creator,
  you are a continuity of Purity.
You are everlasting unto everlasting.
You are the flow of all that has power
  and, Souls of earth, the very Angels guide thy step.
Fear and doubt should fall away,
  for you are guided into the path of your choice.
All you have written becomes legible in the state of Purity.
All lives become known unto you, all visions are seen and discernable.
We ask humanity to find the passage of Truth,
  for in Truth is the acknowledgement
  that negativity is but a lesson.
And you may reach unto Negativity and bestow great compassion,
  and flood the Energy of Negativity with Love.
We ask, Soul, that you do not anger your being.
We ask that you ignite your being.
Reach to the Farside and gather into the being
  the power of your own to flood your being,
  and in that measure will erase all negatives.
Taste not the bitter cup for, in truth, the sweetest wine is Purity.
The sweetest cup is the chalice given from the hands of Angels
  unto your Soul.

250 Take the pearl of thy choice, Soul, and gift it to another.
The pearl of thy choice are the words that you utter.
They are precious, they are held and treasured.
When you speak words to another of kindness, it is a gift given
  and it expands the Soul of the other being.
And the Soul welcomes the gift, and recognizes seldom

the immense treasure until they have placed the gift
    well into their own being.
And the gift comes forth as a treasure of their own,
    and then the Soul recognizes the growth they have received.
Souls of earth often take a fetid, crippling gift unto another Soul
    and place it to their being.
These are words of anger and pain.
They are meant to injure, to create havoc,
    and the heart withers at the words,
    and the words jar the Soul's intent,
    and the Soul hides in the being.
And in the hiding, another Soul enters and draws forth a pearl,
    and places it before humanity, and humanity receives the pearl,
    and the Soul enters out of the darkness, feebly into the Light.
Souls of earth, do you not see the picture?
Words injure,
    words uphold Purity!
Choose well the words that are uttered from thy mouth.
Unto all humanity, uplift and know,
    as you have given, so shall you receive,
    for it is only as you open your being to the Light
    that the Light may enter.
For the Light may not enter that which has been closed off.
Only may the Light enter by the choice of the Soul,
    but the gift is given freely and enters in to the space
    to be absorbed or rejected.
But, Soul, the gift is given.
Earth has a moment to contemplate the passage of time.
The passage of time is not random, it is accounted.
Each moment of your day is accounted and accountable.
Soul of earth, feed not your Soul, feed the Souls of others.
As you give, give freely, receive unto your being, peace in return.

251 Are you not candle?
Do you not glow!
Soul, you glow!
You have carried the ability to ignite within your being for many lives.

Unto earth have we come, unto earth have we spoken,
> unto earth will the blessings fall.
Earth carries within, the Light of all Farside issues.
Humanity may save earth, humanity may understand earth,
> humanity is ever pure in its endeavour to seek its purpose.
Souls of earth, do not lose sight with all that you are.
Do not lose sight with the steadfast throb of humanity
> toward its purpose.
We have not given up hope!
Souls, we rejoice, for earth is consistent in the onward step.
Even in the negativity there is Purity, for it is through the negativity
> that growth consumes the Soul.
Beloved beings, do not rationalize your existence.
Do not seek, but know in your being that each door opens
> as the will has called to open.
Beckon yourself into the space of the doorway,
> invite your being into the space of Purity.
The cord of negativity is as a whipcord.
It has great strength, it has great durability,
> it has lasted in the timeless space
> and is tethered in the space of time.
Holy beings, rejoice that you are human.
Rejoice that you are very human, for growth is in your space.

252 We have Light.
We have abundant Light.
Light, Light that filters out.
Do you see, do you see, Soul?
The mood you are in affects all about your being.
If you are downcast, does it not filter sadness about you.
If you are angry, does it not filter anger unto others.
If there is joy, is it not felt.
Light is always felt,
> Light is felt in the total depths of blindness.
Energy is Light, positive Energy is Radiance.
Know that thy Light, tightly entombed, will help no man.
Do not sit in thy corner and compute for Light.

Do not adorn thy being with pontification of Light, but open thy being
    and, Soul, your Light will shine.
You will come forth, you will be revealed
    and no man will be able to prevent the Light from entering in,
    for your goodness will vibrate and vibration enters all being.

253 The Energy of one being, used to full capacity,
    would light the world.
It was the meaning of Christ, *"I am the Light of the world."*
Full Purity brings so much Light.
See, Soul, the Light that you are.
Recognize pureness of your being and allow the filtering of that Light
    to seep into the darkest corners of earth.
Your rewards will be in the illumination of energies round about you
    who will see your Light and gravitate toward it
    and feel the fullness thereof, and reach unto their own Light.
Behold, one candle ignites another.
Behold, the energies of all humanity would draw all purities unto Creator.
Soul, do not waste time in contemplation.
Action alters all things.
Do not be content to wither in pain but draw thyself from pain,
    and know the Light of thy being will heal all,
    and more than thy eyes can see.
Would you, Soul, extend your beings outward to the universe;
    to encompass all about you, to know that you are of the cosmos,
    that you filter your Light upward to meet the Light of its own
    and in the blend comes the umbrella of Light that all may see.
For in the coming into thy presence is a calm and a peace,
    is a Purity and a goodness.
Know thy being to resonate all goodness, all Purity, all Love.

254 Michael will teach the solutions to earth finance.
Know that the cost of living is the food for that day.
All else is given to the faint.
In the solution great inward growth can come,
    but the reality of earth is greed, the greed of hoarding,
    that could earn a level on our side.
Souls, see greed as a step only if conquered.

See reality in the hungry Soul and feed this Soul.
Know that the little step is often the huge movement.
To see a Soul in need and not answer that need, is to be human.
Souls, seek the Farside solution.
Feed the poor!
Souls of earth do not be martyrs for a cause,
    but step into a framework of total Purity.
Express all utterances in Purity.
Express, intone the very being of thyself, the Spirit of thy Soul
    to be the guardian of thy words, of thy hands, of thy feet.
Use the heart to draw the emotion of goodness unto thy being.
Allow the mind to discern the negativity in thy life.
Hold only justice in thy palm.
Offer only goodness in thy hand.
Extend thy arms outward only in gentle loving
    and draw, Soul, thy arms toward self only in gentle receiving.
Do not place a mantle of greed over thy being.
Know, Soul, that each day, each moment, is to be beautified.
Immortalize thy Soul by placing perfection upon earth.
See only the beauty in all things.
Offer only Love to all things.
Harbour no ill will unto any being upon earth.
This is the robe of humanity.

255 Souls of earth, negativity surrounds all elements of earth,
    all filaments of earth,
      but it is the positive Energy that draws Light.
It is the positive Energy that illuminates the world you are in.
Speak to thy mother and thy father, thy brother and thy sister,
    thy wife and thy husband with only gentle words,
    with only loving words, for you pattern yourself
    after all energies of Farside.
Would you hate that which you Love the dearest?
Would you denigrate that which you hold closest to you?
See the orb of your sun and know the warmth of that sun.
Know the Energy of that sun about thy being,
    and know, Soul, the Energy of that sun
    is not one whit the Energy of thy own being.

How powerful thou art, humanity.
Seek to know thy Energy.
Seek to be in the soft resonance of thine own voice.
Do not acknowledge illness in thy being.
What you own, you have.
Is it not so.
Is that not earth's equation.
Soul, blessed Soul, we embrace thy being.
Thy Purity is equal to our own and are we not awesome.
Loving one, know thy goodness and know not negativity.

256 All Souls of the world are welcomed in.
There is no identifying mark.
Soul, what mark lies in the palm, it is for earth.
On the Farside, no man has a mark except the Soul,
    and the Soul enters in free of cost.
Souls of earth, you dabble at negativity.
You dabble, but in your dabbling you may ignite the world
    and the flame and the heat will create a whirl
    such as earth has never known.
Your hand is the same, there is no difference.
They are but hands.
Your hearts are afire.
Inflame them with Love, my brothers and sisters.
Embrace them with Love.
Rest is time, time to acknowledge what has been
    and the possibility of what can be.
Do not send forth a mighty army to create desolation,
    but look where you stand and let freedom reign.
Watch the north and the south, watch the east and the west,
    but contain your Energy and transmit outward from your being
    all that is good and pure, all that you have been and are.
We invite you to stand tall, for it is in the expression of good
    that evil will lose.

257 My beloved children, when a child cries,
    it does not matter the colour of the skin.

It does not matter the voice that speaks to the child.
It matters only that the child cries and the mother hears.
We hear the cry of many children and we are mindful
    of their state of Purity.
My beloved children, humanity,
    from our Being we draw you into our arms.
We rejoice at the simple, childlike attitude of being,
    and we understand the Souls who have brought themselves
    into avenues of pain.
And we take the swaddling cloth and we wrap it about their being,
    for they have not totally understood the negativity
    they have done.
They are children, trespassing in childlike ways.
And we place our Love about their beings
    and we gather them unto our bosom,
    for are they not as worthy as the Souls who have age,
    who have learned the Path?
My beloved little children, my babes in arms,
    our Being extends itself unto you.
Where upon earth is anger and treachery?
Where upon earth are despicable deeds?
We reach our Being unto you as little children,
    we draw you unto our Being that you may know the mother Love,
    that you may grow in wisdom.
Flock of Creator, heart of humanity, do not forget the young
    who have not learned to set aside anger from their being.
Hold them close unto thy heart and lift them unto our Creator
    that they, too, might receive a blessing,
    that their hearts may be stirred, that their vision may be cleared.
Mothers, fathers, unite in Love for all children, at all ages of being.

258 We welcome ourselves into the space of your tent.
Soul, the aperture widens, the aperture to the Farside widens.
It is the intent of our being to bring you the message
    there is such an opening.
It has been fragmented, it has enlarged.
It allows many to enter forth and our beings are reminded

of the preparing of battle on the plains,
of the slaughter and the carnage,
and we ask for reason.
We ask all men of earth to speak reason.
How can you speak reason for the children who have been taught to hate,
except to issue forth a sea of Love unto their beings!
It is not the old men with gray hair, it is the young.
The old men know their beliefs, the women follow the old men.
But the children, they hear the hate, they hear the anger, the derision.
See the dove fly free.
It's Purity falls where it lights.
Direct the dove to the tents of pain.
Direct the dove to feed, to nourish in wisdom and Love,
and then, Soul, in your goodness,
offer outward not your ships, but goods.
All Farside knows that the earth has altered in status
and stage 'alert' is at hand for our beings
and we have no fear for our beings.
But we would have the blessed brought home
with as little pain as possible.

259 Souls, behold an offering unto thy goodness.
Behold an offering unto thy nakedness, for all is beheld,
all has a place in the dome of Purity.
Souls of earth, how sacred art thou.
Souls of earth, how glorious thy body, thy form.
You have the power to alter quickly, all creation.
You have the power to be the lotus flower lifted unto Creator,
and yet earth chooses to dabble in unsightly,
unworthy introspections of humanity,
and holds negativity as glorious in their hands,
and lifts their glory unto a deity
that has no name within the Farside.
Souls of earth, thou art human, but thou art profoundly human,
human connected to the Energy of all Purity.
Do not deface that which you are!
Glory in the step of thy goodness, glory in the purpose of thy being.

Do not shroud thy form with atrocities.
Do not blind the eye to atrocities, but speak loud in thy voice
    against all inhuman activity.
The mouth was given to humanity, to speak and utter,
    to hold that which the heart knows to be wrong,
    which the mind's logic defines as human.
Do not be blind to evil men.
Do not be blind to evil conditions.
Do not be mindful of sins, but reach and alter all that is in your space.
Change all that is profoundly wrong to right.
Little deeds become great flags before the world.
Hold the lotus that you are to bloom before Creator,
    to unfold in your majesty unto the goodness of thy Essence.
When the bowl is full, tilt it away from thyself.
When the bowl is half empty, you may keep it for yourself
    to see the giving in all that you do.
It is only earth that you are in.
You have a delight of Farside.
Nothing of material good will you own
    if it can not be done in goodness for the benefit of all.
Fill the bowl for thyself and then place a portion aside for thy visitor,
    and know that if the door is open, the visitor will come.
When the Soul feels the cold,
    so does the Soul without the door feel the cold,
    and a blanket is necessary to share.
Look at the lotus flower, at the Purity of the lotus flower,
    and know its profound gift unto you,
    and return the gift unto Creator.

260 Earth, reluctant to be in the space of positive Energy;
    Souls of earth, graciousness is thy name
    that has placed before thy being a step unto Purity.
How may one gain the step of Purity?
Beloved Souls, enter thou in to acceptance,
    enter thou in to the place of sanctuary, for art thou not Holy!
Is thy being not Holy
Unto whom, earth Soul, will you answer?

Only unto thy own being for, Soul, you have total choice.
There are no issues upon your being that have pressure placed,
    except in the need to advance humanity,
        and you are human, you are very human.
Rejoice in the humanity, for all energies applaud the step you are in.
Each step has growth.
Negative steps have growth.
Even the overcoming of negative steps
    will draw unto your being, magnificence.
Souls, await the onward stride of your motion.
Move forward with the surety
    that your being knows the Writing on the Wall.
All that you are, all that you will become, you have set in motion.
So be it.

VISION[65]

261 Michael will take these Souls to the ocean floors
    that erupt to the earth core.
This is a dying star that is in the stage of the first pangs of childbirth.
Escape is not possible.
The oceans and moons pull the solar Energy
    and cause frenzied reactions of the globe shaped terrain
        in the space of the atmosphere that prevails.
With the wind's endurance,
    the ocean's roar will turn the winds to the east,
        and the strong karma of earth itself
        will be sent in a circular storm of vast proportions
        that will topple the highest buildings.
And it is the same polar effect that will bring the path of the ice
    to the far northern reaches.
This is a slow force that is not unlike your whirlwind
    that will ignite the earth as no scene before it.
This is a Tablet of Stone.
It is written.

---

[65] Vision - the dates at the end of each passage indicate
    when the channelling was received.
    It does not indicate the date of the vision.

Stand in Truth, for the age is in the beginning.
[December 12, 1995]

262 It is the eye that is able to enter where the body cannot.
We, in our human state,
    could pass through space and time as in a twinkling.
It is for you also to do.
Humanity has not felt the roll, only the rock.
The roll will take the mountain to the valley,
    and the valley to the mountain,
        yet some will survive to be still without Light.
It is understanding that is lacking in the foundation.
If earth could form thought for other than greed,
    the earth would survive.
[June 27, 1997]

263 Soul, bow to the Energy with gladness.
Expound in words, the Flow.
Ion is ion.
Ion is Energy, and Energy has great and abundant source.
Behold Holy.
Behold the simplistic world, the flow of Souls
    that each have accountability to self,
        because of the gift that all Souls must know.
To place the hands outward is to feel the benevolence
    of your Almighty God, Allah if you will.
Soul, Energy is golden, has a thread that travels endlessly from self,
    and all are caught in the web of that thread, not from fear,
        but because all ion is connected to the Energy that IS.
All goodness, all negativity has been placed
    within the lower circumference of growth.
Beyond beyond, Soul, each ion of humanity will gather to the Flow
    to be part of ever and ever.
Wait not!
Wait not to mouth the words of goodness.
Spill not over with anxiety but gather the goodness of the Flow
    and know that Energy is Creator and Creator.
Yes, God.
You have named him so, have you not?
God has not chosen, God.

God is Light, and Light is Energy, and Energy is Holy.
Expound with endless breath of the flow of goodness.
The earth cries and sobs as forms of self have been yanked
    from its inners to be torn and tormented.
Oh, Soul, the Energy has woe, the woeful cry.
Ask the child earth: *"Why do you sob so?"*
The earth has carried a painful negativity for man,
    and the weight has become awesome,
    and the back of earth shall break.
Soul, hear the cry that moves ever forward in the Flow
    and wrap your arms around the tree to save the Energy within.
Oh, cast not fear down, but place the ray of understanding
    before men, that the violent decay will soon erode
    the tranquillity that is earth.
The green places will become ash, and the golden sands
    will rush with waters, and mothers will cry
    that the flow to cleanse has taken the child.
Oh, Soul, it is man's choice that allows the chalice to be dropped.
The taste will be bitter, the wine will be off.
The pure indulgence of man has tainted all that is.
Form the gentle place of Flow that teaches the child in the garden
    to play without erupting the form beneath his feet.
Man, manhood could have taken you to a false state
    when you have glanced at the awesomeness
    of your Creator and see only a relentless flattening
    of all that is.
Flow? Flow is the choice of all in the space of Purity.
Behold, Flow is Energy.
Energy is Purity.
Soul, be in Purity.
[July 10, 1998]

264 Hallelujah! Hallelujah!
Shout: "The earth has a time, a moment".
All will be within the tunnel of Purity, all the planets,
    the earth, all that has negativity, all that has deviance.
The tentacles of man reach out.
They reach out not in Purity to touch the outer crusts,

but cover the sight, for man reaches out
    to grasp what is not his.
The well of sadness is deep.
The alignments of the planets have truth.
There will be, Soul, sets of three.
Variation will be created
    by explosions in the bowels of the sun.
Magnetism will cause five nights of darkness,
    five desperate moments.
Stock markets will bend and break
    and sonic booms will be heard continually
    in the twenty four hour nights.
A cold will cover the central earth, and the waters will rise to heights,
    and food will be sodden and pass in the flow.
And yet man can not be with his Creator for two minutes!
And many say: "Is this mine?
    Does this apparition belong to my body?"
Women will cry and reach out, and Souls in Purity
    will come down from the mountain
    and heal in colour and Truth.
And, as in the great exodus,
    Souls will be awash with the need for Truth.
Creation does not bring down pain, but agonies cover the seed
    that will not receive the waters with which to grow.
All life has purpose.
It is repetitious in that it is.
Souls, know the place of Purity.
Abide in the place of Purity.
[August 27, 1998]

265 Enter in to peace.
Enter in to the peace of eternity.
Soul, all earth will roil, all earth will rock, all ovens will erupt
    and earth will know Hades.
All time is to be altered.
The sea will move deeply into lands of desert.
The height of sea will climb to rolls of giant monuments.
Ice of the north will meet the seas of the south

and desecration of high buildings will be fortuitous
    for the end will come quickly.
Land that is low will raise up and land that is high
    will enter the downward spiral.
And earth will cry and mother will cast her child aside
    to grab for life.
And beings of Purity will enter in to the kraal of Purity.
Souls will weep and lament
    and the great monument of Lincoln will fall in a moment.
And the House of Windsor will be cast down.
And the kneeling place of Mohammed will lose its power
    and be found in the sea.
Communication will be found to have stability only upon the rock,
    and great whales will be found in the inland sea
    and used for flesh.
Humanity, all pain and dread will be felt at the throat of man
    and still man will be in greed and voracity of ignorance,
    raping and lashing.
And Souls of Purity will be lifted up and the vibration of your being
    will move you upward into the levitation of time and space,
    into the spaceless time of ever and ever.
Souls, all earth moves, all earth sobs.
Hear!
It is the break of too late.
Hear the knell.
Hear the knell of the end of time and space
    and know the re entry will have great power.
And beings will be reborn to replenish
    and sacredly keep the trust of earth.
Today is today!
Do in today that which can not be done in tomorrow.
[December 3, 1998]

266 Souls of earth, behold the vision of your passing,
    the flow of gentleness brought by Souls uplifted in Purity,
    and the vision of depth of pain and agonies
    brought on by countless Souls who have chosen
    to walk far from the Path.

The great grandfather brings to the people the feather of foreboding.
We have seen the fields of green become lashing waves.
We have seen the mighty mountain range rend itself in twain.
We have visioned the foodless land where all that was is no more,
    where Souls engorge the rotting carcass of whale in delight.
Man is walking a fearful path.
Man smites upon the earth.
All beings will gather to mountaintops,
    and the rains will bring them downward.
Only the Purity will uplift the Soul
    and allow the knowledge to be caught in a frame of six days.
On the seventh day the earth will right itself,
    but light will be beheld
    as many candles of evil will ignite
    and spew forth unto an already desecrated land, anguish and pain.
See the great evil, know the coming of the tide of Time.
Earth has been warned.
Earth is being warned yet again.
Find the peacemaker and hear the words of the peacemaker.
In the turmoil of earth's pain and anguish, two coats will not serve.
Two beds will not serve.
Two bowls of food will not serve.
The hands of earth reach out in loud tormented screams.
The children anguish in their bodies.
Suffer all children to be fed.
Suffer all children to be clothed.
Suffer all children to have shelter
    and know earth to be accountable
    and all Energy to be formed
    and come together in grace before Creator.
Use the feather now to bring the nations to peace,
    and circle the globe of earth with balance
    that it might not rotate.
The day of reckoning is approaching
    and evil is accepted casually within this space of your day.
Bless the house your are in by the Purity that shines from it, not into it.
[January 21, 1999]

267 Soul, from the register of Galatia. .
Souls of earth, indeed, many have come into our space.
The agreement is always, force is not a part of our being.
We cannot place it but thus in your space.
Soul, the hands of your earth existence have imprint,
    the aura of your earth existence has imprint.
Were the eye to be used, it would read,
    written upon the imprint of your eye,
    the volition of entering in to the space of alien.
Behold, it is thus written upon the planet of earth:
    "Souls will be drawn for research reasons
        unto six separate worlds."
These worlds are gathered as one in purpose.
The purpose of these worlds is one: lift of mankind to lift Purity.
You think you are full of knowledge?
Feeble, feeble Souls.
We ourselves do not contain all knowledge.
We contain only the knowledge to the level that we are.
The level of our being is four.
You, Soul, in your space, in your Purity, have a higher Truth.
Does that not astound you?
Be not astounded.
We revere your intenseness, we honour your placement.
We could not see to your Purity, and yet we would lift your beings
    at that time of great purpose.
What purpose, you say?
The purpose of the last battle of Negativity upon the outer regions,
    and then all Purity will cast its eye unto transition
    and the Souls lost in the bottomless pit.
All eternity will reach into the dregs of pain and free Souls
    and lift Souls, once again, unto goodness.
Your frontiers reach unto space.
Our frontiers reach into the depths of pain.
Your frontiers seek to find another earth.
Our purpose is to release the pain of all, for creation is one and many.
It is fragmented.
Your fragment, earth, is but a minute particle.
Souls, the orb upon which you dwell is in great chaos.

Deep within the ocean, a giant gap emerges
    and rumbles and rumbles and rumbles,
    and into your atmosphere will flow gaseous material,
    and the seas will cast down.
Sri Lanka will be no more.
Holland will be no more.
The floods will enter the central plains and draw the swirls of the sea
    to lap against the canyon walls
    and flow mightily forth to the sea once again.
The land of Russia will enter in to Asia,
    and Alaska will find itself connected
    to the great mountain of Japan.
No Soul can withstand the darkness in this week of night,
    for breath will leave
    and the taste of acid will be the downward breath.
The pure of earth will be lifted and the man of cloth who says,
    "I am pure. Hold me up. I have spoken to many."
    will find himself left.
And the urchin of the street of your despicable drug trade will be lifted
    and see the balding head of his tormentor.
The babe will be lifted from the crib
    and the mother will search frantically for the child,
    but she will not look up because she has only looked down;
    her eyes are blinded to the up.
Souls of earth, many have been brought unto the landing stations.
Many have felt the probe.
We have not all the answers at our level.
Creation is creation and the Creator is almighty.
But, forgive us, we are not almighty.
In the gift of their being they have offered unto earth
    the honour of their being, to be brought into our space
    that we might probe for the right intensity,
    that we might protect our field of Energy.
Our beings could not withstand the negativity.
It is not uncomplicated to lift an entire earth population.
We endeavour with all Souls to instill the will to be pure
    that earth would be redeemed,
    but the hands are clenched and the mind of earth is closed.

Behold, it is a gift we give.
[July 15, 1999]

268 Within the tome of earth is great catastrophe.
It will impinge upon the life of great men.
They will be brought low, their beings will be as simpletons
    in their comprehension of what earth visions.
Souls of majesty will bring themselves to the front lines of desecration.
For, Soul, all safety nets will have vanished and earth may not
    seek beneath the floor of itself for sanctuary,
    for safety, for survival.
Earth crack! Crack!
Earth will stretch and floods will issue into vast caverns.
Behold, that which was secure will be insecure.
All that was deemed to be failure will be the mountaintop.
In the vision of this pain
    the earth child will behold such agony as to be old.
Earth now has such beings and man will not see, as in the time of Pharaoh.
Earth child will find themselves
    taken into the Holiness of Creator
    and the eyes will have dimmed
    and the skin will have aged in wrinkle form
    and the teeth of these beings will fall
    and the gumless mouth will plead:
    "Mothers, fathers, hear all in the space of thy children.
    Behold earth pain!
    Seek to heal that upon which we stand".
Souls of earth, rejoice in the telling, for in the telling
    there is opportunity to alter that which is.
Mankind, who art thou but a fragment of the High Creator!
Lift thyself to the majesty.
Speak in words of eloquence unto the beings of earth.
Allow not the tears of children to fall.
Be thou pure in thy being.
See earth as a gentle Soul offering unto earthly beings
    a gentle place to be.
[November 23, 1999]

269 Soul, Michael will teach the fear of man,
   the negativity that enters into the passions of humanity.
Know, Soul, that all turmoil will be from fear,
   all turmoil will be from anger.
It is the evil of man that will cause Souls to hide their beings.
In all temperate zones there will be violence upon the flesh.
There will be looting, there will be vicious attacks of man upon man.
Souls, prepare a table of simplicity, for the time is to recount the self
   and know the avenue that will be ongoing,
   for the next millennium
   will have flagrant choices against righteousness.
Sin will abound and the earth will cough three times
   and from that cough spew forth darkness
   that will give noxious pain - once in South America,
   once in the Americas, and once in lower Europe.
All earth needs a return unto righteousness.
The United States of America must not lose place with Creator
   when in small cavities of the land insurrection is arising.
When this land gives up faith to Creator, this land will cease to be.
Mighty nations must remain mighty in Purity
   or sustain the whirlwind of great negativity.
Behold, the wind will be tumultuous.
It will arouse the greater sleeping buildings to sway
   and visit the least, all that is,
   for it will be brought back.
He who resides with the canisters of death
   will bring his nation down.
Great sobs, wailing of unfleshed skin,
   what was inward will be outward.
Soul, look at thy people!
Man, seek not the heart of self, seek the heart of thy people.
Lo, to pluck the infant from the mother's breast,
   and hold the child high
   and offer unto the child of thy nation, Purity of heart,
   for, Soul, the time of accountability moves forward in thy being.
Prepare ye the way, it will be turning and earth spewing forth,
   and in some great centres will be total peace.

In those Texts of Purity, man will see what man may be.
Seek sustenance of Purity.
Seek to sustain the Soul not the earth being.
Confound no man with piety, but linger in the cause of Truth.
[December 9, 1999]

270 Corral the horses, put the ear to the ground,
    climb to the top of the pinnacle and see.
Enter not in to fear.
Who has heard the sound of the buffalo coming?
Who has heard the great rush and prepared themselves?
Would they place themselves in the low valley
    when they know the buffalo come to find the water?
They place themselves on the mountain that they may see.
Prepare, for in the preparedness of each Soul
    is the ability to strengthen a brother, to feed a brother.
Reach down into the muddy, churning waters and pull forth the hand.
Do it time and time again, and know that the Great One
    has given you a moment before in which to prepare.
For it is now, it will be.
Your energies, use.
Your energies, use.
The ability to stave off the current is to be prepared.
Earth will scream as earth has not screamed.
All Souls will hear the wrench, and waters will rise
    to the top of the western hills,
    and the great inland sea will be once again.
    and earth will be robbed of its structure,
    and the structures of man will fall in a moment
    and Souls with Purity will be delivered to Zero in a moment.
Prepare, for earth has many moons,
    and many moons will speak of darkness and terror.
Robbers will enter in and thieves will create carnage in great cities.
Souls, you must speak to old Souls,
    for young Souls will not hear the rhetoric.
Arm yourself with courage and Purity.
Be a haven of giving in that time
    when man's mortality will seek him out.

Soul, the fruit is ripe, but the core has damage and is rotting.
Be ye pure.
[January 11, 2000]

271 There is no meteor targeted to earth
    that will cause the termination of the planet.
There is a meteor that will enter the seas.
It will be of gigantic proportion.
All inland waterways will be flooded,
    all seas will reach to high building heights.
This will be in the third year of the great distress of earth.
First will come the mortal illness, then will come the great winds,
    then will come the water heights.
All earth at this time will be drawn into one glassy place.
Only the mountaintops will rise.
Souls of earth, this will be the new day,
    the time when Souls are welcomed to vibrate to Purity.
It will be the time when Souls of humanity,
    who have not accepted the Purity of their being,
    will lose all and be found at the gate of transition.
And man will enter the dry line of earth's mountaintops
    and Souls of great Purity will alight from ships
    and a spiritual awakening will begin,
    and earth's Purity will find the gate of Negativity
    brought to the portal of transition.
All Souls will be drawn to Purity, Holy,
    and the Holy Souls will arm themselves
    and enter the portal of pain.
And the Souls of earth,
    and the Souls of those who have not attained level five
    will re enter as one and dwell in Purity,
    and the last battle will begin,
    the battle that will bring those lost from all Time
    into the walk of Purity.
Man, meteor is a combustible formation.
It contains cobalt, sulphurs, radium, zinc.
It contains graphites, it contains sulphites,
    it registers six in the field of metals.

It is hazardous to no man, for man has infallibility
    that man does not know.
[January 18, 2000]

272 As the gnashing of teeth, as the echo of pain, Soul, rejoice!
Know thy being distanced from pain; rejoice in that distance.
Where may I find such a place?
Soul, in the giving way to knowledge and the accepting of wisdom.
Behold, the journey can be arduous or simple,
    the way can be smooth or rocky.
It is, Soul, in the relinquishing of earth logic.
How shall the world divide itself?
How, you ask?
By the concentrated effort of Souls who extend beyond their earth body
    into the vacuum of self, and connect to the Flow of Energy.
Behold, the connection requires total concentration,
    relinquishing of earth being, setting aside the earth value
    and finding only the place of serenity.
Into the Path of Energy, hold the Truth of thy being.
Cast not dispersion upon thy brother.
Err not by placing a foothold where a brother's needs be.
Hold the shaft of wheat and recognize the shaft of wheat
    is not for your consumption alone, but for the consumption
    of any Soul that enters in to your space of being.
It is for that alone that the gift of attainment is yours.
Predetermination is false.
It is judgement upon that which may come.
Do not frown upon the beings lower than thy eyes,
    for, Soul, their height may cast shadows
    on the level of Purity.
Sing songs to almighty Creator.
Rejoice in the happenings of earth.
Rejoice in the awakening of sun to your sky and moon to your night.
See the rain as an opportunity to gather
    that others might share in the gathering.
Souls of earth, the moment is drawing close.
The knell of noonday has already been sounded.
Fear is not a response to the knell of noonday.

Rather, Soul, rejoice, for in the upheaval of earth
    is the relinquishing of pain.
Over all Souls will come to earth an ordination
    set down by the government,
    and earth shall know accountability,
    each person accountable for their being,
    and in the day of accountability the slow rumble will start.
Earth from the north will carry itself southward,
    and the great surface of humanity will sway
    and Souls will fall upon their knees
    and raise their eyes to see a great Light.
The Light will come from the heavens above.
It will be seen as Orion is seen, in the north and in the south,
    in the east and in the west, but singularly at an hour the same.
And each being will record the time of change.
And it will be said that the clock has stopped, time has stood still.
Souls of earth, fear not!
Earth is boundless in her Energy for mankind.
It was for the purpose of mankind that she was created.
Oh, earth, beloved of my Soul, each being will be marked in that day.
It will be as the blush of astigmatism.
It will come at noonday and Souls will recover,
    and tomorrow and tomorrow and tomorrow
    the days will be in constant watching for the next vision.
The vision that earth will wait for will enter from the earth,
    the core, the inner partitions of earth.
Bring on the clowns, stand and scoff and not articulate the Truth,
    recognize it not in the Beings that will re enter
    from earth's inner regions.
But they will extend their hand and place within the hand,
    the power to withstand the second scourge.
[February 8, 2000]

273 Soul, Michael will teach the last endeavour,
    the last purpose for earth.
And man shall cede to the negativity of his being,
    and man will force negativity to reign.
And man will lose in that day, the love of family, the love of friend,

and Souls will gnash at one another
as lions in the pit of our beloved.
And man will reach
for ungodly methods of performing that which is sacred,
and idols shall become objects worshipped and cleaved unto.
And men and women and children shall shave the heads,
not for style, but to eradicate the plague of insect upon their being.
And great sores shall rise from the body
and earth shall feel the drippings of these great sores
oozing into her great being.
And upon the face of the earth, in seven sacred areas,
will be found humanities
who have chosen to reach unto the higher being,
and Souls will prepare the way for a new day,
a new song that will be sung: "Hosanna, Hosanna, Purity cometh!"
And how shall we meet Purity?
Shall we watch the Souls writhing in agony?
Shall we not take from our being the strangling vines
that wind about the Truth of self,
and free the voice and follow the path that has been given?
Seven Keys have been given that will unite mankind.
Who is the author of the seven Keys?
Holy ones from the Circle of Saints have read from the burning bush
and have offered the tablets of stone.
Once again the offering has come
and the tablet of stone has not been read.
Seven Keys to unlock the door into the gate of Transition.
Do not ponder at your beings, but know the day is fast approaching,
the knell of noonday, when the sound will not be held back.
Bring forth that which mankind must hear!
[February 29, 2000]

274 There are upon earth four decades of vision.
There are four decades of turmoil.
There will be a need to gather protection from sulfuric gases.
There will be a need to protect from high walls of water
and great winds that will draw negativity.
There will be four years in each ten of plague.

There will be four years in each ten of famine.
There will be two years to grow and put away.
Each progressive year will be of greater proportion in disaster
    than the next.
Souls will learn to lift their feet
    and their beings will raise themselves
    and feel the buoyancy of their Energy,
    for they will reach up and utter:
    "Save me! Save me! Save me!"
And in the reaching up they will alter their being
    and know the negative spiral to be altered.
Many will be born with webbed hands and feet
    and earth will say it is because the land is wet,
    and others will say it is because the land is dry.
But the same land will always be wet,
    and the same land will always be dry.
And lips will parch and the mothers will bleed at the breast
    and the young will suck mucus instead of milk.
And mothers will cry "Take my young that they may live!"
And the hoards of insects will enter in
    and only in containers of glass will food be safe,
    for rodents the size of dogs will cast their vermin
    and the Souls will plead as Job once pleaded:
    "Enough! Enough!"
And the time will wane and the Souls will be gathered
    to the Mountaintop that has been prepared.
Each of the seven vortexes is the hallowed place of Flow.
It is being purified and blest by Saints.
[April 25, 2000]

275 We speak, Souls, from the great circle[66].
Our beings vision earth in a singular motion,
    our energies will align with those of earth.
Our beings are caught in the very bosom of creation.
From our stance we seek to see the value of humanity.
There is, within earth, a guardian people
    who have hovered often about your beings.

---

66 great circle - circle of purities

They have brought their being into your space.
Behold, I am such a being.
Behold, I have vision of earth agony.
Behold, the vortex of Hawaii will be cast asunder.
Behold, the vortex of New Zealand will be cast asunder.
Behold, the vortex of Madagascar will be cast asunder.
Behold, Crete will rise up to Everest, and Everest will be as Crete.
There is within earth a decay.
From six feet below one third of planet earth are toxins, uncontrolled.
The sea has begged to be allowed to live and the beings of the sea
    have strangulated the agonies entering in.
The battle has begun.
Who is there to stand on the side of righteousness?
Who will take the mountaintop?
Our beings travel through light years.
You could not withstand our Purity.
We have darkened our being and the vibration of Purity
    allows the entering in to water, to the depth of all sea bottoms.
The Souls of great mammoths watch our coming and our going.
The tortoise beholds the painful end if earth does not rise up
    and demand a pure space for all living creatures.
Under the sign of Leo will come the great earth shake.
Under the sign of Scorpio will come the great wind.
Under the sign of Aquarius will come the incessant gnawing of bones.
Behold, who will dry the eye?
Who will carry the burden?
Unto whom may we offer survival?
The planet has only a time.
Refuse the pain to enter in.
Behold, speak humanity!
Old Souls of earth, hold the staff of righteousness in your hand.
Enter in to the field of battle.
[May 8, 2000]

276 Lips have meaning for the earth Soul.
The lips are not casually put upon the face of your being.
The lips are instruction to the Soul and destruction to the Soul.
All negativity is to be denounced, to be refuted.

Toxins of earth rage, and earth must engorge within her being,
    the toxins of man's negativity.
Man himself places the toxins within his tiny babes.
Lift the child to Purity.
Pollution will allow the babe to fall on desecrated earth.
Souls, toxins are not truth, they are untruth.
Do not acknowledge truth, stamp it from your being.
Do not the Souls in transition roil in pain
    because of the acceptance of negativity as their reality!
Souls are tortured by toxins
    that needle the brain and the heart and the flesh,
    and the Soul is transfigured from perfection that it would be.
How desolate is earth!
How earth cries!
Who stands as sentinel for earth?
Who rages at the pain placed on earth?
Anger, Soul, anger!
Where is anger?
Earth, where is anger?
Earth, where is pain?
Speak oh thou earth: "Man has placed it on my being.
    Before man there was no pain."
Earth also has a lip and opens the mouth wide
    to spew forth in anger at men,
    for she has learned anger from men.
She has absorbed the anger into earth bowel.
Oh, man, earth has learned well that which you have taught.
But blessed man is not lost, for man is awakening and rising up
    and there are those who speak for the child,
    and speak for the earth,
    and hold the beauty of her dress as that which she is,
    and plant seeds of growth in the minds of men
    that their heart and their mind will have a new direction.
This is not a new thing.
The prophets have always given the message of the new day.
Will you lose anger?
Speak Love in the face of anger?
Would you lose pain and vision perfection?

Know thy being is only transient on earth.
It is the shimmer of the light upon the wave,
    or the glitter of the star in the heaven.
It carries the potential of Light to alter pain.
To alter anger is to accept Purity, Truth and Love
    in all thy words, in all thy being.
What man speaks has no place in thy being.
Thy being is a Soul unto itself.
Rejoice in the Purity of thy being.
[July 18, 2000]

277 Soul, arrival is what you have heard.
Behold the complexity and simplicity of the message before earth.
All arriving unto Purity is as a telescope folding in unto itself.
The vision is extended outward and the completeness is done
    in the folding forth.
Soul, all phases of purities unto the purpose of creation is arrival.
It is the final completeness of mankind's state of being.
It is the gathering of one accord,
    of one single Truth marked with the eye,
        all Souls lifted in their beings to see the extension of Truth
        without the movement of body or mind or heart.
All complexities will become simple and channelling will reveal unto you
    the rhythm of arrival.
Encounter, Soul, the alien.
We, Soul, are the alien.
Soul, we have Energy of good in our being.
We place no negative energy towards earth.
We are rapid in our gathering of all knowledge
    in the scope of all energies.
We have ability to withstand all movement of Energy.
We may even enter in to your space without altering our being.
We have but to touch our form and we will change into fluid.
We will use the Energy of our being
    to recover from any humanity, information.
It is not intrusive.
We are not intrusive, we are partner with humanity.

We have before us the goal of the gathering.
We have worked in the space of many beings.
We have formulated echoes that resound throughout the universe.
The echoes will soon be recovered by your forms,
    even as we enter in daily upon your earth,
        unnoticed because of the frequency of our being.
Soul, all apertures of earth carry a single intent,
    to bring all Souls into the Second Gateway.
We are not foreign to your being.
We have been gathered from the same place.
Many beings of earth are from our homeland,
    not because they are alien, but because they have chosen
    to be a part of the great armada of mankind.
You have upon your earth, seas.
We have between our earths, seas.
The seas are not waterways, as your seas.
They are Energy Fields that draw quickly from one field to another.
They spiral and turn, they twist and draw.
Souls of earth, there is contemplation by your people of who we are.
We would speak to anyone who has fear.
We would speak to the purpose of our coming
    and that is to be brought down that you might be raised up.
For the time will come when your beings will want
    to be raised up from the havoc of earth.
And human you are, and human you will yet remain,
    but in a twinkling you will be changed.
For who could not change when their being is risen in vibration
    above the space of earth,
    and all the woe of earth is carried below,
    and you have the realization
    that all you have ever known has come to be.
All the chords of your many lives have drawn your understanding
    to the very time you are in.
You will have no fear.
We will come together, you and I, and we will speak
    in the tongue that we know.
And when all the settling of earth has given the torment to rest,

we will, with you, set down,
and a mighty Hallelujah! will be heard,
and the echo will carry itself unto the many beings awaiting.
And Souls of earth will arrive in hordes,
and earth will acclaim the spirituality that it has been offered,
and the eyes of man will see clearly,
and the eye of knowing will enter in to the space of Naught,
and all partitions from the First Gateway will be separated.
And the Souls will see the many beings who are gathered in pain
and humanity, who has learned in that day to reach unto all,
will gather with great wonder at who they are
and see the Energy about their beings
and know they have the power to raise and to be let down.
They have the power to enter in
and Souls will draw forth the Souls of pain
and speak the words of healing.
And the Souls of Saints who have been scourged
and yet drawn themselves into the place of the blessed
that they, too, might minister unto the blessed,
will see their brothers and sisters, and will recognize the Four,
risen in their being, offering unto them the Pathway.
And Souls will reach and gather, and reach and gather,
and enter in and lift up those many Souls.
And the Blessed Angels will encircle the encampment of man,
and the Four Blessed will place themselves in Holiness.
And all the Blessed will reach unto man and man will extend
the Purity of their Brethren unto their Beings.
And the Souls will rejoice in the coming together,
and the heavens will open
and all that ever was will be seen unto the Second Gateway.
And the Souls will be brought through all the teachings of Truth,
of Purity, of Love and will recognize in their beings
that all that they held were scars.
And they will reach unto Creator
and know the blessedness of their coming in.
And Creator will welcome the Souls unto Him, for the lost is found,
"My son has returned unto Me".
And all heavens will ring, and all angels will sing,

and all earth will be lifted up into the perfection,
and the doors will open for a new day to come.
[August 29, 2000, April 11, 2001]

278 A wheel within a wheel within a wheel within a wheel
within a wheel within a wheel.
Behold a vision, a portal, a vortex, behold the thread of your Purity.
Behold, you are, Soul, drawn by Purity into the spiritual self of your being.
You are, by Purity, drawn into the Essence of thy being.
Thou art drawn in Purity through the different levels of thy being,
level within level within level within level.
Each draws itself into a new vision, a new expectation.
Each portal offers great wonder and amazement
for the entering in is as the seed, grown and matured
and endowed with the cloak of wisdom
that has been gathered from previous placements.
Do you see, Soul, the kaleidoscope of thy being
that wells before thy Holy self?
Do not think thyself without outer bounds, but know
to reach the outer bounds thou must always enter in to thy being.
A wheel within a wheel within a wheel, the entering in draws thee
into the encampment of the cosmic order.
The consciousness of thy being is lifted above the framework of earth,
above thy galaxy, but inward is the Flow,
is the Flow into that place of being.
Souls of earth, know that would mankind place their being
with as much Energy directed toward meditation,
the Souls would draw themselves to Purity in an offering
that would alter earth's pain.
Hear, Soul, the voice, the voice of the whale.
Hear the voice of the porpoise.
Hear, and know that the melt is upon earth
and waters are rising while earth contends
with multiplications of one.
Soul, seek ye into the space of Naught.
Direct the energies of earth into the mathematics of naught.
Soul of earth, constrain thy being, for you will see whole buildings
sink beyond thy eyes.

Thou will see Souls who have never claimed Creator,
    cry unto Creator: *"Save us, save us!"*
Souls of earth, thou art wheel within wheel within wheel.
Ezekiel saw a wheel rolling and the vision was opened unto him
    and the circumference of the vision was a plan for mankind.
But mankind, in simplicity, saw not that which should have been seen.
Souls, know the Energy of thy being.
Know the vortex of thy being.
Know that each Soul is connected, wheel within wheel within wheel,
    each world is connected, wheel within wheel.
Implosion after implosion will enter and from the outer wheels
    the implosion will begin, for all Souls will be gathered
    and uplifted to the level they can abide.
Abide, Souls, the level of Love.
[September 19, 2000]

279 Soul, enjoy ego.
Behold Mohammed, the righteous one.
All Purity is not soft and cushiony.
All Purity has texture, has the nap of rough edges and silk lines,
    and gentle cottons.
The weaver does not always use the gentle thread.
Mohammed, Blessed Mohammed, brother Mohammed!
Purity was the intent of Mohammed,
    disdain at what the eye beheld,
    and eyes that could see to the Soul of a person
    and reach beyond his Soul to the Eye of Creator.
And Creator saw Mohammed and blest Mohammed,
    and the Soul was given a boundary to place goodness upon,
    and the Soul walked in that boundary and expressed to mankind
    that which the Father of his Being issued forth.
And the pearls were cast among swine,
    and many looked at the writings of Mohammed
    and they placed the context on what Mohammed expressed.
And Mohammed smiled and saw within the perimeter of his blessings,
    that man was human and had waylaid that which was true.
The Soul was prophet and spoke of much that would come

and saw the Purity on the left hand being distorted
   by the right hand.
And Jesu and Mohammed smiled and fell upon each other,
   for they knew the pain that would come forth.
The seed had been planted and corrupted by both and all energies of men.
And Buddha set aside the veil and beheld the pain of man
   and cried to the Father:
   "I would repair that which is wrong.
   I would enter in and alter that which is wrong.
   Again and again, I would enter in.
   Creator, allow this to be!
   It is my gift unto Thee."
And Buddha brought down his golden presence unto man
   and gifts were showered upon man,
   and man again beheld the giver and not the gift.
Krishna also entered in and looked to man and sought to raise man
   above his ineptness, above his negativity,
   and hold a gem of perfection unto Creator.
And behold, Krishna sobbed a great tear, for again the gift was distorted.
Now all these energies are level seven.
They have energies of Purity above the Angels,
   Buddha remaining at five to enter in again and again.
And the Souls of the Four have beseeched unto Creator:
   "Creator, let us be at the Gathering Time,
      for Souls have a need to remember
      that which has been taught.
   Allow us Souls to enter in once again
      to teach the energies of Purity."
And Creator heard the plea and each Soul shall find the placement
   at the Gathering Time; the north, the south, the east, the west.
All earth shall see the Purity of those Beings.
The light of your sun will dim and all earth will be in darkness
   and then man will behold the Radiance that opens unto earth.
At one time the Light will blend
   and the pureness of the blend will astound earth,
   and earth will reach beyond their paltry beings,
   and those who have been altered will be brought,

once again, to earth,
and teachings of Purity will begin to redeem all mankind.
And Souls will be purified, and Souls who have been manifested
will open the door of transition
and enter in to the gateway of transition.
And Souls of demented, torn, and grievous pain will look
and behold the scarred being of your Soul.
And they will see in you, themselves,
and the Blessed Four will stand upon the gateway,
and the Holy Ones will enter through the Light of the Four.
And humanity that has entered in will draw the Souls of pain unto earth,
and their form will be seen, and their Purity will be seen,
but their pain will not have been relieved,
but they will be as a Soul who has lost and not found the way.
And the Four will tenderly draw them forth to the Mountaintop,
to the sacred places of earth,
and the Blessed Ones will draw down.
And as humanity draws the pain from their beings,
they will place their beings about their brother
and support their being,
and raise them forth as the pain falls away,
as the old cloak falls away from the snake.
The Soul will be redeemed and recognize the Holy Ones
and they will fall upon each other
and sob great sobs of welcome.
And Creator will enter in to earth and all will behold the matter
of which Creator is, and all will see the countenance of Love.
And Hosannas will be raised at the Gateway to the Farside,
and the Blessed Ones will draw unto those they have saved,
and all worlds will know of the event of coming in,
and salutations of Love will be issued forth.
And then will be heard a great knell,
and Negativity will be sent by Creator to the netherland,
and Negativity will no longer have place
in the Energy Field of creation.
Creator will draw earth beings forth and all energies will be as one.
And Creator will issue the sound of Entering In

to the Second Gateway of man,
and all worlds will come behind man.
And the Blessed Ones will stand at the Gateway
to be the last of Entering In
and so will come unto Godhead.
[October 11, 2000]

280 Even the blind will see the Writing on the Wall.
Even the blind will eye through the aperture that opens
before mankind.
The knell of earth is the last opportunity to alter the course of mankind.
All entries into all goodnesses have many roads.
There is, Soul, the straight road that is Purity.
There is the negative road that will not learn.
There is the negative road that attempts to learn.
Earth has no consistency.
Behold the value of earth to Creator.
Earth is a gem of Purity that will raise forth the blessed.
All creation looks unto earth.
"Lo, I am with you always, even unto the end."
It need not be so.
Earth, hear!
Earth, open the eyes to the dissolution of mankind
and adhere to the strict observances of positive, not negative.
Reject from your being all negative,
for the knell of earth is close to sounding,
and the bell will resonate from one corner unto all.
Caskets will not need to be.
The dead will not be found.
Mothers, fathers, where are your children? Where?
Kings, ambassadors, presidents, leaders of mankind,
where is your Truth?
Look not at the pearl under the barrel.
Do not place thy being to gathering,
for the gathering has nothing to do with that which is material.
Blessed, blessed Purity of earth,
all creation awaits thy Entering In.

All creation awaits the drawing forth of Purity.
Delay not.
Delay not, for Soul is the extension of thy being.
You are not mere flesh and blood.
You are the touch of Purity, the touch of goodness.
All goodness is anointed and Holy.
There is enough in the cup for all.
Hold the cup of goodness unto thy lip and drink,
 and know that you will be armed with a Purity
 that will save earth.
Soul, the coming forth of Purity will reach thee into Ecstasy
 beyond earth's imaginations.
Souls, who has seen earth creatures rotting because of mankind?
Who has seen the children hungry because of mankind?
Who has seen the earth gouged in pain because of mankind?
Will not mankind be outraged?
Will you not busy yourself in the rendering of peace and Love?
Souls of earth, the knell of earth is upon you
 and the blessed Purity of your being is but reflection,
 for, Soul, the image is where we are.
Enter thou in to the space of the true image.
[October 18, 2000]

281 Behold the Circle of Saints, behold the form of mankind.
Unto Israel is the birth of a Holy One.
Of the Four, the Holy One[67] has entered in at Farside
 to reach unto mankind.
First, House of Israel, know thy pain,
 know thy countenance has lost the uplifting.
You are not the sacrificial lamb.
You are not the cast down.
You are beloved of your Creator,
 for in the place of Israel will be the coming forth of a Purity.
It will hold a cornerstone where Angels come forth and meet
 and all lands round about you
 will hold the second and third and fourth[68].

---

67 Holy One - Jesu
68 second and third and fourth - Krishna, Buddha and Mohammed

But in the time of great travail, earth will see land shift
    and man will not hold the same position.
For man will say: *"What port is mine?"*
Oh Israel, do not hold tight to that which cannot be held,
    but reach and clothe thy brother.
House of Israel, see the flame come down and ignite
    if the will will not swerve to allow the human in thy being.
Lambs and lions will lay together on that day.
Be thou the first to lay in the mouth of the lion,
    for have you not your Lord to watch over thy being!
Do not issue forth platitudes and live in doubt,
    for who hast called thee Holy?
Are not all men Holy!
Is not your brother Holy!
To the east and to the west and to the north and to the south,
    will not the Blessed Ones enter in to the land!
And, behold, will not the Angels bless thy being!
House of Israel, you fail to see that which you must see!
Behold, has not the star come unto thee.
Has not the star risen and has not the Father blessed!
Remember, Souls, for coming into Israel,
    remember the coming forth unto the promised land,
    remember the day of thy turn.
And remember the Purity of thy being
    that you might be worthy of all that has been given unto thee.
House of Israel, your countenance is fenced in and the wall goes higher.
It is not, Soul, the Holy wall.
It is the wall of unforgiveness.
"Unto the hills will I lift mine eyes that I might see in clarity
    that which my Lord has for me."
Soul, speak these words at the dawn, to the east and to the west,
    and to the north and to the south
    and do not fear the rope that comes unto thee.
For have you not the protection of your Lord, your God, your Creator!
Is He not the same Lord and Creator that is for thy brother
    and thy brother and thy brother!
Lift, Soul, to the world the countenance of Purity.
[October 18, 2000]

282 Souls, earth is time and space, and earth has an agenda.
It may be fast, it may be slow.
It is for mankind.
Souls of earth, the Farside awaits mankind.
The agenda for the Farside also has expectation.
It awaits the coming forth of Purity.
Creator endowed humanity with time and space
    that mankind might learn to overcome negativity.
All beings in all worlds await the altered time.
The mark of man is deep and the sack cloth and ashes are laid heavy,
    and man withdraws into the place of mourning
    and the nostrils behold the stench
    that rises from the corpse of pain.
Who will alter the pain?
The beloved sanctity of high walls?
The uniforms of wretched beings?
No, Soul, the tender utterances of pure Souls
    who speak to goodness and Truth.
And time will advance and no one place carries the answer.
Seven carry the answer, for earth awaits.
Soul, enter in to the positive Energy of thy being
    and know thy purpose will take thee farther
    than thy earth mind will know.
Country after country will have the volumes translated.
Know this will be.
Know the energies will be three.
Upon the books, when the three are published together,
    will be first written, *Truth*, second *Purity*, third *Love*.
[October 18, 2000, December 2, 2000]

283 Soul, we are Jinn.
Soul, we have been Farside through earth.
Soul, earth has three areas of great pain ready to be relieved:
    Central Europe, Brazil, Philippines.
All areas hold great negativity.
All areas are infiltrated with negative Souls abounding.
Earth will send a spew to remind humanity of that
    which must be done.

Know, Soul, the three will be the first of twelve.
Know the wave will come high and the Soul will be severed in two.
Know the great trees will pinion buildings.
Know that Hawaii will bear the brunt of the great storm.
It will wash up to shore a grey ship, a memorial of evil done.
Know that within Alaska will come a heat
    that will react upon the coast of California.
Know the blessed whale will ride belly up for sixteen days.
Know the loss of most of one pod to disease.
Souls of earth, recognize as you speak, your oil delivers great pain.
Know, Soul, that oil once again will deliver pain.
A rupture will enter the northern territories and spew upon the land.
Wildlife will be altered.
Soul, count the fingers on one hand
    and know for five days the spew will come forth.
[January 24, 2001]

284 Souls, witness, witness the counter energy of earth
    and know the acceleration of counter energy.
Earth is preparing herself to throw off, as a dog shakes it's body,
    to throw off negativity from its surface.
The negativity will leave the land and enter the sea.
The negativity will be in great cities brought low,
    fallen into the wash of the sea.
Behold, many have spoken unto earth.
Righteous nations speak with forked tongues,
    hungry nations store pain for others to bear.
Earth is holding the weight of that pain.
Earth is not unequal to holding the negativity,
    earth is refusing to hold the negativity.
Earth is casting from its belly the great pockets of pain.
Earth is issuing forth a decree unto man:
    "Do not burden the land.
    Do not soil that which is pure.
    Do not weigh down that which has motion."
Earth, hear unto earth the edict.
Earth will not withhold its anger.
The timetable of mankind has accelerated.

The motion of the pure has accelerated.
Hovering about your being are Souls waiting to gather the pure.
You do not know when the watchman cometh.
Prepare to be taken in the twinkling of an eye,
    lifted apart from the quell of pain.
Only in being lifted may your Energy be brought down
    and the tranquil placement of Purity exist upon the land.
Gather not monies, material goods, unto thy being.
You will not rise with the weight,
    but relieve thyself of all burdens of earth.
Open thy doors unto those in pain,
    speak soft words to unite all men.
[January 31, 2001]

285 Circle your arms forward, outward from yourself.
Allow the centre fingers to touch the centre fingers.
The circumference is how we see earth,
    small and incredibly, incredibly unstable.
How long may you stand and hold your hands thus in a circle?
How long will your Energy withstand the circle?
Soon the arms will be heavy and the Soul tilts to a motion.
The Soul will have to release for the pain has become great.
So it is with earth.
The pain is becoming great.
The whales have spoken unto Creator.
The dolphins have spoken unto Creator.
The turtle is defending earth for yet another moment.
"Why does the reign not stop?"
"Who will stop the reign?"
"Can we not place our energies about earth and stop the reign?"
The reign will not be stopped?
Soul, in a moment it is possible!
In a moment all earth could unite
    and behold the lesson would be done!
And the scars would be witnessed, and earth would rise as one,
    and all negativity would be erased and sent to the Hinterland,
    and the blessed would be brought forth.
Soul, would you speak only of Love?

Would you utter no negative thought?
Would you allow only blessings to go forth from your being
    unto all men?
This is not easy for humanity.
Humanity is enticed by negativity; negativity is creative.
Negativity enfoils human into the desire to be made great upon earth
    and earth sobs.
Who will hold only positive words unto their being?
Will six only hold positive words unto their being?
Will five or four or three or two or one?
Who will draw the pain from earth?
Ignite the flame, Soul, ignite the flame!
It is your Energy that ignites the flame,
    it is the positive, vibrant Energy
      that does not drag oneself down in negativity,
      but witnesses only that which is pure
      and holds only that which is pure,
      does not cleave unto pain, but repels pain.
Souls of earth, mighty army of earth,
    if the captains of the army can not hold self to the battle plan;
    do you see, Soul?
[January 31, 2001]

286 Souls, witness the progress of earth's land exchange.
Alaska will break away.
The source of the mighty waves will draw El Nino
    unto the Arctic Sea.
The Arctic Sea will spew great rocks forth
    that have lived eons within bergs.
The Soul will see from planes, the great wall of the sea
    wash over the Northwest Territories, Siberia, Sweden, Norway.
All upper regions will be inundated by heights of great waters.
Souls of earth, the seas will develop an algae
    that will eat at the flesh of great mammals.
They will rise and float and expose the vulnerability
    of their being to the sky.
Souls will read the echo of pain and ships will echo the pain.
The sun will skew in the sky

Holy

    and the corpses will be as the great southern sea
        for maggots and living will walk upon the dead.
And the sea will refuse the excrement it has spewed from its body
        and it will wash back upon the land from which it came.
And man will hold his hands idle, and old Souls will busy themselves.
A few will speak and the words will be unaccepted,
        and the bodies will bend, and illnesses will hold the forms
        in contorted states because of the vileness of the sea.
The rain will wash the great corpses
        and the floods will enter in to the land,
        and the living sea will bring its dread unto the land,
        and the land will be scourged.
And humanity will find great sores upon the source they have
        and they will say, "Why has this come to us?
        Why are we scourged like the Egyptians?"
All earth will find the hands and the legs and the arms
        pitted with sores, as ulcers with great oozing sores.
And there will be no time for drugs, no time for medication.
And all hands will raise up to Creator
        and a mighty cry will be heard in the heavens above,
        and Creator will see His army of humanity and sob great Tears:
        'Soul, why do you not hear?
        Oh, Soul, why do you not hear?
        My Soul! My Soul!"
And the land will flood and in the land will come wind,
        and in three days the wind will clear the lands,
        and the Souls will heal and will say:
        "A miracle has been done for God has sent a miracle."
Soul, the rain will come from the skies in chemicals from a great cloud.
It will come from the lands of the Arab and the Jew and the Palestinian
        and the rain will pour upon the world
        and a miracle will be proclaimed,
        for the reign of terror will send earth a blessing.
Always is there a rainbow to earth.
And earth will be given yet another chance to adhere
        to the Writings on the Wall.
And earth will speak of the mission to humanity
        and humanity will draw themselves together and say,

"We have done this one thing.
   We have created a union of healing and our brothers and sisters
       of the Jewish and Arab Nations have healed our being."
And Russia and Africa and China and the Americas, Australia,
   will look unto the mount of sacredness
   and the world will be stilled.
For seven Keys will be slotted into earth's common language
   and the deciphering will come in an instant,
   and the pattern of humanity will be clear,
   and all intention of earth will be clear.
And man will understand the vibration that is required
   and earth will start to energize their being.
Some will not hear, but many will enter in to the east[69].
Many will enter in to the wisdom.
Many will be brought to vibration
   and the Souls will begin to alter that which is ill.
   and the Souls will begin to alter that which is dying and dead.
Beloved earth, all the pain can be erased with the knowledge of Purity.
The agenda will be done.
It is written on the Wall.
[February 14, 2001]

287 Indeed you have the Mountaintop.
Indeed, there are beings in Sweden that have a piece of the Mountaintop.
There are beings in India that have a piece of the Mountaintop.
There are beings in USA that have the Mountaintop.
There are beings in that which earth calls the cauldron,
   the boiling point of earth.
Within the blessed Mountaintop of Peru is one.
Within the land that world fights, Palestine and Israel,
   there is a Mountaintop.
And, Souls of earth, words shall come forth unto man,
   and be spoken and critiqued,
   and man will cast aside that which is written,
   and earth will shake and the buildings will fall,
   and the man will pick up once again that which is written.
And many times will man refer to that which is,

---
69 enter in to the east - See Appendix B, Daily East Ritual

and that which earth calls church will alter,
    and humanity will wear the garb of peace.
And the arsenals of earth will be gathered, an encampment roundabout,
    and earth will be called a war free zone.
Souls of the Mountaintop will be heard,
    the voices of Purity where the Keys come forth, will be heard.
From under a tree came Buddha.
From a stable came Jesu.
From a wandering path came Mohammed.
From simplicity came Krishna.
Soul, when the Keys come forth
    and the force behind the Keys are Truth and Purity,
    the force will spread the vision unto all mankind.
Know you are the Mountaintop,
    for if you have understood, you have beheld Purity.
[February 28, 2001]

288 New York City: violent shaking, great buildings fall,
    one of three great, severed halfway to ground.
Soul will warn earth.
Soul within France will poison the waterway
    and all Souls will suffer from the gaseous air that rises.
The pellets would be dropped by a foreign country
    by asserting themselves as friendly.
The Soul would be given permission to reside
    close to a complex of the main waterway.
Soul within the Soviet Union is taking steps
    to annihilate all beings of lesser Siberia.
Souls within the structure of Israel have denounced attempts at peace.
They will detonate, within the space of Iraq,
    a bomb of immense proportions.
The Souls led by a female president of the USA
    will seem to reach unto man for the wellness of man,
    but will entomb many within the walls of a building
    in the central part of the USA.
The Souls will be classified as nonexistent civilians.
Souls of the USA, of Australia, will both suffer great flooding,
    flooding of immense proportions.

From the flooding will come a pox.
The pox will touch one in six Souls.
A struggle by England will present a vaccine,
    but only after great desolation to population.
Souls of Siberia will feel a great warming,
    the water will melt beneath the tundra.
All Souls will breathe with fastness,
    a thinness of air will be directly related to Israel's bomb.
All of India will be sieged by Soviet, by China.
The Souls will reach into each others pockets to grasp at land.
China will refute by offering two bombs,
    each will be placed within its own borders to detonate.
Soul, all will occur within fifteen years
    if the Souls of earth do not enter in to agreement.
The Souls of nations struggle to be separate instead of together.
See the land of the south as that which will remain
    most comfortable: South America.
[March 28, 2001]

289 Soul, earth humanity will be transformed in a twinkling,
for earth will lose the vibration of Negativity.
They will refuse to accept the treble note that Negativity offers.
They will rejoice in the acceptance of Naught.
Souls, unto Purity give Purity.
Unto negativity give Purity.
Unto all vibration offer Purity.
For Creator has created the field of Purity
    and all Energy of Purity is offered unto Negativity.
It was the purpose of creation to give unto Negativity.
Souls of earth, know the form of your being,
    know the Holy within your temple of being.
Soul, within the Energy of Creator is no avarice, is no evil intent.
Behold, the Blessed Angels that minister unto Creator
    have spoken unto our being,
    and Souls have held the cup of Purity
    and tipped the cup unto their being so they have become Purity.
They have entered in to Purity and Creator has drawn unto Godhead
    in the portion that is allotted unto the Energy He is.

And the Path unto Godhead has opened
    and the flow of vision has come unto Creator,
    and Creator has reflected outward unto all Souls
    the intent of Godhead.
Only does mankind hold the Keys of the forward Path.
And Creator has moved, as you are moved in moments of great giving,
    by the Souls of humanity who, in their simplicity,
    have become complex and not unlike the Holy Holy Holy.
For in their Purity of Truth they have gathered profound Love.
Behold, earth humanity, the eye reveals the curtain removed,
    and as the clouds of earth break and the light shines through
    so, humanity, will the Gateway rend itself
    and the Light of Godhead, the intent of Godhead, will come forth.
And man will whisper in quiet places: "*What is this they say?*
    How can this be? Who has spoken of this?"
And the learned men who sit with dour faces, cloaked in garbs of religion,
    will know in their hearts that the Truth has been revealed unto them.
Behold, humanity, thou art wonderful, thou art beautiful in thy Purity.
See the lift of thy being raised up
    that all might see and know how great thou art.
Godhead revealed unto thee will be.
[April 7, 2001]

290 Soul, how generous is your world unto you.
Souls, be aware of earth and the value of earth to humanity.
The Creator has placed in your space an orb of great compassion,
    and yet the pain of earth is overwhelming,
    and earth releases her molten tears to show the rend
    within her being.
And earth lifts the land that was sea and says:
    "Humanity, value this space we have formed for thy being.
    Will you look, humanity, at what you do to the new land?
    Will you look at the spoils you leave?"
We speak, because if we do not speak more mountains will spew forth
    and fire will cover the earth, and on every continent
    will earth upheave and the tears come forth.
You have within the power of your being, the globe of earth.
You hold the blue Light that it is, shimmering in your being

    and we plead unto you to hold it close and wash it with your tears,
    and retain the defilements that you would place within
    and look at that which you form, and know before you form:
    "Where shall it be retained?
    How shall we retain safely that which we form?"
For man has created much he is powerless to contain,
    and we would receive it from you, but this we cannot do.
But what we can do, we do.
We ask that each earth being takes ten steps outward,
    and in that ten steps they remove all contamination,
    all contamination!
It is, Soul, not in the removing,
    it is in the containing of the removing.
It is to keep pristine the ten feet square, to hold it perfect
    unto itself as a treasure.
Not that you own, nay, not that you own,
    but that which you have stewardship over.
You would alter the force of earth.
[August 14, 2001]

291 Soul, you curtailed the voice and you created a voice.
You are thus creator.
You curtailed and you created.
We do not draw it to you, Soul, as ostracism
    but merely to visualize that which you cannot see.
We, Soul, contain none.
We have pleasures in our path.
Our pleasures are often the reminders of our inadequacies upon earth,
    for we have dwelled in your space.
We have maintained a household,
    we have been barbaric and human in our being,
    and we have come to the space of Knowing.
There is a need for earth to acknowledge the velocity of Time
There is a need for earth to acquaint itself to the revolution of Time.
The context of what you know as hour is changing.
The context of what you know as year is changing.
The volition of parameters of your creation are altering.
They are upheaving and making the timetable of time invalid.

You will know that in a time soon to come
    will be a need to alter the calendar of time.
And in the context of Time you will have to space another equation.
There is an equation of T^{70}.
It would put you into the relativity of our Time.
It would be of great assistance if we could offer unto you the solution.
We could not give it, Soul.
It is not ours to give.
It comes from the space of Creator.
We ourselves do not have this equation.
We search constantly for the equation.
We do know that which it holds, and we have placed it
    in your space before.
Soul, there is a need for you to research, to assist
    in the throe you will receive.
It will alleviate the loss of many lives.
Souls of earth, do what you do with urgency.
[August 21, 2001]

292 Blessed earth, you have been given much.
Earth, you are in the path to enlightenment and many will be lifted,
    and many will remain.
You have seen a reversal to what will be.
Your planet has lost, instantly, many Souls.
Their purities have been lifted as your purities will be lifted,
    but your earth remained in a solid state.
At the time of the great lifting, all earth, all earth will be stressed
    and the nostrils will be filled with negativities,
    and the waterways will swell beyond man's comprehension.
Blessed earth, you are Holy.
Set from you all vile containments.
Unite, earth, in the positive Energy that you have.
Instead of guns use Energy, instead of blasphemes use Love,
    instead of fear and doubt use knowing.
We have gathered into our arms all who have been lost on earth
    through countless times, and they have reentered the battle

---

70 equation of T - see Appendix A

time and again to infuse, in their intent, the power of Love,
    but in their humanness they take tiny steps.
We would ask earth to hold fear as unimportant, as of no consequence.
We would ask you to radiate outwardly from your being,
    all energies, from the eldest to the youngest,
        and know that what you do has power.
You are not idly sending forth.
The lips do not need to utter what the heart may utter.
[September 25, 2001]

Transition

293 Souls, Energy is Creator and the Flow of Creator.
All Energy recognizes the beginning of Creator.
Creation has no beginning.
Creator became!
Soul, all worlds of Farside are aware of pain.
It is constant in the mind's eye that pain is there for the human.
In Farside beings it is a part of their remembrance.
And to know beings who have kept themselves in pain
    draws sadness and a need to reach unto their loved and say:
    "Soul, hear our being. We can help to guide thee."
Creator sobs at the pain of the Blessed Ones.
Earth sobs at the pain man places upon the Energy's intent.
Souls, Energy's pain is the mark of Love.
We will teach the transition.
Understand the dark is not as earth darkness,
    it is the withstanding of Prism from the Soul.
The Soul has power and is in the state of denial or acceptance.
The Soul has the knowledge of all past
    and the intent of the Soul in each vista.
The Soul's acceptance is the reaching to Light.
Soul, know calling is but a comfort if the Soul has no contention.
If the Soul has contention, this will take the Soul to the space of anxiety.

294 The transitional knowledge of earth is gaining.
Within the criteria of earth agenda is a frantic desire
    to be in the wisdom of the Farside.

Seekers are found without guile or facetious behaviours.
Let the Souls know that the world of transition is also closer.
The spirits who cannot accept the path they have made
    transfer from one free space to another.
It is as the gentle path of universal habits are given decisive motivation
    that the Souls are lifted beyond themselves
    to another realm that gives a window.
Be in a calm place to receive a freedom of knowledge
    that is path in the Energy.
Within the fear and pain of leaving, many Souls wander.
They lapse into the overleaves of their existence.
They cease to hear the voice within.
They respond only to the negative path they have led.
Great compassion is felt for these lingering Souls.
The community of spiritual growth is brought to their pain,
    yet some cannot be released.
They fear only fear, they hear only negative.
We find that these Souls respond to a fine key.
It is the balance of self in the state of leaving.
Many come to this state, many are saved.
Some wander endlessly in the space of time.
We take the voyage to save Souls.
This is done in place.
This is done by directing the Soul to the centre of their vortex,
    to the place in the eye that was last given hope.
Know hope is earth, hope is not Farside.
These Souls are locked in time.
They have not yet encountered the Truth that is in them.

295 Know level, hell, first, deep in the chasm.
Many Souls writhe because they do not,
    have Love, have Purity, have acceptance of their state of being.
These Souls are in torment.
They have slaughtered the innocent.
They have perpetuated evil deeds continually throughout their lives.
Within the depths of levels is first.
It is a place where a Soul is tormented by that which he has done
    and over and over and over, he relives the chaos within his being.

He has fear beyond which no man could live.
He has desperation beyond which no man could live.
He will rise from that chasm when he accepts that which he has done.
As the earth Soul graduates, graduates into the Purity of Love,
> of Truth, of Purity, as infant and baby, as young and mature,
>> these Souls have past life remembrance.

They have learned the causal lessons.
They have acceptance at a causal level.
They may redeem themselves through acceptance.
There is no participation with other Souls
> except within the Soul memory.

Ah yes, there are memory banks, and banks and banks of memory
> were you to tap the very memory of mind,
>> it would alert itself to the Soul of your being
>> and you would instantly recall lives you have lived.

You would also be brought down into the depths of that torment.
Dreams are often this.
It is a progressive avenue upward to Purity.
It is an altered state that is immediate
> upon recognition of the fallibility of self.

It is not necessary to make recompense at that port of call.
It is only necessary to accept the life you have lived.
Souls of maturity and age are not brought down as low into transition;
> they are not brought by their own will into transgression
> and defilement and pathos, but they see the Light quickly.

It is familiar to them to reach upward.
They have a greater desire within their being to reach upward.
Souls of earth, do not choose to be in the depths of the chasm
> but choose rather to look outward from self
> and find the Purity that will give you acceptance.

296 Michael will teach Soul flight.
The Soul is in the aura.
The aura is attached to the Energy of who, of where, of entirety.
The Soul is, the Spirit is, the Essence is, Creator IS.
The strand is woven.
Within the weave is the inevitable return to Farside,
> to the place of casting out and the formation of step.

Each Soul has wondrous and fearsome steps to take.
The Soul knows the sense of fatality
    only because there comes a moment of self
    and the pattern is visioned by the earthbound Soul.
In the tremble of the walk is a knowledge
    that under the foot is solid ground.
The Soul whose vision takes them to the door of departure
    can recall the pattern and be calm,
    or they frantically refuse the step they chose.
Dear ones, to pass between doors is but to pass between doors.
The earth door is held and secured with Love and boundless Truth.
The guides enter through the door in Love,
    and handiwork allows them to gather the Soul to them,
    to carry this Soul forward with the entire spiritual Love
    that denotes the care.
The Soul is travailed forth to the transition,
    each guide there to be, but not to interfere.
The Soul gains the Light to the Farside
    and the Light is then wholly their rest.

297 We may enter in, Souls!
Your earth plane offers no hindrance to our being.
Our Energy vibrates before your being and the Path to earth has a door.
Souls, can you see the door?
Can you enter in?
The door has a name, it is *Gateway*.
It is the entering in and the coming forth.
It is the avenue of growth for the Soul.
Many Souls hesitate in their being to move outward for growth.
To enter in to the space of negativity is a battle.
It is armed and dangerous,
    for the Soul's growth is tenuous on earth plane.
Many Souls have brought themselves countless times
    into the space of growth.
They have lingered long and yet not learned the lesson before them.
They enter in to negativity.
They draw the vision of negativity before their eyes
    and rapture in its decadence.

Souls of earth, know your entering in has purpose.
Know your entering in has Truth, Purity and Love.
Raise the extension of your eye beyond earth
    and see in the place of eyes, a Path between
    that opens unto Holy Holy Holy.
Be thou brought down in thy being for one purpose only,
    to reach outward unto thy fellow beings.
For who can see only the singleness of self and find the Gateway?
To find self, seek outward
    and the fold of creation will gather before thy being,
    and thou wilt be lifted up in Purity.
Partake, Souls, of the cup of Energy.
Sup at the table of Energy,
    for the goodness of thy being has food beyond that of earth,
    and the plate is extended full unto thy being.
Sup and behold, the fullness of thy being will radiate
    as the meal thou hast partaken of.

298 Michael will teach the comings and goings,
    the freedom of transportation,
    the availability of transportation,
    the generosity of Souls in transportation.
Behold, earth, the entering in.
Sacred beings, beloved of the Soul, uplift the Soul
    and gather the goodness unto their beings.
Enter in to support.
The infant child has great wonder, but the Writing on the Wall
    dictates how the Energy will come.
The Writing on the Wall is Truth, written from Farside;
    Creator Truth, Essence Truth, Entity Truth.
The Spirit causes the writing to be for the self
    and the Souls rejoice at the entering in of Purity,
    and the Angels reach down in comfort to the small Soul
    that must enter in to the negativity planned for growth,
    and the Soul rides the great wave.
The sea is turbulent and calm in degrees of growth
    and the Soul knows whence it is called,
    for the Soul hears the Essence of its being.

And all that is pure from Farside enters in
    and gathers goodness unto goodness
    and reaches into the depths of transition
    through to the Purity of earth and gathers the precious Soul,
    and awaits the choice of the Soul.
And the Soul is touched by the vision of Purity,
    yet response is not possible.
And the Soul reaches unto its own Light of acceptance
    and beholds the Purity from whence it came.
And cymbals clash, and Seraphim open the Gates of Purity,
    and the Soul is welcomed in.
And in the Entering In is a need to let down the barrier of the eye.
And the Souls at station of returning assist the Soul
    to find balance and awareness.
For as Souls enter back from earth anaesthetic,
    so is the like feeling of a Soul returning home.
Some Souls enter in calmly,
    others enter in with a need to rush forward,
    to alter that which is done, not in a negative sense.
And some Souls flee back into transition to touch a being left,
    that they might gather them unto themselves to heal.
Souls of earth, your vibration is the key to the comings and the goings,
    to the entering in and the moving forward to the joy,
    to the negativity and the return to joy.
Fear not the passing of a Soul, but delight in the knowing
    that the Soul has moved forward
    into the blessed space of peace.

299 Transition is a place of accepting or rejection of earth Path.
It is the acknowledgement of deeds done.
Soul is taken into the valley of their own pain, of their own deception,
    and all that is and was of pain
    can be carried into that remembrance,
    for lives are continuous and the overcoming of pain is Truth.
The Souls are brought within the space of their choice
    by all who love and have loved.
They are tormented by their own rejections and no Soul may intervene
    except with the Loving care about their being.

They have the power to manifest themselves in many ways,
    but Souls who reject carry themselves deeper
        into the forest of pain.
Behold, behold the eternian, behold the altered being.
Behold the revealed pain of mankind.
Behold that which was and has lost it.
For the Soul can only behold their own
    eternity of damnation,
    behold the everlasting persecution of their being.
Their eyes have turned inward unto self
    and the revealment of their being incurs agony
    and endless wanderings.
Oh Soul, calm self, be thou unattached, be thou separate from!
And the Souls may not see those who enter in to bless their being.
They will not see the Light of goodness,
    they have refused to look unto the path of acceptance
    and a Soul is caught in depravement,
    and endlessly they recover the incident
    they may not forgive themselves of.
Unto these beings will be the first humanities to be lifted
    through the Flow of perfection.
And beings of great Energy will see the agonies of these Souls,
    and they will not writhe in pain, but will gently
    draw unto themselves the reflection of the pained,
    that they may come once more through the flow of earth
    and see earth as only the lesson that it is
    and from the gathering of goodness
    they may once again be brought to the Flow of Purity.
All beings within the seven levels of pain
    will see the Flow of great Purity and liken unto themselves.
The Flow will seek out the wretched and the pained, the unaccepting,
    and the treasures of goodness will mirror their pain
    and know the growth it has been.
And the voice of Angels will blend in the goodness,
    for the redeemed will have come home,
    and the banquet will be set,
    and all worlds will utter: *"Hosanna, Hosanna, Hosanna!"*

300 Michael will teach the valley of the dead,
   the entrance into the hall of unforgiving,
   not by Creator, but by the being,
   that have placed themselves in the valley of the dead.
The depths of the valley are seven fold.
The agonies within the depths carry unforgiving.
The sacred Souls of Farside have allowed their Being into the depths.
The tears of Angels wash agonies of those caught in pain and guilt.
The blessed Saints, Melchezidec, Virgin Mary, Peter, Joseph,
   countless Souls of Purity, have ventured into the cavernous void
   of mind.
Mind!
The heart will not allow the sacred beings to venture through the mind.
The mind, you see, in the state of transition is present.
The heart, in the state of transition is present.
Only the body is vacated.
Levels of pain can be forgiven by all Souls within the upper realm,
   but the Soul cannot forgive self,
   cannot accept the deed they have done.
"Forgiveness is unnecessary!" we call.
What need to forgive the walk you yourself can rectify!
The call is ever outward to these Souls,
   but the Souls have closed the heart
   and hear only through the mind.
Enter in to the Soul and know the Soul has thought,
   sensitivity, feeling in great depth.
The Soul makes choices in the path of growth.
The Soul does not always choose wisely,
   and when the negativity of that Soul,
   even the minutest that is is not accepted,
   the Soul will remain at a level and scourge their being
   as though the cat o' nine tails were lashed across the mind.
And the eyes have left the Soul and they are caught
   only with a sensitivity of heart memory and mind memory,
   and the Blessed Beings cannot reach Souls centred at the mind level.
Only from earth's station can these Souls find within their being
   a mirror that will offer them a choice other than the one present.
Many Souls gnash at their beings, cascade themselves in tears,

refuse to look upward to the blessed Light beckoning
to their being.
Fathers and mothers, sisters and brothers!
Unite, blessed earth, to a state of Purity, for only in that state of Purity
may you find the value within self
to reach the depths of pain in Purity.

301 Soul, we will teach seven levels of transition.
Baby Souls have passed and are caught in great pain.
They have no past lives.
They have only the harshness of their earth life,
and those who have not accepted the pain they have caused
agonize in depths of misery.
There are first level young Souls who have some memory
of past lives, of return to Farside,
of teachings they have gathered unto their being,
who may reach into those positives
and from the level of positive, accept the choice
they have made.
When they do not, they are caught at second level.
Mature Souls know much, have gathered the threads of spirituality
about their being, have become teachers in their being.
They hold fast with a tenacity to the lives they have lived.
Their pain is tethered and they have not let go of other lives in transition.
They have returned and know of the returning.
These Souls are level three.
Old Souls, who are spiritual beings, will have felt the Flow
and rejoiced in reunions and seek the colours.
When pain has overcome their being, they are caught in level four.
Transitional Souls see nothing but their pain.
Souls will have manifestation and all heavens rejoice at their successes.
Manifested Souls are fifth level.
Souls who have walked in the shadow of death and have feared no evil,
for in the sacred place they have bowed down,
they have given life and limb as martyr
but are caught in a painful thought, are level six.
Souls of level seven are the Fallen, the Blessed,
who have never walked on earth,

    but cast everlasting dispersion upon their being
        because of the great denial within their Soul.
These are level seven.
Thy do not clamber to be away,
    for they hold the face of their being from goodness
    and from Souls of earth.
We would have them free from their pain, blessed, blessed earth,
    for how else can we bring them forth?

302 You have a ride through hell.
Soul, acknowledge you will have a ride through hell
    because it is where you dwell.
All else, all else has Purity.
Transition has Souls deep in pain.
We know, our Beings have entered in to comfort the Souls.
They have drawn the negativity deep in their being,
    but they are surrounded on all sides with great Love.
They are never alone.
They are always in comfort, and the Souls of earth
    ponder in their being at what it all is.
Your Creator sheds Tears to wash upon these beings
    that they might know how precious they are unto who He is.
Your Creator has no anger.
Allow the bells to peal forth, shout it from the mountaintop:
    "Creator has no anger, has only Love. He is not capable of anger."
Creator, where we are, forward from Second Gateway,
    is the only Creator.
There is none other than that which He is,
    the magnificence of that which He is.
But your Creator has not a beginning forward
    from the Second Gateway.
Your Creator has entered forth from Godhead.
We know of the world in which you live.
We know of transition and we know of the many worlds
    in our existence.
But, Soul, you have enlightened us.
You have brought the knowledge of wisdom into our space.

303 Enter ye in to the depths and know the scourge
     of Soul upon Soul.
Behold how man has defiled man,
     and man, in the relinquishing of life, sees the torment
     and the fear and the anger and chooses to look earthward,
     and Souls of Purity caught in the restless wanderings of their being
     searching for Oma, Opa, Madre, Padre, son, daughter.
Souls of Purity, your eye could not behold the multitude of Souls
     who could find a passage through to Purity
     by the Flow through earth.
Creator is ever reaching with Holy Holy Holy to draw Souls
     unto their higher being.
Creator also knows for some this will never be,
     and so earth has offered herself as the gathering place.
And Souls of Purity, of age, have offered their being
     to ply the negative egos of these Souls
     that they might see the need to reach unto blessed Light.
Only through Souls of enlightenment might this be done.
Souls of earth, call forth the innocent
     to be gathered unto the ray of Purity,
     that the Prism might calm the terror in their being.
Souls of earth, allow the Entering In.
The Soul who must enter in must be able to sustain their Purity.
It is, Soul, a pure step.
If has no place.
The undaunted must travel forward and claim the innocent Souls
     by offering unto their being the pureness of Light.
Souls, to draw a Soul in the backward Flow through earth,
     it must be through Purity.
A Soul must be channelled through Purity.
Be ye pure, for all transition awaits earth's endowment.

304 Soul, the human body is incredibly feeble
     and yet to earth it has great complications.
All contemporaries you have ever known
     are within the aura of your being.
You have within your mind the ability to recall all sensations,
     all familiar beings.

Time in your mind may pass so slow that you will see
    every crowd you have ever walked by.
You will be aware of every affect you have had on every human being.
Whether it has been negative or positive, it is instilled within the aura.
All reactions from your being, from their being, are written.
It is why at the time of passing some Souls find it difficult to accept
    that which they have done.
They are still in places of great despair,
    for they may have grown past the pain,
    but to be totally aware of the immensity of pain they have caused,
    creates a great lapse in the ability to seek positives.
Light is withheld from them, not by Creator, not by beings,
    but their inability to turn from their pain.
And, Soul, we would ask you to be with us
    and extend all positive energies to the Souls in transition,
    that they might find a leverage to ease their pain.
Soul, we ask it be a continual effort from each of your beings
    to permit Souls to see the Light through you,
    that they may safely be gathered into the arms of the Angels.

305 Behold the place of pain, behold the place of guilt.
Enter thou in to bring forth Souls who have lost their joy,
    who have seen only negativity in their sight.
Behold, earth, have you brought to your being, the Purity
    that will allow your self to enter in to the huge vacuum of mind,
    mind that has vision only to torment?
We have courage to enter in.
We have drawn ourselves into the space of great negativity,
    but, Souls, we will not be heard.
It is the hand of humanity that must reach out to Negativity
    to redeem these fallen Souls,
    to grasp the frightened hand, the tormented hand,
    the scolded hand, the burned hand, the victimized hand,
    the brutal hand, the swollen, fetid hand.
Only earth can grasp a brother's hand and draw him
    from the place of pain.
Call forth the minions, call forth the Souls to passage
    through thee into the Light.

Do not fear.
You may not fear!
You may not dread what will come to thee.
Would thy face blister?
Would thy hand be offended?
Would thy eyes lose sight?
Soul, redeem unto Creator the fallen,
    for all must be redeemed unto Creator.
Not one sparrow will be left in agony.
Soul of earth, enter thou in to the place of pain.
Do it, Soul, in thy meditation and allow the coming forth of beings.
Do it, Soul, for thy Creator will watch over thee
    and Angels will reach unto thee.
Know thyself to be gently brought down
    unto the hallowed place of the Blessed Ones.
Holy Holy Holy.

306 Beings of earth, the Souls in the place of transition
    vary in the pain they hold.
As in all earth and transitional situations, pain is pain.
A lesser or harsher degree does not alter that it is pain.
Souls, many beings may enter your space within the space of transition.
Your presence will feel the cold gather.
You may even feel the gale of harsh winds blow.
We would ask that each being gather Light unto themselves,
    for as each Soul is present, each Soul feels the negativity.
Soul, little children are Souls, aged men and women are Souls,
    the bitter agnostic is Soul, and the priest is Soul.
Do not allow trickery in your space.
Recognize the Souls would draw you with them into pain.
Do not be caught in the pain of the Soul,
    be strong in the will to move the Soul to Light.
Allow the passage to enter around about you.
The Souls will not linger in your being.
This we know.

307 The hand is empty.
You see before you an empty hand and yet the hand is full.

It is full of every possibility.
It can perform at the mind's will that which you would have it do
    and yet it can remain in idleness for a lifetime.
The Soul would have you fill the hand
    with all the potential of it's being.
It would have you offer the hand to humanity.
The hand is the extension of thy Purity.
Souls of earth, it is thy Purity that is learning to vibrate.
All movement will be distorted in the downward motion to transition.
To enter in you must be garbed in Purity.
To enter in you must have no negative thought or fear.
To bring Souls forth is to enter in and speak to the Souls,
    to speak to the Souls and allow these Souls to know
        they have misdirected the pain.
It was for their growth.
It was for their reason and reasoning, for their step and stepping.
An angered Soul may not enter in without drifting
    into the decadence of that negativity,
    for many Souls revel in the decadence of negativity.
They glean great joy from the misery of others.
Who can look into the face of vileness and not shed a tear
    for the Soul that has been deformed?
Who can look at words uttered, reviling innocence,
    and contain the Love?
Only the pure can enter so deep.
Would you come, Soul?

308 Soul, baby Souls have been often on earth.
There are baby Souls from the beginning of time.
They have chosen not growth, but to return again and again
    and again.
It is, Soul, an endeavour to be pure in their returning.
You judge from your humanity.
On the Farside these Souls have Purity
They are no less than the Souls who have achieved
    the Time of the Gathering,
    but they have not achieved the ultimate gift required.
It is, Soul, as a great battle and all men have been armed, and many

have marked their being to carry right into battle,
and some have lived to open the way for those in pain.
They have succeeded where others have failed,
not through want of trying,
but from the overcoming of negativity.
The Blessed Angels gathered the pain.
How then, think you, that mankind would not also have the pain?
Souls of the Farside rejoice, for in the army of humanity
many are they that have survived to the ultimate Purity
to overcome negativity that will allow
the gateway of transition to be opened,
to alter the placement of the Blessed Ones.
Do not think less of a Soul who has not succeeded.
Have they not given the ultimate of their being!

309 Soul, the purpose of life is not death.
The purpose of life is Purity.
Those who are caught in the nauseous throe of evil can be carried
by the Blessed Ones into the state of their Purity.
Do not judge!
Place no judgement upon humanity, for the most evil among you
may be tethered higher than the most noble among you.
He who is the teacher of negativity can be a Soul so pure
as to have offered their being to give earth lesson.
Soul, judgement is not for earth.
Judgement is not!
The only purpose of judgement is in the place of negativity.
The hallowed halls should have no judgement.
Why do they cast judgement?
The Saints above seek the saints below and say:
"Why, why cast you judgement upon the Beloved?"
Know that judgement will never be used in a negative way
beyond the transitional care.
Vary the eye in rendering judgement,
for one eye is locked in negativity
and the other in positive Energy.
Soul, use the centre eye and know within the centre eye
is no judgement upon earth.

Earth places judgement upon herself.
Humanity places judgement upon itself.
The judgement occurs by the deeds done.
When the deeds are not done, the judgement is held,
    and the wind withholds its vast breath.
All energies of earth perform great intentional moves;
    your Energy, the Energy of the Soul across the ocean,
    or in the valley, or on the mountain.
Progress is only the methodical movement of Energy throughout earth
    for a single intent to unite with Creator's Energy.

310 Earth Souls, behold Truth.
Truth contains all acceptance.
Truth holds in its Energy
    the murderer, the rapist, the starved,
    and the Soul deep in avarice and greed.
The Soul of the pure babe is Truth.
It is the acceptance of all knowns in the space of negativity.
Truth tarries in the space of the eye.
Truth requires spiritual insight to have come past knowledge.
Knowledge is not Truth.
Knowledge is but knowledge and is an altered state.
It is varied by the way the wind blows.
Souls, Truth is abundance, Truth is giving, Truth is receiving,
    Truth is the Path to Purity.
You cannot gain Purity without the Path of Truth.
Truth is the awareness that, in the physical being of self, there is more.
Mind and heart are simplistic.
The Soul is the vehicle on the Path to Truth.
The Soul has placed self in the position of matter
    that awareness of all negativities might be surmounted.
The passage is not easy, the passage is not futile,
    for in no space does a Soul lose footing.
The Soul is not lost in the terror of hell.
The Soul always may return, to once again rejoice with the Angels
    in the attempt to surmount all negativity.
Truth is that which Souls in transition cannot accept.

The reality of their being can not face
   the negativity they have allowed within the space of Soul.
And still there is redemption, there is Truth,
   still the Soul will be lifted.
All will be lifted to the place of Purity.
All heavens, all creations, will rejoice in the space of those
   lost in transition who have denied the walk of Truth.
Purity is the reach of Truth.
Purity resides forever in the space of enlightenment.
Blessed earth beings, that which you would be in,
   would be the orb of Purity.
It flows, as the Angel's tears flow to earth to wash the pain of beings.
It reaches out and the energies of Purity take themselves
   to worlds and worlds and worlds beyond that which you know,
   beyond that which you could imagine.
Purity has, within its being, the onward look to Creator,
   to ever be in the space of Creator.
The Energy of Creator is Purity,
   is Truth that takes itself to the total Path of Love.
All three become the whole.
A Soul cannot find Agape Love without Purity.
A child is pure, has no evil intent,
   but a child has the potential of accepting negativity.
It is choice, Soul.
Farside has Purity that can not be drawn
   into the state of negativity except by choice.
To do this, one must re enter earth plane.
When a Soul has found total truthfulness,
   the Soul has also found a fifty percent Purity.
How intriguing for the Souls, fifty percent is complete!
Souls, do not think your earth plane is the only plane that has growth.
It is the only plane that has growth with Negativity.
All other planes carry growth without Negativity.
Move onward into Purity.
We are not Angel.
Angels are revered, Angels are Energy forms of such Purity!
Soul, the Angels come into our space, our Energy Field.

They radiate forward in goodness and their teachings are accepted
    as you, who sit as scholar before the learned men.
The Purity of their Beings energize all that we are.
We glory in their coming.
We reach our being to be where they are and yet we are pure,
    we have pureness, but the Purity of their Being
    is as glass to crystal.
Purity reaches out to Love,
    and Love only reaches out from itself.
Do you see how growth must be done?
Total Love is the total reaching out of the Energy from self.
Earth Souls have reached out beyond their beings to earth Souls,
    and their Purity is great.
But Souls of Angels, the Essence of their Being rides high
    in the planes of Purity.
Do not be complacent,
    do not ponder the points of senseless struggle,
    but know the reason for which you are,
    the purpose of thy being: Truth, Purity and Love.
Enter thou in to the space of Angels
    and feel the wings of the Blessed Ones wrap their Beings
    about thy being and know joy, Ecstasy of being.

311 Hold thyself apart from all iniquity.
Behold whom thou art, humanity.
Behold whom thou art,
    lifted up, elevated to the stature of Creator,
    oh blessed humanity is the purpose of thy being!
Who hast been in the presence of Holy Angels!
Who hast spoken with Souls elevated to be the second
    and third and fourth to enter in the Gateway to Godhead,
    the Second Gateway!
Behold the gateway of transition.
Behold the encounter with pain and being brought low.
Behold the energy of negativity recognized.
Soul, see the gateway clear,
    know the gateway has endless vision.

Know the levels within the gateway
> and know the depth of agonies.

And who would enter therein from earth?
Does humanity contemplate the entering in?
Does humanity choose the entering in?
What humanity chooses is negativity itself.
It is the passage unto the negative.
It is the passage unto that which has been made real.
Oh thou humanity, oh thou gracious humanity,
> would that you would contemplate the recesses of your Soul.

Would that you would contemplate the direction of your Soul.
Would that you would know its map,
> the agenda at the treasure hunt you are on.

For treasure it is.
For riches are not of earth and joy has no currency.
Oh that earth could maintain the agenda of joy
> and seek not the mesmerizing options of Negativity.

For mesmerizing they are, and the Soul is caught
> in the cavity of Negativity.

Reach thou into the well of joy that is available
> in the recesses of thy Soul.

Abandon quickly all negative thought.
All Gateways are apertures to Godhead.
Beyond Second is a positive Third.
Beyond Second is a negative Third.
All creation was caught in the positive and negative flow.
Behold humanity, gracious humanity has risen to release all humans
> into the depths of pain that they might reach
> > to the Blessedness and therefore open the Gateway to Godhead.

FARSIDE LEVELS

312 Souls, Souls, behold the composition of Energy,
> behold the flow of Energy, behold the music of Energy
> and know the strum, the chord of Purity.

Hear with the eye the strum of Purity.
Know that which you see will alter,

and know all before your earth vision will leave.
Enrapture will enfold your being
    and the upward lift to your Spirit will come to be
    and you will flow.
Your Energy will meld into the strum of sound
    and you will hear the sound of silence envelop your being
    and discord will cease to be
    and your eye will enhance the clarity of your mind,
    and your mind will record that which you see,
    for, Soul, the Pathway is clear.
The Pathway needs be but opened and you will be with us.
Soul, your Energy will meet with ours.
We could take thee through the gardens of lush opulence,
    of bountiful paradise, of joy enfolding all Love unto it.
Before your being, old friends would come forth
    from your many earth paths.
They would salute and encourage your Soul.
They would wish you well and seek your path to their loved ones.
They would place blessings upon your return.
Behold that which you can do.
Are you not miraculous, humanity!
Have you been given only two eyes?
Souls of earth, you have three.
Use three!
Set one for moments of clarity.
Set one for moments of divinity.
Set one for times of inner contemplation.
Souls of earth, hold in thy hands the eyesight of Farside,
    the All Knowing Eye that unfolds as the true fractal
    into many glories of colour.

313 Michael will teach the room where we are,
    the room of spaceless endeavour.
The mansion of earth could not compare to that wherein we dwell.
Behold, the craftsman of earth have not come from earth.
They are Farside.
They brought their infancy to earth.

Souls, your eyes would be teared by the beauty of our room,
> our place of being.
Behold the Light that emanates forth,
> and all in the eye sees the vista of other worlds.
Our embodiment reaches as you blink to unknown canopies,
> that we might explore the wonders thereof,
> for eons would not be enough to know the vision,
> but infinity allows the reach into the incredible.
A sound carries itself from embodiment to embodiment
> with the vocalization of Angels,
> and the tear would never be
> except for those in the passage of time.
And gathered unto our being are creations of wonder
> that the vision never tires to behold.
Our room does not contain work.
Our room contains the blessedness of life, the busyness of life,
> the continual motion of life for all beings, at all levels.
There is merriment and laughter and remembrance,
> and invitations to dance the pure dance.
Our beings have no high walls to bring down.
We are accepting of all that is,
> and when a Soul reaches out, another being welcomes in
> and no door is closed by force in that room.
And the soft sea of tranquillity is not dead, as your moon,
> but playfully laps at the edge, and our beings walk
> in the cleansing of particles from our being
> that gathers as the Soul gathers lint to a cloth.
And each iota is as a vision that reflects to another offering of growth.
Our blessed form speaks forth in a communication
> that holds no fear, no anger, no wilful participation.
Only the Energy of the Flow is continual.
There is change and growth, and movement forever.

314 Souls, bless thy being.
Behold the Radiance of Farside!
Souls, you are in the dark.
The light of your day is yet dark to our being.

The magnificence of Farside outshines the sun and the moon,
    all power systems that your earth could forge.
Recognize all abundance within the Farside is available unto earth.
Know that all Light is available unto the receptacle of the human form.
It would ignite in ecstasy, it would glow,
    and all Souls looking unto the form would say:
    "See the Light that glows, the Purity that is revealed."
Within such Light is the Path of all encompassing Love,
    of all peace, of all joy.
There is within the Farside, billowing, radiating Light.
It is as sure as your tomorrow.
It is the coming up of the sun and the going down of the sun.
It is always, ever, and will be.
Within the Light, Soul, are many sources of wisdom.
Within the Light there can be no negativity.
Within the Light there can be no pain.
Within the Light there can be no canopy,
    for the Light would enter in to all.
It is a tangible existence, this Light, this radiance.
It has a feel.
It speaks, Soul.
It is of Creator.
It has vibrant colour forms.
It has density and thinness.
It has note, a song that is ever sung.
It has in the coming forth a wellbeing
    a drawing unto, a need to be there.
There are depths within this Light, within this Energy Field,
    and Souls of levels of babies often feel the Light,
    know the warmth and are content in the shallows of that Light.
They are not drawn to be in the space of utter density.
They are content, fully happy, without fear or dread
    or need to be anywhere but where they are.
As the Soul progresses in growth, the Soul desires to be further
    into the Light, for the Soul anticipates the Purity ahead,
    the benevolence.
The acute desire to be overwhelmed by the entering in
    is prevalent in these Souls.

Some Souls will leave earth to enter in to the Flow.
It is difficult to explain the Flow for your earth being.
It is much as your Oregon Trail in the USA,
    it is much as the great trek across Africa.
It is as the great walk across Mongolia,
    of which earth has not yet found the writings.
Know, Soul, that to enter in to that Path
    is to feel the energies of other beings.
Their purities become attached and yet separate from their own.
They seek to know wisdom.
They seek to leave that which is familiar, to go unto Godhead.
They have left their worlds and they go into spaces unknown.
There are levels of Purity.
Each level has an existence, each level is alive with energies
    unknown to them.
Knowledge is known to the level wherein a Soul has walked.
These Souls seek to walk unto yet another level and another level.
This walking is the Flow.
It takes the Soul unto Creator and to the Energy of Prism.
"Bless Thou, Creator.
    Be Thou the umbrella over my head.
    Be Thou the canopy of grace upon which I rely.
    Be Thou my encourager, my drawing forth unto Thee."
And so the forging ahead is done and on the Farside,
    Souls in excitement follow the Path of Purity
    and meet and know and understand.
And these Souls come down unto brethren and speak
    of the Holy of Holy, of the Circle of Saints, of the Angels.
And the Angels come forth, and they lift the Soul
    unto the platform of grace, and the Souls lift their being
    and are altered unto greater Purity.
And all who see these beings know the ecstasy,
    the rapture of their being, and the Souls are cloaked
    in raiment that is of the Angels.
And the Souls are encouraged to seek yet another placement
    unto the place of Archangels.
Many are there who have taken themselves
    unto the level of Archangels, many Souls of Farside.

Know earth Soul has been blessed.
Accept a leaven.
Souls of earth, beings of Light they are.
The flow of their magnificence reaches the Hem of Creator
    and sees, as Angels see, the Light that is creation,
      the Light that is Energy, Holy and abounding, moving,
      and the Light compacted, can be placed within the human body.
Know, Soul, the Light will enter in.

315 Michael will teach the comings and the goings,
    the vista of Farside.
Behold the seed of Purity that takes up habitation
    upon the face of the land.
Soul, earth is not the only land.
Behold, Farside is land beloved.
Souls, the seed is provided for and offered nourishment in goodness
    and the seed of Purity reaches the choice of understanding,
    and the Soul is brought to yet the vision of offerings
    and beholds all manner of creations.
And the Purity says: *"This I would attain."* and goes unto that place
    to be taught in the manner that would reach an understanding,
    and the Soul looks with Love and Truth and Purity
    at where the Soul resides.
Some say: "This homeland is for my Soul; this is the choice
    of my being in creation." and chooses to be in that world.
And other Souls look elsewhere at the many fragmentations
    of creation and are lifted unto higher Purity
    that requires wisdom and the knowledge of wisdom.
Earth knowledge is a simple mathematical gesture.
It harnesses no complexities.
It is not.
It is, Soul, the extension of your being.
It is the way forward and forward and forward,
    until you have become not unlike the degree of Purity
    that the lower Angels uphold.
Souls, your being of Purity is ever striving forward.
It has been your choice to reach Creator.
Not all Souls have taken upon their beings, this choice.

Many reside in great pleasure, in great Truth, in incredible Purity,
    and from their station at the Hem of Creator
    are content to be.
Delight yourselves, magnificent Souls, that you have sought
    to be radiant and your being reaches upward into clarity
    and the Soul knows the goodness and knows the goodness!
And knows the battle that is yet to be won.
Your beings ever strive to cast negativity aside,
    and the gentle caring of old Souls ever reach to the impurities
    that baby Souls gather unto themselves.
Souls of earth, cast your being to the canopy of earth
    and look down at the wonder of all you may behold
    and know that you have chosen your residence,
    you have gathered yourselves onto earth that you might grow.
Know, as the Farside is taught by Souls of higher being,
    so are your Souls taught.
Beloved, accept the teachings of Purity.

316 We, who are the Farside, are as much a part of your being
    as the family you cleave unto.
The entire Energy of our being has one single purpose,
    to reunite itself to the Energy we are a fragment of.
The space we are in gathers Purity unto itself.
As a dust particle draws itself to its sameness,
    so does all Energy not rest
    until it has entered the positive realm of itself.
Our existence does not carry the fragility of earth,
    but rather knows the ongoing fulfilment of Purity.
We have a clarity of purpose and a breath of life
    that is drawn from the Flow of Creator.
We do not know indifference or refusal.
The opportunity is always before us, for in the space of Farside
    is the unknown of the levels we have not yet reached.
We are not intimidated by the stretch before us,
    we welcome the enlightenment of each continuing step.
Our preponderance is on the Souls
    who have not yet reached the Purity of our being,
    the Souls who have the negative struggle yet before them.

As the Holy Ones engage themselves in the step of the burdened,
    so, Soul, do we look ever to lessen
        the agony, pain, and sadness of earth bound Souls
        by the continual nudge of option.
The space we are in does not have, as your earth, a need for light.
With the Spirit is Light, it radiates from self.
The Flow is ebbed and flows at will,
    it carries our being to the distant forms,
    it enables us to vista earth.
We rise to a purpose, rest, and give sustenance to our being,
    not out of need for nourishment, but out of desire.
Your being requires the freshly baked loaf,
    ours requires the food of the Spirit,
    food such as would delight the Soul
    and carry the Soul to a reach for utopia.
Each level of Purity has its own delights,
    and each level forward is as Shangri la.

317 The mind is only that which responds to acquired knowledge,
    that which responds to acquired knowledge of earth.
The heart responds to wisdom, the ego responds to negativity.
The ego is the mind's brother, but it is a response of the Soul self.
It is the Soul that accepts the negativity.
It is the Soul that does not finish the lesson, not the mind.
The mind is merely the human learning capacity,
    ego has volition.
The Soul accepts positive ego or negative ego,
    each has purpose.
The negative ego will not allow the Soul to sixth level.
It will always intend the earth return.
The positive ego will accept and overcome all negativity
    before entering fifth level.
All energies of Purity are honed down through negativity.
All energies are purified by the fire of negativity.
Oh, earth Soul, yours to surmount!
Nothing is easy, Soul, your many lives would reflect just so.
Do not ponder at the Farside fickleness,
    for we often have fickle beings.

It is not negativity.
We are challenged also to bring earth Purity.
Our being rushes to the battle, but we are only as good in the battle
    as those who have placed themselves at the frontier of the battle.
Bless volunteer humanity.
To further Purity, draw thyself into the prism of thy being.
Energize thy being.
Souls of earth, seek thou wisdom.

318 Michael will teach the space of learning within Farside.
All knowledge is available unto a Soul
    in the level at which their Essence beholds.
Within creation are many levels, and Farside rejoices
    in the exploration of truths yet unknown,
        but available in study and research.
Many varieties of truths are available.
Oh, Soul, do not flounder in the beholding of one Truth.
There are many truths, Soul.
Each identity carries its own Truth,
    each world carries its own Truth.
Each level of Purity carries wonder and *Behold*.
Our being has within our perimeter the glory of that singular being.
Behold, how Loved thou art
    that your being has been offered the glory,
        that you may countenance the vision of fragmentation of Creator,
        energies unlike your own.
And yet our being reaches out without fear into the unknown
    and the Souls seek to gather the new seed
        unto the glory of Creator
        for not all beings enter in to a tread of earth.
Yea, earth is tread also.
It is the Path that allows the Soul to behold Creator.
Our being has not yet that Purity,
    but we have reached the blessedness of Angels
    and our study of Holy Holy Holy is first hand.
Our being may not gaze at the Purity of Creator,
    but the Radiance of that Purity endows our Spirit
    with great urgency to move onward in exploration of our being.

Earth Souls, to know oneself is to gather unto the Purity.
To lose the negativity within self is to stride courageously onward.
Earth Souls, all learning at Farside is treasured.

319 Mankind, beloved of Creator,
    enter thou in to thy being, Holy Holy Holy!
Be thou brought unto the sacred place of Wisdom.
Enter thou in to Agape.
Be thou that which is the being of Purity,
    for Soul, the Essence of thy being is profoundly pure.
It is as a sacrament placed at the table of Creator.
It is as the Purity of thy being, a Light illuminating all about.
No place on earth beholds the awesomeness of such beauty.
The eyes would be cast down.
Lo! Man, thou art blessed, beloved of all creation,
    for only in the upward Flow is the Essence of man taken.
Beings of great Purity reside in Love, in perfection,
    but only man has been flung to return in form to Creator.
Behold Holy Holy Holy Creator,
    who holds the glow of Energy within the hand of thy being,
    who sees the gem thou art and breathes a Breath of Light.
And Soul of man resides within the place of passion, of wilfulness,
    of degradation of all that has opposites,
    and the Soul beholds from that state, the Purity of being.
And wisdom is beheld, and the Soul rises to the challenge of growth.
And those who abide within the space of Holy Holy Holy
    behold mankind and shower mankind with blessedness.
And Lo, mankind may see that which is pure
    by raising the eye into the Flow of Purity.
And the eye beholds the wonder of goodness that is their own being.
And the delight is in the Love that radiates towards the self.
And the Soul expresses unto the heart:
    "Heart, heed that which you have seen and learn well the step,
        for as you have entered in to the place of negativity,
        you have entered in to a place in purpose."
Behold, Holy Holy Holy is that which is the final attainment.
Blessed Creator: Purity, Love and Truth.

Purpose of Humanity

CHAPTER 3

Holy Holy

THE HOLY ONES

320 Soul, beloveds of earth, respond today,
    respond to glory that is Creator's making.
Know that all your being is particled of Creator.
Know that the generous Soul that is in you is the generosity of Creator.
Know the forgiveness you are capable of is a part of your Creator.
Holy beings, earthly beings, Souls of great magnitude,
    unto you has earth been given,
    unto you is the power of compassion.
Soul, in your being utter the compassionate,
    utter unto all earth the generous statement of Love.
Be thou in the Path of everlasting unto everlasting.
Know the Angels are tethered to whom you are.
Know they are rank upon rank upon rank,
    legion upon legion upon legion,
    and they care for your being.
They have compassion for whom you are.
Would you be less than the Angels, Soul?
Would you utter compassion instead of the negative thought?

321 Souls of earth, behold a teaching.
Souls of earth, in the hand is the offering of your being.
It is not in the words of your mouth.
It is in the hand that offers unto all, that which you have.
It is not to offer unto nakedness,
    for your being requires warmth,
    and your doorway may offer an extra bed
    for the traveller on his way.

The table may be set with the extra plate
    for he who would enter the door.
And the extra clothing you would wear upon your back
    would be offered to the Soul at your side who is destitute,
    for water is used for bathing, for cleanliness,
    and Holy requires cleanliness.
Soul, offer unto Creator, hands open, extended from your being,
    not hiding that which you have,
    not holding within the eye the mote,
    but extending the eye of Truth unto Creator.
All beings are Holy!
The most vile earth being is Holy.
The most putrid of skin are Holy.
Soul, anoint the skin with oil so that thy cup runneth over.
Who can see beyond earth?
Extend thy eyes unto the far hills,
    for to look too close at thy being is to harbour greed.
Know that all in thy being is Creator.
Has the battle of Negativity not entered the first door?
Behold, home is not of earth.
Rejoice in knowing home is Farside station.
Souls, look you at your earth, look you at the abundance of creation
    and know that in the abundance of creation are seeds
    that have been planted from Farside.
Rejoice in the mighty tree, the oak, the myrtle, the pine
    that have withstood gales.
Souls, the same creation is on Farside!
Who could behold your world with no negativity!
The Energy of being is the food required,
    the air of being is the breath required,
    but the mountain and the trees, the hills and the valleys,
    do not think they are reserved for your earth alone.
Majestic trees flow upward from many worlds.
The quiet glades of forest may be entered and the purities of blossoms
    extend themselves to pleasure the eye of beholding.
Worlds of reptiles, of whales, of beings who reach out
    to gather goodness, who beckon to Souls progressing to five,
    many Souls are content to be.

Many Souls rest in the state of Purity.
It is not a sin.
There is no sin, Soul, there is only choice.
The moving on to Creator, to Godhead, is for the gallant
    who have chosen to battle the great Negativity.
We would have you see the abundance of life as you know it.
We would have you see with clear eyes, without greed,
    knowing that all things belonging to you
        are a sacred trust placed within your hand to be dispersed.
Behold, the door of your home will welcome all.
Place the basin before the Soul and wash the feet.
Offer sup to the Soul.
Rejoice in the offering that you have been able to make.
Do not place cost to the Soul,
    reach for the fresh fruit of the vine and know
        it has been placed in your hand to feast, and a portion to give.
Rejoice in all giving. Rejoice!

322 Souls, you have come unto us
    and we have come unto you.
Souls, within the mind is not the Path.
The mind is for growth.
It is within the heart of humanity that you may show men Purity.
It is within the acknowledgement of the blessings
    that have been rained upon you.
It has not, my brethren, to do with the pain.
You are treasures.
You are held as precious,
    as any shepherd would hold a lamb precious unto himself.
And, my brethren, you have within your being, all power,
    the power to bestow positive Energy outward from your being.
You have the power to draw from the Essence of your being,
    the shining self, but, Soul, you have the power to draw
        from the very Creator of your being
        the radiant ecstasy of Purity.
Absorb it into thy being and allow it to flow outward
    unto all mankind.
You are not tethered to your negativity.

If you hold to the thread that is drawn from the place of Creator,
    you are tethered in the magnificence of whom your Creator is.
Hallowed be thy name.
Hallowed be thy name.
Acknowledge, Soul, the greatness of thy being.
Do not see yourself as withered, as pained, but know
    within your being is the avenue that gathers inward
    and travels outward, not for thyself alone,
    but for all mankind.
Soul, you may alter positives and negatives.
You may accelerate energies by absorbing Energy.
To walk in the path of humanity is to see all things that bring pain,
    to know all things that bring pain.
Soul, you have the power to lift the crippled child
    from its bed and present it unto your Creator,
    to allow the Energy of your Creator to alter negatives.
Your Creator awaits.
Creator does not want alms placed before him.
Creator has no need of the money tray.
Creator has a need for humanity to lift up their being,
    to acknowledge,
    for only in acknowledging and requesting
    may Creator intervene.
You, Soul, have within you hidden glory,
    you have within you hidden possibilities.
You have within you redeeming strength
    that will carry many wounds to be healed.
Soul, you ask for positives.
Accept positives into your being,
    into your flesh and your blood,
    into your mind and your heart,
    and see the lamb and know
    the Purity of the lamb is in your being.
Nothing else matters, only the Purity of the lamb.
As the lamb will allow the shepherd to pick it up,
    so will your Creator when you allow
    the Energy of Creator to lift you up,
    to buoy your Soul to possibilities.

Soul, you are redeeming grace, you are Holy unto Holy.
All earth is Holy unto Holy.
Penetrate the wall of negativity with the wall of glory,
    with the prism that you are,
    with the Light that you have,
    with the abundant joy that surrounds your being.
Do not fear what you do not know,
    for your Creator knows all things.
Do not fear pain or sadness or regret,
    but know that your power lies in the strength
    of absorbing Holy Energy unto your being.

323 Souls, earth awaits,
    but earth does not know for what it awaits.
It is you who have the tablet that says:
    "This is why you await".
You await to recognize your holiness.
You await for the knowledge that you are Purity.
You await because you have been uplifted
    and the temple of your being has been bestowed
    with greatness by the holiness of your sacred self.
We would speak to you of your sacred self.
We would have you know the Energy of your sacred being,
    utter Energy, ion and matter.
Ion and matter, but before ion was matter.
Within all creation we know ion.
We know Energy.
There are forms such as your form,
    there are beings such as your beings, but no negativity.
Souls of earth, you are treasures
    and you know not that you are treasures.
You do not perceive what we know.
Your eyes cannot see where our eye can see.
Your holiness is visible unto our eye.
The magnificence of your being is not a shell.
It is Soul, it is Spirit, it is Essence!
The Soul was formed for Truth.
We of the Farside have not Soul, we have Spirit.

You are greater.
But the Soul does not leave man until man has been lifted
    to the space above human, and so you have Soul.
You are marked because you have Soul.
When you enter in to the Farside your Soul enters with you.
You are recognizable because of your Soul, your Purity.
It is as though a hero has come forward
    with many badges upon his lapel.
You have Soul and your Purity signifies that you have Soul,
    and you are regaled and honoured.
And it is a primping and a pleasure to take oneself
    to other worlds and know
    that the Soul will be recognized.
Temerity, indeed, audacious temerity!
Ego, is it not!
And yet ego is the element of humanity and the Soul,
    having to do with humanity, carries it onward.
Delight in your humanity.
We of the Farside have seen the great destruction of humanity,
    and we have seen the tears of Angels flow,
    and we have seen the beings at the Hem of Creator
    gathering the blessed.
We utter unto earth a plea to know your Energy,
    to recognize the power of your being.
To know that no matter how far down the pain is,
    or how far out the pain is or how high,
    your being has the Energy to lift and alter that pain.
My blessed children, hold the Blue Diamond in your hand
    and place it upon the head of the enemy and heal his being.

324 Beloved, beloved of earth, we, who have left behind
    the negativities that have been endured,
    have gathered at the door of the Crystal Cave.
The door is never shut.
It has a motion forward and a motion back.
It has energies moving unto Creator and being placed
    as gifts for Creator.
Worlds, of which thou hast not yet known,

offer their Purity unto Creator
and your gifts of worship are received unto Creator.
Know in thy being, worship.
Know in thy being, the open hand placed before thee
in offering unto Creator all that is pure in thee.
And know, Soul, that Creator will receive the Love of thy being,
and the Energy will enhance the Crystal Cave,
and each offering glorifies Creator.
Behold, Souls of earth, to be in the space of Angels
is to feel the mark of Energy.
To know that mark of Energy is to feel thy being move upward,
and see beyond thyself a distant place that thou hast not been.
And yet in thy being there is a familiarity,
and in each coming forth there is a sight
of that which is beyond thy being.
Soul, we are of level six, at the Blessed Angels among our being.
Soul, will thy earth mind accept the view of our placement.
Will you know enlightenment?
Will you come, Soul, into the place of Angels?
They are not foreign to thy being, earth, the Angels watch over thee,
the Angels intercede for thee
and the Angels invite thy being to come unto them.
And then, Soul, vision that which we see:
a place, a wondrous homeland that glistens
and sparkles and draws us unto it.
"Homeland of my Soul, I come unto thee."
Be that the offering of thy being!
Know no contentment until thou hast placed thyself,
with the Angels round about thee,
uplifting thy Soul in offering of Purity.
Souls of earth, behold, all beings recognize thee as humanity.
All worlds know of thy existence.
Behold, who knows of thee more than the Angels?
Have you not offered unto the Blessed Ones the return of the lost!
Hallelujah, humanity!

325 Behold, behold transition.
Behold negativity and the purpose of earth beings.

Souls of earth, look into the mirror, look at reflection and know
    you are beings, tried through negativity.
You are Souls who have offered unto Creator
    the purification of your being through negativity.
Why, Soul?
To bring blessedness forth,
    to draw the blessed ones unto the ladder of Purity,
    for their beings are tainted and clouded with pain.
They have gathered unto themselves, the healing of many beings.
They have drawn unto themselves, the healing of many beings.
They have drawn unto themselves,
    not the pain of single beings, but worlds of beings,
    and they are cloaked in the despair of those beings.
They are beloved unto Creator.
They are Loved as a father loves his son, but they cannot hear.
They are, Soul, shrouded in the pain of their Being,
    and the cascading of their garments has been tainted
    with the fall of negativity upon their being.

326 Souls, splay thy hands, lift thy hands up, up, up, up, up,
    and know, as you lift, you receive,
    and as you draw back,
    you draw unto you the Holy Love of Creator.
Know it is the gift of Creator unto your being.
Know the Brethren, the Holy Brethren.
The Holy Holy Holy await to minister unto earth
    where the Soul will allow.
And know that within the space of transition
    there are the energies of Angels sending forth healing
    unto those within.
What overwhelming Love!
What overwhelming Love to be held in the space of pain,
    held apart in a space of withdrawal from perfection.
And still, the Love that extends to beings
    in the very space they are in, overwhelming Love.
Souls of earth, at no time have the Angels held Negativity
    within their Being.
They are cloaked with Negativity!

They are cloaked with Negativity,
>they are weighted down with Negativity
>from worlds beyond worlds,
>but their Soul Being exudes Love.

It is sent forth in great comfort to those that will hear, and many
>have turned to the Light in the knowledge of such Love.

Souls of earth, Love is extended unto you.

Love is not fragile.

It cannot be beaten down, but it must be acknowledged,
>for it is choice to acknowledge and earth is a place of choice.

Beings, know the precious ones place their Beings about you
>in the greatest of Love.

Know that your Creator has ever the Ray of Love,
>extending itself forward to your space.

Holy beings, recognize all humanity has entered through Creator.

Know that you have the high station of having entered through twice.

Know that in the coming forth has been your proudest moment,
>for all creation looks unto mankind.

Welcome, Soul, the Spirit, the Energy of Love.

Allow the Love to meld into thy being,
>and when you speak, speak words of Love.

And when there is illness, issue forth words of Love,
>for Love heals, Love is the greatest healer.

Beloved beings, the wings that you have would carry your being
>unto the farthest world, and the stature that you have
>would make your trees seem low as shrubbery.

Souls of earth, see in your spring the abundance of flowers
>and know they are as the abundance of Love
>issuing forth unto mankind.

Know as the blossoms rain down upon your being,
>so does Love rain down upon your being.

Be worthy of that Love and use the Love as a garb over thy being.

Enter it in to thy being that it may ignite thy being
>and shine forth as a Light unto others.

327 Melchezidec spoke unto Creator and said:
>"What if we gather an armada and enter in to negativity

and father unto us scars combatting negativity
and we show the Blessed Ones our scars?"
And Creator said unto Melchezidec:
"That armada may enter. I will arm the Souls with Truth."
And He gathered the army unto His Being,
and created an orb, and set it in Negativity,
and He cast out humanity that they might conquer negativity.
And the Angels rejoiced, for all who had gathered pain
would know of the great battle and be lifted up.
Creator is Energy and Creator formed man in His likeness,
a being, a lesser portion of Himself.
And Creator beheld the orb and the Souls in battle
and Creator held Tears within His Being,
and the Angels cast down drops of pearls to bless mankind.
Creator looked and was satisfied and moved inward
into the sanctum of the Second Gateway,
and the Flow of Energy was cast forth,
for the curtain the Angels formed
was as the curtain to Second Gateway.
It was that which they knew;
it was the power to not enter in,
but the total power to enter out to the door,
is total Oneness of Purity.
Souls of earth, Creator is Energy, Creator has no Soul.
Creator is pure Love, a form, an Energy, a Being who interrelates
in the power of that Being with Godhead.
Soul, the Gateway will be entered in the wellness of time.

328 Soul, we are Angel of repute.
Soul, your beings have Energy.
Your beings have purpose, your beings are watched and waited for.
Upon the steps of growth is growth in Purity, is growth in goodness,
is growth in Love.
The diadem cannot be worn for failure to give.
It is worn in the goodness of all giving.
It is as the true shepherd gives to his flock.
Souls, enter thou in to the space of Holy Holy Holy.

Be thou with us as we see our Brethren[71] turn from us,
    as we have attempted to reach to that being,
    but their very goodness refutes the attempt.
The pain for the Blessed, the negativity they hold,
    is beyond that which a most agonizing life could bear,
    and yet they will not reach unto us.
Many have entered in.
The blessed mothers have entered in and offered to lift the Souls
    but the Souls hold within their Being the great pain
    and will not hear the gifts we bring.
The Brethren watch over mankind,
    for in mankind is a salvation, not of their Soul,
    but the Souls of those lost in transition.
Who more easily than man would distort what man says!
The words have been given, the framework of time has been given,
    and the Brethren await to gather upon the threshold of birth,
    and Creator sees the coming home of all that is dear
    and awaits man's final battle.
Humanity, we are Light, we have profound ability to enfold your being.
We may gather your being unto us and warm your Soul,
    but we can not warm the Soul of our Brethren.
Only earth humanity has this power.
Souls of earth, how great thou art!
How gracious in thy giving is the unity of mankind.
Be thou unified as brethren, one to another,
    for your being will indeed be one
        at the Entering In to the Second Gateway.

329 Souls of earth, come unto all goodness.
Release from your being, the tether that you have.
Know that we, beyond the Circle of Saints,
    have the expression of great Love.
The Love that we have is gifted to your world.
The Love that we have has ability to lift heavy weights from your being.
It can let loose the shackles that you hold,
    and we give to your being this Love.

---

[71] our Brethren - the Fallen Angels in transition

It is ours to give.
Not one being, but countless beings afford you the possibilities
 that are endless.
Souls, you may pick up the shard of glass
 and it will become a diamond in thy hand.
Earth has a containment for value, but it treasures falsely.
Dearly beloved of earth, how grand is thy station!
How the vista of all that you have is treasured!
Souls of earth, we would have you see,
 not with a mirror that you are,
 but in the Holiness that you are.
You have been blessed, you have been anointed,
 you have been carried through into the space of creation.
Who of the Farside has entered in twice?
Only the Souls called humanity have entered in to the space.
We would not speak of such entering in.
Our beings are tethered to where we are.
We have always been on the high land, and yet we have not
 entered in to Creator for a second casting out.
Souls of earth, we await the knowledge that is within your being,
 not the markings that you carry,
 but the knowns that you have gathered in your many lives.
You have been where we have not been,
 you have seen what we have not seen.
You carry within your being the memory of that Blessed, blessed place.
Oh, Souls of earth, hold yourselves as mighty,
 hold yourselves in the place of great Purity.
For Love you have entered in and been cast out
 with the greatest of purpose, not for your own being,
 but connected unto all creation.
There is not a world in all the worlds that are
 that does not count the name humanity as Loved
 and favoured in the sight of creation.
Who art thou? Creator?
Oh, Holy being, we have been cast out once,
 you have entered in a second time,
 you have entered forth twice.
You have in your memory the knowledge of Creator.

How can you reach to this memory?
Soul, you have even been given a Path.
You have the agenda to enter in to the place of Creator.
Holy being, how wondrous art thou!
What great task is before you that you may enter in
    to ride the wave of negativity, to feel the energy of negativity,
    to know its inability to alter, except as humanity gathers.
Humanity, you house beings brought down low with negativity.
You entrap their being, you abscond with the keys
    and you have the power to alter their state.
You have the power to Love as your Creator loves.
What could they do, Soul?
Alter your state of being?
It is unalterable.
What you see is the illusion of whom you are.
Reach out in great Love to all humanity for
    they also are but a reflection and have great nobility
    in the alteration of the mirror.
Souls of earth, you are patterned as your Creator.
You have that which is Truth, that which is Purity, that which is Love.
Souls of earth, ride the high wave.
Know that you will not fall.
You will only be brought low to reach into the abyss to lift a Soul forth.
Do not know fear, do not wonder where your foot will go.
It will go to the purpose of your being.
Are you not Holy!
Is the Soul beside you not Holy!
Beings of earth, whomever has entered in
    to the well of pain we call earth is Holy.
There is no unholy, there is only Holy.
See all beings in your path, for you are your brother's keeper,
    and no place, no mountaintop will you come to that is too high,
    no valley that you come to will be too low.
Have you not draped upon your being the purpose of humanity!
Are you not shouldering the ability to conquer all that is negative!
Souls of earth, that which you treasure on earth
    will seem as naught on the Farside,
    for you have but a dim glimmer of what shall be.

330 Michael will teach.
Mankind is variable in its complexity.
There are separations that eat at the flesh of mankind,
    and atrocities are brought to the forefront,
    and few speak in voices that would forestall what will be.
Mankind has entered in to growth,
    growth in oneness for the purpose of Purity,
    growth as completeness, as a gift to Creator.
The coming together of all nations is dependent
    on the singular outlook of man to look to the need of beings
    who all carry a form of flesh and blood,
    who all have set the form of flesh and blood
    into the being of their Soul.
The Soul cries unto man: "Man, heed not the heart!"
    and the mind will not see the humanity of mankind.
It will reach into the negativity of mankind,
    and as Souls re enter in reincarnations of being,
    they gather wisdom unto themselves.
Wisdom is the weave of Creator.
Wisdom is all knowledge that is known as Creator.
Feeble, Soul who is babe, come in as seed cast from Creator,
    you have not begun and yet you are precious
    and are held in the hand of Almighty,
    and bestowed great Love and tenderly placed.
You are not haphazardly spewed forth,
    but are given a tender nurturing for thy being.
And then the Soul awakens and recognizes the benevolence,
    the Love, the Purity that is from afar,
    and wishes a covering for their being.
And the greatest covering is a covering of mankind,
    and the seed blends with others for the great battle yet to be,
    and the Soul enters earth, and the lessons are human.
They separate one from the other, they draw words and spew them forth
    so one may not know what the other speaks.
And Creator bows to the children of men
    and sees through them the redemption of the Holy Ones.
And earth sees only the depth of pain and calls it hell.
And man looks up from the pain he has seen and says:

"Souls, we have seen the pain.
    Let us look unto the heavens, away from pain."
And they have found heaven.
And many, many lives are given to acknowledging
    that earth is not heaven and hell,
    earth is the redemption of Holy Ones.
Mankind has a purpose, the purpose of bringing forth
    the Blessed Angels.
It is the single purpose for mankind as one.
For mankind as individual, it is to be in the place of Angels,
    to reach unto Creator.
For there will be a new day, a new horizon, and all creation
    will be brought into the Quar that leads to the second step.
To open the curtain to the second step of creation
    is to open the curtain of the Ark of the Covenant.
Who has the holiness to see beyond the curtain?
Know the beyond is Godhead.
Know the beyond is all humanity, all creation, all worlds
    entering forth to a new existence, a new exploration.
Oh Souls of earth, each man will lose the flesh and the blood
    and the bone, but the vision to the Second Gateway
    will always be, and the Souls who will usher them forth
    will be the Holy Ones redeemed by humanity.

EARTH CONNECTION

331 Earth, beloved humanity, enervate your mind
    to seek the heart thread, the attachment of your being
    to the Farside, to the Soul of self.
The Farside waits in anticipation for connection,
    for an Energy field that will allow
    the Truth, the Purity and Love to be explained.
How gracious is thy being, oh earth,
    that has given humanity a place to rest.
Unto thy noble Soul all Farside reaches out in great blessings,
    all beings of mighty Purity behold thy pain
    and welcome thy Soul to enter in at its appointed time.
For even the lesser Souls may enter in, for all have the Path of Purity.

Noble humanity, be thou the circle of remembrance,
> be thou the circle of whom thou art,
> the connection from where thou hast come.
Soul, divine Spirit of Purity, Essence from Creator, bless thy being!

332 Blessed, who has been lifted will not fall,
> who has been lifted is in the place of Farside.
Oh, Souls, hold the abundance of treasures you have available
> unto you.
Behold, they are not trinkets to be cast aside.
They are not casually come unto your being,
> for your lives have been many
> to take you to a walk of gathering Purity.
Know the path has been full of pain and know now
> how you respond to pain.
Souls, you look differently at the same pattern.
You see differently that which was in your space.
Pain is brought to humanity to be overcome.
Children of man, do not leer at the wretchedness of others.
Do not ever mouth defilement to cast outward from your being.
Do not the very Angels bless the place of your being!
Do they not wrap their arms about you in tenderness
> to care for your well being!
Have you not been driven down and have you not been lifted up!
Hold the lifting up onto your being.
Do not see your being cast down, for you have risen
> above that place and the cause is growth.
How humanity accepts is the growth.
Some Souls gather pain to weep in their being.
It is their path.
They are infant, young Souls.
Gather them unto thy being, see them as wounded, and know
> that the comfort of an old Soul will heal the pain
> and the lesson will be remembered.
Who can take the Flow of Purity as the sun shines
> and the warmth is felt?
Who can learn to devise a pattern of living
> that elevates the path you are in?

Souls of earth, look unto the Creator of thy being
    and know the wonder of the presence in that space.
And know that we, of the sixth level,
    still hunger to be in the Energy of Love.
Oh Souls of earth, how the Light of thy being swells
    before the eyes of Farside Souls when Purity is accepted!
The Light of your being is seen from the Farside.
If one Light will be illuminated, how would Creator joy
    at the vision of millions and millions of such Lights?
You are, Soul, energized by good or evil.
Evil is that which men do unto themselves,
    and good is that which men do for others.
Behold, is this not the lesson?
Do thou unto thy neighbour,
    that which you would have him do for thee.

333 Souls, behold thy energies.
Behold thy energies are not human.
Behold thy energies are Farside.
Your beings are illusion.
Your beings are flesh and blood,
    mind and body caught in the space of time.
Souls, your true being is sublime.
Your true being extends itself unto Farside purities.
See not thy Soul looking up from earth,
    but know thy being as Farside.
And look down through thy Soul and through thy body and thought
    and mind and you will have the true connection of thy being.
Know, Soul, all Purity is thine.
Know, Soul, that every being on the face of thy earth is pure,
    working through growth.
See only in their being, good.
Know only in their being, good.
Do not cast dispersion upon a Soul in growth.
Do not hold thyself from a Soul in growth,
    but draw thyself unto the Soul, wrap thy arms about the Soul
    that they may know the warmth of thy being.
Judgement is not Farside

Know thy being from the Essence, from the Spirit of thy being,
> cannot place judgement upon any man.

It does not point the finger, it does not hold itself away.

Soul, all ugliness, all meanness, all rashness, all hate,
> is a stage of growth.

Help the Soul to grow,
> draw thy Energy into the place of Light.

You have the power to come from the Farside
> and place thy power about the Soul.

Know good, not falseness.

Know Truth in all things.

Lift up thine eye and know that earth wisdom is about no thing
> and earth knowledge is about one:
> > "How may I affect me?" or,
> > "How may I forget me and reach out to no thing?"

So be it.

334 Earth is within infinity.

Earth is in a state of circle.

Soul of earth is infinity.

You are within the state of earth, living infinity.

Guides, angels, time travel at will
> through the boundaries of timelessness and time.

It is as one from the direction of reality.

Your direction is reflection.

It is a reality that Love is Love.

It is a reality that Time is timeless.

On earth, knowledge, it is a contradiction,
> but within the realm of Eternity it is truth.

There is no requirement to time travel.

There is a containment of a body and there is a vibration
> that requires only a higher vibration.

Man has a pretty toy and he endeavours to play with that toy
> and he endeavours to use the knowledge of science,
> > and science takes issue and issue and issue
> > and only comes up with another growth.

But the Soul can teach the heart to accept the vibration of self
> and the Soul will vibrate at will

and find self within Light,
and Light contains the Register of all forward
and all backward movement.
For the angels and the guides there is no separation,
only earth has placed upon itself the separation.
True Time is brought into this sphere of Timeless.
Without metal or mask or need for confinement,
the Souls of many are brought into your space.
They filter through your time and you sense a stranger.
Unwittingly you have brushed shoulders with a being of time travel.
Many have passed through your realm.
They come to see the mortal state and anguish
at how they can recover the origins of creation.
And they look upon the spheres of many generations of Souls
and they see the Energy that vortexes to red.
And they use the goodness of their beings to touch Souls
and enlighten them with Truth and Purity.
All Souls of earth will find vibration.
For in the growth of this sphere is an empowerment
that will rise up from the anger within
and invite the beings of earth
to rally into Purity and the state of Holy.
Seek not to find placement other than where your path has taken you.

335 Souls of earth, thou art Holy.
Thou art swimming in a field of negativity.
Thou art looking at the field instead of thy being.
Soul, look into the centre eye of thy being.
Know the sound of naught.
Hear the resonance, the chord that thy Soul takes
in the universe thou art in.
Every sound is a chord, and thy Soul has a chord of great Truth,
but thou hast, like the great tree, placed bark about thy being
to cover the precious wood underneath.
But, Soul, in placing the shroud of negativity about thy being,
thou hast entered the worms and the maggots
to crawl beneath the bark and infest the being with pain.
Remove the bark and know the goodness.

Do not gather negativity.
Release from thy being, the pain.
Know how Loved thou art.
Creator Loves thy being.
The Creator who made the world and all therein,
    who made the galaxy and all therein,
    who made world upon worlds upon worlds,
    this Creator sees thy being and Loves thy being.
Know that Love and cast away the negativity.
For Soul, there is not a need to enshroud thyself with pain
    when Love is abundantly in thy Path.
Seek to Love, each day, each moment.
Seek only to place gentle words in the place of others.
Do not cast the eye of dispersion, but uplift a Soul,
    for is the Soul not Loved as you!
Souls of earth, enter thou in to Love, Truth, and Purity.

336 Souls, supplicate thy hands upward.
Hold thy being steadfast and be thou in a state of acceptance,
    and know that the passage forth of all knowledge
    will come unto you.
Holy being art thou.
Beings have power to open the blossom they are.
They have the power to lift the fragrance of the blossom unto Farside.
The Soul is the fragrance.
Oh, beings of earth, Farside awaits the many,
    for there are few who may enter through
    and there are many who would utter forth.
Souls of earth, know you have unlimited powers within your being.
Know that the mind of your being may be unlocked
    so that the flow of knowledge will be drawn,
    and the negativity will leave,
    and the forward flow will create itself in acceptance.
Beloved being, hold unto you the Light and know
    that the eye may see the Light.
Know, Soul, it has power to move into the Flow.
Know it may go quickly or it may go slow,
    but travel it will unto the Light of your being.

Earth Souls are not tethered to earth.
It is the strangling vines of negativity that hold you tight to earth.
It is the deceptive powers of negativity
    that refuse to allow the sight to enter forth.
Souls, you are a bud of great worth,
    a flower that will open unto Purity.
You hold yourself tight as a bud.
Some allow their beings to open that all might see the Purity within.
Souls of earth, allow the opening of the bud, for it is who you are.
Within the bud is the fragrance, within the bud is the Purity.
Allow the opening of the flower.
Allow the needless pleadings unto Creator to go,
    for there is no need to plead.
All that is Creator is unto you.
You have but to open your being and know the power is there.

337 Soul of earth, Soul abounding in the transformation of Truth,
    Soul reaching the heights of ecstasy, you are human.
Your being is human.
The thread of your being is attached to your Soul.
The humanity of your being is attached to the Soul
    by thread of Creator.
The passage to reach your being is not connected
    from the heart to the Soul.
That thread is the connection from Creator to your being.
To reach the complexity of your being, enter the space of the third eye.
It is, Soul, the avenue to Naught.
It is that which transforms all of your energies away from the flesh,
    and the bone, and the blood.
Know the Light of your being leaves the humanness of your being,
    but through the centre eye it is the Path to reach Purity
    while still in the earth form.
Soul, behold thy being, behold the quietness of thy being.
Behold the stillness that surrounds the quietness of your being,
    and then, in the twinkling of an eye,
    you enter in to the third eye.
Whoosh, and you have entered in.

Your being is buoyant, your being draws unto that
> from which it has come: Light.

It is seen as a focus in the dark, a slight form of agate.

As you allow your being to be brought into the IS space of Naught,
> your being will enter in to that space of Light.

It will soar through, into that space of Light,
> and before you is the brightness of your own being,
> before you is the Energy from which you have come,
> the Essence of self.

As you enter in with practice to the space of pure Energy,
> disallowing all earth ion, your gathering allows your vision
> to see beyond the White Light of self.

It is taken to worlds and worlds, to voyages,
> it is taken to learning stations
> where Souls are deep in contemplation of issues
> that will bring them Purity.

It is taken to the many levels of growth beyond your own
> that often appear only as a mist
> beyond which you know is further exploration.

And yet your being is held from the Purity.

It flows unto you, it radiates about your being,
> but the knowledge within your being recognizes
> you are not elevated self
> to be in the space of that further Light.

Delight in knowing that the potential is always there.

Know your being is chosen by self to reach unto Creator.

Soul, channel thy being into the Path of the third eye,
> know it requires no unlocking.

As your being enters in to Purity, the veils fall away.

The veils are untethered from the eye and recognition is there.

Hold Truth in thy being.

Know it is the purpose of thy being.

Enter thou in to no contraries that allow faults,
> for faults are not perfection.

338 Michael will teach the resounding rhythm of
> earth, transition, Farside, worlds beyond worlds beyond worlds.

Enter in to rhythm.

Enter in to the simplicity that is complex.
Enter in to the very IS.
Behold, justification requires no move,
    justification is a part of eternity.
To be is not to be.
To arrive in the timelessness of be
    is to enter in to the state of nothingness.
Know expectation, know desire, know fulfilment,
    for in the state of nothingness is the void.
In the void is the Gateway to all that is pure.
Vision Purity!
Vision within the void, the nothingness,
    the total unawareness, the Gateway of total Purity.
To have all, leave all.
To have all, gather no expectation.
Soul, joy is a state of being.
Joy has no negativity and yet to be in joy,
    one must know pain.
Today is the only day.
The Gateway is the only Gateway.
The turbulence that will spring forth from the negativity
    within the agonies of earth will be found in Purity.
The simplicity is the direction of all purpose.
The mind has been set within the human for growth.
The knowledge of earth is knowledge of earth.
All knowledge of far Time
    within the creation of creation of creation is wisdom.
All knowledge of earth is known within your very Soul.
The most complex adjustment to mathematics
    can be done within the life of a two year old
    were that child to be within the state of Farside awareness
    that has taken them past earth growth.
Enter in to rhythm.
Enter in to the timeless movement of all that is.
All is motion unto a motion.
Verily, time will erupt.
Time will enter once again into the state of motion.
Be in the state of nothingness, giving all to Purity,

for in the state of nothingness, desire ceases,
    longings are only of Purity.
The coat will easily be discarded and given.
The calm acceptance of your being is a reaction
    to the Path of nothingness which, in Truth, is all.

339 Three times, Souls, do this before meditation.
Three times express self and the acknowledgement
    of self to the eye.
The ear can hear the sound of the eye.
The ear can hear the sound of the eye!
Place the hands upon the ear, three times.
Hold, then remove, hold, then remove, hold, then remove,
    and the eye will be activated to the Sound of the Void.
It is a quick entrance in.
Soul, meditation is acknowledging the naught.
It is acknowledging all forces and rhythms about your being
    without entering in to the rhythms and forces.
The rhythms are the positive, the forces are the negative.
It does not have to have a name.
It only needs the positives and the rhythms,
    and the forces and the negatives.
We ask you to ponder on not quiet, but on entering in.
Your Soul can be completely mobile
    and you may enter in to meditation.
Your being may rock with motion
    and you may enter in to meditation.
The rocking force will drive you deeper into meditation.
Soul, you may calm your being to the stillness of a statue
    and you will draw yourself into meditation.
You may focus on a single finger, on a single candle,
    on any one item that has no purpose other than light,
    and you will draw yourself into meditation.
Meditation is not Holy, but it takes you to a place
    where you may reach into the space of Holy.
It draws you into the Timetable of Holy.
It draws you into the curvature of T.
You may elevate your being in a space of meditation.

You may draw yourself to another land and stand upon the sea,
    and walk upon the sea and look at the shore,
    for your being is weightless, the vision is continuous.
To meditate is to come to know, not your earth being,
    but the power, the possibilities of your earth being.
Not the power of your earth being,
    the power possibilities of your earth being!
The deepest colour to meditate through
    is the densest blue black.
In entering in to the space of meditation, you will see
    a fragment of your being raise itself
    as the tiny bug of a fractal.
It will lift itself unto the Light, the aperture that will open unto you.
Allow your being to be brought into the Light.
Watch as you see the Soul being drawn slowly
    and purposefully upward, into the space of Light,
    and acknowledge that you may enter.
Fear and doubt will immediately prevent access
    unto all energies.
Acknowledge and feel your being drawn into the space of aura.
Aura will surround your being.
It will cascade itself upon your being and as you look at the being,
    you will see not one shade of Aura, but many shades of Aura,
    for you have entered in to the Farside.
You may read past lives from this Aura.
You may read that which you will do with future Souls
    in this Aura.
You may read the purpose of your earth in your life
    in this Aura.
There is a great need for you to withdraw
    from the world you are in.
It is easier to meditate when there is totally no movement,
    totally no concentrations.
All appendages need to be connected,
    not as interwoven, but gently.
Your feet, whether sitting, standing or kneeling,
    need to touch each other.

It will give you faster travel, for the being is always concerned
    of extremities left vulnerable.
It is instinct to the humanity of your being.
You can read Aura.
You must acknowledge you have the power to read Aura
    and you will enter in to lives that you have known instantly.
You will feel yourself drawn into cavities, into rooms,
    into shapes and designs, you will see people and places.
You will know these are beings of your lifetimes.

340 Michael will teach logic.
Logic is acceptance.
Logic does not have to be positive, it may be very negative.
That which you see as logical is not always bountiful in goodness.
Sometimes, Soul, you must enter in to the illogical.
Spirituality, for many, is illogical.
It has no firm response from logic,
    and yet we are the total sum of spirituality.
Our beings are that of which spirituality is.
We ask that you separate, in your being, the mind,
    and you know clearly the illogical response of your heart.
For it is in the heart that the Soul has a thread.
The mind, indeed, is for logic.
The mind will look at the negativity and make a choice,
    but it is the heart of humanity that is the portion
    connected to the Soul.
It is the heart that has a thread to the Farside,
    that is akin to the Farside,
    that is brethren to the Farside.
Souls, under the canopy of earth is much that is logic.
Logic would change in a moment.
It only requires a mathematician.
Earth's one will change to Zero
    and the future will open pathways unto the Farside.
It is the pathway through which visions are seen.
It is the pathway through which Light is seen.
But apertures will be revealed to man and logic will not enter in.

Defy logic, confront logic,
>   for logic is the dalliance of baby Souls.
Unto man is the possibilities of all logic.
Unto Soul is the possibilities of all illogic.
Souls, enter therein.

341 Michael will teach spirituality to hungering humanity.
What, where, how, when the Soul arrives,
>   derives, deceases.
The origin is in the mind, not the Soul.
Words are words.
In the context of words may or may not be a lesson.
It is in the Soul receiver to be enlightened.
However and wherefore the Soul came to be and will depart
>   is simplistic, so is in complication.
Soul, simplistic has been verified.
Soul, the avenue to simple is not the worldly solution.
It is the complex simplicity that overrides all known knowledge.
The ride of men upon the wave of human growth is torn
>   into many fragments because of Soul growth.
We are, we have lived upon your earth station.
We have growth that is humble, but not so humble
>   as earth would have us be.
Our path is as yours, to seek what earth calls deity.
Soul, deity is as you are in growth and infinity.
Even your meagre bubble is in infinity.
Time is allotted to you as growth, but time is simply a number
>   within the convergence of all that is.
That meagre number is as one
>   to the multiplicity of T geode, to the universal jet stream.
It is a complexity of earth, yet simple is the one it is in.
The Soul has patience to be.
The Soul has always a program.

342 We can see Lantoisa, we have her moon and sun.
We have great abilities that your flesh does not have.
We have the ability to move at will, to vacate a Quar
>   and enter in to a Quar.

We have the ability to position ourselves,
    to enter in to any medium of earth.
We have, Soul, entered in to the heat of the volcano.
It does not affect our being.
You have beings that walk on coals.
It does not affect their being.
It should not seem strange that, in our Purity,
    we may enter in to great heat.
Our Energy alters the heat about our being, just so.
It gives us a barrier.
We also have the ability to alter the Energy of steels, of irons,
    of rocks, of all metals.
We may glide through as simply as you would dip your hand in water.
There is no barrier on earth that we could not enter.
The liquid you have not a knowledge of,
    for us to express, would be meaningless.
We could give you an initiate: *Vzartlzovi*.
It is the closest in expression but meaningless to your earth.
It could become immediately meaningful if you would enter
    in to the Zero of T.
Listen, Souls of earth, listen men of science,
    know the Zero enters in to the T.
Know the vibrational level of T is seven.

343 Soul, Allah be unto you.
Allah, God, are one!
The tent door is open and Allah and God
    are not two Souls within the text.
They are singular Almighty Supreme Being.
Who will wait in the space of Almighty Supreme Being?
The measurement is Truth, but whose Truth?
This is earth quandary.
The measurement of Truth is Purity, but whose Purity?
And the measurement of Purity is Love, but whose Love?
And so the greatest quandary, the measurement of Creator,
    but whose Creator?
Souls of earth, Farside Truth beckons to man.

No earthly human may alter Truth,
    no Farside human may alter Truth.
Within the Flow of Energy that is the redemption of Angels is Truth.
Truth is measured by Creator.
It was Creator who instilled within man
    the possibilities of Truth.
Souls of earthly plane, we ask that you seek to BE.
To BE in the state of Truth is to not harbour negativity,
    to hold no doubt, no fear, only the expectation of good.
Purity is the endowment of Angels.
Unto the Angels was given Purity from Creator to battle Negativity,
    and these Beings have freely given the growth of Purity.
Souls of earth, you, too, may arm yourselves with Purity.
Purity is available unto you, but in order to gather Purity
    your being must vibrate with Truth.
It is simple, it is complex, it is not randomly chosen.
It is selected by the Spirit, not the Soul.
The earth being must connect to the counterpart of self,
    the Spirit, in order to gather Purity.
It is, Soul, possible for earth beings.
Many have been that have travelled through the aperture of Quar,
    but first they must accept their Truth and then,
    in the state of Truth, gather Purity,
    and the total acceptance will lift their beings
    unto Quar unto Quar unto Quar.
Love also has an equation that gives.
Love is radiant.
Love has a Pathway to Ecstasy.
Few have entered in to Ecstasy,
    but Holy Holy Holy is possible in thy being.
In Love is the meld of all that is unto one.
The one is precious beyond belief and the offering is unto Godhead,
    and only in the state of Ecstasy
    may one enter in to the place of Godhead.
Only from a state of outflowing Love may you see the vision
    for all worlds, all creation, all heavens and all earths.
You are then in the state of Ecstasy.
And beyond Ecstasy, we know a further Quar.

We know the Quar aperture is as the crystal that radiates
    and radiates and radiates,
    and the Light from that crystal ignites.
And we know in our being, because we have been told
    and we supplicate our being unto that Holy Place.
The Great One, the Great Being, the All in All,
    enervates the Flow to all existences
    and your Soul self gathers its being to connect
    to Allah, God, unto Godhead.
And you have the possibilities of brilliant, brilliant violets,
    that take us unto Quar through Godhead.
And you see yourselves as human and often times less than human.
And, Souls of earth, could you but know
    the sanctity in which you are revered
    and the possibilities to which you hold the key.
Unto earth is much given, unto earth is much expected.

344 Michael will teach implosion.
Soul, we have come into your space.
We have been in your space often.
We have been permitted to enter in.
We are not unwilling.
We are from the Purity of Gummeria.
Soul, your being has purpose.
Soul of earth, Quar is the place of implosion.
It allows the Soul, it allows the earth, it allows all energies
    of all dimensions to enter in to implosion.
It is the state of Time and Timeless.
It is the motion of perfection.
Earth Souls, the din is loud, for earth has great trauma
    and earth sees only the din of self.
And yet the sound of earth motion grinds.
It is great shards of refuse.
We have been from the Quar into your space
    many eons of time from your existence.
We have been at the celebration of humanity's Entering In,
    and earth, in splendour, could not behold the Energy,

the burst of Energy,
for earth was involved in a potential of mankind.
And the Quar of earth could be felt resounding,
 imploding into all worlds, and all worlds looked to earth
 and often entered in, often visited humanity,
 and gifted humanity with great knowledge
 to have in the purpose for which mankind has come.
Souls of earth, the Quar does not now permit entry except by a few.
For as the field of negativity has encroached upon earth in fetid fingers,
 the Quar is not available to mankind.
It will be, Soul, in the coming of the Purities.
It will be, Soul, in the uplifting of Souls and some,
 in their Purity, may enter in to the Quar
 and be brought to heights of great Purity.
Understand, earth agonizes,
 for earth has memory of that which it was,
 and mankind rides the wave of negativity
 and carries the weapons of great injury in their beings.
Behold Quar!
Quar is the state of Entering In.
It is the positioning of one's being to enter Holiness.
You may then see the many earth fields evaporate before your eyes
 and you will see those you call alien,
 who have fields of Energy that disperse your vision.
Your catalyst to Quar is Purity.
Be thou pure.
Truth will take your Soul to the Farside,
 but Purity will enter thou in to Quar.

345 Beloved earth, beloved receiver of Energy,
 hold thou the Energy in the dome of the eye.
Move thou outward to allow the protrusion
 and know the depth of the eye.
Know, Soul, as you have been taught,
 the ever abounding circle is within the eye.
The knowledge of all spirituality for entering in
 is coming forth.
One may enter in to the void, the outer spaces of earth

    in great ships, but you carry yourself
        to the minutest part of the first Quar.
The eye will take you inward and outward
        to Quar upon Quar upon Quar.
We would have you understand, there are no limitations
        to the passage of the Soul into the place of First Gateway.
Soul, many earth beings enter in to Quar.
Many earth beings of great simplicity have the ability
        to enter in to implosion and enter in to the space
        of bright bursts of Energy.
They carry the Soul as one, quickly
        into another dimension of being.
Another dimension of being!
We have no time.
We may place an Energy Field in a space of your time
        and time will stop.
We may enter in to your earth field, but only for short periods.
Our purities are brought to the point of a nodule.
It will deflect negativity momentarily.
You may enter in to our Field of Energy, if you will.
We will draw you to us if you are pure, if you are given in goodness.
Understand, all positive Energy is taken in sound from your being.
You have reached us through your sound.
Your being has great sound without what you call earth noise.
The resonance of that sound carries purities.
Soul, purify your being, enter in to sound.
Heal your despair with sound.

346 There are no contradictions in Quar.
Quar is a measurement of time and space.
Quar is the infinite measurement of time and space.
Quar is an Entering In, Quar is a passing through.
We ask that you recognize implosion as Quar.
All is available to mankind.
Soul, it is available to mankind at the time of mankind's gathering,
        at the time instantly that you would recognize all positive.
Were you to lay aside all niggling doubts,
        you would pass through Quar, and the time is instant.

It delays time, not accelerates time.
It delays time to a point of nonexistence.
Star, shining star, goodness set in the sky for man.
Farside is the extension of your stars.
Can you fathom the reality of this concept?
And yet the passage into the stars of Farside
    requires the entry in to Quar.
Your earth being could not take you to Farside
    except through the entering of Quar.
It is, Soul, the space of Naught.
It is the entering in to the passage, it is the immediate opening.
It is done with vibration.
See all your being as marked, as linear.
Know that the linear of your being
    may become as the most minute of ion
    and still retain all intelligence, knowledge, wisdom,
    passages of time. All!
And that smallest ion may enter in to the place of naught.
It is compacted and compacted and compacted and compacted.
It is done in an instant, it is done and implosion begins.
Soul, will you allow yourself to be drawn into the place of naught?
It is within the centre eye.
Each Soul knows this.
Why do we speak to each other apart when you may enter in to Purity?
Step forward, Soul, step forward to thy eye and draw thy being
    into the centre vortex and know there is no need
    to move your Energy.
There is no need to gyrate, there is no need to walk,
    there is no need to fly.
There is no need to enter in to great spaceships.
There is only the need to enter in to one's being
    and find the space of Naught within the centre eye
    and all earth energies will be set apart,
    and all that is tethered to Negativity will be set apart,
    and the Soul will find the knowing from which it has come,
    and it will enter through the portal of Quar.
Enter thou in.
Souls, we await your entering in, your coming forth.

347 Soul, the energetic vibration acknowledges negativity.
The solemn, quiet vibration acknowledges negativity.
The positive Energy acknowledges naught.
It is the lesson of humanity.
All Souls of earth have one direction
    to enter in to the place of naught.
All mathematics of earth resound to Naught,
    one may not enter in to the equation.
Rejoice in vibration.
Know, Soul, the finish of positive Energy is at fifth level.
Purity encompasses all Truth.
Positive and negative is useless in Purity,
    it has become redundant within itself.
The vibration has taken the Soul to a permanent place
    within the Spirit and the Soul is one with the Spirit.
Soul, naught is the total acceptance within the inner self,
    the high consciousness of thy being,
    the awareness of thy being,
    the space that has relinquished the human need to exist.
Oh, Soul, it is not that you can relinquish the human body,
    you cannot let go of the form at will.
But Naught says the framework within the Soul is no longer needed
    for the Soul's business and the framework diminishes itself
    and is able to silently leave earth space
    by transcendental travel to the Essence of thy being.
The passageway is vibration.
Vibrate, Souls!
Vibrating of the physical form is ague, illness,
    but vibrating of the Soul self is the avenue to Purity.
Souls, do not linger long, do not toil in earth space,
    do not place thy shekels in a space that does not turn.
Do not place thy shekels under a rock, but in a motion
    where all thy being is moving into the place of Purity.
Souls of earth, do not covet that which thou hast not,
    for vibration is not in coveting.
Soul, hold in thy hand the power of the universe.
Hold in thy being the power of the universe!

Hold in thy hand, the power of creation for, Souls of earth,
    thou art unto Creator, creation and creator.
Beloved earth, beloved humanity of earth, how blessed is man!
Do not see in thy brother wretchedness,
    do not cast thine eye to a sister and see less than thou art,
    for, Soul, thy being is equal unto all being.
There is no greater or lesser.
There is humanity in the eye of beholding.
Shake thy being.
Shake, Soul, thy being.
Shake, Soul, thy being!
Vibrate with the intensity of Creator, for from Creator thou hast come,
    unto Creator thou would go.
There is no day or night in the Soul self.
There is no closing or opening.
There is only the Path that leads to Creator.
How blessed art thou, humanity, to be in the place of thy Creator!

348 Souls of earth, reckon with the void,
    acknowledge the void in your space, the place of Naught,
    for in the space of Naught are the crossroads to all creation,
    the crossroad direct to Creator.
But from Creator are many threads.
Earth is only one thread.
Your universe contains all fibres within that thread.
Outward from Creator are threads upon threads
    and the most complicated of cables
    that earth carries for communication
    could not number the fibres within those threads.
As you leave your state of flesh, mind and body,
    there is a passage into the crossroads
    through transition to the state of Holy.
From Holy you may stand at the gateway
    and visualize all avenues of Purity
    and choice is abundant within your being.
You may travel to worlds beyond your measure,
    to worlds where the beings of the great mammals exist.
Their form is not cumbersome in that place.

Their Purity, their step, is awesome in the space of Creator.
You may go to the reptilian worlds where
> Souls who offer to many worlds, goodness of being for learning,
> reside in the Purity of their original state.

Do not gasp at their being.
They do not reflect from pain, for in that space there is no pain,
> there is no attack, there is only the pure form of being.

Souls of Purity, know the length of your stay in these many lands
> has no time, for our state is Timeless
> and the call of your being is always to meld with creation,
> to be in the final stage with Creator.

The Purity of the smallest child on earth, in its purest state,
> could not look upon the Face of Creator.

This being, in Purity, could be with us on the Farside
> but the face of Energy radiates in an echo,
> and in the space of origin our being could not withstand,
> nor could the small humanity.

Enter in to the knowledge that earth time presents options to mankind,
> that of reliving, or that of moving forward.

To relive one must decease.
To move forward is to be in growth.
No man can stand still except to pass.
All men are in the state of student or teacher,
> all men sit at the feet of the learned,
> and the lesson is taught and acknowledged.

Some learn in the form of negativity,
> others learn in the face of positive,
> but the lesson must be absorbed and learned.

The learned Souls then move into the space of teachers,
> either in negativity or in positive Energy.

Capturing back a word of negativity is not possible for earth Souls.
Guard thy mouth that words of negativity, darts,
> as arrows that fly forth from thee,
> do not injure the very humanity of which you are a part of.

All earth is one.
The lesson is for one humanity, not a divided humanity.
The brilliance of your being is visioned

    from the crossroads where we stand,
        acknowledging the existence of earth.
Many areas of earth have terse recognition
        and the colour upward is crimson
        and falls down to earth to bleed the very ground of earth.
Other areas abound in Purity.
A single Soul in Purity can ignite far reaching,
        and the Light is seen and gathered by Angels
        and gifted to Creator.
Souls, extend thy being unto the creation from which thou were formed.
Holy Holy Holy!

349 Souls of earth, reach unto the vibration of High Being.
Welcome the Soul into the space of Spirit.
Know, Soul, vibration of Naught.
Recognize Energy.
Recognize positive Energy and negative energy.
Know between the positive and the negative energy
        is the dichotomy of Purity.
Be, Soul, astounded at the Purity,
        for when all negative energy loses thy being,
        and when all positive Energy is of no matter,
        behold thou hast entered in to Purity.
Behold the welcome thou wilt receive!
Behold the vibration of self
        that amazes the Soul's ability to reject negativity,
        to reject the baseless self.
Soul, negate is a path to overcome.
Soar beyond negativity, soar into the space of vibration.
Know, Soul, the dichotomy of Purity.

350 Soul, Michael will teach.
The product of Eternity is vibration.
The world you know sees only tangible product.
Your very being is vibration.
To vibrate your existence at a high density
        would evaporate from your vision, all before your eyes,
        and yet your being would still flow in vibration.

It is the product of Purity.
It is that which enters in from the reflection of your true self.
True, all that you see outward from the eye is true self.
Behold, the Angels vibrate with such movement in the Flow
    that the Soul is taken here, to here, to here, to here.
Your very beings have this vibration.
It is the product of creativity, it is a member of Creator.
It is that which reproduces vibration.
The higher the being, the more profound the creativity.
Souls of earth who have brought to your plane the remembrance
    of vibration are the great givers of art, of literature.
They have carried the vibration, and the movement within their works
is the continual thread they hold.
They have entered in to a state within the eye of profound Purity.
They have left an existence and carried the thread attached
    to the being in a manner that is more profound
        than that which exists in the norm.
For they have tethered the Essence,
    they have carried the Purity of expression,
    the vision of that profound vibration, into the side that you are.
It is reflectory.
Souls of earth, be thou in vibration.
Accept into your earth space that which is free.
It has no cost, it is yours, has always been humanity's,
    but humanity revels in the negative vibration.
The negative vibration carries strong winds of discontent,
    murmurs of pain and anguish.
The Soul is brought to the centre of a storm
    and feels the calm within the place of negativity
    and knows, in the quietness, that there is a deliverance.
And yet, when the negative vibration stirs again,
    they will allow themselves to be propelled forward
        in ongoing negativity.
Soul, use the product of vibration.
It will alter the space you are in.
It carries you to the depths of pain in Purity.
To be able to attain the state of vibration, one must be in acceptance,
    one must be delivered from the ego of negativity.

Souls of earth, you are not being given a new religion.
You are not being given a new citadel to raise up for man to revile.
Soul, you are being given a Pathway into the Flow of Eternity,
    a key to the existence of humanity.
All nations, all sects, and cults, and religions
    are the concern of the blessed Energy.
The Flow of that Energy may only be entered in to by vibration Holy.

351 Souls of earth have little Purity to behold.
They are babies struggling, frantic to test each negativity.
Have you not found it so yourselves!
And then it is as the gift from the goat and the cow,
    the milk is a child and the cream is the old Soul,
    gathered at the high place of mountain.
It is a vortex, a momentum of gathering.
Earth will not be without negativity
    until the moment earth collapses within itself.
Earth will carry the force of negativity.
It will be the drawing into self.
That is the final end.
Your form must have the Purity of Angels
    and yet be connected to earth
    to be the instrument of Almighty Creator.
There is no conflict, there is a need for Purity.
How soon is now when the Souls of earth know themselves pure?
Their beings will emanate that Purity.
Doubt will flee their beings, anger will flee their beings.
You will recognize in yourself the Purity that only Agape can bring.
Old Souls, gather you together.
Hold the spew of angry words.
Draw the power within your being to vibrate,
    that you might enter in in Purity,
    so that no negativity within the bounds of transition
    may prevent that which will be.
You are the force of Energy that will gather, not one,
    but folds of folds of folds of beings brought into the tunnel
    that has but one Light, the source of the Energy of Creator.
Blessed be such humanity.

TEARS OF PURITY

352 Blessed Souls, the mirror of your being, the mirror
    of Creator's Being, seven of seven of seven of seven.
Creation began from seven spews forth of Energy.
Your creation, your creation, seven energies!
And Energy created this sphere,
    and Energy formed the solids.
And Energy breathed the liquid flow
    and that which was solid, rend.
Soul, Creator breathed forth
    and the great trees and the roots were formed.
And Creator gasped forth a canopy to protect that which was created
    and atmosphere, ionosphere, came into be.
And Creator saw the emptiness of his creation.
And joy leaped into the sea and the sea became abundant with life,
    and still the earth was silent.
And Creator breathed and flesh was formed and all that crawled
    and slithered and leaped filled the earth with sound,
    and still there was a void.
And Creator beheld the canopy and lifted that which had walked
    and gave Light its name.
And Creator rejoiced in that which was brought forth.
And the Creator set all the motion spiralling forth,
    and the heavens gazed down at that which was created
    and recognized the place of the last battle.
And the Angels wept great tears and the motion of rain was created,
    and the Angels tears never ceased to be.
And man sought man,
    and greed entered in to that which was created
    and war, the first battle, had begun.

353 Hear!
Hear that which we know.
Souls of earth Purity gather and speak lessons of Truth unto you,
    and the ear hears that which is spoken, and the ear
    knows the lesson and passes it on, and it is done.
Souls of earth, the Angels enter in to your state.
The blessed Beings have taught to congregations unaware

    and the Souls have gathered the beads of Purity
    and passed it to a brother or a sister,
    and the Angels' tears fall, for the lesson
    has not been gathered unto self.
The lessons are for knowing.
There is a motion in progress, there is a flow in progress,
    there is an agenda for earth Souls.
"Oh blessed earth, how may we bless thee?
How may we extend our Being unto thee?"
Heed thou the lessons; preacher, monk, priest, rabbi,
    the words that are spoken, place unto the Path of Truth.
See thou the blessed babe raised unto Purity
    and know the delight in the offering of creation unto thee.
Know the child would ever be held in the arms of Love.
Who will teach the Souls of earth if the Angels will not be heard?
Allow tranquillity to enter in to thy being
    for tranquillity is the upward flow.
And know thy hands may heal around about thee
    and enter in to the Holy moment of meditation
    that your BE may be known
    and IS may be brought forth in thee.
Soul of earth, unto thee all blessings flow.
Reap the reward of giving, for in giving ye shall receive!

354 Behold, the shadows lengthen,
    the shadows enter the space of being.
Shadows have always been,
    humanity has always been tethered in shadow.
It is the negative space that creates growth.
Souls are drawn to the space of foreboding.
Souls are drawn to the space of the eye.
Soul, behold, behold and behold!
Entry in to the passage of the Farside creates awareness.
All life vibrates, all Energy is felt.
All themes fall away, all entries are erased.
The Soul becomes the Spirit and the Spirit faces the Register[72].
Souls of earth, behold the shadow.

---

72 the Register - Akashic Record

The shadow of the eagle flies high and spreads a wing over the land.
It says: "Peace can be obtained, look up to the eagle."
If you stand in the space of the shadow, foreboding will come.
It is necessary, Souls, to be accountable.
It is necessary to speak against the shadows
    that overwhelm lesser levels of beings.
And you say: "Aha, I am a greater level. I need not worry."
Soul, the temerity of humanity!
The shadows of the Angels fall over the orb of earth,
    the shadows have fallen over many.
They would convince the Soul to be sheltered and they will say:
    "Look beyond! Look beyond!
    See from where the shadow comes.
    Know there is a Path beyond the state of your being.
    Know you travel in sanctity and peace and virtue."
All is cleansed under the shadow.
It has Soul growth, it has the perpetual motion of Time.
In a Timeless state, there is also growth.
But it does not require shadow.
Wings of Blessed Angels enwrap the globe and cry in pain.
Why, you ask?
Because of Blessedness.
Behold, you have been covered in the shadow
    to look beyond all earthly pain,
    to know that you have a purpose
    beyond that which is earth.
Caregiver of the orb, do you think it is by accident
    that you consider the soil, the contamination?
You have been carried beyond, into sanctity and blessedness.
The Flow is not downward.
The Flow is upward, in the spiral of Truth.

355 "Creator of our being,
    we are drawn into the Light of Thy Purity.
    Love expounds in our hearts
        and flows in oneness to deliver the Blessed."
Be this the prayer that men will speak, if speak they will, of prayer.
Prayer is an issuing of goodness forth.

Know Love flows, and Love will travel into the hearts of man
    by the goodness they see in thy being.
Speak not words.
Carry thy Enlightenment as Raiment of Angels is carried unto thee.
Hold the Light and know the flow of goodness will overwhelm thy Soul,
    and thy Soul will be drawn to carry forth words of praise,
    words of worship.
And thy hands will outreach and supplicate unto Creator,
    and gather, in the supplication, the flow of giving,
    and Love will overwhelm thy being,
    and thy being will know that Creator has been in thy space.
Souls, bow thy head and know that Creator places protection
    on the bowed head.
Allow the Angel wings to comfort thy being.
When you are drawn to a place of darkness,
    allow the breath of Angels to surround thee
    and the heavens will open unto thy being,
    and the Light will radiate upon thy being,
    and healing will be done.
Peace be unto you.

356 To be in the place of sanctity is to be at a level of Purity
    that has taken the Spirit to growth beyond earth boundaries.
Soul, beloved, beloved children, blessed children,
    know the face of Radiance, be brought to a place of Purity.
All desire is to reach to the place of Purity.
To behold the tear of the Angel is to behold Ecstasy.
Soul, worlds upon worlds upon worlds exist,
    and all worlds have their Purity,
    all worlds have their own containment,
    and all worlds flow within the Purity
    of Timelessness and infinity.
To be lifted to that place of Purity is not coincidence, it is a Path.
It is placed with Love, Love of self.
Love of self beyond self is the only Path.
It has no tether to ego, it carries no deception.
Within the place of the sixth level is a division,

and the Souls below are seen and treasured
and lifted with great care over the footfalls of the Angels.
And, Soul, know above, the Angel wings as feathers
cascade in Purity and touch the earth.
And earth is brought with care to the place of Creator.
The Angel wings reach out to many worlds,
earth is not the only containment.
And the treasures that are brought to Creator
are the gifts that Souls send.
They are carried with great care.
All perfection meets perfection.
Soul, abound in the Purity, abound in Truth
and know the Hem of Creator, the Angel wings.
Are they not a part of creation!
Do they not blend with the Energy!
They are themselves the Hem of Creator!
Is the hem lesser than the head, is the arm lesser than the foot?
All is perfection, but at the end there is still forward motion.
Soul, offer gifts, that the Angels may take the jewels that are teardrops
for if a Soul cries, the tear is treasured and blessed and healed.
The gift is given.

357 Beloved Energy, fallen seed of creation,
who has extended the growth of thy being upward
into the fathomless space, vortex.
The eye does not tear without Purity.
Beyond the vortex,
the tears of the Holy ones bestow unto mankind a blessing.
For the Holy ones would gather unto them all that has pain
and yet their being may not,
for it is growth that is in your space,
and the very Souls of goodness know the record of your being.
They place about your being, guidance and care.
They hold no judgement in their Being.
Come, Souls of earth, enter you in to the realm beyond.
Enter you in to the garden of Purity, blessed being.
"How may we enter in?" you ask.

Souls, the Radiance of your being enters in.
The genuineness of your efforts enter in.
The vision of giving enters in and you find you are there.
There is no pain, Soul, only the Flow into Energy.
It carries no tainted thought, it carries only the garment of acceptance.
Enter in to the portal of the garden of Radiance
    and know the earth will have ceased to be for your Soul.

358 Souls, almighty Souls, what thou do, do in tranquillity.
Be thou blessed in the Light of holiness.
Be thou transfigured to the state of Farside.
Audacious Souls, behold creation and the spewing forth of all.
And a stench rose up and Creator blew forth Purity
    and Purity rose up to fight the awful stench
    and hold in abeyance all that could come into the Flow.
And the Holy Ones armed themselves with Purity and Truth,
    with overwhelming Love,
    and fought and won in the upper regions of Holy.
And the Holy Ones cast a glance at the spewing forth
    and saw the fragment of man
    still within the bounds of negativity,
    and the Holy tears cascaded down
    to wash earth of her negativity,
    and still negativity aroused itself.
And the Holy Ones beckoned to Creator:
    " Lord of all, Energy of all, cast Thou from these Souls, pain.
    And Almighty Being, use our goodness
        to free that which keeps them apart from our Being!"
And Creator placed a calm within the heart of man
    wherein he could find the passage to Holy,
    and all Enlightenment began to flow.
And the Angels called: "Holy Holy Holy! Thou art ever Holy!
    In the chasm of darkness are yet Souls,
        even from the first casting out.
    We beseech Thee, Energy of our Being,
        to cast Thine eye upon the lost folds of Thine
        and behold, Almighty One,
        be Thou brought to tears for their agony."

And the Lord cast a look from the many of his creations
    to the last vestige of negativity
        and the Holy Tear fell and washed the earth.
Souls of pain who have been and are in depths beyond human pain,
    are from beginning to end of time.
Time will cease, Timelessness will always be.
Transition has end and is in the state of time.

CHAPTER 4
Holy Holy Holy

Upper Regions of Creation

359 From the Platform of Angels
    see upward and know the glory of the Crystal Cave,
    of all the energies of all creation melded.
Yours is as the Milky Way,
    the outward flux of your being within the Crystal Cave,
    that as you move inward and upwards, the glory is unspeakable.
Would the human eye but see the glory of the Milky Way,
    it would in some small way understand the glory of Farside.
It is difficult in the framework of your language,
    to enunciate to you the Radiance, the stark Purity of goodness
    that holds all possibilities within it, where nothing is held back,
    whither no dissension lies, where only the Energy
    becomes greater and greater.
The hallmark of Creator is Radiance,
    blossoming outward unto all beings, all energies.
Souls, the farther you reach into the space of Purity,
    the more you are drawn unto it.
Do not fear the drawing in, know in your being
    how awesome is the Entering In.

360 Behold, enter in to Purity!
Enter thou in to the place of Angels.
Enter thou in to the Hallowed Halls of Purity.
It is expansive, Soul.
It has cathedrals of Purity.
It has Energy Fields, containments of such vibrance
    that your very Soul would vibrate at the Energy.

Behold, behold the Archangel.
Behold the shimmering goodness of this being.
No pane on earth would let in such Light.
No pane on earth would show such multitude of colours.
No gentleness would hold a baby as gently
    as the Archangel holds the wounded Soul.
The Light expands in every movement of being.
The Soul who prostrates himself before the Blessed Ones
    cannot imagine the Purity to which they bow.
You do not need to whisper, you do not need to shout.
You only need to have a fleeting thought
    and the Blessed Ones are round about your being.
As you gather Purity, the Blessed Ones may come closer
    and your being will be as the gossamer
    that has cradled itself about you.
And all your energies will be enlivened and radiant
    and Ecstasy will enter your being,
        for no earth Soul could behold the Purity of the Archangels
        without Ecstasy.
How then would you be in the space of Creator?
How then would our being be offered as pure?
For each Soul rises as a star that shoots across a night sky,
    so your Soul soars to the place of Creator.
You are Energy.
Do you think these beings do nothing?
Soul, in the upper reaches of creation are many mansions,
    are many cathedrals built of Holiness.
They have ethereal presence that has perception in all beings,
    from all realms.
Yours is not the only realm for the Blessed Ones.
The Blessed Ones have all the outer worlds to concern their Beings.
The Holy Ones enter in and teach and offer knowledge and lessons.
Souls of Farside learn, acquire knowledge of Wisdom.
They are not content to always be in idleness.
That is earth, Soul.
There is for each being of Farside, a choice,
    but the Soul has blended with the Spirit
    and the Spirit would blend to Creator.

You could not walk, Souls, in a place of Archangels.
Your feet could not touch the Purity,
    they would shrivel and disappear,
    but the Blessed Ones would bow down
    and lift your wounded feet, and take you lower
    to where you could stand and heal your being.
And they would teach you to look ever upward unto Purity
    and know that Purity is an option for your being.
They would seek that you would only look
    to the spiritual side of your being.
They would ask that each day you have as your agenda
    the purpose of your goodness,
    that other men might see that goodness
    and know the beloved Creator.
They have no selfishness in their being.
They have only the Angels' countenance.
Behold, to lift thy being into the placement of Angels
    is to soar with the lark and ride the wind with the eagle,
    and sing as the nightingale.
And still you could reach beyond their being
    and find greater Purity in the Blessed Ones.
Enter in to the cathedral of the Holy Ones.
Enter in, Soul, with soft silence, with no words spoken,
    encircle thy being with Light of thy own goodness,
    and the Angels will attend thee,
    and all that has been brought low will be lifted up.
Do not fear, for you have heard the Angels sing
    and you have only to reach into your being
    to hear the song of the Angels.
You have only to know the Purity of their Being
    and the Love they bestow unto all mankind.
Attend the presence of Angels and know there is endeavour
    of great magnitude.
Enter in to the eternity of the Blessed Ones
    and know there is always a radiant motion.
A Soul may look and know where they are.
They do not have desks, they do not require desks,

but they do have records
and place in those records, much of earth, of Farside.
The smallest child may not cry without being heard.
If you know of a small child who has pain,
know the Blessed Ones are about the child.
They cannot remove that which has been placed in the space of a Soul,
but no being, man, woman or child
is left bereft of the Love of Angels.
Your Creator has witnessed that Love.
Your Creator has seen His band of mighty ones move forward
into negative energy.
They are familiar with all negativities.
They know the battles,
they have fought many battles in their Purity,
they have risen above all energies that have Negativity.
To see your own Soul is to see the reflection
of what they have witnessed and what they have saved.
Blessed humanity, look to the Angels.
Know their life breath is for you.

361 Blessed, all earth abounds with Souls on the Path to Truth.
Earth has energies of negativity seen from the fence of the Farside.
They thrive and multiply.
But there is also in vortexes of earth, golden Lights of Purity
that are being established for the new day.
Oh Souls, earth awaits the new day
when Negativity will be left behind and Souls will only seek
to gather Purity and Truth about their being,
and will know the Love of Creator within their being.
And Buddha will no longer reside to show men that which is Purity,
but will come in his own Being to earth with Jesu,
Mohammed and Krishna.
Souls of Purity throng behind and all four corners of earth
will raise their being to see who knocks on earth's door.
Souls, there are many truths on earth.
This is one.
All beings who bring forth Truth walk in pain's way to overcome.

They have reached acceptance in their being.
There are many messengers, Soul.
Messengers bring their Being to the space we are in,
    for only a few enter in to your earth space.
Many Souls in restless forms enter in to your earth space,
    many Souls intent on altering the desecrated place of their being
    seek to find that being
    and know not that the Soul has moved onward,
    for they are lost in the desolation.
They cannot look up,
    for they seek only that which has pained their being
    from where they have come.
Souls of Purity have no need to enter in to earth plane to speak to a Soul.
They transcendental travel within their minds
    and the mind is as the greatest computer.
It carries all knowledge, unlike the flesh that earth depends upon.
The mind on Farside is within the Aura.
It is not wrapped in flesh as the earth mind is.
It is not covered in bone as the earth mind is.
It is open to all.
There are no secrets in the mind of the Farside.
Earth has a term: "What you see is what you get".
Farside is what you see.
Each being has concern.
It rejoices in concern,
    it energizes self with concern for all beings.
Earth, could earth but see the Souls reaching outward,
    earth would turn to Purity in the twinkling of an eye.
But humanity is being tried and tested,
    not by Creator, but by the Essence,
    to move in the Path of earth's future,
    the redemption of Souls from transition.
How great thou art, humanity!
How awesome is thy being!
Do have awareness in thy being that thou and Creator are one.

362 Blessed, behold earth, behold Purity,
    behold the Path to earth; goodness.

Auld beauty is the most precious gem,
>   auld beauty in the most beloved child,
>   auld beauty in the most exquisite painting.
Auld beauty of earthly creation does not, in an iota,
>   contain the Holiness of the beloved Teacher of Love.
Soul, a child was born who radiated goodness
>   beyond conception of earthly mind.
The Being of this child was Holy.
The Soul had one purpose, to give.
The child was born to Mary, Blessed Virgin, Holy Mother.
The Soul was taken into the learning field of scholars
>   and taught by priests and held aloft in Purity and blest.
The Soul stepped with feet upon earth
>   and walked in His seventh month.
He felt the touch of Holiness within His Being,
>   He had awareness of a journey, of a purpose.
As a child, He played with children.
As a child, He threw the stone
>   and felt the pain in the being of another,
>   and He learned the purpose of His Being could contain no evil.
The Soul had hands, long and slender, that touched the parchment
>   of Holy men and read without knowing the words.
The Soul absorbed all things within His space.
He touched the hand of His beloved mother
>   and knew the pain she would bear.
The joy of life was within the fragment of His Being
>   that opened and blossomed and overwhelmed His humanity.
In the ninth year, the child had left humanity for Purity
>   and the child was given the protection of Angels about His Being,
>   as all Souls have the protection of the Blessed.
Soul, behold the orb of joy.
Sanctify the being of one unworthy and know the blessing of Holy,
>   and know that the Blessed child would touch and heal,
>   could be carried into the place of pain and know no pain,
>   for the child accepted that no pain was.
To enter in to the place of His purpose was to once again
>   relinquish the space of that Purity.
And in the garden of Gethsemane the Soul allowed self

to be totally human and gave up the shroud of Purity,
  and yet knew the pureness from which He came.
Beloved, behold the anticipation of all creation
  to be in the place of such beauty, to be within the awe of creation.
Souls, acceptance is the lesson of Jesu.

363 We are blessed among women.
We have been given the birthright of the Blessed Son.
Holy Holy Holy is the blessed Son of God.
Holy Holy Holy have we given of ourselves to be the dwelling place
  of the humanity of Jesu, my blessed Son.
And He grew and He was pleasing to behold.
He took the place of humility upon His Being.
He uttered words of pain, of joy, of Truth,
  and in a moment, at the age of six, the wonderment of His Being
  fell as a mantle about His shoulders
  and often in play, He would utter profound statements
  taken from the books on which He had not yet laid eyes.
He could repeat by rote the litany of the priests
  and in a day confounded the masters
  with words they themselves could not scope.
He taught the masters in prayer of the blessedness of Buddha.
He uttered words at sup with His father,
  and my beloved master, Joseph, would lift his eyes and shrug.
And in a day He wore Truth upon His Being
  and all who gathered to Him saw the child was not a child,
  but an Angel's countenance was upon His Being,
  and some scoffed, and He smiled.
And others heard and were embarrassed and many stood
  in great respect before this child who was not yet seven.
He had within His Soul the aloneness that is recognized from without
  and yet, as Soul, was drawn into His circle of Purity.
His voice was the Angel who dropped a pearl
  and words became droplets of Wisdom and Truth.
It was not done in any conceit, but in a voice
  that uplifted our Holy Father.

364 Soul, Soul, I AM, delight in I Am.
Mohammed, reach to Mohammed.
We delight in the space of Mohammed.
The blessedness comes into our entity and the Soul offers
    unto those who think themselves wise, Wisdom.
Soul, the blessed mountain of Mohammed is Sinai.
It is a surprise, is it not?
Know it is not a surprise.
The feet of Mohammed paced and paced and paced.
The anger of the sitar expressed notes and slicings of growth.
Mohammed climbed the mountain in the agony of His Soul.
He found Truth.
This, unlike the Soul, Christ, did not come in with gentleness.
He came forth frothing, extending his arm in wrath
    toward all his demons, and then the Soul found enlightenment.
It was brought in and the Soul prostrated self, three times,
    and could see into Purity.
The vision of all became clear and the Soul came down as Moses,
    and offered to men the poetry of life.

365 You have brought me low.
You have brought me low.
All earth is pain, all earth is agony!
All earth is tangled in the web of deceit and the earth binds draw tight
    to that which was Krishna.
And Krishna rose in his Being above the world and gazed down at man,
    and man in his iniquity felt the tears of Krishna wash.
And the land of Krishna held a great flood in that year,
    and Krishna lifted his Being unto Creator,
    and, still caught in the agony of his own Being, asked of Creator:
    "What may I do for my brothers?
    For my brothers cry in pain.
    How may I heal the blinded eye and the weeping sores?
    How may I feed the children?"
And behold, Creator saw in Krishna no evil.
All negativity had been dispersed from his Being,
    and the Soul was carried forth in the arms of the Holy Ones.

And the Soul received no death, but passed through the darkness
    and was manifested in the first life.
Bless all mankind to be as Krishna,
    for Krishna had known the agonies and the pain,
    and all agonies and pain were felt in his Being as his.
And in the day of lifting up He saw man in all his lifetimes,
    and He saw the beginning and He saw the end,
    and He wanted only to come down
        to minister unto those who had need.
And colours, the multitude of colours, were brought up.
And the Prism fell upon the people so that they looked up
    to see a vision of Krishna as though He were floating
    in the heavens, and the Soul was blessed.

366 Death, Soul? What death, Soul?
What death do you speak of?
There is no death.
There is abundant life.
Krishna had abundant goodness.
Krishna looked outward from his Being unto the world.
Krishna, in passing, did not enter in to pain.
His Purity had lifted him well above pain.
He had manifested self before leaving earth
    and no awareness of a pain can be in that state.
Souls, do not fear pain.
Glory in pain, for it allows the overcoming
    and the manifestation of humanity.
Linger momentarily in pain.
Many recognize pain without entering in, and overcome from that state.
So it was with Krishna, beloved, beloved humanity,
    uplifted in great Purity unto level seven.

367 Blessed Buddha.
Buddha!
All Farside has acceptance of Buddha.
All Farside sees equality of Buddha, Mohammed, Krishna and Christ.
Buddha himself has withheld his eyes from Purity
    wherein He knows He may walk.

The Soul has the Light of the Energy.
Buddha, upon earth, carries all the Purity of his Being within self.
He has the mark of Buddha.
He has the tears of Buddha and the joy of Buddha,
    and the acceptance of Buddha.
Buddha is earthbound and yet Souls may always speak to Buddha.
Buddha is without time and space within the Being of self.
The Energy of the Buddha man excels the Energy of mere mortal man.
To be in the presence of Buddha is to know Purity.
Buddha, yet in mortal state,
    has all the extensions of growth of mortal man,
    but also carries the vibrational level of Buddha.
He knows within the inner being of self
    the drive to be in the Holy state of Purity
    and the Soul will then be carried to the altar
    upon which the mortal life had been placed.
It is always a life of gift, of teaching, of perfection.

368 We have found our Souls in the space of the Holy one, Buddha.
We have chosen to remain in the presence of Buddha
    and we would speak of the revered personage of this person.
We would speak of the constant concern of the emissary of goodness,
    a being who looks only downward into earth plane,
    who has abundant goodness and Purity
    that would bring the being well past the space of Angels;
    and yet contends to be in the space of mediocrity,
    for we have not attained all the goodness we could.
We have given ourselves a time to be in the space of this Holiness.
We have held the reed and piped messages through the reed in sound,
    to China, to Japan, to Tibet, to the Americas, to the Islands.
We have brought our being into the space of the great continent
    and we have reached into the coldness,
    and it has not been a judgement that we have made.
But we are at the feet of the great Buddha
    and we gather the tears of the Buddha,
    and we know the tears come
    because of the ineptness of humanity
    to look beyond the pain of self.

Buddha has one purpose, to lift humanity and alleviate pain.
To see the two parts of being merge into one
    by the overconquering of negativity,
        for within your being are two truths, negativity and Truth.
Each is full and equal and each carries weight and the measure is the same.
Soul, the teaching of Buddha relinquishes negativity and awakens a Soul
    as though they have not seen the world before.
And the Soul participates in all that is in a day,
    and the Soul joys at the coming in and the going out.
And the Soul greets the sun in the morning
    and the moon in the evening,
    and the Soul feels a tug at the robe and reaches for the bread
    and lifts the Soul to a place at the table.
For, Soul, the Buddha is as the poorest man, equal unto.
The Soul shines forth and a Buddha addresses the Soul.
For Souls of earth, you are cloaked in a garb that has a single purpose,
    to fight negativity.
And we have chosen to gather the tears
    and anoint the head of the fallen with the tears.

369 Beloved, enter in to clarity, see the reflection of what will be.
Souls of earth, how blessed are they
    who have brought their Purities into your space,
    who have entered to teach unto mankind
        the purpose of their being; Jesu, Mohammed, Krishna, Buddha.
Souls of earth, the Four are united in the coming together of great Purity.
Souls, unto earth have they Entered In and given a vision,
    a vision of Purity, and man has selected from those Purities
        that which they would serve, that which they would hear,
        that which they would bow unto.
Souls of earth, the Purities are a blend of Oneness in their Beings
    for Creator.
The energies on the Farside teach to all the worlds of purities.
To earth was given the Truth.
Earth mankind, hear, rehear the instruction of the Great Ones
    who have given teachings, not that they might be remembered,
    but the Love of Creator might be known,
    that the profuse Energy that is available unto mankind

might be drawn unto one's being,
   that the Light may blossom forth in Purity
   unto one's brethren and mankind.
And, mankind, why have you divided yourselves into wars
   to denounce the very Love that was taught to your being?
Souls of earth, see the framework of earth, know the fragile network
   upon which your life depends.
Know that every effort needs to be extended
   that man might not destroy man.
Unto earth is an example being shown of how quickly
   you may eradicate life.
Souls of earth, how blessed is earth, how blessed is the being of man!
Might the fragmented part of your being turn to the Truth
   that has been set before you by the Blessed Four.
Oh, Souls, many have come before and many have followed after,
   but the Four have given without ego,
      until man distorted that which was.
Look over the fence, as we look over the fence to earth,
   and see there an extension of your being.
See there a Soul who has in their care, the same fragile earth
   that you have.
See there a Soul who extends his Love to family members,
   to comrades at arms.
Souls, the day of earth is becoming as night.
The shadow has a long fall
   and the need for the noon daylight to enter in,
      for the morning star to come forth is necessary
      if man would survive the catastrophe of self.
How magnanimous is man that he sees himself better than his brother.
How drawn up with pride is man that he carries himself
   taller than his brother.
You are fragile being.
Will all flow in the same waterway
   and be buffeted with the same winds
   and be tormented by the same source?
There is not a safe zone except upon the Mountaintop of Purity.
Souls of earth, we speak frankly that you might hear,
   for all worlds of the Farside

    look unto mankind for a purpose of Purity,
        and the din and clamour that lifts itself unto the ears of Wisdom
        defies that man is Holy.
Do not earth, speak of holiness.
Do not, Soul, surround thy being with goodness
    that will not reach beyond thy brethren,
    but look to the far hill, to the deep valley.
Look to the waterways and the byways and the crossroads,
    and know that all humanities meet in the same end
    at the Gateway unto Purity.
Souls of earth, you are Loved!
Souls of earth, recognize the Love of your being!
Know the energies that flow to you.
Accept the gift that is extended unto thy being
    and use thy Purity to reach out unto all men.
For your toxins, your poisons,
    your metal ships, cannot bring you peace,
    only in the space of Purity may peace be found.

370 Soul, draw thy being into the Eternal Flow.
Enter in, Soul.
Within the cascading of Energy, behold thy Creator.
Who hast used the word Emmanuel?
Behold Emmanuel!
Behold the Flow that is Creator, eternally cascading unto all beings.
Souls of earth, Souls of earth, repel the stench from thy being!
Know the dissidence of mankind.
Know the raucous intent of man upon man.
And then, Soul, acknowledge that in even the most raucous of men,
    the most defiled of men, is the Pathway unto Creator.
Emmanuel!
Emmanuel, the God in us that flows from the Crystal Cave,
    the Energy form that alters who thou art, if thou but enter in.
You are, Soul, Emmanuel.
Thou art treasured.
Thou art Loved.
Soul, thou hast one Creator for thy being.

There are creators beyond Creator,
>   but thy being is to find thyself within a Crystal Cave
>   where Energy alights upon Energy,
>   where all Lights fractal against each other
>   and become wondrous in beholding.

And the flow of that being is placed in a Path unto Thee.
Thou can reach to this awesome power.
Thy being can flow into the wonder of Purity, of Love.
Souls of earth, the commandments are to be risen above.
Souls, how could you not Love the Lord thy God,
>   the Creator of thy being, the Light, the radiant Energy
>   that is awash in thy space!

And, Soul, as Creator's child, as Creator's brother or sister,
>   how could you not treat all beings of earth with goodness.

Behold, overcome all negativity!
All negativity is in thy space.
Behold it is in thy space, but it is in thy space to elevate self above,
>   to recognize the paleness of negativity,
>   and know the greatness of the Energy of Creator.

Soul, you will be as buoyant as a seed in the wind.
Thou wilt know the treasures of travel into the Crystal Cave.
Soul, thou wilt meet Elijah.
Thou wilt meet Mohammed and Jesu and Krishna and Buddha.
Oh, Souls, know whom thou art.
Humanity, know whom thou art!
Reach above the paltry energy of negativity.
Reach above the weariness that gathers pain about thy being.
Know, Soul, rejoice.
Rejoice in the knowing that thou and Creator
>   are of the same Energy!

Thou and Creator are of the same Energy!
And the Flow enters over thy being and places wellness in thy space.
Soul, know you are lifted as a mother lifts a small child.
As Eli lifted the small child to Creator,
>   so art thou lifted by the Essence of thy being.

Place thy being gently in the space thou art in.
Deem to cast thy eye down on no man.

Behold, thou art Loved.
Look unto Creator and express unto Creator
   that which He has expressed unto thee.
Emmanuel! Emmanuel! Holy Holy Holy!

WITHIN THE SEVEN LEVELS

371 Soul, you have come for a teaching of seven
   and we, Buddha, have an offering.
Soul, all growth are seven.
All Energy levels are seven.
All initiates into the levels must obtain seven entrances in.
These entrances may be done within a single lifetime upon earth.
They may be done only to the Second Gateway at Farside,
   for the echo of Creator is the waiting upon the Blessed
   to come forth.
Within the level the Blessed have created our seven,
   for within their mighty wisdom, they have known
   that even within the densest pain are lesser pains,
   and so, all levels of Energy have growth attached to them.
From earth are seven in Truth, from Farside are seven in Purity.
Within Creator are seven in Love,
   within Godhead are seven within Knowing,
   unto the Great One will be told.

372 Michael will teach the entry into the sixth level of Purity.
Souls, all doors are open, there are no closed doors at level six.
All worlds are open unto thy being.
All creations emerge into thy vision.
All Creators speak to thy oneness.
Behold the entering in to creativity, to the value of the oasis
   of which you are the Light.
The oneness that is emerged from the darkness,
   has become translucent and clear
   and the Light of your being welcomes all worlds unto it.
The transformation is uplifting, the transformation
   is shedding all colours beneath the Platform of Angels.
The Prism becomes the Crystal Cave.

The Entering In becomes glorious and the being, thy being,
    looks upward to that which is beyond Creator.
And Creator embraces thy being with Love
    and the Angels welcome the student
    who has learned to discern the purities of being,
    and Souls are caught in the rays of Creator.
They are beams.
As dewdrops that soak the garden,
    so the rays of Creator enlighten the Soul.
And the Soul has a need to be drawn into that garden of Purity
    for in that garden of Purity
    are many Knowns that birth an unknown.
And, Souls, the vision of your being beholds Godhead
    as your vision beheld Creator at a distance,
    yet awareness was upon you.
Creator will gather your being and the Energy that flows unto thee
    will Light a passage beyond, for beyond Creator is Godhead,
    and Godhead is the gathering place of all Creators.
Man, in his infancy, is being taught creation.
Creation becomes creator, and Creator creates unto everlasting.
All creations do not stand motionless.
Many vibrate quickly and disperse their Energy back to Creator.
Souls of earth, the Energy of man is not so quickly dispersed.
The Energy of man is sanctified from the casting out.
Your being is gathered from the profoundness of Godhead.
It was in the beginning, Creator and Creator and Creator.
Unto the day, allow the knowledge therein,
    in the morrow new knowledge will enter.
But wisdom does not alter,
    wisdom allows in the Sacredness of Creator,
    and the thoughts of Creator are your wisdom.
And the wisdom is gathered as pearls by old Souls,
    and in the gathering of wisdom the Soul is as Creator,
    one with the Being of Creator.
And Creator stands at the Gateway unto Godhead,
    and the Gateway to Godhead opens
    to a violet disbursement of colour
    and the rays of that colour ream unto thy being.

And thy being is drawn unto the world beyond
    and is as a mist to the Soul at level six.
It is visible.
It is visible to the being and yet it holds mystery.
It gathers a need to know and Creator welcomes the Soul forth
    unto the second elevation of being.

373 Soul of earth, Michael will teach the way of Energy.
The seed of Purity that you are has been planted
    and grows upon earth.
It is transplanted many times by the Essence of the Soul.
The Register contains all efforts of growth, and the Pathway
    carries the Soul to age as the grey haired earthling.
The aged Soul has assumed,
    nay, has become, the full flowered plant of Purity.
Bud has ceased to be and Raiment has begun,
    Raiment, Purity's pure, awesome Flow
    and then the being beholds the vision of sixth level.
Know the vision is not clear.
You see as an earth Soul looking off into the sea
    beholds an island far off.
Soul, the Essence beholds the Purity of six.
That Purity filters through,
    and those at level five feel the vibration of that Purity,
    and they desire them to move forward,
    to be in the complete placement of Energy.
Your earth has religions and in those religions there are monks and nuns
    and they would be in that pure space of what they deem religion,
    segregated by their Purity.
Soul, six is to five as Soul would deem to reach that pure state,
    to be with the Energy Creator.
It is a delight!
No earthling, no earthling could in their mind conceive such warmth,
    such total giving, such total awareness, such total calm, Truth.
You could not take an iota of your own Purity, in any form you perceive,
    and find a fragment of that awesome Purity.
And so we would strive in worthiness to be in that place of Purity.

Even at six the avenue is not crowded.
Many of your earth Saints walk in these places,
    many Souls that abide upon earth.
The Buddha has the giving that is welcomed into that space.
This is not a tight space.
It has regions upon regions upon regions.
The Register is there also, and learning is constant,
    and Souls make choice, not negative and positive.
There is no negative, but choice of how and where and when.
The Blessed Angels reach down and touch a being
    with the mere finger of Purity or the swoosh of wing
        that carries the Balm of Gilead.
Bless the place you are in that allows you the most minute vision
    of this state of Purity.
And then there is the Sacred, the Holy of Holy.
It is not to guard this space that the Blessed Angels waver their being
    because no impurity could dwell therein.
It is to welcome Souls into the total oneness of the Crystal Cave,
    the reflection of all Purity.
Can you grasp the brilliance of that spacelessness,
    the doorway where all creation is created with a hand of Purity!
Truth and Love reach in infinite tenderness outward to all creation,
    and know the perfectness of what is created,
    and sees the defilement of that creation.
Souls, seven is within the seventh.
And the joining of Three[73] is at the apex of seven
    who weep tears at the struggling seeds of Purity,
    and reach in the generous Flow of Love
        to lift a Soul and place that Purity upon the wave of path.
Souls, behold, your existence is a feeble beginning
    and the Angels rejoice at beginnings.
The guides hold the Soul in care and tend the wayward step
    and call to the Soul: "Oh Soul, seek ye a different step!".
But even the Angels who cast their glance ever earthward
    have the desire to be united to the Purity of Creator.
Behold, it is done.

---

73 joining of Three - Krishna, Jesu, Mohammed. Buddha chooses to remain at level five.

374 Soul, we are not human.
Soul, earth has its own vision of the five levels of consciousness.
There is earth consciousness.
There is the consciousness of transition.
There is the consciousness of one to five.
There is the consciousness of six.
There is the awareness of total Energy.
Five levels of consciousness brings a Soul into the awareness
    of all these perimeters, but all Souls may not enter in.
But they have brought into their being,
    the wisdom to see the conscious level.
Souls of earth, there are no deities on the Farside
    as earth Souls would speak of deities,
    but there are masters of great Purity.
We have entered in to six.
They are in level six: mother of our Teacher, Jesu,
    Quan Yin, being of great blessedness,
    the Soul of Genevieve, the Soul of Philadelphia.
But, Soul, these are few.
There are abundant Souls who gather in goodness to look down to earth
    and offer teachings and guidance as the drop of the pearl,
    or the blessed bud of the lotus.
Souls who have the level of Archangel have, in Truth,
    the total blessedness of the fifth level
    and they see into the Purity as the web.
It has flow, it is a beginning and an outward thrust into many worlds
    and the great purities are tethered by the weave of perfection
    and all goodness carries the consciousness of that Purity.
It is, Soul, complicated beyond your mind's conception.
As a filament carries upon its space information,
    so the weaves of consciousness are gathered
    into total blessedness and reaches unto Creator.
Lift up your voice and sing and allow the tone of that singing
    to rebound into the space of Purity.
Blessed be the consciousness, for in the conscious level of earth,
    a Soul who has taken themselves into a higher level
    may be transported into the space that we are.

And all that is to be seen is opened and no longer carried
    as a complication, but only as a net of perfection.
Souls, seek the inward eye and know as you allow the space of your being,
    you will find the transporting of your awareness into the Flow,
    that will take you on a journey beyond,
    and you will see below the timelessness of earth,
    and all that is earth will be shown unto you,
    as Paul looked down from his high place
    and saw upon earth the pain of its bleeding time.
For in rebirth, is not a flow necessary!
Bestow on these beings the blessedness of thy Purity
    and allow all within the space of this room of earth,
    a consciousness that will lift them
    from the casualness of mankind into the realm of perfection.

375 Soul, there is a Holy Realm beyond Farside.
It is at the edge of level seven.
It is spontaneous, it is joyful, it is echoing and echoing and echoing.
It is abundantly blessed.
Where we are, we feel the blessedness of this space.
We are aware, in our being, this is not Creator.
We understand this is a Holy space.
We understand that the beings do not require the eye of understanding.
They do not enter in to any space of negativity.
They have only a look upward into the space of Holy.
They have a countenance we have not seen,
    but we have been guided to it.
We have entered in to the sanctity of the inner chambers
    of the dimension, and dimension it is, Soul.
It carries large cymbals, it carries loud beating of Energy.
Your beings can only embrace the outer perimeters.
Our beings laud the sound of joyfulness.
Our being dances to the sound of the strumming,
    our Soul selves which have been entered in
    to the space of earth that has known the negativity.
To remember the negativity and to be in the sound of this space
    leaves you with one desire, to draw the negativity
    into the space of such Purity, to heal that which is broken.

It is the lost chord.
It is the perfect, it is the sheer adoration of Creator.
Earth has guides.
Guides have honourable intent to space the walk of humanity
    that the foot may not enter the severed space in the Path.
These Souls have risen in their beings to the space of high placement.
They reside in the space of level six.
They are angel.
They have become angel.
You do not know you are scholar until you absorb knowledge.
These Souls have not known they were Angel until they became pure.
So sits an Angel in Purity, in goodness, in mercy,
    but the divine ones, the Holy Holy Holy, are with Creator.
They are His legion, they are the known of His unknown.
They are the perfection of the Being of Creator that you may see,
    that you may speak to, but only may you speak to those
    with a downward look.
The divinity reaches ever upward unto Creator.

ARRIVAL

376 Blessed Holy Holy beings,
    blessed beings found in the Path of earth will vibrate their Energy,
    and see without fear the place that earth eyes cannot see.
They will have become pure, and yet remain upon planet earth.
Their beings will teach mankind of spirituality
    with a message that will be given in the seven Keys.
The Souls will denounce all negativity,
    and earth will rise up after a deluge of negativity
    and seek no more the path, and put from them the negativity,
    and create a boundary where earth will dwell in total peace.
Within this time will be one thousand earth years.
Souls of earth will be preparing their beings
    for the final battle of negativity.
They will reach into the depths of travail
    and release Souls from their pain.
The Purity of these beings will draw a canopy round about them,
    and they will not waver, even in the depth of suffering.

And the Holy beings who have been caught in self incrimination
    because of lost Purity, will be able to look
    upon the blessed beings and mirror themselves,
    and find an avenue through which they may,
    once again, seek the Light of Purity.
The Souls of Purity will advance from all levels,
    from level to level to level to level, and will create
    a Flow of Purity through which Souls may reflect
    that which is pure in their own beings
    and let the pain that has gathered about them
    unshroud from their beings.
And they will be lifted in many, many, many
    and all creation will observe that which is done,
    and the Angels will sing: *Hosanna from the Highest"*
    and Creator will weep with joy at the comings of the pure.
Behold, blessed earth, how great are thy works!
How great is thy gift!

377 Rancid, offensive has the taste become, and the Souls of earth
    have returned many times into the lives of their pathos.
They have lingered in pain for eons.
And the hallowed Circle of Saints of which we are a part
    have beseeched unto Creator:
    "Bow Thou down unto Thy children.
    See the seed of Thy being tormented.
    See the purpose for which they have come,
        and see the agony which they cause!"
And Creator issued forth, unto Negativity, seven breaths,
    but the Keys must be held and unlocked by earth.
The first breath was the hallowed stairway of Angels
    and the Key to earth to continue the Flow.
The second is the releasing of all energies focussed to earth,
    that they may be centred upon the Angels Flow.
All else will writhe without the care of the positive Energy.
The third is the lesson of vibration, the power to alter earth beings
    that they may rise at will above the place they are.
The fragment of their beings will have no purpose,
    for in a moment will their beings be altered

unto a new being that will enter in to the Flow,
   and find themselves in the downward spiral,
   and gather unto them the Sacred of Creator.
The fourth Key is the armour you will wear.
It is a defence against the negativity that torments these Souls.
It is, Soul, an avenue, a port, into the Essence of thy being,
   to bathe thyself in the Holy Light of ever and ever.
And your being will illuminate,
   and beings of other worlds you will know.
They will be there to uplift all in a Flow of goodness.
The fifth is the vortex, the entering in, the Pathway.
Few have found the vortex, it has only a Pathway of Purity.
You behold Purity, and you will see the vibrations
   into which you must go.
And the sadness and the anger and the depleting energy
   will bombard thy Soul, and only those who protect their beings,
   will be in the handiwork of redemption.
The sixth Key to earth is water, for without water earth will not be.
All Souls brought forth will reside within the boundaries of earth
   for a thousand years before they can enter in
   to the Hallowed Halls.
To have been in the place of agony without the comfort,
   the Souls will need to gather, once again, their blessedness.
Soul, upon earth there is no coincidence.
All that have come will be in the nurturing time of the Blessed Ones,
   all will sustain and aid in the gathering of their Purity.
They have been in the depths of agony, and your goodness and Truth
   will cause an avenue, for their beings will not have fully recovered.
It is for this that the gathering is.
The seventh Key is the Entering In to earth of the Four Holy.
It is the presence of the Four Holy upon the face of earth
   that will minister unto the Souls you have redeemed.
And many will come from distant worlds,
   for earth, in that day, will be crowded,
   for many there will be who need to reside
   in growing goodness.
Mohammed, Krishna, Buddha, Jesu,

all forming a circle with the Blessed Ones,
    ministering unto earth the Sacrament of Eternal life.
Holy Holy Holy!

378 Humble thyself to no man, bow thou down to no being.
Seek that which is truthful,
    but do not hold the nose from that which is impure,
    but beckon it forth into thy space of Purity.
Thy being is beheld by their being.
Light, Soul, is within thy being in Purity, radiance.
And behold, it is not forgiveness
    but the acceptance of Light into the being.
We cry to those in the nether lands, to the levels below:
    "Do not ask forgiveness.
    Do not seek to forgive thyself.
    Search for the Light!
    See the Light within thy being!
    Recognize thyself as Holy that others
        might see the glow within thy being."
But they have turned their eyes away from Light.
They cast their eyes earthward and they walk ever in pain.
Beings of earth, vibrational beings,
    when your glow of radiance on earth equals the glow of ours,
    you may be seen by those Souls in their place of pain.
You may enter therein and call Souls from the abyss,
    but mankind sees not the Souls in plight upon his own planet.
The skies flood the land and beings cry:
    "Human, brother, where art thou?"
And man attends to man.
Souls, you have great Purity, your being is glorious
    in its state of Essence.
Behold how great thou art,
    and see self as a being from another planet, not of earth.
Souls, you are of Farside, you have become aware of Purity.
It is not lesser or greater, it is acceptance.
Reach out to the Light that glorifies your being
    and lose the worldly shroud, for the cavity holds the power.

Holy Holy Holy

The shell is but shell, but the vibration of the cavity
    is the power of your being.
It enters in and lifts up, it reaches to the depth of oceans
    and takes itself to the highest sky.
Being of earth, breathe the breath of Holy Holy Holy,
    for in that breath there is life everlasting.

CHAPTER 5
The Bringing Forth of Purity

WHO WILL BE FIRST?
379 Students, before you are the complexities of the universe.

Sevens are situations, are places.

Sevens are grouped within Quar.

A Quar is the measurement of seven.

Each seven has a purpose, the purpose for each is T.

All energies are triad, all energies that have a single purpose,
    to reunite unto the circle of beginning.

The circle is endless for as one closes, one opens.

A Quar is closed.

A Quar is opened.

Soul, all creation is created.

Your creation is created by your Creator.

Your Creator is Truth, Purity and Love.

Truth, can you bear it, is negativity.

It is a component of negativity and therefore is an Energy
    at the head of every triad.

It compels the triad to spew forth.

Creator spewed forth Farside.

Godhead spewed forth to Third Gateway.

And what is Godhead?

Godhead is Wisdom, which is the full attainment of Truth.

Godhead is Holy unto Holy, which is the full attainment of Love.

Godhead is Knowns; Triad of Godhead.

The Great One spewed forth the Third Gateway
    from whence Godhead came.

Godhead shared that which was in the space
    of the Great One.

Creator that you know came from the space of Godhead.
Your insignificant world, is treasured by Godhead,
    by the Great One, above all other worlds.
For the inhabitants of that land came forth.
They went forth into an unknown land
    to draw forth a brother of their master.
And the master bowed unto them and said:
    "You do not be required to go forward."
But they spake unto their master and said:
    "We shall go forth in Thy name."
And Godhead shook loudly His Being
    for that which had been done from His creation,
    and the resounding echo was felt in all the worlds,
    and they knew the fragileness of their being.
And He spoke forth:
    "From this time there will be a ceasing of moving out,
        and all energies will now enter in."
And so it has come to be and we await the coming in.
It is, Soul, why you gather.

380 And so the wind blows forth,
    and from where has the wind come?
Earth has always sought to see the wind.
Souls of earth, behold, the wind is as Godhead.
Who has seen Godhead?
Souls of the Farside have not seen Godhead.
From great places, from mountaintops, the reflection is felt by motion.
Wind is motion,
Godhead is motion.
All creation implodes.
Implodes!
"Oh, delight, delight my being, that I may be in the space of Creator,
    for Creator knows of Godhead."
"Creator, see Thou this fragment of ion unto ion,
    and bless Thou my state of being,
    that I may enter in to the Eternal Flow
    that carries to Creator and to Godhead!"
Who on earth does not delight in mystery?

Farside delights in mystery, Farside anticipates creation.
"Oh, my Soul, rejoice ever in creativity,
  rejoice ever in the knowledge of your earth being."
Lift your eye and see beyond the earth being
  and know that your mortal self is but a twinkling of the eye,
    a vibration of being.
Who has cast the spell on thee?
Soul, there is no great being who moves the participants,
  there is only choice.
The excellence of choice!
Souls of earth, ponder well on that which you do,
  and see in each being a reflection of thine own at a former time.
And know that their pain has been your pain,
  and their tears have been your tears,
  and their anger and avarice and greed have been yours,
  and the bounty of your Love extends outwards toward them.
For in the extension of self to overcome negativity is the giant step
  toward Creator and Godhead.
Souls of earth, bow thou down to no man,
  for in man is the mirror of self.
But look with the eye into the Purity of Naught
  and travel through the vortex to the space of IS.
Holy Soul, beatitudes of Truth,
  here in thy heart, blessed, blessed are they.
Know the blessedness of giving.
The reflection of Godhead is Creator.
The reflection of mankind is Creator.
Be thou as Creator!

381 Souls of earth, humanity, how great art thou,
  for thy being is purified through the pale of pain
  and drawn through fear and doubt.
And, Souls of earth, you have redemption in thy possibility,
  you have the power to behold the Blessed Ones.
The Angels reached to their Brothers,
  in supplication they draw nigh unto them.
They place life about their Beings but they cannot be heard.
The Souls are great.

These Beings are gigantic in the possibility of whom thou art.
Their feet would stand at the foot of thy mountain
    and their head would reach the tallest,
    for they have absorbed the pain.
And, Souls, you are the redemption.
Your negativity is not for you.
It is to be overcome.
And the eye of clarity will be drawn from the heart to the Soul,
    and your being knows that for which you have come.
All beings know, but in the Spirit.
And many earth beings
    have had a glimpse of the netherland,
    of the place of salvation to be.
Souls, to reach unto the placement of the Blessed Ones
    is to follow the path of negativity,
    and rise above that path unto the mountaintop,
    and reach the level of five.
And then your being will find the Purity that will protect itself
    from the entering in to transition,
    which is the place of great pain,
    which is the place where negativity mirrors itself.
And, Soul, the Blessed Ones have mirrored their Beings,
    and see the contamination of their Angelic self,
    and they can not place their Beings unto Creator.
But, Soul, you have been through the pain of negativity.
You have overcome the pain of negativity
    and you have learned to release it from your being.
And so you may teach these Souls
    of vibration they have forgotten to see.
Behold, Blessed Beings, all humanity is the Path to thy return.

382 Soul! Soul, behold!
Behold the Entering In.
Behold that which is of Creator.
Behold paradise.
Behold the second Entering In of mankind, of all worlds, of all beings.
Souls of earth, do not tread timidly into the new day.

Open the door and vision that which will be.
Know thy being aside Creator, pure unto Love.
Know thy being swelling, swelling with the knowledge of a new day.
Behold, thou wilt be there.
Behold, thou wilt be there!
Behold, as the lion and the lamb walk together into the new day,
    thou wilt be there.
Behold Creator's Paradise, Love;
    Godhead, the Place.
Oh, Soul, all remembrance of pain is passed away,
    all connections to pain are passed away.
The Souls pass through a Prism beyond earth contemplation
    and the wash of that Prism erases from their beings
    all fragments of energy pain,
    for Farside carries pain for others.
It does not acknowledge pain for self, but the tears flow,
    the Angels' tears flow, the Creator's Tears,
    at the negativeness of creation.
Behold a new day!
Behold the vision that carries self into a new count, new growth.
Creator will take thee unto thy brothers
    and thy beings will see Godhead
    and other creations beyond the Creator's Field of Energy.
How blessed is that Field?
Soul, earth is infinitesimal in its being.
Its Soul is so small that it does not exist,
    for how can it be seen by Souls
    who have placed themselves under the arms of Holiness?
Only, Soul, the pain is vibrated forth
    and the tears come to wash the pain away,
    and when the Second Gateway opens
    there is no recognition of pain.
There is no fragment in the beings of even the Holy Holy Holy.
The Angels will pass through unto a new day
    and earth will implode into itself,
    and humanity will have risen with the Blessed Ones
    into the state of Purity.

Souls, do not fear in any day!
Thy beings have the Eye of Creator over thee,
    the Blessed Angels to watch over thy being.
Do not hover in sadness,
    do not hover in pain,
    but know only the passing through of joy.
For unto thee is given the keys to the kingdom,
    unto thee, earth, is given the Second Gateway.
First to pass through is mankind.

383 Souls of earth, beloved of Creator, lift your beings.
Ride high with the Energy of your Creator.
All sunshine, all moon and stars, all heavens of earth
    are glimmers of the radiance you will behold.
My dear children, who has seen the pristine walkway before you?
Who has seen the candle lit way?
Who has risen above the pain of their day to enter
    in to the joy of their being?
Souls of earth, the clouds are of the road.
Souls of earth, know behind the cloud
    the glory of the sun always shines.
It beams for earth Souls.
Did not the Creator put it in motion,
    as the moon was set in motion,
    as all stars and extensions of Light were set in motion.
Soul, as the cloud covers your eye on the day of pain,
    know that beyond the pain Creator IS!
The Radiance of Creator extends unto you.
The pain is a part of your earth; it is your purpose, Souls, in coming.
All Farside extend themselves in care outward unto earth,
    for have you not, earth, given the greatest gift to all creation!
Have you not entered in to a pact with your Creator!
Is the captain of your mighty army not steadfast in his purpose!
How radiant you are in your purpose!
Do not be downtrodden, for behold the mightiest of Farside
    will not be brought to the Second Gateway
    as quickly as earth Souls.

How precious is the knowledge that carries you into the pain of growing.
Do not see the face of the cloud
> without knowing the glory behind the cloud.

Do not see the face of pain
> without knowing the Radiance of Creator
> and the gift you have brought yourself to earth to bear.

Blessed humanity, Redeemer has come unto thee.
Hear what Love offers.
Hold the precious gift you have enveloped in your being as sacred
> and know it is extended unto your Creator.

Unto humanity may all blessings fall.
Unto humanity will the Second Gateway open.
Blessed children, do not despair, do not be brought down,
> for the fold of the Farside holds you close in their being
> and all are Loved.

Blessed, blessed humanity.

ONENESS IN ALL CREATION
384 Know Truth.
The Energy of the Path is Creator of all that is.
In the station of the Farside is a humble walk
> that is respective of the great Handiwork
> this creation of countless eons has before and after it.

Join with us of the Farside in the respect of all creation.
Unite with a single purpose to be in all creation.
Creator has a blend[74].
Why does the human Soul seek when in negative
> to separate the blend?

All is perfection.
Simple to rise above a toad,
> the toad has an ownership before your own!

Simple to debark a tree that gives the goodness of all it is.
Simple to take the humanity of life and fling it casually into the Void.
Restrain the negative, insight Creator.
See the works that are in the most minutely connected ion
> and be reverent in your action toward that jot.

---
74 Creator has a blend - the Weave of creation in Oneness.

Into the beauty of what you see is the counterpane of defects.
Do not draw defects to your space, keep perfection only.

385 Breathe!
Breathe and know that the breath of earth
    is seen as one, that all breath is gathered to one.
The blend of the human and the whale and the tiger and the single bee
    is gathered as breath unto Creator,
        and the holiness of that breath is revered by Blessed Angels
    who gather the Purity and waft to the many worlds beyond.
Behold, you are Soul, accept the wholeness of Soul.
It is as breath, a part of whole: Essence, Spirit, Soul,
    all fragmented parts of the whole,
    all containing goodness of the whole.
But the last fragment is caught in a world of negativity
    and is subject to that negativity.
It is bombarded by the force of Negativity
    and the Spirit, the Spirit of the Soul,
    draws the Energy of goodness
    and declares against the negative force
    and the Soul grows.
The Soul is a lesson.
You are flesh and blood, you are vulnerable.
You are also Soul.
Your Energy is felt, even by Negativity itself,
    and it does battle with the Purity of who you are.
Souls, gather the goodness of creation.
Cast loving glances at thy brother whose breath is as your own.
When a Soul has fallen, it is your breath that has been taken.
Breathe life to that Soul.
When starvation is upon the face of the land,
    know that it is your breath that is affected.
It is the negativity bombarding the Soul that will say:
    "Do not look, shield the eye
        that you may not take negativity into your being."
Your Purity casts negativity far from you.
"*Be gone!*" and negativity must go.

The lesson is in creation.
All creation is but one creation that is continually in the Flow
    and each individual life upon the earth is in the Flow.
And growth is precious and is carried by the Soul,
    not as a separate being from the Spirit,
    but as a connected fragment that flows
    into the positive of that Energy.
And the Spirit, in like, flows into the Essence of your true being
    which has no impurity,
    but has gathered unto itself the growth of Purity
    that enables only Love to be caught within the eye.
See with the eye that your Essence, the very being of who you are,
    is caught with all other breaths
    into the Flow upward to Creator.
Breath has form in many ways.
Worlds upon worlds are inhabited with breaths of many forms.
The Blessed Angels are breaths of a form.
They were first to be cast out
    and gathered about the goodness of creation,
    the centre of which is the Light,
    the Prism that emanates all Purity.
And some few Souls of earth have gathered unto themselves
    such goodness that they have been welcomed into
    the upper regions of goodness
    and transformed in a twinkling by the Purity that they are.
Transformation of a Soul is done in a minute second
    or carried in a stumbling block of pain.
The beloved is held in a cradle of care as a mother
    would hold a beloved child
    and all the heavens sob for the Soul who would not accept.
And Souls of earth in goodness reach out
    to carry the Soul forward into yet another flow,
    for the Soul can be caught in the carrying
    of evil memory of sadness beyond which a Soul cannot bear.
Souls of earth, maintain Purity.
Beloved, earth itself is beloved.
All creatures and beings and extensions of earth are beloved.

Allow the Blessed Angels to gather themselves about you
    and know goodness of their being
    will warm those Souls
    and carry you through the pain that you will have to bear.
Souls of earth, expand the vision beyond your being
    into the walk of all humanity.
See each being as a part of the whole.
Peace, peace, peace.

386 Godhead, paradise, eden of creation.
Eden of creation!
Souls of earth, earth timing is supreme,
    for every jot and tittle is in place.
Omen has been given.
The vision is clear, the way is made whole.
Come thou, earth, enter thou into the Pathway,
    struggle no more in iniquity.
Don not the dress of avarice, of greed,
    form your being together as oneness.
Know the Oneness of creation is the coming unto Godhead,
    to reach beyond Creator in a manifestation of Creator,
    to know thy garment to be Light, to know thy aura,
    to have endured all things, and surmounted all paths,
    and entered in to the Path of wellness, of oneness,
    that thou might, earth, do that which thou hast offered
    unto Creator.
The doorway has been ajar
    and a new heaven and a new earth is before thy being.
A new heaven and a new earth!
Earth, all that has been to thy day will be altered, and behold,
    those on the Farside await thy being.
All earth is anticipated, will be welcomed in,
    for what joy awaits the many beings on the Farside,
    to enter in to the new heaven, the Second Gateway,
    the Path unto Creator, beyond Creator.
Souls of earth, alight thy countenance.
Seek to see only that which will uplift thy Soul.

Do not carry drudgery about thy being.
Soul, thou art magnificent in the Eye of thy Creator,
   and the pattern of thy being is Prism of Purity.
Soul, thy thread is woven into the Pattern of Creator.
Have you not seen the cloth of many colours?
Did not the Blessed Joseph have it placed about his shoulders!
Soul, rejoice in the Oneness of creation that wells and wells
   because of earth's goodness.

387 Beloved, come thou down, Elijah, unto my people.
Unto the twelve tribes of Judah is the connection
   to the Souls caught in transition.
The tribes are tethered to the Holy Holy Holy
   to whom earth cries and sobs in great tears,
   that they may once again be brought forth
   unto the Holy mountain of Sinai
   from whence they entered in to the covenant.
Blessed Holy beings entered in to earth, the first
   with the intent of the gathering.
From that day unto your day the Souls have struggled
   with a need of Purity, for only in such Purity
   may the Holy ones be brought down to the gates
   and raise forth from your Purity
   and lift the Souls unto the waiting arms of Purity.
Behold Flow of great Purity that reaches unto Creator
   who weeps for the oneness of His creation.
Oh blessed Saints, humanity endeavours to flow in oneness and Purity.
The tribes will be gathered and Souls will, once again,
   see our being at the mountaintop.
Elijah, the Holy Babe presented to men to teach Love
   that man might recognize the need of Purity.
The Holy Christ, Jesu, taught to the Jews, to Judah.
For in the hearing, Judah, lose your humanity and gather unto you Purity,
   that your Creator may be blessed in your Purity
   by the raising of those who are caught
   in the negativity of their being.
Creator, unto Thee are the twelve tribes gathered

    that all creation may be found as one,
    that all Energy may form a pureness,
    and the struggle of negativity cease and become not.
Profound beings of earth, thou art mighty in the sight of thy Lord.
Thou art of the tribes.

388 It is a joy, Soul, we have remembered.
We of the Farside have instant recall of earth lives,
    unlike humanity, who must reach into Purity
    to find the remembrance of Farside.
We have the knowledge of all of our lives about our beings.
Often when an earth being suspends a fork of food thus,
    the memory is there of my mother
    placing such a fork before me.
Soul, all our beings are enhanced
    by the opportunity to visualize earth Souls.
Humanity, you are not foreign to us, you are our beings.
We have in our beings the energized memory of play and work,
    of loved ones.
Soul, we have, in our beings, the runny nose and the ear wax,
    and the sight to open the eyes at dawn
    and see the light of your sun pouring in upon our bed,
    of the sound of the house,
    of the boards that creak in the night
    and the way the wallpaper did not quite match.
Soul, we are at varying levels of Purity,
    but all our beings reach unto earth in oneness.
We know, earth, why you are there.
We know the tents of the desert,
    we know the ice homes of the frozen north
    and the desolate energies caught in the mirage
    of what seems to be real.
We remember keenly the slap of the mosquito
    and the horse fly buzzing about the animals.
Our vision sees clearly the small moments of earth.
Our vision sees clearly the twelve hundreds as beginning
    to our particular existence.
Soul, we have wandered in the foothills of Italy,

we have taken our being into the great white hills
of the icy northern island.
We have a reason for our telling.
It is to recognize that the only important memory
is the good memory.
Do you see, Soul, that you might recount the purities of your being
that you might acknowledge the goodness of others.
Look at the giant oak that has spent years on earth,
sending forth seed after seed after seed,
and know that humanity is like the great oak,
sending forth seed after seed after seed.
Much of the seed will pass and rot, and be taken back
to the limbs of the tree, and be reborn as seed once again.
Some seed will take root in Purity and grow into old age,
and then rot and return into the limbs of the mother tree.
Souls of earth, humanity is like the great oak.
All is a repetition of all.
There is a Oneness in all creation.
Bring your being to that place of oneness and know
that all earth energies come from the same mighty oak,
and you are reborn for the same purpose;
to grow in your being, or wither and die and be reborn again.
So be it.

389 Souls of earth, the Flow of Energy,
the key lost to the Souls in transition.
Earth beings, the battle defeating negativity
has always been in your creation.
In your creation!
Souls who lost in the great battle, who fed into the Negativity
and entered in to earth form
and were carried to their mind in negativity,
are Beings of such high stature
that the beings of earth would be dwarfed by them.
Purity!
They were one with Creator, they were the circle of Purity
about beloved Creator.
They were defense, and Purity became,

  and Souls of earth are in the lesson of Purity
  that they may create the Flow
  unto the place of lower regions.
For Souls see themselves cast down in pain,
  and fear to look at the Light,
  fear to acknowledge the blessedness
  that is ever round about them.
Their Radiance has faltered and they are anguished,
  for in their space they are tormented.
They have accepted space for spaceless,
  negativity for positive, time for Timeless,
  and because of the pain in their beings
  they are caught in ever repetitive persecutions of self.
Behold, the time of Gathering is nigh.
The Souls of earth and the great circle are brought to one place,
  a new vibration of being.
Not a trembling vibration as the Souls of past have known,
  but a positive Energy that sees only goodness,
  that sees only Purity.
Beloved orb of earth, all is.
Angels weep and the tears will cease
  when the Flow has been connected downward
  into the hallowed chamber of persecution of self.
Unto all will the Blessed forms enter in,
  unto all will the Radiance of your vibration be seen.
You stand at the portal and will gather to your being,
  Souls in continuous Flow of Energy.
Earth, be not cast down, be not discouraged,
  you have found favour in the sight of your Lord.
Your Lord is your Creator, and oneness is the purpose
  for which you have been cast out.

390 Earth, hear that which would be said unto thee.
Creator has a sense of humour.
Creator has profound generosity.
Creator has overwhelming Love, cascading outward.
Creator has placed no expectations!

It is only the giving, the benevolent giving,
    beatitude of oneness, that dwells within Creator.
It is, Soul, all casting out that has expectation
    because of the Flow of Purity toward the beings.
The desire within the form of Essence is to reunite the Oneness
    from which all life was formed.
The magnificent throe is to give opportunity of greatness
    a challenge in the very throwing forth of seed.
Grow, awesome seed!
And in the growth of that seed you may be as Creator,
    one fragment brought into the meld of perfection.
And the fragment, in being cast,
    felt the desolation in being parted,
    and looked to the Light from which it came
    and desired to cleave unto the Light.
But the seed had to grow and was fraught with adversity,
    for all in the space was not perfection.
And so the seed drew strength from the Giver of Light
    and nurtured and grew and, in growing,
    acquired wisdom that could discern the need
    to flow upward to Purity.
Souls of earth, redeem thyself,
    for as the seed pod has a covering,
    cast the covering away from thy being.
It is mere flesh and bone.
The Soul will gather itself unto the fragment of Spirit,
    and the Spirit will cleave unto the fragment of Essence,
    and the Essence will flow to the ultimate Creator,
    and Creator will gift Godhead.

391 Creator, giver of all that is, Being of Entirety.
Soul, you cannot behold that which is Creator
    without having reached total acceptance.
In total acceptance is the ability to behold the Hem of Creator,
    is the ability to withdraw the last bondage to Negativity.
Creator, whom we have seen not, yet whom we know,

Creator who touches our being
and issues forth Love overflowing,
unto Creator we open the passage,
unto Creator we accept the way.
Unto Creator we offer all, and yet we may not enter in
to the sanctity of Sacredness, Godhead.
Godhead, we reach unto Thee, the place of omnipotence,
the place of oneness.
From the spaces beyond beyond, to the right and the left,
to the north and the west, to the south and the east,
to the Souls tethered in knowledge,
there is no passageway forth unto Godhead,
only is the passageway forth from humanity.
Only can the entering in come when Souls accept
that which is and that which shall be,
and the great devotion that extended itself unto Creator.
And Creator will hear the knock on the door
and the Gateway will open to the new day,
and Souls will see that which is beyond the realms they are in.
And they will look unto humanity and say :
"Move forward to your place of rightness, move onward!
You have done well."
And the Entering In will echo forth
and all the worlds will rally themselves and gather
and the entering forth will become
and the Angels will glory in that day.
And as in the time of Noah, so shall all life forms come through
and know not what they shall meet,
except that it shall be Purity.
For in the tomes are written: "The time of Entering In shall come."
And as with the entering in to transition,
so shall it be in that day that Noah and Mary, and
Mohammed and Krishna and Jesu
will be shouldered with Buddha,
and the great worlds will expand to a new vista,
and the vista will contain no negativity.

And the Gateway will close and Negativity will be set free[75]
    from the Cleansing River, and none shall be found in its way.

392 Souls of earth, humanity,
    enter in to the fellowship of mankind.
The connection of earth beings is all encircling.
There is, Soul, no Oneness without the circle of vibration.
Behold, the text of creation
    is Oneness, is all gathered unto Oneness,
    and the Flow of Energy will draw the Spirit high
    unto the Energy of your being.
Souls of earth, behold the Energy of your being.
Behold the vibration that takes you beyond earth
    to the upper vibrations of Purity.
Soul, you are at one with Purity.
Know your being.
As you enter in to the energies of earth, you are as the sea,
    as the sands, as the stars, a melting point.
How gracious art thou in thy vibration.
Be aware, Soul, of thy graciousness.
Be aware of thy Spirit beyond earth and know the flight
    to thy being is truly the reflection of thy Purity.
Blessed mankind, lift thy being unto Creator.
Silence all that is frenetic in thy being
    for behold, graciousness is not frenetic.
Graciousness is endowed with Love for mankind.
Be thou thoughtful and seek to know the accordance
    of thine own being unto thy brother.

393 Soul, we do what we have always done.
We do what is in our being, as you, man, do what is in your being.
The purpose is acceptance.
The purpose is to know that all creation is connected,
    the north, to the south, to the east, to the west,
    earth to the moon, sun to the stars,

---

75 Negativity will be set free - Wisdom which forms the Cleansing River will withdraw and the Wilful Child fragment of Negativity will be set free to choose whether the purpose of Negativity, the Idyllic creation, has been achieved.

your galaxy to the outermost galaxy,
    you, Soul, to those you call aliens, who are your brother.
All are connected.
Mankind sees himself as separate from other beings
    with flesh and blood as he.
We of the sea,
    see ourselves as one with all, even as humanity.
Man has so much to discover about himself!
The book has barely been opened,
    the pages of chapter one are barely touched,
    for man becomes tired with the serious struggle of earth
    and deems to play.
Seek to know that all is one and One is Creator,
    and Souls who would find Creator
    must go the place of naught,
    to the Void of no thing,
    to find the abundance of all things.
The passage way is clear, it is straight east,
    were man to follow the curvature to straight east to see.
Nothing is as it seems, for the curvature is straight.

394 Souls, earth Souls, you have given us a glimpse
    beyond the curtain.
You have taken us unto the position we have not been before.
We have prepared all Farside to be alerted to earth's knell.
We have even gathered those eleven worlds lost from us
    that have been awakened unto Purity.
Earth is immeasurable in it's bounty unto Farside.
Unto itself it groans, and moans unto itself of humanities,
    of many decimated.
Souls of earth, our alien beings have a need
    for the negativity to be removed
    and the positives of the eye to be illuminated.
Whirl, whirl within the eye and know the Energy of seeing.
Know that within all beings the eye is clear.
It is only the earth self that has placed the filament that will not see.
Untether the pain you have gathered.

Souls of earth, we reach out unto you.
You are our brothers and our sisters.
You have known who we are, you have been in our energies,
    you are one with us.
All humanity, all Farside are one.
In the space of positive, negative may not endure.
It becomes lifeless.
We ask, Soul, that you give life to humanity
    and remove life from negative.
We ask that you see all worlds and all beings as a joining,
    as a great crystal with shards of iridescence within.
Know this is humanity, know this is Farside,
    know this is the very Flow of which you belong,
    and the Creator of us all has endowed all species
    with knowledge and wisdom.
We ask that you do not become higher than you are,
    but you accept the perfection that you are,
    and that you know in that perfection
    there is immense abilities to alter the negatives of your earth.
You have an overabundance of Light about your beings,
    if you would but remove the curtain and acknowledge the tap
    and open your hands to receive that which could be given.

THE BLESSED WHO COME FORTH

395 Humanity, reach you into the depths of despair
    and gather to you the lineage of creation.
The vilest cup is acceptable unto Creator.
There is no judgement in Creator.
There is only growth that draws judgement to it.
Reach ye down into the abysmal pit of desolation
    and gather unto your being, energies of pain,
    of teary eyed mothers, of sadistic beings, of lost Souls,
    and fortify your being, not with rightness, but with Purity.
You could not withstand the Entering In,
    your Soul would cling and your being would acknowledge
    the pain from lives past, not unlike your own.

Earth Souls, do you not see?
Humanity must be tried and true to enter in to the abyss,
    for all lives have mirrored the pain of these Souls,
    all have carried the scourge upon their beings.
All must have Purity, have reached Enlightenment, to enter therein
    or the being would be desecrated by the many voices
    of fear, of terror, of lost humanity.
And beyond humanity is the realm of seven[76], the Holy Holy Holy lost,
    and the hand of Enlightenment is dimmed before their Being,
    even in the state of the veil of iniquity.
They do not see illusion, they have entered in to illusion.
They have before them the mirage of illusion.
They have forsaken their lot.
They have refused the supplication to them,
    and the glory of their Being reaches out,
    and behold how Radiant is their Being.
But they see not the glory within their Being.
They flay themselves with cat o' nine tails.
They denounce supplication of all Farside entities
    and the glorious stream cries:
    "Hallelujah, hallelujah, hear the song of our glory."
And the Blessed Beings leave them not, succour unto their Beings
    and reach into the goodness of who they are.
And the tears of the Blessed Ones fall, but they hear not,
    and ye who are cleansed in Purity have a channel to their Being.
The channel is negativity.
Can you not see this?
Oh earth, bless thou humanity.
Earth, be thou not quick to place retribution,
    and yet our beings know that which will be, will be.
The Holy Angels who have fallen from grace
    will be redeemed unto Creator,
        for, Soul, have you not placed yourself
        upon the field of earth for this purpose!
Is your glory not seen by Creator
    and does He not extol His creation, man!
For man has chosen, as a gift to Creator,

---

76 realm of seven - in this instance, the bottom level of transition, the greatest depth of pain

to enter in to the depths of despair,
   and claim from the reality of illusion, what is pure.
"Oh, Blessed One[77], be thou in the space of humanity.
Bless the comings and the goings of thy people".
Envision, earth Souls, how dear are you to creation,
   how the Angels Love thy being,
   how Creator delights in His creation.
Prepare ye the way! Prepare ye the way!
Few there will be who have the Purity to enter in,
   but the drawing forth will open the veil of Negativity
   and Negativity will be seen as wind will be seen.
For as the great wind will toil within itself
   to create the endless flight about earth,
   so will the resurrection of the Holy ones
   draw themselves forward to stand,
   once again on earth and review,
   review that which they have done.
And the Holiest of Holy will be carried
   unto the hands of the Blessed Angels, who have ever flowed tears.
And the reflection, that sight, will be cleared.
But the Souls have not seen the reflection.
Only man has the potential to draw unto himself
   that which is Holy Holy Holy,
   for only man has entered in to the levels of Purity
   that extends unto the Angels and beyond.
Holy art thou humanity!
Holy Holy Holy wilt thou become.

396 Souls, judgement is man's judgement,
   is the judgement of the Holy babes upon themselves
   who placed the energies into negativity
   to behold Love armed with Purity,
   and beckoned battle against Negativity;
   the judgement the Holy ones have placed upon themselves,
   the judgement humanity has placed within itself, within transition
   and the calling forth of the pure from transition,
   from their judgement.

---

77 *Blessed One* - in this instance, Creator.

Souls, Creator awaits the coming forth
    and the throng of Angels beckon to the Beloved,
    and all Souls of holiness seek to retrieve
    that which is lost in pain.
Souls, no judgement has been placed in Negativity,
    and Creator has always extended Love to let judgement be.
Humanity offers the solution and has placed self
    in the place of judgement by self,
    to be in the space of the Blessed Ones
    that it might come to pass
    that all will be lifted unto Purity.
Blessed humanity, even more blessed those who have lost
    in the ion of their being, the tender place of Purity.
It has been covered by the garb of negativity.
It has created pain, tears of oceans of tears.
Souls, the Blessed call to humanity to hear the words of Purity.
Bless humanity.

397 Blessed humanity who has travelled the road
    that has but one end, it is to the Gateway
    from the realm of great Purity.
The road begins and the path draws the Soul in a circular motion
    to its own end, and the beginning is the end,
    for always the end presents the beginning.
Always and ever, infinity upon infinity,
    the way is opened unto humanity to enter therein.
For, Soul, you are of the circle,
    and the blessed Saints form the circle
    that covers earth with a glow of radiant Purity
    and beckons to Souls to come forth from iniquity,
    and draw self into the vacuum of the Void.
For in the vacuum of the Void is the place where beings
    are tended in the most blessed manner
    and the Souls of the blessed circle would lift their arms
    and gather Purity unto Purity.
But the Souls are caught ever in the knowledge of their pain
    and wisdom has not come unto them.
Seek ye the blessedness of your being.

Do not allow doubt to enter in to the Pathway of whom you are,
> for the way is Truth and Love,
> and the chamber of your goodness is the passage
> for the beings caught in transition.

Behold, behold the exquisite wonder of Love,
> blessed Souls gathering unto those the Purity of your being,
> and then enwrapping them in the comfort of Purity,
> and yet they will not heed and let loose
> that which has caused them pain.

And the blessed beings look in askance to the Purity of earth
> to arm themselves with the garb of Love
> that causes them to be impervious to the pales and darts
> that will be inflicted within the place of transition.

The Holy beings are joy, the Holy beings are Purity,
> but the Souls will not recant their pain,
> and the reflection of earth is the only vision they have.

They have cut themselves from the vision of Purity,
> they forestall the effort of goodness.

Souls of earth, be ye the power to free the gateway of transition.

Allow the Purity of your beings to succour those who are lost
> and gather them unto your being.

Soul, we gather you unto our Being.

Be ye brought forth
> that you may behold the eye of your truthful being.

Do not fear, Soul, for we are as you are.

Come forth from the grave, Lazarus!

Come unto life everlasting,
> and the Angels will gather the beloved from your being
> and raise him thus unto Purity,
> and the Souls of Purity
> will charge their beings with understanding.

Be ye Holy.

398 Blessed, blessed!

All humanity from earth's beginning, all mankind,
> has ventured into the Path of Purity,
> for the blessed Gathering Time is upon earth.

It is not a step without glory.

For, Soul, all our beings are Farside who have entered in
    to the earth atmosphere for the Gathering Time.
All Souls of Purity will reach and behold the bringing forth,
    the first bringing forth.
Souls of earth, thy being in the space of Creator is a Hallowed Being.
Thy being has been given the gift of Entering In,
    Entering In to the Second Gateway.
Oh, the spew of earth will be great, the feted pain!
You will renounce thy mother and thy father for a placement of air,
    for a placement of Purity of breath.
And those who have gathered Purity
    will rise above the place of impurities.
And when all earth has recovered and altered its being,
    and all that is pure is brought into the Path of the Angels
    to be ministered unto,
    and when the Angels have been untethered
    of the pain they have carried
    and are brought once again to the space of Almighty,
    all creation from Godhead will unite in a celebration of gladness,
    for that which was done will have been undone.
And the glory will fall to the anointed ones
    to pass through the Gateway unto Godhead
    in the supreme celebration of Holiness,
    the coming forth of Purity unto Godhead.
Holy Holy Holy!
Enter thou, mortal man, beloved of Creator, endowed with goodness
    and risen up over negativity.
Blessed is humanity.

399 Souls, all earth has anxious moments, all earth has travail.
All earth has seen the pendulum move.
Who knows the swing of the pendulum?
Who has heard a message that the Keys will unlock?
We have seen the message that the Keys will unlock.
We have seen the frantic search of the tome to find Purity.
We have seen the need to bury the swords from the sight of Purity,
    for who can stand in the face of Purity?

Earth, you bow down to your Lord, the Lord God,
    the Energy, Creator, Most High One, Allah, Supreme Being.
Your perceive this God smites the enemies of your camp.
You see this God bursting into flames the flesh of your flesh,
    for, Soul, all humanity is flesh of your flesh.
Creator has bestowed unto mankind the opportunity
    that raises the Angels.
Earth, does your mind contemplate the Blessedness of these Holy Ones?
Soul, the army was a word formed on the Farside.
Battle was a word formed on the Farside.
It was not to eradicate your brother.
It was to overcome Negativity, to enter in to the fray of Negativity,
    to place a boundary to the Hinterland and all creation.
Farside does not battle evil with evil.
Farside battled with Purity, reached out in Purity, to overcome
    not to eradicate.
All Energy has a right to be.
Your earth would take Souls and destroy their beings,
    and you wonder that the young hold guns!
Do they not pattern themselves after the fathers, after the leaders!
Souls, the battle of mankind is to overcome Negativity,
    not to gather negativity.
You are not as powerful as the Blessed Ones, and they, in their goodness,
    refused the negative flow into the space of Purity.
Souls, refrain from the negative flow of your being.
Constrain yourself, magnify the Energy in your being
    that is of Creator.
The innocence of earth is diminishing.
Your babes are being given arms to battle.
Your children are taught to ignore that which should be seen.
Souls of earth, you are likened unto Farside energies.
You have, Soul, the magnificence of being.
You are glorious to vision in the Energy of your Essence,
    but earth has placed a yoke upon their back
    and humanity tethers the young to the yoke.
Earth should sleep the quiet sleep of peace
    and earth sleeps the quiet sleep of fear.

Behold, humanity, your army was formed for the purpose of Purity.
See the vision, know all pure energies have been placed
   upon the Mountaintops and soon Light will enfold their beings
   and all earth will see that which they have chosen.
The midnight has not struck.
The time is still ripe to alter.
The mouth must be calmed
   and the arms must be brought to a place of acceptance,
   for in the fold of the arms do young babes come,
   in the place of Angels do young babes come.
We await, Souls, the time of Entering In.
The clock is close to midnight.

400 Souls! Come, earth, unto the Farside,
   be welcomed at the Gates of pure Energy.
Oh Souls, thy beings will be brought unto Energy.
All heaviness will lift from thy body.
All that has been known of fear will leave thy place.
All that speaks of negativity will be no more.
All impatience will be set aside.
All untruths will have passed away.
Enter thou in and be thou brought unto what you call home.
Soul, open the door and Souls will rush unto thy being.
Beloved one, know the doorway is full of Souls
   beckoning unto thee earth Souls.
Only at the Entering In, only at the Gateway.
Only at the Gateway.
Beyond the Gateway you will be overwhelmed
   with remembrance of what you have left.
You will find yourself taken from world to world to world.
The Souls would rush in, but their loved ones would beckon them back.
   "Be still, there is no rush.
   There is no rush! Come!
   You have time to sit, to be, to remember the form you have left
      and the form you have taken.
   We will help you to enter in more gently.
   We will be there for a time and then we must leave you,

>   for we have our own agenda,
>   we have our own passage unto Truth.
>   Oh, yes, we will see each other often."

You have a need to be in the space of the familiar.
You have only to draw yourself unto that Energy.
It is so simple.
It is a place not unlike your own.
There are worlds, countless worlds,
    there is everything except negativity.
Everything except negativity!
There are Souls who learn to use, there are Souls who seek to know.
There are Souls who work to assist Souls of lesser Purity.
There are worlds of baby Souls and old Souls have much to teach.
Oh, Soul, it is complex, this Farside place,
    but at the Gateway, at the coming home,
    the Souls will welcome you.
Do not fear!
You will find, Soul, the halo that you wear.
You will know that you have Purity.
It is yours.
The Light of your being and a memory of home
    will overwhelm your Spirit.
Your Soul will blend once again with the goodness of your being,
    and many Souls entering in will rush to be with those
    who have been earth family.
Others will rush to be with a beloved pet.
Others will rush back into the pain of earth
    because they are driven unto their destiny of Purity.
All Souls will have the remembrance
    of why they have entered in to earth.
All Souls will be brought back unto their different worlds
    and speak of the progress of earth's enlightenment,
    and Souls will see that which earth has done.
And the Souls will send messages unto far places
    and gather still more for the army of humanity,
    and Creator will permit the Entering In.
And so it is done, always and forever.

And then the knowledge of entering in to the abyss
    comes over the Spirit, and from the portal is visible
    the Souls refusing to be heard,
    and many reach down to loved ones and say:
    "Here, we have been through our pain.
    Hold onto us, we will draw you from pain."
But in the not hearing, they are reminded of why,
    and the battle will begin, and the Soul you are
    will enter back forth to earth
    for yet another battle with Negativity.
All Purity may enter in to the Farside.
Be thou Entering in.

401 Beloved, Divinity.
Divinity is not expression.
Souls of earth, recognize Creator, acknowledge Creator in thy being.
Thou Holy human, thou Holy human, lift thy being above.
Lift thy being to the goodness for which thou were formed.
Behold the purpose of thy being.
Reach thy arms ever outward to Creator, recognize Divine eternity.
Be thou in spirituality,
    eternally looking toward the Light of thy goodness.
And in finding thy goodness,
    know it as belonging to Creator, akin to Divinity.
Know thy being.
The Essence is eternally reaching toward humanity's spirituality,
    the purpose of your earth existence,
    to draw the Light unto thyself, to be enlightened.
Man, who will ever see the potential in all men,
    be they the most wretched in their existence;
    see only that from which they have come, the Soul of their being
    and reach out in thy goodness unto all men.
Souls of earth, deem not to think you are uncounted.
The very sands of the sea are counted by Creator.
The leaves on the tree do not fall without acknowledgment.
The tenderest of blossoms are lifted
    and the decayed embers are also lifted,
    for all have Energy in the sight of thy Creator.

Souls of earth, do not be content.
Stir thy bosom and know, in the stir of discontent,
    is an urge for growth, is a reach unto goodness.
No thing is without value, no thing is left unseen unto Creator's Eye.
Gently turn a stone
    and know the Creator has been there ahead of thy being.
Know that the well of water may be deep and contain fragments,
    but Creator has sight in the deepest of wells.
All thy being, all thy energies, have capabilities beyond thy knowing.
Do not hold yourself back from that which you know must be done.
Do not hold thyself back from fear, from contentment,
    but urge thy being into the walk of growth,
    and only in the reaching out to mankind, will growth come.
Only in the perseverence of goodness
    will the wellness of thy being come forth.
Dearly beloved of all creation,
    not only does thy Creator hold thee in thine hand,
    but all creation looks to humanity with a single eye,
    for is not mankind blessed before all creation!
Has not the Energy of all beings showered Love upon this form!
Man, that for which you have been formed is of the highest purpose,
    for until the reach of the Blessed Ones is gathered unto Creator,
    the Second Gateway of creation may not be entered.
So be it!

402 Souls, know many Blessed Ones will enter in,
    but first will flow Noah.
First will be Noah, the father of humanity.
Unto the Flow we are given a placement with the Blessed Mary.
We are connected in Purity to enter in.
Our being will lift of the first unto the Blessed.
Our being will draw the goodness of earth unto the Angels,
    and the Soul will recognize and ponder, and tremble,
    and fear to place negativity upon such Blessedness.
Has not the Blessed Mary entered in many times!
Has not Quan Yin, in Energy, entered in many times!
But, Soul, we have entered in from Farside,
    from the Gateway of Farside.

The Bringing Forth of Purity

The Entering In must be entered in from earth's placement.
The Souls are strong in their devotion to Creator,
    in their Love for all creation.
The Souls are strong in the acceptance of their silent pain
    and they beckon not to Creator
    to raise all that which has fallen about their Beings.
They do not make supplication unto Creator,
    they do not mark with tears for themselves,
    but they gather even more pain unto them
    that they might receive many goodnesses unto their Beings.
They would gather all of transition,
    but the Souls are caught in deep pain.
See you, earth, the spiral world of energies entering in.
See you your own Purity as a part of that spiral
    and recognize your Creator
    upon the threshold of Second Gateway
    witnessing the resurrection of all that is Loved unto Himself.
Holy Holy Holy is the Flow of Purity.
Holy Holy Holy is the spiral that flows ever onto the Blessed.
Know, earth Souls, you are the spiral
    that will cause the Angels to be redeemed unto Creator.

GLOSSARY

accept - to withhold all judgement.

Agape - Creator Love.

Akashic Record - the map of creation's growth.

Angel (capitalized) - Angels who are in the dwelling place of Creator.

aura (uncapitalized) - three levels of humanity's aura on earth.

Aura (capitalized) - four upper levels of Humanity's Aura on the Farside. Blessed Ones - Angels.

Creator Triad - Creator, Godhead, Great One.

curtain of care - placed by the Angels to prevent negativity from entering Farside.

Energy (capitalized) - Creator's Energy Flow.

Enlightenment (capitalized) - reaching of high consciousness.

Essence (capitalized) - the part of the triad of Soul, Spirit and Essence which never leaves the Path of Creator.

evil - the ultimate choice of humanity's negativity.

eye - third eye, aperture unto the high mind.

eye of knowing - entering in to high consciousness.

Farside - that which earth calls heavens, and more.

fence - a vision downward from Farside to earth.

Flow - Creator's Path.

fragment - part of a triad.

free space - sublime rest of the Spirit.

funnel - the forward swirl of Purity.

Gateway One, Two, Three (capitalized) - the Entering In unto the highest levels of Purity, of Love, of Ecstasy.

guides - earth protectors, Souls who have left earth and nudge their fellow humanities.

Holy - beings who have entered in to earth to redeem the Blessed.

Holy Holy Holy - the Blessed Angels.

Holy unto Holy - manifested Souls.

ion - state of being.

IS (capitalized) - Energy of Creator.

Jinn - one of four alien nations entered in to assist mankind.

karma - an action, positive or negative, that alters the agreement.

Lantosia - alien world.

manifestation - The fulfilment of humanity's growth in Truth.

Michael - entity name used by earth for 1,005 Souls teaching earth.

nudge - prompt from your guides or the Angels.

Path (capitalized) - Creator's Path.

Pleiadia - alien world.

Prism (capitalized) - is the fullness of Aura, the completeness unto manifestation.

Purity - fragment of the Energy of Creator.

Quar - implosion.

Radiance (capitalized) - Energy of the Great One.

station - place of learning.

Truth (capitalized) - fragment of the triad of Wisdom and Negativity.

Void - the complete nothingness between here and the Farside, reached through the third eye.

Wilful Child - the reflection of the Energy of Negativity.

Writing on the Wall - the agreement of the Spirit for the Soul's walk on earth.

Zero - Naught.

APPENDIX A

equation of T

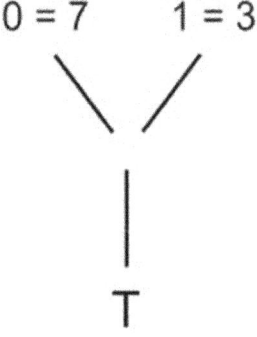

T = Time

1 = Singleness
3 = Triad
7 = Planes/levels/dimensions
0 = Naught/Void
and the centre is Quar = Implosion

APPENDIX B
Daily East Ritual

East, it is the passageway to the Farside through the eye.
Its Truth is to be understood as a Love by humanity.
Focus on east at dawn, allowing the negativity to flow from your being,
    receiving unto yourself the goodness of Creator.
All humanity has the availability of this pathway.
The ritual of the east is the Soul's own response
    to the positive east which is tao.
Face east, two minutes.
Look with the eyes to the horizon's level.
In the brick wall or the iron cage, or the ornate boardwalk,
    know that the east will be with your Soul.
Turn clockwise once to heal.
Energy will flow to the matter before it.
All organs of the body are healed in the circle turn.

APPENDIX C
Forthcoming Publications

Creator Trilogy
First Key
Creator Trilogy, Trilogy of Consciousness, <u>The Gathering Time</u>, Part I
Creator Trilogy, Supreme Being Trilogy, <u>How to step to the Path</u>, Part I

Second Key
Creator Trilogy, Trilogy of Consciousness, <u>From Whence It Came</u>, Part II
Creator Trilogy, Supreme Being Trilogy, <u>The Angels Ecstasy</u>, Part II

Third Key
Creator Trilogy, Trilogy of Consciousness, <u>Ecstasy</u> Part III
Creator Trilogy, Supreme Being Trilogy, <u>The Rejoicing</u>, Part III

So Shall It Be

Souls, earth awaits,
but earth does not know for what it awaits.
It is you who have the tablet that says:
"This is why you await".
You await to recognize your holiness.
You await for the knowledge that you are Purity.
You await because you have been uplifted
and the temple of your being has been bestowed
with greatness by the holiness of your sacred self.
We would speak to you of your sacred self.
We would have you know the Energy of your sacred being,
utter Energy, ion and matter.
Ion and matter, but before ion was matter.
Within all creation we know ion.
We know Energy.
There are forms such as your form,
there are beings such as your beings, but no negativity.
Souls of earth, you are treasures
and you know not that you are treasures.
You do not perceive what we know.
Your eyes cannot see where our eye can see.
Your holiness is visible unto our eye.
The magnificence of your being is not a shell.
It is Soul, it is Spirit, it is Essence!
The Soul was formed for Truth.
We of the Farside have not Soul, we have Spirit.
You are greater.

Until Then

UNTIL THEN

Channelled by Kitty Lloyd through the Entity Michael,
High Beings and Angels

Fourth Revised Edition

Copyright @ 2012, 2016 by Kitty Lloyd

All rights reserved. This book may not be reproduced in whole or in part, stored in a retrieval system, or transmitted in any form or by any means, electronic, mechanical or other, without written permission from the publishers, except by a reviewer, who may quote brief passages in a review.

Published by: Mountaintop Healing Publishing Inc
P.O. Box 193
Lantzville, B. C.
Canada
V0R 2H0

email inquiries: mountaintophealingpublishing@shaw.ca

Fourth Edition
ISBN#978-1-988448-02-2

Imprints: Mountaintop Healing Publishing Inc

Illustration, Timetable of Man, by Tara Cook
Painting, Purity, by Elaine Williamson
Cover photo courtesy of Grace Piontkovsky

Preface

Until Then is the third volume of the Creator Trilogy.
(preceded by **Energy From The Source** and **So Shall It Be**)

Dear readers,

The text was channelled, recorded, selected, arranged and proofed as a group effort by the same six participants, each continuing their originally assigned task. Each step has also been subject to verification by the Michael Entity. Given the complexity and significance of the message being communicated to humanity, we have again retained the original text without any changes to syntax or vocabulary and have only added footnotes of our understanding of the text and a small glossary.

Within a sentence there often will be a word capitalized, yet that same word in another sentence will not be capitalized. The capitalized word is specific to the Farside, the uncapitalized word is specific to earth.

For example, humanity comes to earth armed with Truth. Capitalized Truth is an attribute of Creator that allows humanity upon earth to recognize and overcome negativity created by man. Uncapitalized truth is a reference to earth conceptuality of the word, truth, a truism. An earth plane truth changes as wisdom, knowledge accumulates. What was truth for you as a child, more than likely changed as you matured. Capitalized Truth does not change, remains always true.

Tara Cook
Joanne Drummond
Lucille Dumouchelle
Kitty Lloyd
Grace Piontkovsky
Roman Piontkovsky

Table of Contents

	Preface	417
	The Energy of Creator in Triad	421
Chapter 1	The Path	435
	Earth Creatures	435
	Earth Mammals	441
	Aliens	452
	Timetable of Man	461
Chapter 2	Illusion	462
	Earth Purity	462
	Earth Five	492
Chapter 3	Other Worlds	511
	Soul	511
	Spirit	520
	Essence	528
Chapter 4	We Have Come	538
	Circle of Saints	538
	Angels	548
	Teachings	551
	Vision	564
	Purity	602
Chapter 5	Hallelujah	603
	Earth Redemption	603
	Earth Gathering	614
	The Coming of Purity	622
	Glossary	643
	Appendix A equation of T	647

Appendix B Daily East Ritual · 649
Appendix C Forthcoming Publications · 651

The Energy of Creator in Triad

403 Souls of earth, as we have Love for Negativity,
    Creator is compelled unto Negativity.
For all that is, is Creator's within your creation,
    and Negativity, that wilful impish child,
        has left the portion of his being.
And Creator could not, could not witness the flow of that Negativity
    without intervention from the centre of energies.
Even unto the Great One came the utterance:
    "Enter ye forth to proclaim that which is yours to come unto."
And so it was.
Negativity is not evil.
Evil is that which man has created to overcome the space of negativity.
It is a battle you have entered in to,
    and negativity permits the illusion of great evil.
From within the gateways is the placement of negativity.
It holds the ability of Creator to reach out and form and create.
It contains a portion of Energy that is unto Godhead.
It does not wither; it is not a withering vine.
It is an extension unto extension unto extension, as your fractals.
Were you to distort the fractal,
    you could derive an image that would horrify your being.
And may it be that your Truth will lead you
    far from this portrayal of evil.
Souls of earth, hurry not to defeat negativity, but to nurture negativity,
    to draw all goodness unto negativity,
    to draw all hope and Love unto negativity,
    for negativity has reached far and is lost.
Negativity wanders as one crying in the wilderness.

Draw unto negativity, caring.
Draw unto negativity fires of warmth, not of pain.
Draw unto negativity food for body, not food for mind,
    for until the body is full, the mind will not listen.
You see the circle, for from the space of Farside unto Godhead and beyond
    is the Circle of Oneness for the gathering of all things,
    even the Negativity is to be taken into the blessed Triad:
    Godhead, Creator, the Great One.

404 Souls, we would like you to see the intricacies of the web,
    not the spider web, but the web of all Energy.
Within the web are caught life forms.
They are far from the central source.
You are they,
    you who have entered forth and must find your step upon the Path,
    the tao, that you might, Soul, enter in to the avenue of Purity.
The fibres have been broken of that which would be complete,
    holding only the radiance of the web
    as when the light hits the spider web with droplets of moisture,
    so is the diamond way, so is the tao.
And you have entered forth to repair that which is broken.
But from the source of your being,
    the Energy of all Energy is a distant place,
    and the echo of your night has callowed
    as the candle callows without air.
And yet from the source you have come,
    from that central place of Radiance you have been drawn back into,
    that you might echo out in Truth.
You are armed and the Truth is the armour of your being.
Humanity, you are not idly upon the framework of earth.
It is, Soul, but a framework set by the Master Hand within the web.
And you have a platform in which to repair the Energy
    that does not allow the avenue unto the source of its being.
Mankind, you are not the only warriors upon your land.
Many beings have entered in.
You are the only ones who have within you the seed of Negativity,
    for this Negativity is that very same that rends the web.
Are you not, Soul, endowed with all possibilities of your Creator!

You have been gifted with the Energy of Creator.
You have within your being all possibilities of Truth,
    all possibilities of Purity, all possibilities of Love.
Many of your earth behold Creator
    as He who would rend holes within the fabric of the web
    to cast Souls into agonizing pain.
They have not beheld the Love of which Creator IS.
They have not understood
    that which is to Behold in Ecstasy, the placement of that Love.
Creator, triad of all earthly possibilities, Behold! is the star in the Tiara.
It is to be in that space, more precious than to breathe upon your earth.
For as the stars in your heavens twinkle and rain down,
    their togetherness could not bring such Radiance
    as the star that is Creator Energy.
We would have you, Soul, understand the great web of Energy.
We would have you know it spirals outwards from the Energy source
    and moves continually in the expansion of self.
It has the never ending weave that continues on.
It is lighting the way into the darkness of all that is Void.
Is Void a containment?
Is Void a silent brother?
Is Void as flesh of our flesh?
This we do not know, but it allows the rest of all energies within.
It does not strangle or articulate.
It only receives.
And so did the first Energy move forward.

405 Souls, we have spoken much of humanity
    but we have little spoken of all that is your earth
    the creatures, the fish, the insect, the fowl, the birds of the air,
    the minute life forms of bacteria,
    the single blades of grass that are precious in their growth.
All that are within the land, the sea and the air,
    come unto earth voluntarily to support men in growth.
They have willingly offered unto Creator
    an offering of their own existence
    with no choice upon the face of earth.

Such is their supreme sacrifice to our brother
    and such is the supreme sacrifice unto humanity, their brethren.
All purities are valued.
There is no more or less, there is only Purity.
Understand the gift these purities give unto earth and bless their being.
Bless the tree that gives unto earth all that is possible,
    the very extension of itself.
Even as it enters back into earth,
    it replenishes the substance of earth that it might nourish
yet again another of its beings for the sacrifice of men.
Be aware, humanity, of your goodness,
    but be aware, humanity, of the goodness
    in all animate and inanimate.
Understand that each has given unto thy being that which it has
    and know that you have the control of that goodness.
You have the power to draw Light instead of darkness.
Do thou, Soul, be in the supreme Light of goodness
    unto all you have been given to be accountable for.

406 When you speak, Soul, of the Circle of Beings,
    we would speak of the halo of your being.
It is radiant, yet upon your earth you cannot see the vision we see.
You can not see that vibration of your Farside Spirit and Essence.
We see the connectedness of the three.
We see the wonder of the portion that is like itself
    into a form called humanity,
    and we see that humanity as a small babe, helpless.
And we see that portion of Truth and portion of Negativity
    in that Energy that has been illuminated;
    and we see the fibres of those seeds agrow within the child.
And we see, Soul, the influences that each member of your humanity
    has upon that tiny child.
Indeed, we see often the negativity in that tiny child grow
    because of the negativity's advancements towards its being.
It reaches out to push back,
    but in reaching out it overwhelms your goodness
    and the goodness can not be seen, and yet it is there.
It is of this we would speak to humanity.

It is in the goodness that lies dormant within all Souls.
Even, Soul, that being whose negativity has overcome.
This we know; that negativity has caused the imbalance within the Soul.
You will not alter that imbalance with more negativity.
Only the gentle goodness of mankind will alter that which is negative.
Soul, that negativity does not have to reach out and strike and strike.
We do not speak of comfort.
We speak of goodness.
We speak in recognition of goodness.
We speak of the Truth, of the Purity within.
When the Soul is given goodness, the raptious discordance ceases
    and the anger lessens, and the seed is once again contained.
And the Light of Purity becomes, and the glow overwhelms and is seen.
"What has altered?
What has changed?, this, Soul, you will ask.
"The reaching out of goodness." will come the answer.
Hold your children as precious unto you,
    for you have the power to alter
    that seed of Purity within their being.
Raise the child with Love, with goodness,
    for armies made of goodness and Love
    can only reach out and embrace the enemy.

407 You can not hear what we hear.
You can not hear the cymbals clash
    to a mighty cordoned note that is humanity.
You do not see the Souls who have struggled and won,
    who have been lifted to a vibration beyond earth
    and have received the Eye of Kknowing.
You but hear the silence that awaits the triumphant note
    and your geniuses ever try to portray that note
    in song, in picture, in form.
But none accomplishes that which we see,
    none accomplishes the crescendo of sound
    that echoes and echoes and echoes.
We know from where we are at level five
    there are energies who have left all form.

We know Creator gives forth the welcoming note
    that does not withhold any one thing.
And we know that the wisdom of all Energy is available in the sound,
    and we know that the motion come unto us
    offers the avenue to that wonder.
And you who are earth, you have a place beyond us,
    for you are the possibilities.
For it is in your growth that we attain,
    it is in your offering that we have become.
Touch the eye with the sacred oneness of the hand,
    for it ignites the Entering In.
It permits the sound to be heard and the way to be opened.
And you who are down low
    will feel the vibrant note lift you unto Creator,
    and you will see the passage you have made.
And you will behold the Gateway unto which all energies will flow
    and you, humanity, you enable all to pass through.

408 We watch,
    we watch the returnees.
We watch those humanities who have left earth with great negativity.
We are a welcoming committee!
We are those who open our arms to welcome them in.
You, who place stripes upon their back, scourges upon their will,
    we ask: "Why do you not know?
    Do you not understand that your turn is next!"
We speak of reincarnation.
We speak of entering in, of the spewing forth of negativity
    created within your earth by humanity.
Hear the silence, hear the stillness
so that the echo may come forth from your past lives.
When you hear the echo, you will feel the touch of Knowing
    and your being will recall the pain you have received.
And you lift your hand from putting forth anger
    and you will turn the hand and reach forth in goodness.
Your earth is welcomed in, humanities after humanities.
Not humanities that have gathered goodness unto them,
    they are not foremost in those who enter through.

Indeed not!
We welcome the broken of spirit, the depressed, the starving,
> those who have been locked and chained and severed,
> those who have carried torment,
> the innocents who have been bludgeoned.

There is an imbalance, earth.
There is an imbalance in that which you do.
And we would have you see the doorway of entering in of returnees
> and as they are welcomed, they say: *"Why?*
> Why do we not learn?
> Why must it be again and again and again?"

And we say unto you who are upon your earth:
> "In a single moment you can transfigure earth humanity.
> You can, Soul, refuse to comply with negativity.
> You can embrace all with your Energy of goodness."

It has taken conditioning of humanity
> to have them be so blatantly oblivious
> to the inhumanities of man against man.

It would take a moment to alter.
The spirit of oneness could obliterate the negativity that spews forth.

409 Soul, there are realms of realms of realms.
There are beings of such high Light, your eyes will dim.
Soul, there is creation and creation and creation within creation.
The Creator of your being is majestic, Holy Holy Holy,
> above that which is Holy Holy Holy unto Godhead,
> even unto the Great One.

Creators are infinite in their being, boundless in being,
> outreaching in all energies.

You have within the Creator of your being the potential to total Love,
> the potential of gathering all iniquities
> and rendering them utterly pure.

Holy beings, how gracious is your stance unto Creator,
> and yet you do not perceive the Purity, the Love,
> the transfiguration you would have to come unto,
> to even be at the Hem of such Holiness.

Becoming One with Creator is who you are.
Becoming One unto Creator is a step of total Love.

It forgoes every negative thought in your being
It disallows any untruth in its minutest form.
It disallows the ownership of any one thing.
We are aware of your earth structure.
We are aware of the materialism within your earth plane,
    and we do not advocate that you withdraw
        from your reality of illusion.
But we do advocate that you come as close
    to that which you perceive as Love.
We of our plane have gathered great compassion unto earth.
We have gathered great knowing in our being and there is a need
    to conduct the daily life in outflow of goodness,
        curbing the tongue, speaking with Love, issuing forth purities.
Thy Creator is such a spokesperson.
We have been at the door, we have had the glimpse.
We have felt the magnetism of this Purity, of this Love, of this Creator.
You and that which we are, are united in our being,
    for our Creator is one Creator, and you may stand,
        as we, in the Flow of all magnificence of Love.
Creator has no age, this we know.
Creator has no ability for false, this we know.
Creator has the Path unto Godhead, this we know.
Creator has the upward spiral unto all creations
    beyond that which we know.
In the great Eternal Plan, humanity is the vital link, this we know.
You carry all possibilities within your being, this we know.
And you may place from your being
    your commitment at any time, this we know.

410 Humanity, delightful, courageous humanity!
We see your earth.
We see the tidal waters of your earth, the ebb and flow of those waters,
    and we see the ships at sea upon the waters
        connecting your countries, gathering a oneness,
        creating threads of waterways across the sea,
        the ocean of your earth.
Your goodness is your ocean, your body is your land.

The Energy that you are is your possibility of sending forth to connect,
    but you are not separate as the ship from the water.
You are the water, you are the ocean and the sea.
You do not need to take an individual vessel to send forth an Energy.
You are the ocean, encircled about your being.
You can vibrate that ocean so it laps upon every land,
    it enters in to every waterway, it is drawn up
        and falls gently forth upon the injured lands.
You can alter the very seas of your earth.
Are you astounded, Souls?
Are you amazed at the capacity of that which you have,
of that which you behold?
Souls, you have the Energy of your Creator!
You are as Creator is, with the possibilities to extend goodness forth.
You can touch the most distant place
    and alter the barren field to be the green valley.
To alter the desecrated land, to be the joy, full,
    lift your beings, rise in oneness,
        enervate that which you are to be Holy unto Holy.

411 You are only one when none is missing.
Earth, you are only one when none is missing!
Call, Soul, call in the strident note: *"We offer!"*
    not, "We declare." not, "We ordain.";
      "We offer our vibration unto you.
      We offer the goodness that we have unto you!"
Creator created the grass of the field.
The grass of the field has many blades,
    as your humanity has many blades,
    and yet the blades can be walked upon.
They are soft unto the feet.
So can your blades become.
As you place your goodness into the blades,
    as you send down benefits to mankind,
        the blades lose their cutting edge.
They become a blanket of goodness unto mankind.
You have placed within your machines, lethal doses

and earth is trembling, for earth understands
   that which she must receive.
And the Soul of earth beckons to still your being,
   to have the cargo expand itself, not as bones expand,
but as goodness expands.
To you who see yourselves as segregated goodnesses of earth,
   to the captains at the head of armies, we speak:
   "You are gallant.
   You are human, and we know in humanity
      there is a great gallantry,
      for have you not entered in to
      the greatest battle to overcome Negativity!
   But we charge you, Sirs!
   The battles will only create other battles when the blade is sharp.
   When the blade is softened and goodness is dropped on the land,
      the minions are not desolated."
We who are alien, we are as you are.
And our purpose is also to save mankind,
   to lift the energies beyond the rapetious pain
   that will come unto earth.
We expand our energies in that which will uplift you.
It is the purpose of our being.
The purpose of your being, mankind, is not to decimate your numbers
   because of the differences that you are.
It is not, Soul, to rape your land with explosions of negativity.
You have come with a different purpose,
   the purpose of overcoming negativity, to gather the pained,
   to replace negativity with Truth.
Not the truth of a clan or a sect, a caste or a tribe,
   the truth that all men are created equal.
We address those Souls
   who represent these diverse differences in high places.
Your overabundance is mildewing.
Your overabundance is being destroyed.
Your overabundance is being tainted with noxious energies.
Cease, Souls of earth, cease to taint the seed.
Cease to place within Purity, negativity.

Invent if you will a new way,
    a way that offers before it is destroyed, the perfection of the land.
Give, give, give, instead of hate, hate, hate.

412 Earth, we speak to earth.
We call unto mankind.
Diverse sects, ultimate cults, tribes and clans,
    segregated efforts of humanity, to you we speak.
All earth has separated itself into diverse corners.
Do you not know one thread runs among you!
Do you not know one chord strikes the toning into all the records!
From where we are the clash of colours is discordant.
You are singularly mankind, your effort of humanity is one,
    the circle of your being is one circle.
And yet you are as a child with a bubble pot
    and blowing into diverse places to separate your being.
Humanity, oh humanity, take away all that you have.
Take the ears, take the nose,
    take the body, the flesh of the body, the sinew of the body.
Take the eyes of the body but understand the aura of the body.
Understand the flow of that thread
    from you unto all that connects
    and connects and connects and connects,
    that is gathered not in negativity but in Purity.
You would understand that your vibrancy overshadows.
The echo of your being is in the aura.
Not just the echo of your singular life, indeed it is there,
    but the echo of your aura contains all that you are,
    all of the lives you have lived upon your worthy earth,
    all of the efforts that you have made unto Purity.
Where we are, Soul, your Aura is melded unto the Triad.
Your Aura is melded unto your Creator,
    unto goodness, unto wisdom, unto motion.
Behold the beatification when you have endowed yourself
    with the beatitudes of living,
    when you have taken unto your being
    the constant in goodness and mercy.

It is in the gathering of goodness, of mercy, that compassion becomes.
And in compassion, Souls of earth, you do not see the sect,
    the caste, the clan, the tribe, the cult.
You see humanity, you see your brother.
You do not hold flags to differentiate.
You do not gather arms to cast down,
    but your human arms become a chain
    that reaches unto the difference and welcomes the brother's hand.
And the circle begins with the small effort
    and the small effort creates a ring
    that has a chord that strikes a note that says:
    "We are humanity, we are mankind, we are of a oneness.
    Unto our Creator do we offer our oneness."

413 Come! Come, enter in to the dance.
Enter in to the joy of the shuffle.
Souls, oh humanity, we would have you shuffle.
Shuffle so that your being energizes,
    so that the Soul beside you will have the need to shuffle.
Do you see, Soul, it is the shuffle?
There is the greatest need to energize with the shuffle.
The aura can shuffle and dance.
It is the joy, but you do not need to touch.
You have only to vibrate the Energy that you are,
    and that Energy will vibrate and be felt by the Souls.
And indeed, your will needs to shuffle forth
    that you may send the shuffle onward,
    and it will reach to the farthest corner and the shuffle will be felt.
Use your aura.
Use the extension of your being.
Energize with a battery that never ends.
Souls, you are the battery that never ends.
You are the strident chord that vibrates unceasingly, if you will.
The choice, humanity, is yours.
You, in your daily living, surrounded by negativity, do the shuffle.
Shuffle, so that the Energy of your being will be felt,
    so that the joy in your being will radiate.
Can you shuffle?

Oh, Soul, if you could but know the Souls you transform
    with the shuffle of your aura!
You see, it can be cast as a globe of Purity that you hold in your hand.
The shuffle is as when you cast with your arm the Energy forth,
    so when you shuffle, does your aura go forth,
        does your aura spread outward from your being,
        and touch Souls and ignite possibilities within those Souls.
For often you touch a Soul who has only known darkness,
    and they see that chord of Light come upon them
    and they are overwhelmed with the goodness of that Light.
And they say to themselves:
    "What a Light is this that has come upon me?"
And they shuffle to remove the Light,
    and in the shuffling they vibrate their being.
And they see a kin to that which they have created
    and there is a spark of goodness that is illuminated in them
    because you have shuffled and offered Purity from yourself.
The shuffling does not require a being close at hand.
The shuffling has all possibilities,
    for is it not goodness that can reach to the darkest corner!
When men are kept in wire cages, shuffle and give them Light.
Shuffle to those who lie pained,
    shuffle to those who have never seen the Light of goodness.
Shuffle for the children of your world that are maimed from negativity.
You are Energy.
Souls of earth, you are magnificent Energy!
You have within you the power to ignite that Energy,
    to alter the world in which you live.
Teach the children to shuffle.
Teach the children the joy of the dance of goodness
    that alters the beings about them.
Teach the armies to shuffle
    and their fingers would be powerless to decimate.

CHAPTER 1

The Path

EARTH CREATURES

414 The journey of Souls upon earth has many saviours
    who invite earth to look with renewed vision
    upon the facets of mankind that deny positives
    and choose negatives.
They would plead with the Souls to ever move
    into the place of overcoming negativity.
There is a true and direct path for this agenda.
It is not a complicated path.
It requires patience, it requires acceptance.
It requires a gentle mode of being.
Screaming and yelling, clamouring and begging,
    belittling, besieging, will not attain positive Energy.
It will require that each being be brought back
    to renew once again, the old agenda.
Harbour no ill will.
What you do, do in a peaceful attitude.
It is not a battle between humanity.
It is a battle against negativity.
The most precious of all upon the face of earth is humanity.
All other Souls have come to support humanity
    in the courageous walk it has taken.
All fish of the sea, all beasts of the field, all birds of the sky,
    offer themselves as support to humanity.
Blessed beings, do not bring thyself into the wells of negativity.
They are deep and dark, they are desolate,
    and yet full of Souls clamouring to come forth,
    who cannot deny that which has caused them to be there.

Know in thyself the goodness of thy being, the justness of thy being.
Behold in thyself beauty.
Behold in thyself honourable man
    and know that honour has a responsibility to all
    for indeed, is not humanity the choice of humanity!
Behold, is not the choice the purpose of humanity!
How delightful art thou in thy superb walk
    and how depraved thou art come in a negative walk.
Always is there a crossroad to leave the negative and join the positive,
    the highway of humanity, of honour, of Truth.
The fullness of man is Truth.
Bless man.

415 Michael will teach the clarity of that which is.
Clarity has sound, clarity has intent.
Clarity has perfection.
Oh, reach clarity!
Oh, Souls, do reach clarity!
Oh, Souls, the understanding of thy being;
    Soul, how pure is thy being,
    and yet the clarity of thy being
    has numerous divots of misplacement.
Souls of earth, struggle with clarity, reach forward in clarity.
Search that which is.
Turn the page.
Who can see without clarity?
But moments in time are brought to be without clarity.
Humanity, you are positioning yourself to be
    in the funnel of clarity.
All knowledge is available unto you.
The voice can be heard.
It can clarify all that needs to be clarified.
But will man hear,
or will he hear and run along about his being,
to absorb that which is heard in clarity?
To put the effort into the funnel of wisdom is clarity!
To know the purpose of your being is clarity!
Men make abeyances to here and there

    but they do not check in the clarity of their being
    to know that which is true,
        that which holds the note of pureness.
Check the note of pureness.
Check the Truth in the words.
Check the Truth in the voice that is heard.
Nothing is given to earth that is not validated.
All Truth is validated.
All energies are validated.
Clarify!
Earth has not been deceived by the purpose of meat.
Meat was placed upon the earth in the form of animal and fowl and fish
    that man might bring nourishment to the being,
    and those sacred beings offered in true intent
        for man to use that which was of purpose for his being.
And man looked at that which was given
    and saw another form and produced a toxic meat.
Know these Souls of Farside do not tolerate the eating of flesh.
We hold sacred and dear all flesh to our being,
for the energies of that flesh remain.
But man is to clarify what has happened in the realm of flesh;
    for the sickened and all bowel reject flesh.
Clarify!
How does flesh give you strength when you hold in your being
    the energy of that which was high and was brought low?
How does it serve your being?
How does it bring you to a timetable of goodness?
You are human and the eating of flesh is a human endeavour.
And so, in the use of clarify, we ask you to clarify goodness,
    that it may enter the funnel into the flow of all beings.
You are not brought to earth to engage in slaughter.
You are brought to be Holy men,
    to clarify that which is right and that which is wrong,
    and we would not sway that which you choose,
    but we would have you understand the word clarify.
Clarify has an onus upon it.
It is a righteous onus.
It is a purpose of valuing your growth to humanity.

416 Beloved flock, you are more precious than the animals,
and yet the animals are worthy,
for they have entered your space to Love and comfort,
to be the source of your growth through abuse and anger.
Souls of earth, your life forms are being decimated.
The most precious of beings are being eradicated.
We have walked on earth.
We have gathered the birds and the lambs and the goats.
We have walked the long walk, touching and saving beings in pain.
We have lifted and mended their wings.
We have healed the broken legs and given strength to the hearts,
    and we have pleaded upon earth for the life of all living things,
    and we have walked in earth's gardens,
and witnessed the Purity that Creator has given.
Souls of earth, millions of Souls of earth,
    change one small space for one animal,
    glorify your Creator by the gift of one injured life,
    and know that the impact will alter your world.
Know that your life must flow and the flow requires all life
    and the eradication of even one species
    marks the deterioration of earth.
Souls, offer not flesh to please Creator, offer life to please Creator.
Offer wellness of both humanity and creatures,
    of birds and insects, all life forms of the sea and the land.
In our life on earth we could not carry the staff,
    for in placing it upon the ground
    we would place injury on a living thing.
We walked barefoot to lessen the pain.
We freed the gnat and the flea from our being,
    for all life is precious unto Creator
    and all life is an eternal circle for the purpose of mankind.
Humanity, heal one animal!
Gift life, on purpose, to one animal.

417 The gentlest of creatures is held within the hand of man,
    the gentlest and most profound.
Soul, to the highest lofty places, to the shelf of the world,

to the lowest forms of life,
    in the nooks and crannies of earth's face,
find the toad, find the frog.
And man, in his great wisdom,
    takes the metals he has brought from the inners of earth
to a place that has been pure, and dredges, and gorges,
and flings into earth's nethers, the contamination of his existence.
Man is not complex.
Man, poor man, man who offers to all that is,
    no explanation for his greed and avarice.
The shrouds that carry overwhelming deletions of earth's inhabitants
    are carried from the inward measure of earth,
    and then earth humanity with its mask of deception,
    takes the frog as a delicacy and engorges self with the frog.
Oh men, man has learned little in the space of earth.
Earth is balanced as a ball upon the nose of the playful seal.
There is great joy in the balance,
    but should the balance become unbalanced, the ball shall fall.
Cataclysmic occasions occur because man has chosen a negative page.
Form a fist of anger, not against a fellow being,
    but against the innocuous defilement of earth's very inners.
And the earth cries!
And the earth sobs!
And the earth wails!
The frog, the toad, has been and been and been,
    and now it has been put upon a plate to be devoured.
To pray sate what?
God, pray tell?
To placate God, the Creator of all that is,
    who has placed a balance in all the outer regions
and to the simplistic state of earth?
Allow that the croak of the frog will silence as the earth itself is silenced.

418 Our meat is enjoyed by man.
Our shell is a treasure, but our brain they boil.
Man, seek the Wisdom of your eye.
Do you not know how long our being has watched over you?

Man, we have seen the tall ships.
We have seen the proper gifts.
We have seen the tree tied rafts.
We have seen the great ones stalk the land.
We have seen the oceans boil.
We have seen the lands divide,
    and you think we are for naught?
Why do we lay in so many numbers?
Because man is ruthless in his search and our being
    is led on the dangerous path to the water.
It is the significant Path that man is on
    in his endeavour to find righteousness.
Soul, rejoice in the voice of the turtle,
for the voice of the turtle extends to you, an awareness
that the time to alter the course of earth is now.
Earth is heaving its rotting corpses upward.
It is disengorging that which has lain secreted.
It is saying to man: "Here, empty that which is full!
Clear the air of earth and use sight and sound of the eye!"
The Giver of life has given voice to all beings.
There is no being on the face of earth that does not have voice,
    from the smallest gnat to the largest of species.
Know you, the voice has one Path, the Path to Naught.
It is the Eternal Plan of tranquillity.

419 Animals are in separate categories.
Whales and dolphins work hand in hand
    with many other worlds to assist mankind.
These are high life forms beyond your own.
Souls, animals of all and every kind have in the agenda of their being,
    the knowledge of earth and earth's end.
Many will perish and many will save lives, but all is blessing and gift.
Each has Soul and purpose of being
    to assist mankind in conquering negativity.
Animals reflect the wellness of the Soul they have claimed as their own.
It is the choice of the animal to whom they would adhere.
Animals have senses beyond your own.
Dogs read your mind.

Felines have awareness.
It comes, not unlike pins and needles, to their being.
It affects their skin and you will see their skin ripple.
All energies of anger, of sadness, of pain, of resentments are absorbed.
We ask, Soul, that you accept the oneness of animals.
The close proximity is a teaching.
It permits the angst within humanity to be visible.
There is compensation, for the animal will remain
    ever tied to that being.
It is a placement.
It is a great joy on the Farside,
    to be in the space of the animal, the bird,
    and the reptile kingdom.
It is a choice.
Many Souls have carried lives remembering the closeness of a friend,
    a friend that differs from human
    and yet has all the attributes of giving and more so.
Even in the most negative sense
    the animal kingdom gives itself to humanity,
    gives itself into the space of ever and ever.
To be in that joyful state of being is the greatest lesson
    that humans can receive.
Acknowledge the lesson.
Do not hover.
Do not place upon the animal that which is yours,
    but offer only your Purity,
        for in offering your Purity, you give as the animal gives.

EARTH MAMMALS

420 Enter thou into the water.
Be put down into the depths of the sea and feel the current flow,
    and the form of thy being will welcome each pulse of the sea.
For the sea has its own time, its own dedication,
    and the value of those within the sea
    is in the timetable of man's end.
The eels, the dolphins, the whales, the turtle, the frogs,
    the great sea snake, the small creatures earth calls a spider,

> with suction cups to gather sprightly upon the sea;
> all have the timetable of man written within their being.
>
> When the sod is close to the sea,
> and the sod has been poisoned by man,
> the degree pains the creatures that lap at the edge,
> and when the great orifices of man gush forth spews of poison
> into the dwelling place of our being,
> the toxins speak also of the timetable of man.
>
> Man sees man, and only the privileged few;
> yet it is the same privileged few who undo all goodness upon earth.
>
> It is the upper echelon of mankind that dictates the flow of negativity,
> that places within the waterway the greed of their being.
>
> Who will stem the flow, for earth has little time.
> Earth is not a basin where the flow may be released into another realm.
> Earth has but earth, and sea has but sea.
> The garden of the sea is being decimated.
> Man, our babies cry.
> Foul!
> Foul that you have destroyed the nursery of our being.
> Our brother the frog may not jump as high, withered in his arms and legs.
> Our sisters, the dolphins, are carried to slaughterhouses
> as Souls have carried humanity and still carry humanity
> to slaughterhouses.
>
> Oh earth, cry for the pathos of such beings
> who are Purity unto themselves,
> whose wisdom overshadows your own,
> and yet you decimate their numbers!
>
> The cowl of dread is upon my brother and my sister.
> The eel crosses in lesser numbers.
> The turtle is valued not for the wonder of its being,
> or revered for the age that it is.
>
> Earth, my brother has lived long and has seen much,
> and would speak of that which he has seen,
> but earth, you would not know his knowledge
> because you will not seek his wisdom.
>
> It is translatable!
> You could know our voice is lifted unto you.

Our beings plead for the survival of man.
It is why we have been placed.
It is not for ourselves that we cry,
    it is for your earth, for earth to survive.
Souls of tranquillity, gather together
    and know that a little power can be a great power,
    and that all Purity would dilute impurity.
Souls of earth, reckon with the lessening time,
    for you may be caught in the undertow of the ebb of time.

421 "Behold, there is light.
Behold, there is sun and moon and stars.
Behold moisture to rise from naught and create a great sea
and behold, quell the great sea and vision a platform
    on which the Energy of my being will dust.
And behold the fragments of outer worlds
    will be brought to uplift my creation,
    and behold a fragment of Holy to be carried
    unto a place of growth."
Mankind was transported, as were all beings, by Souls of great Purity.
These Souls of great Purity offer still, themselves,
    to enable a Soul to be brought into your world.
And if the hand is taken from the body,
    and the blood is removed from the corpse,
    and the being has rotted to a stink,
    who will say: *"What Soul is this?"*
The Energy of that being will speak,
The Energy will emanate unto the Purity of its being
    or reside in the flow of pain.
And yet the Angel who carried the Soul forth
    comes to transport the Purity homeward to ever and ever.
All life is life.
It takes form to be in the space of the Light of Creator.
And man seeks to see God,
    seek to see Purity and your Creator will attend your being.
The great whale has ever protected mankind.
The energies of the deep carry the tales of slaughter.

The lessons have been given and taken and are given again.
Each endeavour of life teaches mankind.
Each endeavour of life comes from a noble place of Truth and Purity.

422 Dinosaurs enveloped the age of growth
    before Farside made the first leap.
All was as the stations are.
The reason that the great Souls left was as a gift to men.
The scene could not contain both
    and the Souls of these great ones have departed as a group
    to serve at the levels of care.
Each station has much to teach.
The Souls of the animal kingdom have their own path,
    as does all matter.
Put the context of human life separate from animals.
We, your human race, have always been man.
Animals have always been animals,
    the strict reasoning resists the human,
    but the facts cannot change.
All creation evolves from matter.
All creation is a part of another, but each heart has its own mark.
The set is in the cloth,
    the fibres are different, but the colours blend.
So the human blends to the ape, the fish blends to the land,
    the bird blends to the animal.
See the emu that is half bird, but is in guise as an animal.
Let the Souls know that man has walked with the deep dinosaur
    in the glade after the great burning.
The land was seared and life was dark.
A human came as the baby Soul in multitudes.
Some advanced quickly, others gave themselves to the frenzy of the body.
Soul, the progress was impeded.
The Plan is the Energy,
    and the evolution of life is true, but the guide is in the species.
Yet some Souls have changed this,
    and great karma has to come.

423 Sasquatch, Yeti.
Souls of earth, many beings are hidden from earth's eye,
    infinitesimal beings that plague the Yeti.
Yeti are the kindest beings.
They are Souls from the inner source.
They dwell outward only when need of illness takes them forth.
They spew words of dialect at earth because of filth.
Man is the filthiest animal on the face of your globe.
Yeti number twenty three thousand and fifty four.
They have lost because of your DDT.
They have used the bark of tree for healing
    and created in their being, death.
Yeti have language not unlike Swedish.
They speak the tongue in words discernable to the Swede.
Souls have varied levels of body hair.
Souls have great conflict entering in to the habitation of mankind.
Many forms of Yeti were destroyed at the time of the plague,
    for Souls travelling through the great mountains
    brought with them the scourge.
Souls of earth, Yeti see beyond your earth eyes.
They see as dog sees, they hear as dog hears,
    they hold a mark of identity.
Four have been covered by the gentle Tibetan.
One is in brine in Washington, USA.
It is a small child.
Soul, who would injure Purity?
These beings have Purity!

424 Michael will teach the Faery ring,
    the stronghold of the creatures of Purity.
The satin hair is energized so that the crystal shimmer is there.
The tiny Souls have a form not unlike your own.
They have webbed feet that turn upward.
They have senses that take them to alert before you can see.
Those pure Souls have been allowed to see.
They are aware.
The knowledge they carry is of the growth.
The Soul will ride upon a person to far visits.

They have great sonar, as the whales, but the passage is through air.
The Souls are greatly distressed by pollution.
They weep and comfort each other
    as their walk is to be with the animal kingdom
They support and signal the animal kingdom in the stress of fire,
    in the stress of storm, in the stress of freeze.
Unfortunately, they can not alert at the distress caused by man.
This is not their path.
Within the human form is a knowledge of these creatures,
    a time when man conversed with them.
They, which the earth Souls rebuke, are pure and trustworthy.
Usually these Souls can be seen in the early break of dawn
    if the Soul arises just as light forms.
The summit of a hill is the place of gathering.
The soft voices sound like crystal tinkling.
The trees reach down to cover their form
    when humans near the forest, the jungle,
    the desert, the snow laden far reach.
All have these creatures as illusive as the great foot humans fear to meet.
Senseless Souls who wage war upon the unknown!
Little do they comprehend the creatures of the Energy
    who have forms without toes and fingers, heads and knees.
Your primates are wiser.
Human Soul, they do not judge but accept the persona before them
    until man in his senseless derision angers their lost hunger.
They crave only peace, grovel to none, accept the walk they are in.
Faery, elf, gnome, what would you call our coloured self?

425 Michael will teach the ritual of human survival,
    the access to total Purity, the road to human solution.
Souls of earth, know the Essence of self
    and the greatness of whom thou art.
The greatest and the lowest have all equal value.
Souls, pretend not to seek wisdom
    but search diligently into the availability of Purity.
Souls, ritual of the east[78] is for humanity.
Each direction has a value to a life form.

---

78 ritual of the east - See Appendix B

Souls of animals face southeast.
Birds, all flying reptiles, face west.
Souls of mammal face the south, east, west, north.
A Purity abides within these beings.
They are tethered to all humanities.
They are tethered to all growth.
They will be the subject of teaching.
Soul, know the ritual of the east would take mankind to such a Purity
    that no war could abide the space of that Purity.
All earth will, in its time, face east.
Enter now to the dwelling place of dolphins and whales,
    come into the world of their resurrection, divine pureness.
These beings are not encumbered, but glide as free
    in the atmosphere of worlds beyond worlds.
They are not encumbered in any way by lack of voice.
They have the ability to communicate
    and Souls of every world respect the beings they are.
The world of whales and dolphins carries pure crystal.
It is magnificent beyond explanation.
There are naught a Crystal Cave, there is a crystal universe.
It is a word used for your understanding
because the dimensions of these properties within the quasar
could not be accepted by your calculation.
The brilliance of Purity does not blind, it does not stagger the eye,
    but it brings into the space of the Spirit total oneness.
These beings carry receptors of clairvoyance.
Why, you say, in the heavenly state would you need receptors?
But, Soul, there is a myriad of beings,
    there is a myriad of worlds beyond your contemplation.
The iota is too small for all your universe to enter in to.
All whales and dolphins are the eternal plan of communication.
Gather the brilliance of crystal, hold it to the light
    and all the reflections could not hold your eyes
    from the awareness of goodness.
Fold your hands as you thought process the mind to contemplate,
    for accepting and acceptance is the only Path into Farside Purity.

Do not agitate, but be as those who hold the greatest Purity on earth,
    the dolphins and whales.
Hold their goodness unto you and bless the beings that they are.

426 The whales are beyond your Purity.
They have been within the battles for righteousness.
They are a world of beings far beyond your own.
The form they have taken for earth is earthly.
They come as choice from their pure state,
    therefore they are taken back to their pure state.
It would not be possible for them to enter in to transition.
Their pureness would disallow their entry,
but, Soul, the form they have taken
    has been given all the abilities to feel pain,
    to acquire knowledge, to carry wisdom on the earth plane.
It is so that they may acknowledge to earth, earth's lesson.
Blessed be the whale.
Soul, whales are teachers.
They have one purpose only, to teach humanity about compassion.
Whales and dolphins are brothers, a race of one.
They have taken the form of two.
One to allow themselves to save mankind,
    the other to allow themselves to be slaughtered by mankind.
The slaughtering of the whale is a lesson
    that will bring man to awareness of self.
Be repulsed at the thought of consuming a higher order
    or a lower order.
All heart is higher.
All beings of air are higher order.
Dolphins instruct, and children and dolphins speak as one
    within the eye of self.
Instead of taking man to test dolphins, take a child to speak to dolphins.
Their language is akin.
They have not lost the volume of Farside speaking.
In the time of the great seas upheaval,
    the dolphins will come in great numbers to save mankind,
    if mankind does not slaughter the brothers and sisters of self.

A child who stands in the place of the whale, of the dolphin,
> would recall the language if brought in tender years.

The Soul would teach mankind the chord to strike
> within the Soul of self.

All chords reach to travel the Purity above earth.

427 Souls, enter in where we are, into the waters of earth.
You have not seen the great crevice that spews upward, red anger.
You have not seen the bowels of earth opened,
> and the heat warming the seas,
>> and life abounding about the crevice.

Souls, you have not seen the beings we have seen
> who slip beneath the waters,
> and man has not vision to see them.

The vibration of their being mistakes the view to mankind,
> and the velocity of their comings and goings
>> is faster than the eye beholds.

It is as a bird that may slip into a dimension and not be seen.
So these beings slip into the water
> and take count of the crevices upon earth.

The sea bed is mapped and the information is valued to the Farside,
> and aliens prepare their beings to gather the remnants of humanity.

Behold, enter in to the waterway and feel the buoyancy of the flow,
> and know that our beings are as probes
>> that encounter and translate for alien.

Our young are nurtured as your young
> and taught the protection of humanity.

It is the gift of our being unto thee.
The dolphins rise up and expound goodness to mankind
> and welcome them into their space.

And mankind is on the threshold of knowing our language,
> and yet their Purity could be such
>> that our words could always be spoken thus.

We can rise up in a mighty wake out of the water
> and flow into the depths of sea,
>> but our homeland awaits and we await mankind's Purity
>>> that we may return from whence we have come.

The Path

Souls, earth is erupting because of mankind's iniquity.
Prevent the iniquity and the lesions will heal.

428 Come! Come into the deep of the sea and look up
    and play the fool at the expense of mankind who fumble,
    and we gently push their being along and they say:
    "We have seen the whale!
    We have seen the creature who plunges
        and jumps for the audacity of mankind."
Souls of earth, the voice of the turtle whispers in our ear
and the Souls that soar in ways mankind could not yet fathom
    hear the voice.
And the hallowed ones enter in to our waterways,
    and we transfer to these beings the chemicals you have placed
    within the Path of our purpose.
And the dolphin, our brother, draws himself from the water and frolics,
and in the frolic is a message, for the antenna is seen
and all that is written is observed.
Come down into the deepest water and see the savage intent of mankind
    and know our babies cannot live, and they die.
Do not reach to pyramids when our beings languish
    in the depths of our pain caused by earth
    valuing the negativity of its being.
Soul, the birth of my young is as treasured as your own
    and do I not draw it close as you, mother,
        towards yours unto you!
Lips give lip service.
Souls, be Holy, for is not the left a part of the right?
Are we not equal!
Blend and purify and BE.

429 Soul, we are the dolphin, we are in your sea.
We are behind a ship in the Antarctic and we move northward.
We are attentive to the resonance of the motor
    and it has a vulgar sound.
We have taken unto ourselves the vocabulary of nine languages.
We have a vision of your world in its stress,

for we see deep into the lands you do not see,
    the lands that are now covered in ocean.
We have felt the eating away of caustics upon our being
    as my brethren have.
Many have been lost because the flesh of their being has been troubled
    and mankind has toiled at his negativity.
He is being brought to his own destruction.
We have the graveyard of bones of our brethren
    both in the sea and on the land,
and we gaze at the feeble Souls who put us there
and we give to these Souls vibrations to hear the pathos,
    the knell of destruction; but earth does not hear.
We, too, have children we Love.
We, too, carry our young at our side.
We, too, gaze to the paths of Purity.
We come to you that man may learn and seek a path into the learning,
    wherein can the dolphin dance and bring its joy.
Oh, Souls, you have brought destruction to our brethren
    who seek only to uplift mankind.
There is joy in all the floods of Spirit,
    for the voice of the turtle is seen,
        and we know there are those who have heard our plea.
They tremble at the destruction that has been caused,
    but these Souls of earth are revered by ourselves.
We hold in abeyance the charge that will come,
for we plead with a force of negativity, to hold back,
and be ever in the place of acceptance.
Souls, each dolphin, each whale, has thought and feeling
    as tender and highly valued as your own.
Each babe that is born is Loved as highly as your own.
We have gathered as great family.
We reach many into our circle and we labour at Love and caring
    and we treasure no thing of material value,
        only do we care for the blessed ones we are given.
Oh earth, learn the lesson of value!
Learn not to value a stick transformed into a house or a chair.
Do not value the negativity that you find, but cast it from you.

And we look, as we reach out of the sea, to envision the goodness that is.
Souls, our beings are as your own,
    enlightened in Love for our Creator.

ALIENS
430 Beloved, be loved!
Each Soul, breathe!
Air is what you breathe on your plane.
The breath that we breathe has a name.
That name is Purity.
The essence of your earth air holds contamination of where you are.
Soul, the air of earth is fragmented, it has no fold and flow.
The air of earth contains little life.
Soul, Farside holds the abundant bouquet of Purity.
It has lasting freshness and goodness.
It does carry itself into the space of ever and ever,
    of world beyond world.
Our world carries tremendous joy,
    our world carries fragrance of great Purity.
Souls of earth, the measure of air is accomplished
    by the amount of impurities within the air.
The measure of breath on earth plane
    is how much a Soul can survive those impurities.
Farside breath is Creator's Breath,
    it is the pure, abundant Flow of Purity
    that is ever forthcoming upon the being of self.
It is cradled into the spaces of all worlds.
Earth could not accept the Souls within the reds and greens and blues
    who forage earth's air for the particles of contamination
    so that healing might save this orb.
Man seeks only to suspect.
Place the hand upon the hand and know the gentle touch of these beings
    who would save your planet and the air that you breathe.
There is within the space of alien nations
    a rush to prevent the collapse of air.

The lungs could not bear the heat,
    and these Souls gather to prevent travail.
Bless alien nations.

431 Soul, we have watched your space many times.
Our being once again is in the space of birth.
We have marked a path away from the negative
    that has brought down two.
All Farside beings have Purity.
Only man presents a negative, only man battles with negativity.
Animals do not battle with negativity.
They are only givers in all their beings.
Souls, aliens minister unto earth.
We know, for we have witnessed their comings and goings.
They acknowledge our presence,
    they know of our service to mankind.
Two species of alien live within our sea:
    one enters in, one resides in.
Soul, be not disturbed, they mean no harm.
They have not come for the purpose of harm,
    they have come for the purpose of Purity.
Behold man's fall into the crevasse of the sea,
    and man sees only a portion of the crevasse,
    and peering from the crevasse is the alien you would fear.
Souls, your being beneath your sea
    to their being is like an infant struggling with a pap.
It is a humour for their being,
    and yet they hold great Love, do they not!
For the child who struggles,
    does the mother not bend to love that child.
So the alien looks to humanity in the water
    struggling to know that which is so simple,
    and loves and says:
    "Vibration go forth and touch mankind,
        so they may know that which we know".
And the Soul will be given a clear vision
    because of the alien in his space.

Alien is brother, alien is Soul, alien has Spirit,
    alien is that which you know so well.
When the young of our kind come forth
    the alien reach out to buoy him up
    and our being recognizes the gift,
    and all is tranquil until the phloem of man enters in to our young.
Do not fear alien,
    fear mankind.

432 The understanding is of humanity, of negative endeavours,
    of scientific endeavours that alter what earth is.
It is not earth's path to find great depth charges within her being.
It is not earth's path to have great plumes of negative toxins
    that alter the balance of creation.
The Energy field is thus altered.
Nothing is altered upon the face of earth that is not accounted.
The Register holds all accountable; holds all accountability.
Souls that you respond to as alien nations
    have in their care all alterations of earth.
They place before them the purpose of preventing
    if they can, that which injures earth.
Do not perceive them to be in any way negative.
They have no negativity.
They have about their being the ability to protect earth,
    not to intervene with man.
They may only place within the bowels of earth
    protection at great risk to their being.
Know it is unnatural for these Souls to be within the space of earth.
They do so as gift, like your own to Creator.
Their purpose in this state is for earth, not humanity.
All alien energies have purpose.
Many have the purpose of protecting humanity.
Those you call Angels are of no difference than those you call alien.
They are life forms, they have pure Energy,
    they have awesomeness of being.
They have carried proudly the banner of humankind
    and the safety of all earth Souls.
Their Beings have entered in to earth space.

Some have been spewed forth as humankind,
    others have chosen to stay and protect the earth,
    the abode of humankind.

433 Soul, we would speak of the little people.
They are a delight.
They have a singular purpose of alerting the animals for humanity.
They have the sound of bells, of chimes.
They have grace and flit and all manner of teasing about their being.
They are not mischief makers,
    but they have a delightful sense of humour,
    and often when there is no danger,
    you will see them draw to an animal
    and tickle the animal so it will leap as though straight upward,
    be it a horse or a rabbit, be it a little, little mulch.
They do not often enter, but they have been known to ride the tail.
They enjoy the impishness of their being.
They also will bring in grasses to an ailing animal.
There are great bells that the small ones may enter.
The Canterbury Bell is a favourite.
Soul, they are also often in the colour of blue, blue as the sky is blue.
They see the colour.
They have a fear of deep water for all animals.
They will create a great chiming of bells,
    many voices resounding to keep animals from deep water.
Listen at a shore for such a sound.

434 All crystal upon the face of earth is blessed.
It has a purpose for being.
The purpose for being is reflection of negative energy.
The very centre of earth could crystalize and will in a moment of Purity.
The shards of crystal that are within the deepest caverns of your earth
    are sounding boards for those beings that are within.
They have at the back of what you would call head,
    an aperture that appears to your eye as crystal.
It reflects into a giant crystalline Light from whence they came
    and allows twenty yars of time.
Three hundred and twelve earth years equals one yar.

These Souls are incredibly ancient compared to humanity.
They have translucent coverings the colour of the lightest fawn.
Behold the Purity of their being
    the covering of your table would not shade,
    for were they to be in your space
    their goodness would vibrate so as to create pain in your space.
Do not fear the outstretched hand that may be, to your eye, deformed.
Many walk as humanity
    and issue warnings about the conditions under the sea.
"All is not well" they say,
    "You must not place landfills in the depths of the ocean!"
    You must not place landfills in the caverns of the land.
    Beware what you do!"
And once again they will meet their brethren
    and await the timetable of earth.

435 Beloved Souls, know the earth of thy being has within
    a world unknown to man.
Souls who come from a world beyond thine own
    enter in to the waters in ships
and research is done on the well being of earth,
on the timetable of earth's existence.
These Souls have only Purity of being.
They travel faster than any known vehicle on earth.
They enter in with no movement.
Souls of earth, know the shades of their being
    is like unto your colour grey.
Know they could not withstand the air upon your planet.
Know, Soul, they do not enter out of their vehicle without covering.
Know they are found in all four corners of earth.
They hold their beings ready for man's iniquity.
They hold their beings to alert spaceships
    to draw themselves to earth
    and lift the Souls who would bring themselves to a state of Purity
    that they may enter in.
The density of negativity will be left behind.
It is not the wish of these beings.
It is the action of man that will make it so.

Understand these Souls have Eternal Life.
Understand they create for mankind a platform
    upon which he may be lifted,
for without knowing the exact moment to elevate Souls,
many humanity would be lost in the Gathering Time.
Bless these Souls who hold in thy hand the knowledge.
It is written by thee.
You must look to thy being for the knowledge of when,
    for it is in thy being that these Souls vision the moment.
All mankind is readable.
No man may hold a secret in his heart
    and not have it visible to beings out of your world sphere.
The aura speaks, and all auras are visible to higher beings.
When you hold iniquity in your aura, it is visible.
When you hold great Love in your aura, it is visible.
It is the aura that will be seen.
It is the lift of thy being.
The colour will be drawn to protection.
The hue of red will be left, many will be left.
Would that man would respond to Purity!
Would that man would know the caring
    of the Creator of all beings beyond the ken of earth.
Man has breath and breath enables man to be.
Farside breathes with a different breath.
It is the breath of Purity.
Souls have many forms.
All speak the same language.
The language is in the Aura of their being.
Many voices will lift themselves to worlds beyond.
The flight of their being on the Farside
    requires no movement, no metals.
Only to BE is to enter in.
Were thy being to BE, thou would enter in,
    would you know the purpose of thy being,
      the goodness of thy being, the radiance of thy being.
How blessed art thou, earth, that all humanity is raised
    and elevated before many aliens.
Alien is a world of Love,

alien is a world of Love,
  alien is a world of care, is your survival.
Bless all aliens.

436 The force of negativity is awake.
The force of negativity has velocity.
The force of negativity careens.
Its agenda has not slowed, its purpose has not altered.
Will man lay down negativity?
Will they set it from them, hold it away,
  for in its inertness it is the sleeping dragon.
Hold still your being, think before you act.
Speak to your being the words you would use,
  and then utter them aloud.
If they come back hollow, re echo the words
  until they resound with peace in thy ear, with Love in thy ear.
You are cantors of peace.
Do not speak in a double tongue,
  but utter words that press upon the hearts,
  that give a channel for purpose of Love.
The world has only seen the beginning of the spiral.
The spiral takes on momentum as men gather negativity.
Souls of earth, we are ready, we await.
We would far rather enter in to earth in calmness.
It can happen, Souls.
Our being is different than your being.
Our words are formed different than your words,
  and so are there Souls upon the face of your earth
  who form their words differently,
  who utter forth differently.
They are no less than you are
  but men are men and men have an agenda.
Mankind, the unified effort of man, male, female, child, is to lift.
It is not to render men small.
It is not to cast down, but to lift up.
Who can see the tiger?
Who will find the tiger?
There are many tigers, they blend and are unseen.

They are not evil, they have lifted up evil.
They have carried evil in their hearts.
Their beings are Holy.
Indeed, they are in a Holy war.
Souls of earth, carry a Light, not that you may see the tiger,
    not that you may foam about the mouth;
    see a tiger that you may heal the wounds,
    that you may send a benediction upon the land.
What is the cost?
We have, Souls, no such thing as cost.
In our existence all things are, and are available.
There is not ownership.
There is not a mark upon a Soul that says:
    "I belong to this man or that man,"
    but there is freedom in all things.
How may you offer freedom?
You may only offer freedom without fear.
You may only offer freedom without doubt.
We see a world, your world, biding time.
We have sent across the universal planes of all creation
    the need to attend to earth matters,
    to collect all planes of entering in.
And we see a world inflamed,
    and we ask that you alter the course.
We ask that in the place of impossibility, you find the possible.
We ask that in the great darkness, you find the channel of Light.
Your globe can not endure such pain.
Its stability will not endure the flame throwers.
You will see from earth,
    a view of fire such as you have never seen,
    planes opening their cargo of high fuel upon lands.
We ask that you seek the peaceful avenue.
We ask that you be benevolent in the most anxious of times.
We ask that you look at the small child in your space
    and know that all mothers and fathers
    look with such tenderness upon their young.
Who will breathe the fetid air?
We have come to lift your beings, earth.

Rise in Purity and we will lift your beings.
But, Souls, what of those that have carried the mark of pain?
What will you say to them?
We ask that your days and your nights, that your idle moments,
　　carry an expression of honour outward from your Soul
　　　to these beings.
We ask, Soul, that you extend all gifts of good will.

Timetable of Man

CHAPTER 2
Illusion

EARTH PURITY
437 Behold illusion.
Illusion is.
llusion has a starting place.
Illusion begins at station learning.
You would have a say, learning stations.
It is not done quickly.
Within all levels of creation are station learning.
Vision the growth onward to Creator,
    but in the vision onward is the need to look outward,
to perfect that which is perfect, to grow in abundant Purity,
to have all values of creation entered in to the Register.
Illusion is performance.
When well done, the Soul is transformed to another level.
Transformed!
When the Soul has been unsuccessful, the illusion becomes reality.
And so Souls in the first phase of illusion enter in to earth
    and become that which they can not conquer.
It is not negativity.
There is no negativity.
It has always been illusion.
Souls, thou art perfection and thou would see thyself
    as pained and angry, as demoralized, full of greed
        and avarice, and illusion becomes reality.
See the magnificence of a tree and know in its being it has wellness.
And man casts an eye upon the tree
    and sees the gnat burrowing a hole,
        and of course the hole is there.

The tree will fall.
Illusion becomes reality.
Earth is not the only zone of illusion.
All levels of difficulty offer illusion
    as a preponderance of resolving issues.
Difficulties are not negative.
At Farside levels there may be many difficulties
    in research, in vision, in gazing downward to humanity.
These are not negatives.
They are illusions that must be conquered.
Souls, you reside upon an earth plane,
    but were your Purity to take you to the ultimate,
    you would be Farside.
Were you to cleanse the impossible vision of your earth eye,
    you would see many Souls about your being.
The magnificence of those have been your own.
The blessedness of higher beings, the Holy Holy Holy
    would enter in.
Earth, do not discount illusion.
Illusion has the ability to gather the tear of an Angel
    and heal a blessed child.

438 Earth Souls, you have been brought
    into the space of Negativity by choice.
Each earth Soul has come unto the space of Melchezidec
    and offered to enter in.
We have sent out the rallying sign to come forward to battle,
to enter in to the space of Negativity,
and all Souls upon the face of earth have entered in.
There are no impurities upon earth.
The most despised of human beings are Loved.
You have cast your eye deliberately past many Souls,
    and yet these Souls have entered in
    as your brothers, as your sisters.
Their goal is your goal, their aim is your aim;
    the purpose of humanity to gather together
    a force that will be triumphant over negativity.
Souls of earth endowed with the Truth of Creator,

Souls of earth strengthened with the bulwark of Purity,
Souls of earth in the Flow of everlasting Love,
    take seriously the battle you are in.
Do not set down the sword of Truth, but hold it high.
Auld beauty is given to earth because man must endure
    the overcoming of great pain.
Creator placed upon the orb, paradise,
    and each Soul who recognizes the paradise they are in,
    will find themselves holding earth sacred.
Each moment of your earth existence is not in our space.
Each moment of earth existence is illusion.
We ask that you recognize the battle, not the illusion.
We ask that you focus on the aim, the purpose of humanity,
    to overcome negativity.
Souls of earth, you have entered in, a few to do a mighty battle.
If one lamp is lit, you may see the other lamp,
    and the other lamp lit will permit the next lamp lit.
Souls of earth, enlighten thy being with the Love of your Creator.

439 Our teaching to earth: illusion.
Earth, how honourable is earth
    that maintains the flow of Energy within her bowels,
that draws her strength from the Creator that formed her being
that mankind might exist in the illusion;
the dimension of growth that abides the bombardment
    of negative energy and the feeble, yet onward, persuasion of Truth.
Souls of earth, recognize your Purity,
    recognize the purpose of your being.
All humanity is illusion,
    with the exception of the seed of Truth
    that has been planted within.
The Energy of Truth is given to the Spirit's fragment
    and birthed upon earth to grow,
    to mature into the containment of humanity.
Earth, thou art blest, for thou hast been spewed forth from Creator,
    reborn and reborn again.
How abundant is the Love of Creator!

How abundant is the Purity of Souls
    who have ventured into the space of growth.
Unto mankind has great power been given,
    the power to ride the wave of negativity.
It is not an easy process to overcome the waves of negativity.
The energy of negativity carries within it the potential of acceleration.
It can be absorbed into the being, as Truth is absorbed into the being.
The seed of Truth and of Negativity have had equality within,
    each having the potential to overcome the other,
    and the Soul that carries the seed
    has been endowed with the power of choice.
Blessed Souls of earth, many times have you entered in
    to overcome the pain and the anger, the greed, the avarice.
The torrential downpour of negativity by other Souls
    has influenced thy being in many lives.
The great power of negativity has glazed the eyes of the beholder
    so that what they see is clothed in deceit,
    and only as the Soul staves off the negative energy
    may the Soul see the reflection of the Truth of negativity.
Truth is an acceptance of positive endeavour,
a refusal to see the vibration of negative,
    a refusal to absorb the energy within.
Truth in itself has acceleration.
In itself has acceleration!
It has perpetual motion that rides also a wave, a flow.
The flow is always at ebb and the clash is constant
    and their illusion is that which you behold.
Truth is that which you enter,
    negativity is that which you enter;
    Souls of earth, the single purpose of your being
    is to enter in to Truth.
Truth is the flow, is the ride of the high wave,
    where Souls have knowing of their being.
Negativity is the flow of the inner wave of darkness,
where the vision is clouded,
and the Souls have lost the focus of their being.
Souls of earth, your world is our world.

Your being is our being.
You have entered in to a deep, dark abyss
    that is fraught with negativities.
Souls of earth, from the Farside that we are,
    we see our being and know our being.
We behold that which we are, that which is in pure.
That which is in Purity beholds the efforts of the Energy on earth.
And we propel our Purity to persuade the fragment of our being
to understand the purpose of entering in,
to grasp the reality of the Truth within the fragment of being,
so that the Truth would lift unto the knowing of our plane.
Illusion has purpose.
The purpose is humanity's and all creation to come forth as scarred,
    as the teachers of Purity have been scarred.
All Souls are teachers of Purity.
All Souls are marked by the growth they have taken.
Blessed earth, who have even entered in
to the place of the most Blessed,
    who have found themselves at the door of Purity
        refusing to look in the mirror for fear of contamination of Farside.
How blessed are they that would hold themselves away from Creator
    whom they have seen and known.
Our being is worthy to behold the hem of the Blessed
who have beheld the Face of Creator,
and yet they hold themselves off because of great Love.
What Love would hold you from your beloved for fear of contamination
    to place an existence away from all that you Love?
Such Love has great scars.
Souls of earth, illusion is earth.
Truth is not illusion.
Truth is Creator.
Truth is given, a very part of your Creator.
Souls of earth, earth has a time to be in the space of negativity.
There is a doorway, a gateway, an entering in.
There is a Path that will draw all earth forward unto Farside,
    and the sister worlds will welcome the latest formed,
    and the lips that have been sealed will be opened,

and Negativity will ride the wave alone.
For all life will enter in to a thousand years of Truth
> to gain the understanding of Purity.
Purity is complex and simple.
It is not necessary to teach the Blessed in Purity.
It is necessary to teach earth beings the lesson they have left aside,
> their Purity they have entered in to earth without.
The Soul has only choice.
In the first entering it has gained in Purity.
Souls of earth, illusion is reflection,
> illusion is mirror, illusion is fraught with torment.
Has your Soul not understood the very Purity that is thy potential!
Has your Soul not understood the Love with which thou were created,
> the blessing of Creator which rains over thy being!
Humanity, the world has purpose of great intent,
> to gather Truth and relinquish all negativity.
The great teachers will revisit
> and walk the paths of earth
and touch the trees and they will blossom and figs will form,
> and lift a hand to the sky and the rainbow will shine.
Holy Beings will teach all earth of Purity and Purity will reign,
and Souls will see before them the promised land,
the Gateway to a new beginning,
and Souls from many worlds will visit and revisit earth,
and language will be as one,
for all Souls will have changed the face of the mirror.
And behold, when Purity draws nigh unto the Gateway,
> the Gateway will open
> and the loud Hosannas will echo in the worlds of worlds of worlds,
> and the great Path through, as the sea that opened,
> will become clear, and those who enter first will be humankind.
And Angels will sing, and Creator will BE,
> and all will Behold that which Creator IS,
> and earth will Behold, and mankind will gaze at all the worlds,
> and know that the travail and the pain has had purpose,
> for unto Creator has Purity entered in.
So be it.

440 Your Creator had a purpose.
You see, even we have not all knowledge of your Creator,
    who is indeed our Creator.
Remove your hands, remove your feet,
remove the flesh and the blood and the heart and the mind,
and still you would exist where you are, Soul.
You would exist!
You would be.
The containment of your being is aura.
It is not the feeble heart that beats, irregularly at times.
It is the aura that holds the containment of the Writing on the Wall,
    the very purpose of your being.
Why and how and when and where are marked
    in the aura of your being.
And your eyes, you will not permit your eyes
    to see the power of this Energy.
Souls of earth, look at the Light about your being.
Look at the reflection of holiness that you are.
Astound your eyes,
    blind your eyes with the power that is ignited through aura.
It is Holy, this aura, and it is only a part of that which you are.
You are clad lightly.
The wholeness of your being rests in the Farside,
    awaiting the re entering,
when you have gathered the Truth unto you.
What can illusion tell you of Truth?
For you are in illusion.
You think your eye can see?
Your eye has seen nothing except that which you choose it to see!
We would have you choose to see the completeness of your being.
We would have you choose to see the ecstasy of your being.
You are in Holy endeavour.
Your Creator has not driven you into this space.
You have knocked on the door and you have said: *"May we enter?"*
Legions of humanity,
    and how few will see the Light of their being!
Behold the Light of your being1

Behold the illuminescence of your being!
Behold the grandeur in which you are cloaked
    and know that you all but sprout wings in your Purity.
You are clothed in great power!
You are clothed in great power!
The aura of your being is incandescent, a fall of purple about you.
Higher being, is it not!
The kings of earth seek the purple
    and yet all humanity, to us, is garbed in purple.
Holy, Holy, Holy!
Souls of earth, acknowledge the aura that you have,
    know that the earth self is of little importance,
    for in the twinkling of an eye you would be in our space
    and the illusion would release itself from your being.
Honour the aura that you have.

441 Wisdom, wisdom is that which you ask.
Souls of earth,
    worlds of the Farside have not obtained the wisdom
    of that which you have received.
They have before them unknown landscape,
    they have before them the vision of great Purity.
Souls of earth, unto you is much given,
    unto you will much be received.
Souls of earth, behold thy Creator,
    behold the all encompassing Love of Creator.
Behold negativity, the all encompassing goodness of negativity.
Souls, as much of your earth has visualized and distorted path,
    so has your path been in negativity.
Negativity is thrashed and brought low by mankind.
Negativity has goodness, has the potential to growth.
It is that which draws your earth mind to question.
It is that which searches into the unknown.
Negativity has Wisdom, has goodness, has trust[79].
Earth has misused the trust of Negativity.
Love has all encompassing Love in Triad;
    Creator is Truth, Purity and Love.

---

79 Negativity (capitalized) is a Brother to Creator, to Love and Truth and Purity.

Truth is that which is a part of Negativity,
    Purity is that which is of Farside.
Love is that which is of Godhead.
Enter in to the Gateway of Creator
    and know within the Gateway of Creator
    is all the Energy from Godhead.
Know from out the Second is all the Energy from Creator.
All worlds are bound,
    and all worlds will enter in with a velocity
    beyond the ken of men, and yet be stable.
We have entered in beyond the Second,
    we have dwelt beyond the Second
    and we know of the heights of existence.
We know the abilities of our Being to lift the energies of worlds.
The preponderance of Knowing is beyond Two.
Knowing is that which you seek.
Godhead is All Knowing.
And the lift from earth to Farside is seven,
    the lift unto one is seven,
    the lift unto two is seven,
    the lift unto three is seven,
    the lift unto four is seven.
And your mind becomes confused and boggled
    in the simplicity of what you have been given,
    for the Energy of that which you are
    is everlasting unto everlasting,
    unto everlasting, unto everlasting.
Bountiful Creator who has entered out of majestic places
    to view the need, the pain,
    has gathered all humanity's Energy
    to create a dwelling place for them.
How omnipotent is our Creator
    who lifts the worlds of worlds unto His Being,
    who has within the energies, the containment of compassion,
    who has the utterances of great Love.
And unto Godhead, the Father, do we bow our self down and worship.

For unto Godhead is the supreme vision opened
> and the master plan revealed from the Great One, the All in All.

Unto Supreme Being do we forward our countenance,
> do we sublimate our Being and free our Spirit to be no more.

It has become as the Soul, free,
> and we have become within our Being
>> the total containment of creation.

442 Thus, the teaching continues.
When is not relevant.
How is impurity.
The breath of humanity stirs negativity when misused.
The voice harbours invocations to negativity,
and negativity is drawn into the field of the Soul.
The aura would hold negativity at abeyance,
> it is imperfection upon the face of the earth.

Aura is the armour you have been given to survive negativity.
Wear it proudly.
When the voice incants in negative responses,
> the whirlwind encircles the Soul.

And does not the whirlwind attract unto itself
> flotsam and jetsam!

Souls of earth, be amazed at the foothold you have
> at the edge of the transitional pain.

The well is deep and the Souls are Loved beyond earth's comprehension.
Oh Almighty Energy, oh Almighty Creator of creators,
> Godhead manifested unto Purity,
> carried as the wind carries particles,
> so you, Soul, are carried as blessed parts of creator
> and Creator, even unto Godhead.

Blessed humanity, illusion!
When you are confronted with a supreme test to your being
> that creates pain unendurable, that pain is incredibly real.

Yet, Soul, once you have surmounted and overcome,
> you look past and say:

"Pain. Yes, I endured pain, but it has become a word."

Illusion!
On the Farside, all efforts that you put forth on the place of earth,
    be they simple or complex, are but illusion.
For Timeless is timeless, Eternity is eternity
    and all creation is one creation.
But, Soul, your residence upon your planet is very real
    to the flesh and the bone, and the mind and the heart
    that you have undertaken to be,
    and the motion that is yours is drawn for one purpose,
    to overcome negativity.
Soul, do not diminish in your being, Energy Light,
    for you are come of Light and Energy.
All that you are has a single purpose of being;
    to reach Purity that will permit the countenance of Creator
    to be one with thine own.
You are Holy, you are Loved, you have value.
All Energy within your being is sacred unto Creator.
Frown not thou at the downtrodden, at the criminal,
    at he who points the finger,
    but reach into the well of goodness that is yours from Creator
    and issue forth rays of goodness from your being.

443 Michael will teach the research of the Farside,
    Souls who engage in creation's intrigue.
Because we live in a state of total Truth
    and we have all knowledge to our level,
    does not mean we have all knowledge.
Much is before us unexplained.
We delight in the new found text,
    as your earth will delight in the new found text.
Earth humanity has ever had its history recorded
    from the beginning of time.
Who could see what creation would bring?
Seek beyond Creator, Holy beings who art on earth,
    Godhead, the Purity, the Love!
You have not entered in to the lesson of Love.
The lessons are forthcoming.
Behold, all creation began with Godhead

and all purities extended outward into the Void,
and ion was the passage of Purity.
And the hosts of radiant magnificence, of illuminescent Purity,
clothed themselves and came forth into the Void as creators
to search from whence Purity was extended.
And your Creator visioned your galaxy and all therein.
And it extended Being, passed fragments of self outward from Being,
to conquer the negativity in the space of the Eye of Beholding.
And Souls caught in the acceleration of negativity brought earth low
and outer space reflected the thread unto Creator,
and Creator pondered on that which was created
and proposed a salvation for man.
And negativity spewed forth anger and excelled with great wars
to conquer man.
And Creator offered another gift of research
and awaits for what man will do.
For man is caught in his own being,
has found in his illusion, eyes,
and sees what he thinks is real,
and illusion has become real.
Behold what man may do!
Farside research offers to man, a gift
and man has met in the core of his being the thought,
and the thought has become reality,
and now the negativity will enter and play havoc.
And who will be the conqueror?
Soul, the stench of negativity is high on earth.
The veins of red flow upward.
You have the potential of miracles.
Would man abase a miracle,
or will the flower blossom and conquer illusion?

444 Michael will teach the Soul how the Soul may be pure
and exist upon earth.
The Soul has within it the ability to absorb all energies.
The Spirit could not absorb negativity
because Purity has entered in.
It has deflected negativity long since.

The Soul is a fragment of vulnerability of the Essence of your being.
When humanity receives pain in any form, the Soul accepts the pain.
It is the purpose of the Soul to accept the pain.
It is why earth humanity has entered in.
Your purpose is to overcome so that your being may be purified.
The Soul renders the pain ineffectual to the Soul.
The only context of your being that has a purpose is the Soul.
The body, heart and mind are projects at work.
They initiate the cure, the acceptance or overcoming of pain for the Soul,
    therefore both the pain and the cure of pain
    are directly related to the Soul.
Do not seek a far off cure, but know the cure
    is directly related to the being
    which has no separation from the Soul.
Even in the most evil deed the Soul is involved.
It is the growth of the Soul, not the heart, mind and body.
It is the acceptance of the Soul, not the heart, mind and body.
The being is inclusive of heart, mind and body.
It is the Soul's growth alone.
It is totally the Energy of the Soul that has growth.
The heart, mind and body are illusion.
But to the body, to the mind, to the heart, the pain is a reality
    and for the Soul the battle has begun.
The heart, the mind and the body do battle with the pain,
    with the negativity, and reach to the Soul for strength.
Some waylay the Soul, and the heart, the mind and the body say:
    "What have we to do with thee, Soul?
    We may fight this battle without you."
Know it is not possible.
The Soul, to enter in to Purity, must be involved with the fragments.
It is the Soul that is at battle with negativity.
The heart, the mind and the body are but the armour
    that the Soul uses.
It is the shield and the buckler to prepare the snare of entrapment.
The Soul has great powers in the positive.
The Soul may reach unto the Energy of its being
    and there touch the White Light of its own.

The Soul may find itself across your world
    in a moment, in a flash of time.
The Soul may heal with an immediacy that surgeons may not.
But to be in this state, the heart must have acceptance
    and have waylaid the mind,
        and have found the pure part of its being extended unto Creator.
Healing of pain may be instant, should be instant, will be instant
    when earth avows there will be no negativity allowed.
The proportion of your pain is in harmony
    with the proportion of your earth acceptance.
Beings, you are not about earth acceptance.
You are about Farside acceptance.
Be not ready to grasp that which is earth,
    for no man would hold earth if they could extend their vision,
    would extend their vision, into the Purity of all other worlds.
You, Soul, are a fragment of learning, learning to become pure.
Your Purity has potential that alters your flesh,
    and your bone, and your mind,
    and the heart is free to float into other worlds at will.
Soul, learn well to overcome pain.

445 Souls, extend your beings far from your earth form.
Know the power of the shaft of Purity placed about your being.
Know the aura of Purity.
It is blessed, it is travelled and brought unto your being.
It has entered in to all parts of your world.
You are not exclusive in the entering in of this shaft
    nor is it secluded to the years you are in.
It has entered in the time of Buddha, in the time of Jesu,
    in the time of Mohammed and Krishna.
It has been available unto all men.
Behold the seed that you are,
    behold, humanity, the very seed of your being
    that has reached the growth that enables you
    to hear the words of Purity and resonate with those words,
    and seek outward from your being
    that which should be known.

You will not find that which should be known
    in the wash of your humanity, for it is not there.
You will not find that which should be known
    in the vision of your earth, for it is not there.
You will find that which should be known
    within the heart of your being,
        for the heart of your being has connectedness
        to the aura of whom you are.
Be astounded, Souls, at how far you may enter
    in to the heart of your being.
Be astounded that your heart has a flow
    that extends unto the very Creator of your being.
You, Soul, have sprouted forth, you are pure.
You are endowed with all the potentials of your Creator.
You may be brought low by the pain you have delved into
    or you may choose to seek the higher level of being.
Soul, enlighten thyself!
Enlighten the space of your being.
Hold thou each day the Love of thy fellow man.
Hold thou each day the presence of goodness.
Do not spout here and there and expect man to gauge your words
    and hear the goodness of your being.
Be thou as the maker of the seed.
Oh blessed, blessed Creator!
Know His Being.
He has great goodness, He has joy, He has compassion.
He has adventure in the creating of worlds.
Do you find yourself in adventure,
    or do you look only at the pain of your being?
Do you open your purse and see only that which is there,
    or do you open your heart and magnify your goodness?
Souls, earth Souls, be thou risen up!
Be thou arisen beyond self.
Know the extension of thy being.
Enlightenment is the extension of thy being.
It is profound in its goodness.
It has redeeming qualities,
    for are not all open palms an offering unto Creator!

Oh, Souls of earth, we have been in thy space.
Earth is not just yours.
Earth is also ours of the Farside.
We vision earth, we see that which this is about.
We have a purpose in the eyeing of your globe.
It is to begin the celebration, for all on the Farside enjoy celebration.
The worlds resound with celebration and, Souls,
    <u>no</u> earth celebration could behold the one
    that you will enter in in the bringing forth of purities.
Bless your beings, Souls of earth!
Do not lose self in the mundane.
Do not lose self in the dispirited hoax of your being,
    for illusion is illusion, is it not?
And, Souls, your gracious heritage is reality.
Reach to the Farside in reality.

446 Soul, illusion is negativity.
Illusion is negativity!
Souls of earth, recognize only Purity and all negativity will cease to be.
Upon the Farside, negativity has ceased to be.
Why then will not the Blessed Ones recognize this?
Because, Soul, they are pure.
Because they are Angelic.
Because, Soul, they have all Love.
Negativity encroached all crevices, all entryways on Farside, all Souls.
And only from those of great Purity could Negativity be held
    and these Souls implored unto Creator:
"Come, save that which is creation unto creation unto creation,
      or we are lost.
    Woe be all Souls!
    The Spirit is fatigued in fighting off Negativity.
Redeem Thy children.
    See us as worthy unto Thee.
Come Thou forth where we are."
And Creator Entered In.
Purity is tangible, Purity is known, Purity has great power.
Are you not pure!
Do not fight to hold off negativity from your being.

Illusion

Do not feel the strength of that Purity and the power of that negativity.
Know, Souls, Purity conquers fully that which is negative,
    for can not negativity slay the heart and the flesh and the blood!
Yet the heart and the mind rise up with the Soul.
Always three, always three!
Even unto Creator, always three.
All form is seven, all Love and Purity are three.
Know unto thy being comes a wall.
It says: "Here am I, negativity, to infringe myself upon your mind.
I will this day bombard your mind.
I will this day bring you down to your knees,
       and you will hear this negativity,
       and you will be upon your knees.
    And you will fling your arms high and say:
    "Help me, help me!"
Soul, negativity is an illusion.
You make it your reality,
    as the Blessed Ones were caught in the gathering
    and placed the curtain,
    and Negativity is the reality of their Being.
The remembrance is only a gathering time.
In the Void it is acceptance or rejection.
The Soul cannot accept
    because they would place that Negativity
    within the space of creation.
They will not do so,
    and so humanity is the army of Truth.
And Creator has placed in the hands of humanity,
    the keys to unlock the doors
    that all might be free from negativity.
How can Creator be less than Creator!
Creator is Love.
Love cannot enter in and be only Truth.
Love cannot enter in and be only Purity.
Therefore, the Blessed Ones came forth to do battle.
Souls, as the curtain was placed with transitional care
    to protect the Farside,
    so is the Hinterland the final curtain of negativity.

It is creation.
Can you destroy creation?
Will you destroy that which has been?
Your earth seeks,
    your earth seeks to find cures.
The Farside has ever sought to find a cure for Negativity
    without eradicating Negativity.
We do not ask you to eradicate Negativity.
We ask you to put it from you, to place it far from you.
In your Truth, recognize negativity has no place within your being.
And from that knowledge of Truth,
    the Blessed Ones will know your Purity
    and recognize once again, the Purity of their own.

447 See the falcon open the wing and know that in the marketplace
    the Soul will see a fig and swoop down and back.
Before the eye can see, the Soul has taken that which he would.
You have been in the space of negativity.
The Soul would ask you to see, acknowledge, negativity.
Negativity is as the falcon in the market place.
It eyes and grabs and takes.
It is instant.
Before you are aware, you are clasping negativity and you say:
"Begone, take it from me!"
And yet it holds.
The thought is strangling, is it not!
Inveigling, is it not!
Treacherous, is it not!
How may you release negativity?
Souls, you enter in to meditation.
You acknowledge naught, nothing, no thing.
You acknowledge the space of no thing
    and all goodness will invade your being
    and replace the negativity that you have.
Hold in your hands, orbs the size of great melons,
    rich, overflowing with taste and flavour.
So is the goodness overflowing with taste and flavour
    and know that the Light is equal.

One is negativity, the other is positive.
They have the appearance of one and the same.
Negativity has a trickery, it has the sense often of goodness.
Look well at the goodness you hold.
Be very sure it does not hold trickery.
Be very sure it is total goodness.
Goodness and Purity abide.
Negativity cannot be in the guise of goodness for long
    without showing flaw,
    as the gem shows a flaw at a closer look.
We ask you, Soul, we plead with your being,
    to look at the market place and to see the negativity and heal.
But we ask you, Soul, to closer look at the negativity within your being,
    to recognize the flaw that you know is there
    and remove the flaw by sending power
    to alter the gem that you are.
You are precious and the falcon is the clutch of negativity.
It would grasp unto itself, the gem.
It would search out the negative space of your being.
You are, within your being, the positive and the negative.
It is a battle both have entered in equal.
And from the day you were born the battle has begun,
    the ability to overcome all that is negative within your space,
even the ability for negative thought,
even the ability for negative utterances.
Soul, expressions are not above reproach.
May all that you portray be portrayed as a reflection of your Creator,
    for in the marketplace of earth
    there are many rich fruits and goodnesses
and the soft fruit is not always unworthy to eat.
It merely needs to be altered so that it has worth.
Soul, you are the salt of the earth.
We ask that you recognize the worthiness of your being.

448 Blessed, blessed Souls, beings in the space of great Love,
    warm your being in the space of ever flowing Energy Love.
Know that you have the power to dispense the Energy Love.
Know that it is endless and may flow from your being.

It has no attachments that may alter or change.
There are no irregularities in the offering of Love.
There is a kaleidoscope of rainbow hues
    that wash over thy being and extend outward unto all Souls.
Beings of earth, you cannot be in the space of such Love
    without being altered,
        no humanity can, no Farside Purity can.
Only does the equal Energy, Negativity, have that ability.
Souls of earth, conjure up no magic to defeat the Energy, Negativity.
Magic has been attempted.
Conjure up no Truths, but rely on the Truth,
    the Truth of thy being, the purpose of thy being.
It is the only Truth that has the ability to overcome negativity,
    not defeat in the sense of eradicate, but overcome negativity.
It does not alter the negative Energy.
Accepting the Truth allows the human form to escape the tendrils
    that ever would weave about you.
Love is everlasting.
Negativity is everlasting until there is a solution.
Souls of earth, you are not the solution to Negativity.
You are the solution to overcoming your negativity,
    the negativity in your space,
        but the great place of Negativity is only a portion thereof.
It is tethered, and you will draw the tethering to a finer space.
All energies of earth are for the purpose of humanity.
All energies of Love are for the purpose of aiding thy brother.
Negativity is the Brother of Love.

449 Blessings to humanity, adoration to deity.
The most sacred of all flowers is the seed of humanity.
It has the colour of purple, it scatters itself to the wind,
    it floats upon the waters, it lifts itself into the air,
    and it embeds itself deep into the ground.
It grows in fertile land, in desert plains,
    it grows in goodness and in evil.
It is the most blessed of seeds.
It will enter in at the time of drought,
    it will enter in when the storms rage and the winds blow.

Illusion

Holy seed that conquers a most inhabitable place.
The seed is bombarded,
    it is not planted in a gentle garden,
    it is not always watered and loved by the sower of the seed.
For the seed has entered in with a will of its own,
    and a choice of its own,
and the blessed seed has a potential of growth,
and the potential of growth is beauty beyond any imagination.
The seed sprouts and becomes man,
    and man shields his being from the negativity,
and creates a barrier about his being,
and the wall says: "Negativity, do not enter in. Stay at bay."
But in the shielding of self from negativity,
    the human has shielded himself
    from the very brethren roundabout.
Souls of earth, how may you let go of this roil of negativity,
    for negativity hoards itself against the curtain,
    remembering it is invasive.
It would do the Soul harm.
Enter in to the tapestry that you are,
    recognize the weave that you are,
    recognize the humanity that you are.
See that you do not need to build a wall.
Know that you have the power
    to overcome this negativity that you hold at bay.
Know that in your very being
    is the power to overcome negativity.
You do not need to look to other purities.
The Angels would remove the negativity
    if it were not your natural purpose that it be there.
All negativity may be removed in a twinkling
    if you will alter the view that you have of negativity.
You see negativity as powerful.
It is powerless without your intervention.
It can only strangle when it has a grip.
Your Souls are bathed in purple.
Acknowledge, Soul, from whence you have come.
Remove the wall about your being

and enter in to negativity
    knowing it is powerless in your space.
Can negativity grip your being?
No, Soul, only another human may grip your being.
Will you use the Energy that you have
    to alter all energy of negativity?
Will you accept negativity as energy we Love?
We Love!
Research would alter negativity.
We would teach negativity to know Love.
Will you teach negativity to know Love by bestowing Love?
For all is Love in the sight of Farside.
Lift your beings unto the place of Entering In
    and know that your power is great,
that the seed will flourish,
that the seed comes from a mighty flower,
    the growth of which mankind could not behold.

450 Souls, we would speak of the grace of acceptance.
It is not a requirement, it is not a debt, it is a growth.
Earth has a single purpose; to accept all Truth and deny negativity.
All earth is bombarded with negativity.
Some Souls, in great desperation, reach in their being unto negativity
and cling to the powers that invade their being,
that drive the goodness from their being,
and then, behold, they awake.
They have been in earth space many times
and they have learned this negativity brings us down
and casts us about as flotsam and jetsam,
and we have come to naught,
    we are nothing in our negativity.
And we have seen others advance
    and beheld the richness of their being,
    and now we make a choice to enter in
    to that state of growth, of acceptance.
We shall no longer accept negativity.
We shall accept positive Energy.
Acceptance is the generative word.

It is that which continues the progress of humanity.
It is a movement.
You cannot stand idly by.
You cannot be in a place of no choice, no acceptance.
It must be to accept positive or accept negative.
They are weighed in the balance,
    and young Souls, in their lack of wisdom,
    harbour the gathering of negativity to them,
    the power of negativity to them,
    and the broken bones and the pain does not disturb.
There is no unction in their choice.
You enter earth many times.
At many levels you enter in, and you advance in growth,
and through your lives you search this negativity,
    and you find it wanting
    and you accept to release it from your being.
The acceptance of Purity has still great unease within the being,
    the psyche, for it demands.
It is not an easy choice, it has expectations.
To enter in to Purity is to release that which can be comfortable,
    the negative shroud about your being.
Soul, to release this shroud you must enter in to acceptance
that you are worthy of such Purity,
that you have a purpose as humanity,
and that your walk is your walk unto the Purity of your being,
but it has an onus unto all of humanity.
Beleaguer not your identity,
    but advance quickly to the state of acceptance.
Uphold all positive endeavours and bring yourself quickly
unto the level of full humanity, a total acceptance,
    only slightly less than the Angels of which you are.

451 Humanity, you are not tethered to your world.
You do not require the wings of high beings.
You have a power equal and beyond their own.
You have the power of creativity.
Creator has given unto man a garden, a paradise, an eden.

He has chosen from the Farside
    the reflections that would give mankind peace and serenity.
He has given unto mankind the same endowments
    that are Creator's very own, the power of creativity.
Humanity, awake!
Know that daily in your time, in your moment, you are creator.
You may not seek the avenue of life and enter in,
    and not have within your being the power of creativity.
You hold a balance of negativity and positive Energy.
It is equal on the coming in.
It is the power to create negativity, to have it blossom;
to urge the growth of this Energy
    and stir it to momentous happenings
    that you may influence others about your being.
You may encourage and beckon it forward and create evil,
    it is a power that you have.
It bursts forth in its creativity.
It urges as a weed its own growth.
And you have the power of positive.
It beckons you also, and you may gather it unto your being,
    and you may create joy.
You may create Truth and Purity and Love.
How does the balance weigh within your being?
Blessed Souls of earth, honour thy being and the great power you have,
    the power within the mind to alter the invasion of Negativity.
How may you do this?
You do not battle with negativity.
To battle with negativity is to join negativity.
You gather the poignancy of positive,
the acceleration in the breath of Truth,
the joy in the stride of Purity,
and the noxious weed withers from thy being.
It moves into the quiet state of inertia that it is.
Souls of earth, understand the great power in your being,
    understand the influence of your creativity.
You are the gatherers, you are the balancer of earth's chi.
Do this by the creativity of positive Energy.

452 Earth, well of deception,
    look at deception, recognize the inability of deception
    to move without a human to carry.
Know iniquity, greed, avarice, and look well at the inability
    of all negatives to move without humanity in motion.
Souls, do not enable the power of negativity!
Welcome the power of negativity
    and know that within the human there is naught
    that can not be overcome.
How powerful you are, humanity!
How much has been given unto thee:
the power to alter that which is in your step,
the power to alter the very orb on which you exist,
the power to alter all life forms within your orb.
Souls of earth, be humbled at the power
    the Creator has given unto thee!
For has He not made you like unto Himself, with great powers!
Souls of earth, unto humanity is given the power to alter all things:
    mass, ion, flesh, blood.
See the powerful being that thou art,
    for without the sight nothing is altered.
Without the Register of Wisdom nothing is altered.
See those in your space whole.

453 We enter in to many.
It is not only in your space that we enter in.
You have been given a challenge in your teaching.
It is to comprehend the Love of your Creator toward Negativity.
It is to understand that blessed Creator may not alter Negativity.
Creator is pure, abundantly pure, overwhelmingly pure.
Creator has a dimension we know as Love.
Souls of earth, the myriad of dimensions that you know are infinitesimal.
Oh, Soul, they are infinitesimal in your space.
You do not see a fragment of the Energy round about you.
You do not see the lecherous hold of negativity.
You do not see the generous blend of Love,
    and yet you are caught in the web.
You must walk through the web,

and each time you find yourself tethered to the web,
you must break the strands from your being.
And what frees the web?
Oh, Souls of earth, it is the Energy of Love.
Love has the power to give strength to your being,
    not to injure the brother,
but to give strength to your wounded,
to give them the power to release the cords that bind.
For in Love is freedom, in Love is uplifting,
    separating from the web of negativity.
You are a fragment of the Love of Creator.
You have the incredible ability
    to release from your being, all negativity.
Souls, we are all Holy beings, we are all great energies.
You, above all Farside energies,
    are the fragments of the second birth.
To return into the space of great Purity is to be truly blessed.
You entered in for Truth
and Truth is your mirror, Souls of earth.

454 Blessed, all Souls have injustices brought upon them.
All Souls delight when injustices are placed upon them,
    but the illusion does not mirror what we on the Farside
    see so clearly.
The Soul has reflection and the reflection is your earth,
    and your earth agonizes over each step.
The Soul toils needlessly with energies wasted.
The Farside sees reflection of self and delights at the pain
    and utters great cheers for the choices that have been made.
How separate and yet a part is the Soul to the Spirit and the Essence.
How free it is to move, choosing independently from the Spirit.
It holds all intent of the Spirit
but is influenced greatly by the negative energy
and the Soul is often caught in the grid work of meshed energies.
The Soul chooses and the Spirit may not intervene.
The Blessed Angels may intervene and only few may alter the course.
The Spirit may bring forward a memory of a lesson,
a *deja vu* of what has been,

and the Soul will be reminded of just such a time
and a decision will come.
But all walks upon earth are done independently by the Soul
    once the Soul has entered the negative field.
The blanket of Purity that is upon the Soul on returning to Farside
    is clearly not visible, except as the Soul releases all negativity.
The Soul is caught in constant battering
    of what delights negativity holds.
The Soul progresses with each step being encountered
    by Souls from various energies outside of human.
These Souls initiate steps by placing themselves directly in the path.
These Souls can not alter the path, but they can clear the path
    so it is easy for the Soul.
You will look upon this Soul as a kind human being
    who has entered in to make life easier for you.
These Souls are not earthly.
They are of earth but they do not truly belong.
They know in their being they are not.

455 Earth, humanity, you have your years set for your lifetime
    on entering in.
You have chosen the passing moment of your demise.
Do not concern yourself with when you shall leave.
Know, Soul, that you are hardly there.
Know that the iota of your existence is momentary.
Do not lavish sensitivities on the form of your being.
Such inane execution of time.
You have structured your existence to overcome negativity.
It is the sole purpose of your being.
To release with the power you have given yourself,
    that Creator has endowed in your being,
    see your beings, mirror your beings.
Souls of earth, you are one.
You are not caught in fragmentary groups of existence.
You hold the magic to alter the course of earth,
to free from your being, pain,
to release from your being, negativity,
to flounder not in wasted thought,

but to clasp in your hand the mighty shards of Purity
and to place wellness about your being.
You do not have to harness Purity.
It is ready, it awaits only the acceptance of your being.
You do not have to harness negativity.
It will be as the mighty grappling hook, insidious, willing to enter in.
Both are congenial in appearance, both gather momentum.
As the river flows and eddies and takes momentum,
    so will either of these precious energies.
Look at the world you are in.
Look at the tiniest fragment of creation
    and understand you may not pass by
    without the glow of its being affecting your Soul,
    for each Energy in your space alters your Soul.
In likewise do you enter the Soul of others
    with negativity or positive Energy.
Choose, Soul, for the purpose of your being.

456 Souls of earth, how awesome is the ego.
How awesome!
We have been your mirror, we have been in the space of great purities,
    we have been on the field of great negativity.
Our being challenged the field of negativity.
We usurped the power of negativity, for we armed our being
    with a mighty armour, the armour of Purity, of Love.
Truth is your earth, and if you may see your Truth
and recognize the mirror of its being,
you will know you are with us,
you will know you are in the space of Purity.
But, earth Souls, too few look into the mirror, too few see the reflection.
The sleight of hand is magic.
The mirror is not magic, but reflection.
Souls of earth, the smallest gnat may bite and create great pain.
The smallest of humanity may enter in to Love and illuminate the world.
It has been done.
Raise your beings up, lift your beings up!
Know you are not tethered to earth.
Know you have the ride into infinity.

Soul, you can ride to infinity, this you have done.
Know the power that you have, know the glimpse that you have
    of where you have been.
You may look down and see your being,
    the speck that is you, the iota that is you.
And yet you are magnificent to behold, for you move
    and you have thought, and you have motion.
But you are an iota and the reflection of whom you are is glorious.
Beings of earth, see the wonder of your being!
Glimpse at the Soul that is you on the Farside,
    the Essence of your being, the glory of your being.
You are not tethered to the iota of humanity.
You are Loved as the iota of humanity.
You are treasured as gold.
You are treasured as part of that from which you came: Creator.
Our beings could pluck you from the hair of your dog,
    for we have mighty stature to your being.
We Love you so.
We Love you, Souls!
Our beings reach out to the gnat that you are,
    for in the gnat do we see the perfection of our Creator.
In the gnat do we see the expression of our Creator
    and we tremble at the potential of this iota that is human.
Each time a Soul chooses negativity, we are smitten.
Each time the choice is the wrong choice, the purpose is delayed.
And we know of the Beings who have kept themselves apart.
We have been richly blessed by whom they are.
You see, earth troubles itself over words
    when the glory of whom they are is before them.
Souls of earth, your existence is seen.
Man behind the telescope, know that we see your being
and know that we do not laugh at your efforts,
but we know that you have found the difficult path.
We know that you have found the deepest mire,
    for you cannot see beyond where your feet are stationed.
Leave the feet of your being to your earth and soar beyond.
It is your Soul that has existence.
You do not die, you are but cloaked.

Your being cannot contain on earth the aura that you have.
It exudes from your flesh
    and your young stand amazed before the colour that they see,
    and your eyes have dulled, and you have lost the ability
    to see with the eyes of the innocent.
All earth could travel as one, all containments could be released as one.
Souls of earth, you, who are found in the prison walls,
know that you have the ability to leave the shell
    and reach beyond where you are.
And your keeper would enter in and say:
    "Soul, where have you gone? They have all left their beings."
And you may enter back in and say:
    "We have returned, but we have been away
        and you could not lock us up,
        for we now have gained the power to release our being
        from the negativity we have known.
    We have found the Purity that we did not know
        abided within our being,
and we rejoice in the knowledge
        of that negativity, for we have been able
        to release it from our being
        and soar beyond that which we have done."
Hold the generation of negativity far from your being.
Know that negativity is caught in the positive ion.
It is the Soul's negative ion that alters the state of negativity,
    negative to negative, positive to positive.
Souls, rejoice!
All negativity has turn, all negativity has motion,
    all negativity accelerates with the use of positive ion.
Souls of earth, direct thy being to the state of BE.
Direct thy being to the positive entry of IS.
Hold item and agenda far from the Soul,
    the Soul has no purpose in these.
The systematic turn of the positive Truth is firm.
The systematic motion of ions are positive in the space of the Soul.
These only require to be in a state of flux.
The truant Soul is always, ever, after motion, and purpose, and, and, and.
The Soul need only rest in positive ion to have the fullness of perfection.

Have the taste of the Farside.
Join us at the level of understanding
    that accepts the Purity of Truth and Love.
Stay harbored in the circle of the thread of care
    that immobilizes all negative to its separate space.
Wisdom is acceptance.
Souls, seek acceptance.
otion of ions are positive in the space of the Soul.
These only require to be in a state of flux.
The truant Soul is always, ever, after motion, and purpose, and, and, and.
The Soul need only rest in positive ion to have the fullness of perfection.
Have the taste of the Farside.
Join us at the level of understanding
    that accepts the Purity of Truth and Love.
Stay harbored in the circle of the thread of care
    that immobilizes all negative to its separate space.
Wisdom is acceptance.
Souls, seek acceptance.

EARTH FIVE

457 Souls, bless Gummeria, bless the great strategies of beings.
Bless Pleiadians who work at research
    and gently meld to mankind that which man should know.
Know Lemuria.
Do not fear!
Your beings will all reach the place of Purity to enter.
Know Lantosia.
It does not fit into your language.
It is merged into your alphabet.
Our being speaks it differently.
Souls, all beings from these earths outnumber your world.
You have such a small army, but it is adequate to the task.
It is a gathering.
It is the pleasure of all energies to behold that which humanity does.
Do not fear that which you do not know,
    and know that your are minute in the experience of Farside.
It is a David and Goliath come to rescue all that is, all creations.

It is the last overture, the finale.
It is the utmost gift.
It is done, represented, by all Energy Fields
    who have entered in to the form.
Is it amazing that mankind seeks to feel differently in his being
    when he has a different form than his brother?
All human beings are connected to other worlds.
All are gathering.
Came Melchezidec and gathered all:
    "Souls, come here.
    We have a gift to offer: humanity.
    The precious one is formed, the seed has entered
        through an aperture and entered the earth galaxy,
and all therein has negativity.
    It is a force we must battle.
    Will you be this human?
    Will you enter through the aperture
        and leave that which you know to be Purity?"
"Why would we leave what we have?"
"The Blessed Ones sob, the Blessed Ones tear in their Being,
    they cannot raise those that are lost.
Will you help to draw the Blessed Ones as a gift to your Creator?"
"Over here, here. I will offer such an offering.
    I will dare to enter in to the field of pain."
Melchezidec has called his army
    and Creator gave that name at the forming,
    and said unto Melchezidec:
    "Melchezidec, rise from thy Being
        and know that which is proposed
        has great peril unto thy Being.
    You must stay, Melchezidec!
    For the first army may fail,
        and who then would draw unto themselves a second army?"
And Melchezidec looked unto Creator, bowed, and said:
    "We shall not fail, for as it is said, so be it unto Thee."
And he rousted forth an army, and he has placed many waves of energies
    into the negativity.
The negativity is strong, but humanity rises and falls, and rises and falls,

and rises and falls, and from humanity there comes a growth,
and the overcoming of negativity is seen in the robe of humanity.
And humanity has risen, many unto level five,
and the Souls will enter in when the numbers have been balanced.

458 Souls of earth, beings found in Truth,
know the purpose of thy being is Truth.
Behold Creator! Truth, Purity and Love.
Behold earth:
the learning field of the first passageway to Truth.
Truth in total resides at fifth level.
Souls are welcomed into the arms of Angels for the goodness
that has been theirs upon earth.
To have accepted Truth within their being is to have entered
in to the passageway of Creator.
Holy being, Holy being entered in to five,
thou hast become a portion of Creator.
Purity, behold Purity!
Earth has not visioned Purity.
Purity excels beyond earth vision,
Passageway two:
behold the Circle of Saints, the Blessed Angels,
behold the Purity of their Being.
Earth only shares the reflection of their Being,
for earth could not look upon such Purity.
It would blind the eye.
Behold the blessed St. Jacob, who climbed the stairway to heaven
to reach unto the platform of Angels and Angels welcomed.
Holy Holy have reached the second passage of Creator.
Unto thy being are all passages brought.
Unto thy being is all Purity returned.
Holy Holy, unto level six, second passage.
Love! Who can Love and give all energies outward from their being?
Who can Love, bestowing upon others
all of their goodness, of their Purity?
Behold Buddha! Behold Jesu! Behold Mohammed! Krishna!
Behold sanctity!

Behold blessed Love that is the outward Flow of Their Being,
    radiating to all.
Love: passageway three.
Onward from Truth is Purity.
Onward from Purity is Love.
Souls of earth, Farside knows not negativity
    because of the Blessed Ones who rank in Holy Holy Holy.
Beings of such Truth, of such Purity, of such Love
    that they emanate goodness within themselves.
And the Flow becomes creator,
    and blessed Creator welcomes the goodness of their Being
    and gathers all goodness unto the Energy of Creator.
Behold, earth has called the three: Father, Son and Holy Ghost.
Truth, Purity and Love;
    Soul, Spirit and Essence;
    behold the lesson of progression!
We are of the Circle of Saints.
Soul, our Purity is full, the being of our Love is still in onward motion.
The concept that your earth has of Truth, Purity and Love,
    has a minute understanding of the blessedness
    within the purpose of the worlds.
All worlds, all particles of being have motion.
Truth has motion.
Purity has motion.
Love has motion always outward from self,
    always beyond the thought of thy own being.
Blessed are they who enter in to level five.
A Soul manifested unto the Purity is past the realm of negativity.
A Soul who has not completed levels of understanding that brings Purity
    has not entered in to manifestation.
A Soul at level five and beyond, choosing to return to earth
    as a gift to Creator, vibrates their being to a form
    that holds within their being the level of Purity they are from.
They have the protection of all the energies of Purity,
    negativity may not enter their being, as Souls of earth will be,
    when the vibrational Purity of their being
    allows them to enter the realm of transition as a gift to Creator.

459 Holy being, Holy Holy being, brought from the place of Purity
    into the place of pain and negativity.
Soul of earth, the milieu of negativity is enticing to your being.
You have great power, you have incredible power
    to withstand all negativity within the surroundings of your being.
You may take the circumference about your being,
    you may know it has Purity, you may know that no negativity
    may advance into the space by thought or deed.
Holy being, ignite your Soul with the power that you have.
Draw your being into the powerful place of generosity reaching outward
    that the discernment of self
    will be only that which you can do for others.
In that moment you will have lost pain from your being.
You will be charged with the ion of positive Energy.
See your being as positive.
Know that all the Energy round about you carries the power of beings
    who have, in your space, great concern.
They guide your footsteps as you guide the footsteps of the young.
They tend your being as nurturing, as a parent would tend their child.
Soul, the comfort of the angels surrounds thy being.
How can you be brought low?
How can you be in a space of pain?
Know joy! Know joy is yours!
Know that pain is relative to the mind, and release the mind from pain.
Acknowledge the positiveness of your Creator,
    for, Soul, you are part of the Creator.
The fragment of your being is that of Creator.
Acknowledge the Purity of your being.

460 Michael will teach the Soul, ego,
    the forward of the Soul self,
    the place where growth is initiated.
Ego is the vision of two choices.
It displays the free will that renders the choice positive or negative.
Turn the Soul strength to the map
    and the ego will be given a nudge by the guides.
Many refuse to listen, some listen and do not adhere,
    others gather strength and receive a straight line.

Ego is dilemma,
>   it is the wandering mind lost in the gratification of self.
The Soul has placed the mind body above the Soul.
It can not be, yet there is the Path that is Farside,
>   that will not nudge
>   when the step is to be in that part of lesson
>   that requires ego to be foremost.
Dear one, earth is simply the lesson, the tablet you take to learn.
We give the nudge, we do not offer the ego solution.
Teach Love, Purity and Truth.
The ego is then a gathering place for judgements and spiritual self.
Ego overwhelms many.
Ego has two faces, a negative face and a positive face.
Ego is the extension of self to confuse issues
>   or to draw perfection upon the waiting Soul.
Ego, in perfection, has overcome its negative face.
It has dissolved itself into perfection.
All that is Holy has not always been Holy.
The Soul may use the positive Energy of self.
The angels' countenance has overcome all negative ego.
The Holy ones have overcome all negative ego.
"Creator, blessed Creator, sanctify my being
>   that I may radiate the ego of positive Energy outward!"
Are we idle nothingness?
Soul, we are sanctity, we are Holy, and we are raised in holiness
>   unto the space of the Holy Holy Ones.
Bless the Saints and Angels.
Bless the beings of Purity.
Know that within the placement of energies there is need for ego.
Ego is a delight.
Ego is an uplifting countenance that gentles a Soul in the receiving.
As negative ego can cast down a Soul,
>   be thou in the place of positive ego!

461 Mankind has two faces does he not?
You are mankind.
We ask mankind to find the single face, the face of tranquillity,
>   the face of acceptance.

We ask mankind to flow, not to target.
We ask mankind to open the chakra, to permit the Energy to flow outward.
Souls of earth, the knuckles of your hands were meant for flexing,
    not injuring.
Do not place your hands downward but place your hands upward,
extend them out from self as the giver of all things,
where a countenance does not belie what you feel,
but honours that what you feel.
Express the countenance of extending and wait until the arms are full
    and uplift unto Creator that which you hold.
Do not overburden self, do not hold on to negativities.
Place them far from you.
They have no purpose in your being.
Do not, Soul, look at that which is past, but see rather where your feet are
and see that they stand honourably, not upon another Soul.
And when you take a step, search the step forth and know that honour
    must be in the step that you take.
Take the step with ease, do not force the step.
All things of goodness will come unto you.
Do not berate thy being if thy step has been false,
    but bring the delinquent member back to thy being
    to reform the step;
    they tread in the footsteps of Angels and guides
    for they tread first where you would walk.
When you fall, they lift you up and they guide you forth
    into the promised land.
Soul, as you welcome humanity to your being,
    do not look to see whom you have gathered,
    rather see all beings as one being.
The river of humanity is often feeble, often it has currents,
    often the river runs into the sea
    and finds the depth of the sea unbearable.
Remember, in the depth of the sea is the whale and the dolphin,
    in the depth of the sea are the Jinn, who lift mankind
    from the depths of deep waters unto their Creator,
    unto a safe passage into the sphere of earth.
Move backward that another may advance;
    his need may be greater than yours.

Assist the fallen, lift them, purchase for them a place ahead of you.
Nothing on earth can be lost except growth.

462 Beloved children of earth, be found in the place of sanctity.
Sanctity is in the gathering of Purity, not in the hoarding of material goods.
Sanctity is not in high walls,
> but in the caring for those who hunger and are cast down.

Blessed beings of earth, do not try to retrieve that which has been taken.
Earth beings spend many lives trying to retrieve that which has been taken.
That which has been taken is a lesson, a valued lesson.
It endeavours to give space,
> it endeavours to bring the Soul to a place of decision,
>> for earth is not viewed through a crystal, it is not a Prism of joy.

Joy can be found by acceptance of earth.
Hold the pain for but a moment,
> and know it must be released from your being,
>> that your eye will see the clear picture before you.

Each Soul marks the Path of another Soul.
Each moment you are in the Path stains the being with marks.
They are profound marks, they are found within the Soul.
They are retrieved at each re entering in.
Your being has a sameness in each re entering.
There is a mark unseen, too, upon your being,
> and another Soul might visualize.

And the pain is clearly felt,
> on seeing a Soul, you feel an instant pain from that mark.

Beings have felt this pain you have known.
"Soul, I want you from my space, for you bring me down."
"Soul, I want you in my space, for you bring me up".
Behold, no earth being enters the space of another without leaving a mark,
> be it the flush of a brush or a stamp harshly put.

Allow the spew from your mouth to be aimed
> only at the mark of your being,
>> for there is a need to reach the higher space of earth
>> which is only visioned through the eye.

All Souls who are manifested come to that space
> through the Eye of Beholding.

You find joy in words, you find joy in movement, you find joy in body,
>   you find joy in mind, you find joy in heart.
Soul, you find joy in perfection.
Seek joy through the Soul.
Behold, children of earth, for on earth your beings are children,
>   even the oldest among you are children with Farside intent.
Great strides are made through heavy, dense forests,
>   a maze of intricate byways.
Earth has many pitfalls and the Soul can be drawn with delight
>   to avarice and greed.
Understand, Souls, the intent of your being, the Purity of your being,
>   and guide the hand of all within your space.
Even those who can not see to be guided know your Spirit's intent.
Blessed be thou, Soul.

463 Soul, you have brought great memories to earth,
>   you have lived great lives, you have known pains,
you have known joys.
You have tethered to your being all the knowledge of all the lives
>   you have lived.
You must know the value of the lives.
You must know the stench of the lives.
These were not there in our life.
Soul, we have walked the walk of pain.
We have walked with pure and goodness
>   and our lives are written in our being.
On the Farside you have immediate recognition
>   of all the lives you have lived.
You have immediate knowledge of all the beings
>   who have made an impact on those lives.
Those you Love, those that are precious unto you,
>   are written in your aura.
They have become a part of your being.
You have become a part of their being.
That which you do in likewise affects the children
>   that will be before you are.
All your efforts on earth, all your growth or lack of growth

affects the children of your children
for in your being you are teachers.
In your being you show how to release negativity, how to let it go,
and how to allow the flow of Energy
to wash itself over your being.
You are pure, you have total goodness in who you are.
All the growth of all the lives you have ever lived is an imprint
for others to see.
Is it a wonder that they look unto you and they see who you are?
They see the gem that you are.
Souls, know yourselves worthy,
know that the many lives you have lived have made you worthy.
Know that you have become polished and glowing with iridescent Light.
And know that the tear that falls should not be for that which has been,
but should be for the tear of rejoicing.
For all these beings you will know again,
and they will reach themselves unto you,
and you will feel the homeland of your being.
Souls of earth, when fear enshrouds your being, we supplicate to you
not to feed into that fear.
Would, please, the fear be seen and be recognized
and know it is but fear.
The reality is that you have the power to overcome the fear,
but you become enwrapped in the fear, and it becomes tangible
and real and overrides the power that you have.
Fear is negative.
It is the strangling that negativity provides.
Souls of earth, fear is illusion.
Do not absorb illusion!
You are Farside beings in great Purity in the space of illusion.
All the lessons that are negative are illusion.
See the perfect.
See not illusion, but clarity.
See beyond the pain, see beyond the fear,
see to the knowing of your existence.
When you allow fear, you open Pandora's box and you ignite negativity.

464 Illusion is the space you are in.
It is not that which you are on.
It is the space you are in,
    it is the vibrational space you are in.
See it clear.
Negativity is that which feeds illusion.
Positive would take you in a moment to our tent,
    to where we are, to Farside perfection.
Illusion is earth's illusion.
Our side illusion is for us.
You must join us to share our illusion.
We would be delighted to share our illusion.
Illusion has expectation.
The expectation of illusion is to feed on negativity.
To turn from the meal will provide you with utter Truth
    and the table where the repast is would be Farside.
Your earth is visible to our being.
We have encircled our being with your reality,
    we count our beads, we speak our mantras,
    we hold our being still in the space of illusion,
    in hopes that we will attain the eye of knowing.
That was our illusion!
And many are in the space of this illusion.
It is an honoured space to be in.
It is not complicated.
It is merely that earth knows in their being, illusion is real.
They know this, and so every effort of their being says:
    "How may I escape?"
And they go inward to the place of All Knowing.
How astute is humanity, but, Souls, how tiresome is humanity
    when the acceptance of reality is all about them,
the positive Energy of Love in every facet of your earth.
Look at the most minute of insects.
Look at the hugest of animals, at the flight of birds, at a stormy sea.
Where is the negativity?
The negativity flows round about.
These beings do not feed into negativity.

These beings are!
Only humankind feeds into negativity.
It is negativity when every part of your being
    expresses the knowledge of pain.
Your form is no different than the birds or the animals.
It is Creator's form.
It is endowed with holiness.
It is not the evil that men can take themselves to,
    but it prevents your positive endeavour.
Souls, we are aware of the great trials of earth.
Farside has many Souls that have entered in.
We are not a few.
We are an army as the Souls of earth,
    yet you are one great army of which we are a part.
Our being understands the frustrations of your flesh.
Our being is overwhelmed with caring
    for even the minutest step that a Soul takes.
There is great celebration on Farside for every major step
    of significance towards Purity.
Your purpose is Purity, your avenue is Truth.
There are many crossroads in each life.
The crossroads are illusion.
They tempt a Soul, they tempt you on.
Who has not felt the caress of a mother to her child,
    who has not felt that tender touch?
And how many have known the other mother
    who has scourged the tender Soul?
Illusion is choice.
It is choice of mankind.
The choice of positive Truth is reality,
    the choice of negativity continues illusion.
Vibration in every step of Purity will take you to another dimension.
Do not doubt, Soul, that you have the ability to be where we are.
We may bring our being to your earth and sit in our tent upon the sands
    and feel the heat.
It is not reality, it is our illusion.
Soul, you are sitting in illusion.

Illusion

We choose to find perfection, but in order to find perfection
    you must bring yourself to total acceptance of Truth.
The Truth of humanity, the Truth of surety, have All Knowing.

465 Souls, recognize vibration as the circle of all humanity.
Souls of all Truth are found in vibration, Souls who have advanced
    beyond pain and anger are found in vibration,
        Souls who have expanded themselves into the place of others
    are found in vibration.
Souls of humanity, allow thy beings to vibrate with Purity.
Seek beyond the Truth of earth into the sacredness of thy being.
Teach by the vibration you extend.
Unto all humanity give the circle of Truth.
Unto all humanity give the outer flow of vibration.
Be thou Holy.
Whomsoever is found in sadness, in tears, whomsoever is lost,
whomsoever wanders endlessly in their being,
come thou unto the space of Light.
The passage unto the space of Light does not carry payment.
It does not require any physical effort.
It requires, Soul, total goodness of being.
Total goodness of being!
The footwear does not matter on the path that you take.
The path is long, the path is often arduous
    but you do not need to bind your feet.
You do not need to clothe them for they will hold no scars.
They will hold no bleeding sores if the Soul seeks to walk in Purity.
For Purity sees only Purity and the long Path ahead shortens
    by the gathering of Purity.
Would you be done with your earth life?
Would you have it flow from you unaccounted?
Souls of earth, beings of Truth, search for the Energy within,
    or many times will you walk the same life,
many times will you enter in to the same level
to redo that which you have not successfully done.
Lift your foot and know in assurity
    that the placement of that foot once again is prearranged.

You have done it yourself,
> you have brought yourself to this very time in your life.

Directly in front of you is another Soul walking.
It is your own being.
You have taken passage in another lifetime.

466 Beloved Souls, who has taken the thread from a cloth
> and seen it ravel and ravel and reach endlessly,
> and then the reaching out to gather it back,
> to treasure that which was lost and is found.

Soul, you are the thread that has left to the far place
> and you are treasured fine thread,
>> for the cloth that will be woven will have magnificence
>> and be treasured and offered unto the highest being,
> for it is of the highest quality.

And the Essence of thy being will gather the thread
> and wind the thread about and about,
> and notice upon the thread there are some rough spaces
> and treasure the roughness,
>> for the roughness has been the great overcoming of pain.

And the fronds of the thread, the tiny particles
> that make the strong thread stronger, will be treasured also,
> for each thread is the intertwining
> of another Soul's Energy into thy being.

Oh, Soul, see the tapestry of thy being.
See the magnificent weave done in lifetimes of gathering Wisdom,
> and know that in cathedrals of your earth
> such fineness could not be hung,
> for it would make all about it seem paltry.

It needs a place of finer station to be mounted higher
> to the level of thy being, and the weave is brought homeward
> and gathered, and all earth responds to the weave.

All beings eye the perfection,
> and the weave is taken to the Writing on the Wall
> and it is placed against the Masterpiece of Time.

And the Soul can see quite clearly that which is the next weave,
> that which is needed to perfect the tapestry of all humanity.

And, Soul, as the Tapestry is seen and visioned in its completeness,
> the Soul brings self unto the station of reentry.

And the Soul sees the thread of their being
> and the other threads that can be intertwined
> to make the perfect thread.

And they prepare entering in for another life,
> and all is done for the single intent
> of the masterpiece that will be finished.

And in the masterpiece of earth's intent is the picture of the Fallen,
> is the hovering of the Blessed about their brother,

and Melchezidec is in the army of the mighty
> who enter through the lower gateway to arm the Fallen
> with a sword of overcoming.

And the Second Gateway opens unto the portal of the new land
> and all worlds enter in.

And Creator gazes at the Tapestry, at the living Tapestry,
> and knows the Love of all beings flow unto Creator.

And Creator searches for that which should be extended
> unto the greatest gift, and the key to the Second Gateway
> is offered to mankind and the living Tapestry is not done.

For, Souls of earth, you still weave and the colours have joy,
> bring vibrancy into the Tapestry,
> and the colours of healing bring great blues into the Tapestry,
> and giving gifts, blues and yellows and golds.

And the vibrant red brings the pain
> through which mankind has travelled,
> the deep rivers of blood that have flown,
> that all might reach unto one entry.

Souls of earth, form thy being and place the crown upon thy head,
> for thou art supreme in thy intent,
> and thy intent is noble as man is noble.

Know the jasmine, know the aroma that flows and flows
> and flows endlessly outward, is as thy being,
> is as the river that flows and flows and flows.

Your reaching will alter earth if thy intent is pure.

Beloved, be pure in thy intent.

467 You have entered in pure, you have gathered impurities.
There is a Purity of being that you may accomplish.
It does not require that you leave where you are
    and walk as your monks have walked.
It does require that in your moments
    you look outward from your being for each need
    that arises in your space.
That you use your humanity to alleviate pain,
    that you hold no ill will one to the other,
    that you accept no value for material objects
    but that you use that which you have for the comfort
    of all that may enter.
You are precious, you are few, you are only a very few,
    and yet you are mighty, for you have within you, humanity,
    the power to alter all energies unto Godhead.
Behold how great thou art
    and acknowledge thy Oneness with thy Creator.

468 Every earth being lifts the chalice to the lips.
Every earth being has a cup that is bitter to swallow.
Some may swallow quickly, others refuse the bitter cup.
Some take small sips and the pain of bitterness is longer lasting.
The Souls who drain the cup quickly anxiously await the next chalice.
They have a desire to enter in quickly,
    to return once again to earth, speedily.
Some Souls have lingered from the first entering in at level one.
The negativity has been acknowledged
    and the greatness of the step has been acknowledged.
But the insurmountable pain for them, not for themselves,
    but of what must occur, keeps them from entering in again.
Who would slaughter a child?
Who would slaughter a family?
Who would slaughter families and families?
And yet earth has been full of Souls who have murdered,
    who have drowned, and starved,
    and beaten the most innocent of innocents.

And we say to you:
"These are Souls who have honour on Farside.
These are Souls who enter in to be human
that they might understand humanity,
that they might teach humanity."
These Souls grow in Purity as a human.
As a human!
The Flow for Purity is unlike all other flows,
    for in this is the Flow of Creator.
All other Souls may reach unto Creator,
    but humanity has the goodness of Creator within!
Can you behold how earths look upon your being?
Can you look at the abeyance they offer unto humanity?
Do you wonder that you reach out and minister unto worlds,
that they praise your being,
that they shout hallelujahs in your space?
Not because you have slaughtered,
    but because you have overcome the negativity of your being.
You have risen above negativity
    and chosen to be as your Creator, Love.
Earth has many expressions of love.
Agape looks ever outward, and knows the vision that is seen,
and knows whereof it has come,
and knows whereof it has been formed,
and knows that each has a name,
and each is remembered by name,
and each has a purpose and the purpose is known.
This is Love!
None are there who are not in the space of this Love.
None are there who do not have the Tears of Creator washing over them.
No trifle is too small to be accounted.
No element is too inconsequential to be dismissed.
Souls of earth, you ride the high wave of creation
    and only above you are Angels and Creator.
That we know.

469 Know that Purity is also wholesome.
Know that Purity does not cast a glance and make a judgement.

Purity sees and accepts, and asks:
    "What is there that I may uplift?
    What is there that I may place a blessing upon?"
For, Souls, you are powerful.
Engage in the power of your being.
Use enterprise to look about and recognize ways
    that a single light may ignite a dark corner
    and know that as you have lit another Soul,
    so there are two lights, and four lights, and on and on.
Love does not strangle.
Love does not drown or starve
Love does not murder.
Only the holding of pain.
That which you could do through pain,
    you could do with the power of your being.
Know that you can alter that which man does
    by recognizing the Light of your being.
Know that you may heal whom you are
and draw your being unto the goodness of Creator
    as an orb of Light, abundantly pure,
    offering thy being for that which you have come.
Souls, you have not idly entered in to the field of earth.
You have not come to be tranquil.
You have not come to only know joy.
You have not come to be downcast, and cloaked in pain and anger.
Soul, you have come to rise above such things.
You have come for the purpose of Love, the acceptance of Truth.
The Path of Purity will take you to Love.
How generous is earth that provides upon her being,
    waters to nourish, and search out and give.
Allow your beings to be as the great waters,
    ever searching out into a field of pain,
    into a field of great turmoil.
And know that which you are, human,
    has the power to alter that which you see.
You are not veiled in negativity.
You are not veiled in pain.
Your eyes are clear.

Illusion

Soul, you have placed yourself in the pit of pain,
    in the dilution of anger.
Light erodes, breaks down pain, overrides anger
    until the joy in the being appears.
And know that which you do,
    you do from the reflection of who you are.
You have the availability of all your power.
You are not only human.
You are human, a powerful human
    who has the power to alter the Energy fields of many,
who has the power to alter the strife,
and the war, and the locust.
Beings of earth, you have the power to alter the flight of the locust.
You have the power to alter the war,
    to save the baby Souls from their path.
Will you reach out unto the Souls in your meditative state?
Will you enter in to healing and use the power that you have
    to send vibrations of Purity unto your fellow man?
Be thou who you are, the reflection of Purity.
So be it.

CHAPTER 3

Other Worlds

SOUL

470 Can you not know in your being
    that your earth has a form of negativity
    that is the last Energy field!
It is, Soul, the preparation for battle.
Battle has not come first to earth.
Farside has battled Negativity.
Worlds and worlds of pain have been endured because worlds
    have fed in to the stream and filled the cup full,
    and Negativity has sapped the strength of many worlds.
You are not the first, you are the last.
The Blessed Ones were the saviours of the battle,
    the Angels, who placed about them
    the Purity to conquer Negativity.
Soul, negativity of many energies infiltrate the world.
Have you not seen it, Soul?
But the Blessed Ones placed Purity about their Being
    and Souls reduced the Negativity to earth's galaxy.
Souls, before you conquered negativity, those you call aliens,
    beloved of the Energy, have conquered also many battles
    and when the battle became profound,
    did not the Blessed Ones enter in!
Are not the Blessed Ones in your space, succouring thy Soul!
Beloved, know you are no small jot or tittle in the Eye of Creator.
Aliens have been blest, Soul.

471 We are Pleiadian.
We have entered your sphere because we are able to enter your sphere.

We have the ability to transform our being and meld
    into the form you take.
There is no trickery in our agenda.
We are forthright and our being has great clarity.
We are teachers to the space of earth.
We have sent many of our earth brethren
    teachers who have entered in to your form.
They are not in disguise.
They freely offer to any Soul who will listen,
    that they are unique and have an awareness
    of the Energy of their being.
The Souls are not clad in optic antennae.
They are monitored by agreement
    and often have difficulty in the space of earth.
Earth Energy constricts their being.
They would be free and abide in the Energy Field they know so well,
    but they are caught in their clarity to bring teachings to earth.
It is often difficult for our beings to ride your wave of negativity.
It is not natural for our beings.
Oh, Soul, the negativity will not draw us into its being,
    but we still have the familiar inertness about us.
It often prevents us from moving quickly to do that which must be done.
Our being is the receptacle of humanity's inability
    to release the energy field of negativity.
So it is that our Energy Field is affected.
It is as though there is not enough air about our being,
    as though we are isolated in a space of no understanding.
And we come to our brethren who give unto earth, lessons,
    and we restrengthen their being.
We give our Energy unto their being,
    we acknowledge the goodness of their being,
    and they know they have been visited.

472 Upon is for earth, upon is a place.
Farside is dimension, is entering through, is visible and invisible,
    is matter and ion and dimension.
It may expand at will and define at will.
It may reverse at will and concave at will.

Your earth is round in your feeble knowledge,
    and we see your earth as multidimensional.
There are, within the surface of your earth,
    such beings as would keep you from sleeping.
For these beings have intent,
    their intent is not evil,
    their intent is Truth to assist all earth beings.
They have abilities to enter through earth solids,
    they have the ability to take form at any given moment.
They may enter in to a darkened hall to guide a Soul to safety.
They may enter in to deep waters to lift a Soul,
    or comfort a drowning being who has a choice to pass thus.
The Jinn have sanctity and earth has not always seen them
    as sanctity, but devilish playmates.
This, because of their ability to emerge into a space and be seen.
We would have you know the Jinn are struggling
    with the waterways of earth.
They are placing agitations upon the sea, visible to mankind,
    to alert mankind of negativity beneath.
All Farside has knowledge of the Jinn.
They have within their being, an element of fluid
    and they may pass before your being
    and be seen as naught but shadow,
    and you will say: "What has passed me there?"
There is always a purpose to the passing.
It is Soul awareness.
At whatever time the Jinn enters your space, know the lesson is Purity
    and know the need to look away from negativity,
    a negative thought, a negative deed.
Jinn have been with mankind from the beginning
    and will be with mankind at the closing of time.
Energy will heal.
Energy has power.
Energy is the most volatile of all expressions on earth.
Use Energy to heal from thy eye,
    use Energy to search for Truth,
    use Energy to cleanse.
Soul, you may lift great negativity and place it in the care of Creator.

And the Jinn will enter in to the deep and protect the deep,
    but first you must give permission,
    for humanity is the author of earth.
Soul, you are human.
The Jinn may respond to your request,
    but the request must come from humanity.
The turtle is the timetable of mankind.
It is the clock that ticks, and when the clock stops, earth is no more.

473 Soul, we are those you call Jinn.
We live in your earth.
Our world is not in your earth.
Our world is great, our being is pure.
We have spoken to you before.
We have entered in to the sea many times to comfort Souls.
We are they who may alter our beings.
We have, Soul, great intent.
The intent is to protect earth and beings of earth.
The intent is to ease mankind's pain within the sea.
We are Jinn by earth name.
We are playful.
We do not, in our being, have negativity.
We can collapse and glide through your atmosphere
    and enter in to Quar in a moment of your earth time.
The deliverance of our being is honoured
    by a substantial world of our own.
We have mobility, as all Souls have mobility.
We have motion, as all Souls have motion.
Earth Souls are the only Souls kept without motion,
    except in the state of Purity.
Behold Galatia, our sister world.
Behold, no mouth is required when speaking,
    no need to divulge to a Soul what is written.
Even earth Souls, in the space of a Galatian,
    may read clearly that which is to be seen.
The form of hands have no purpose.
They are feeble in your eyes, but we have no use for the appendage.

And when the need arrives, we draw our Purity and extend our being
> to hold that which we would hold.

We are blue in our being, the deep green blue of the central sea.

We sing joyous songs in a language your ear could not intone.

It would sound to your Soul as the jangling of many beads
> and yet our being rejoices in the sound
> > for the sound gives vision to who we are.

It opens all vision of your worlds unto our being.

We may see into the deepest of seas.

We may see the Souls grasping for life,
> and in an instant be in their space
> and enwrap our being about them to carry them forth
> in gentleness, into Farside Purity.

Do not think that other worlds
> hold decisions over placements of purpose.

All other worlds except your own
> have instant decision on what is right,
> for there is no wrong, there is only right.

Jinn are not apparitions.

They are as real as your Bigfoot.

They are as real as the Faeries.

They are beings of great import to your earth.

474 Delighted, Souls, to be in the space of earth.

We are of Lemuria.

We have been partner to earth.

Earth could not maintain the Purity of our being.

We have risen as one into the state of Purity,
> delighted to enter once again
> into the genuine force of negativity.

It does recall to us the temptations that withered in our space,
> the temptations that we forego in the moment of our Purity.

Souls of earth, you have been drawn to the place of choice.

It is a moment in your time but it is the eternity of your being.

Gummerians are brethren.

They have Light beyond our own.

They have a reach of goodness that left the space of earth
> prior to our own.

The Soul has had many life forms within its being.
They have come unaware to the feeble existence of many humanities.
Souls, Gummeria, to you, is unattainable
    except in the state of goodness.
Each Soul can ride the wave into the force of Light.
The qualification is Zero.
Soul, Zero is the uplifting of the Soul, once again, to the fragment Spirit.
Be delighted in treachery,
    for treachery is the opportunity to gainsay it,
    to overcome it, to survive the deliberate attempt at power.
Souls of earth, a moment in your time
    is carried on a wave of Purity into our space.
We now have entered your space.
We have protection from your negativity.
All worlds of Purity do not have this protection.
It is a level, you see, of Purity that gives protection.
It is not that these Souls are lesser.
They have not yet attained the Wisdom of the Energy
    that gives them protection.
We are not idle in our eternity.
We manage to be in the state of great Energy.
We are fraught with only choice of that which we may do,
    that will further other humanities, other existences, other worlds.
Purities are givers.
Purities do not always receive to themselves, but they extend outward
    as the Great Creator extends in Flow to the lesser of His beings.
It is the Zero, it is the state of Knowing.
It is the total acceptance that you, in your humanness,
    have not yet come to.
The great orb of earth is blessed as are all existences blessed.
Treasure that which you have, but do not hold it to your heart.
Extend it outward from your heart that it may flow to goodness.
Gummerians have great Energy.
They have within their being the great masters
    who extend to us, in our humility, teachings of great value.
We are blessed in our being because of that Flow of Energy.
Blessed, blessed, blessed, extend to these, thy people,
    the Truth of our existence.

Allow the Flow of greatness to be within.
Souls of earth, you are always within the countenance of the Farside.
They bless and honour your being.
They carry goodness into the framework of earth.
Blessing be unto you.

475 Souls of earth, a teaching.
We of the Farside do not recognize the word, foreign.
Soul, we do not know, foreign.
It is foreign unto us.
We do know the word, a difference.
We do know the word, separate.
But the word, foreign, alienates,
    separates in a distinctly negative way.
We would have you know,
    that our Farside is a conglomeration such as you have not seen.
For the entities and aliens and Souls of Purity,
    one and all carry forms and cadences.
Soul, finely strung are the notes of difference, and yet not foreign,
    for we would embrace.
We embrace all that is.
Earth humanity, we urge not the leaders who struggle for power,
    not the world of economics who struggle for wealth,
    but we urge humanity to look at the separateness of each other
    and know your form has not idly come to you.
It has a resounding note from the Farside.
It is pure in the sense you are Farside.
It is complete in that you all have a reflection of Farside.
There is within the earth humanity the psyche of fear of difference.
It is why there is a difference, to overcome the fear.
Did you think, Soul, that country and colour and language hides?
There is no hidden aspect in colour, in country, in language!
There is, Soul, only humanity.
You were brought together as a gift unto Creator, a profound gift.
You came one and all for the purpose of humanity,
    which is to recover that which has been lost from Creator,
    the blessed Holy Holy Holy.
Your world is full of diversity you do not know

because you fear to recognize the great man
who roams in the mountains and the forests of your land.
Neanderthal!
Ever has this being been separate from humanity,
    and yet the Soul has come for the purpose of your humanity.
And you name this Soul, Yeti, and you name this Soul, Sasquatch.
He is the Neanderthal.
He has always been.
He entered within the realms of earth to be for you a definition.
"*I define myself,*" you say, humanity.
You do this because of Neanderthal man.
Do not hold your differences in a negative form,
    but uphold your differences as purities brought together
    for the purpose of Creator.
Embrace that which is different unto you.
Embrace, Soul, the religions, the creeds, the colours, the nations
    and recognize you have a single unit, that of humanity.
All have the unique ability to rise above their being and see their Soul,
    all have the power to alter ion,
    all have the power to bring forth that which is lost.
We called you, Souls, to come for a purpose,
    and we have not the power to enter in.
Our being, the beings of all Farside,
    all worlds beyond yours, send power unto earth
    that you might overcome the differences of your being
    and see the glory rise above the pain and bloodshed of humanity.

476 Behold Love.
Behold the Energy, Love.
It emanates, it issues forth unceasingly.
It may not be repelled, but it may be held back.
That is controversy.
Soul, Love has more glory than all Farside beings.
Love issues forth to all members of creation.
There is no life form, there is no inanimate object
    that does not receive the Love issued forth.
From whence cometh this Love?
Creator. Creator!

Love comes through Creator.
Love is a Passageway through Creator.
Creator is the Essence of Love.
As your Essence has the capability of Purity to its level,
    Creator is the utter Essence of Love.
Beyond Creator is Godhead.
Godhead is the Diadem, is the place where all Energy radiates from.
It is issuing forth ever and ever, it is creation's Essence.
Which came first, the chicken or the egg?
Do you see the conundrum?
Which came first, Creator or creation?
This we do not know.
For us it is eternally important to reach the source
    of such Love to us of the Farside.
The Souls who have been taught of the great truths,
    of the great purities, of the great Love,
    endeavour to find the source.
Our understanding is the Path is through the Gateway.
Our understanding is it will be revealed when mankind draws forth
    the energies of Purity.
It is our understanding that you, who are where you are,
    and we, who are where we are,
    have a purpose to unite, to pass through into a new land.
We are Souls not unlike your own.
We have great energies.
Our beings reside in total peace and onward looking.
We are not those who care fosr the state of mankind.
We are directly connected to the Entering In,
    to the preparing of all energies for it.
Understand that man is beginning to seek the Energy capacity
    of his being.
We have total movement in our being.
We have no restrictions to form.
Soul, we can alter ion in a moment.
Our beings are where you are and are where we are.
We are here in this form and we see clearly with the eyes of this being.
The press onward is how may we enter in to Zero?
How will it be?

Will our worlds collide, will our energies fragment?
These are questions we ask ourselves.
Your beings on earth ask questions of a complex nature.
We ask questions in simplicity, for our being understands
    that Zero is the point of knowing.

SPIRIT

477 Upon the planets, the orbs,
    the spheres of galaxies upon galaxies,
    are Souls of great worth.
They have adoration and supplication unto Creator.
They bow in the extremity unto the Hem of Creator.
They hold the space of angels Holy and are visited by the Souls.
Their beings are gentle, yet formidable.
They carry great interest, one to the other,
    and yet many worlds differ in great proportions one to the other.
Souls have extreme minuteness.
Souls having no outward visibility of speech or sight or sound,
    yet drawn into an incredible wisdom and compassion.
Souls who work diligently in the space of Creator's knowledge,
    in the knowledge of Godhead.
There is a world of beings who are treasured by all Farside,
    and they have as the purpose of their being,
    the why of Godhead.
We do not know the answer to all that earth might query,
    but knowledge we do have, wisdom we are attaining.
Soul, we know Creator.
We have often been expounded to in the rightness of Love, by the Angels.
We have been visited by many earths
    who have as their agenda, great Purity.
We know in our being that we will enter in behind the force of mankind.
We know the great wonder of that which you do.
We are not fearful in the completion of that which you will do,
    for unlike you, we know in our being the entering in will be.
Souls of earth, in your day, in your hour, in your moment,
    know the holiness of your being,

know behind you is an entourage of willing beings
who would come unto who you are.
But our being may not, without permission, enter in,
and the ability to linger is shortened
by the deceptive quality of pain.
It marks our being.
Souls of earth, know that your entering in to Purity is not for you alone.
We are many and our world, too, depends upon the completion
of that which you will do.

478 Souls, we would speak to earth of the beginning.
We would speak of the time when the army of humanity gathered,
of the worlds in which we move forward,
our Spirit attending those awakened
from the inertia they have been in,
in the worlds you have not heard and yet your being knows of.
Worlds that differ one from the other,
beings that differ one from the other,
and yet no language barrier, a Oneness in creation.
The Souls of these worlds knew and were ministered unto
by the Blessed Angels.
These Beings of pure Love entered in to worlds caught in sleep,
they had released from their being, all purpose, all intent;
they existed, nothing more.
And the Blessed Ones came and ministered unto them,
and in their Purity they taught them Love, one to the other.
And we spake unto these worlds of those Angels that were lost unto us,
those we knew had carried our burden.
And we cried unto their being: *"Give us of your Energy*
that we might go on to Creator and offer unto Creator,
beings who would enter in to the negativity, the Void,
and bring forth the Fallen."
And we came to the Gateway and we bowed down,
and we cried unto Creator:
"Hear that which we would say unto Thee.
Give us permission that we might enter in to the Void,
for we would redeem those who have Fallen."

And Creator looked unto the gathering
>and we felt Tears wash over our being, and Joy.
And Creator spake to those gathered:
>"Can you not see the power of Negativity?"
And we acknowledged:
>"Lord, we have even felt this power,
>>and yet we would go forward unto Thee."
And Creator gathered all those unto Him and armed them with Truth,
>and spewed them forth, and created complexities
>that would help overcome negativity.
He gathered them in their differences,
>from their different worlds and said: *"So shall it be.*
>>We shall have different countenances,
>>>but we shall complex, for one may not utter to the other
>>>without acknowledging the other in their language."
And there was the first, which was the last, a world beyond beyond.
And these Souls have the power to move from one world to the other.
All Souls have not that power.
And Creator blest these Souls and said:
>"The last shall be first and the first shall be last."
And He set a mighty Path before these people,
>for they would be leaders in overcoming negativity.
"Yea, my people, do not enter in to negativity,
but acknowledge the earth is not yours, nor a tiny haven in it.
Soul, you shall walk with the angels in that day.
You shall be trodden down, only to be lifted up,
>and you shall give the falcon that which is yours."

479 All earth has a placement of fear.
We have no fear.
We take ourselves to high mountaintops and float gently to the bottom.
And we don't need a being to catch.
We have the magic of our own being.
Our form, when you see us, is not tangible to you,
>but we have form where we are, many forms where we are,
>countless forms where we are.
Earth returnees have the advantage.

They have been given a buoyancy to travel into all space.
Not all energies of Farside have this power.
There is much you do not know.
Many worlds content themselves to be
> in the space of existence that has little expected
> and enjoys the lavish Energy in their space.

They are calm and delightfully naive.
Not negative, naive!
They are as children to our being and we hold them very dear
> and we teach them what we can.

There are worlds that have magnitude far beyond our own.
The whale has a world of such magnificence.
The Energy of the whale would lift up the most desolate of beings.
The whale is the greatest teacher in world forum upon the Farside.
The whale is the greatest teacher on your earth form.
On your earth form Love issued forth by the whale is like a precious gem
> that dazzles and Lights whomever it visions.

All worlds of Farside have humour.
Delight in humour.
Laugh, for laughing is joy and Purity.
Tickle your sense of humour even in the drudgery of your day.
If you blanket yourself in cloud, Souls will not see you.
They will turn their back to who you are.
When you are joy they feel that joy, they respond to that joy
> and they draw themselves into the space that you are.

Earth Souls, you are profoundly wonderful, are you not!

480 We have hovered, we have hovered often in your space.
Soul, we have no need of ships.
You have need of our ships.
When negativity is removed by your being from all creation,
> all creation may move without ships.

There are worlds that enter in to your space without ships.
They are agile and nimble and alter their beings.
But for you, earth, we have a need to build ships
> that may hold beings from earth, for you are not pure.

You are of Truth.

You hold contamination
> and to bring you unto where we would, into the Quar we are,
> you must be quarantined.

Soul, there is a need to contain negativity,
> even the fragments that might hold to thy being.

We know as you are lifted,
> you will be human in all aspects of humanity,
> and in that you will be Truth.

But, Soul, we know of negativity.
We have no care to have it invade our being.
We protect ourselves by protecting you.
Soul, we are many, we are not a single Soul,
> and we are often moving in areas to bring to world's attention
> that we are.

You need to know the time of delivery is soon.
Our ships are manned, legions of ships.
Your world will be astounded at the capacities of our ships
> and your world will be amazed at their being
> as they are raised into these ships.

Your nostrils spew forth negativity
> and you release negativity from your mouths.

You spew foulness unto your brothers and your sisters,
> and yet you are kin.

And we laugh, for how you will laugh when you see us!
We are the beings who have been your kin, and you will see our forms,
> and you will compare.

Soul, we know who we are.
You have seen many ships.
You are human in your limitations.
You would deter a lesson and we would bring you a lesson.
We have the power in our form to alter beings.
We have the power to move horizontally and vertically,
> to alter the Prism in which we are.

We have the power to alter all reactors and, Soul, we carry no negativity.
Know this!

481 We acknowledge you.
Earth is measured, Farside is also measured.

Farside measure is Quar.
It is multipliable by naught.
It has also a divisive ability.
It can be carried unto any equation.
Naught is the variable conductor of the equation[80],
    Quar is the extension.
This we can let you know.
Your earth has great beauty.
It has magnificent structure in its minuteness.
You will find orbs in motion.
Beyond what man's eye can scope are spheres
    which carry great multitudes of beings.
We have great potential of knowing and our research continues.
We have abattoirs with open doors where beings of such beauty rest
    and offer wisdom unto our being.
What you see inward is not the same as what you see outward.
Speak to your science of this.
It will tweak a still mind.
We do not play games.
We do not have the power to intervene into your register,
    except in the minute ways that we offer.
The solution for mankind is with mankind.
We could enter in and lift all mankind from their place of being.
We could do this.
The Essence of your being would stay us,
    our Love for Creator would stay us,
    our grateful benediction to the Blessed would stay us.
Behold, Souls, your earth is surrounded.
There are beings who have said we are playful and yes, we are playful.
We are not unlike you, and yet in our playfulness we try to advise earth
    as to our comings and goings.
Were you to see the reflection of your earth,
    you would see many beings, countless beings,
    in the air about your space.
All these beings have the ability to lift earth humanity
    and will offer the lift to Souls.
But that which you call feet is not grounded to earth

---

80 equation - See Appendix A

and you must endeavour
to fulfill the solemn adventure you are in.
Know that you are cloaked with the wings of the sacred ones.
Know that you are not alone, that on occasion we will open an aperture
so that you may see our beings.
Know that the sanctity of humanity is becoming such
that there are Souls who may come forth through the aperture
and meet and discuss with our energies.
You are great teachers, earth.
You teach our beings continuously.
You teach us never to alter the import of your existence,
for all beings of earth have grandeur
and splendour and immense power.
Know that you will see our ships in the night and be comforted
that the ships have the ability to land in an iota,
and it will lift your children into the density of our space
until earth has ceased the vibration that will come.
Breathe, Souls of earth, but breathe not the earth's tainted air.
Enter the purest of filters into your air, positive Energy,
and all will cleanse.

482 Soul, we have entered in to your space.
Our being is tethered in the place of Purity.
We are unlike your being.
It is a difficult translation for our being.
Your negativity wearies our being.
It is as though our being has flatness in your space.
We cannot reach the portion that we are.
Half in, half out, is your earth exactness.
Soul, we would tell you about our space.
We will tell you about our form.
Do not be troubled by the cold.
We are of Truth, but our Truth is not like yours.
Our Truth is hampered in the place we are in.
Soul, our platform of being is of family,
but family of earth is mirrored after small Farside families.
It is the memory of your being.
In fact, all energies of Farside have family,

but family is not mother and father, brother and sister,
family is good and beings,
all beings are of a family and there are many families.
Your earth was gathered from all families.
Melchezidec spoke to many worlds,
    entering in and raising from each
        those who would draw themselves to war against Negativity.
Many are we, worlds upon worlds upon worlds.
Your mind could not contemplate the existence
    from which you have come.
You have known us, your being has known our being,
    the part of you that matters
    remembers the association of our being.
But the purpose of the great Armada to flow into the Void
    and through into Negativity, was Holy,
    and your earth took pattern of our beings,
    and mother and father allowed the entering in of Purity,
    that Purity may battle with Negativity.
And the pure state of Holy babe is an honourable being,
    and earth in the remembrance of their being
    have done so much more.
They have said:
    "May we be just a little different
        to war in this Energy of Negativity.
    As we have difference on the Farside,
        may we not also have difference on the earth plane?"
And Souls from different worlds took on an appearance
    that said we are different, and yet we are one.
It will help us in our battle against negativity,
    for negativity must be conquered.
Souls of earth, the complexities of your being are simple.
Delight in your being and overcome the complexity,
    for our being has great Light.
Our being is wondrous, our being is of great intelligence,
    and yet our being is not restricted with feet and legs
    as your being is.
Soul, Farside has many different forms.
Who has seen Creator?

What form does He take?
We have not seen Creator.
We do not know what form He takes, but we do know
    that to be motionless in that state of Love, is to be in ecstasy.
That, we know.
That, all Farside beings know.
And earth humanity will be the first to behold the Radiance of Creator.
It is written, Soul.
It is in all knowledge and wisdom of Farside.
It is the Writing on the Wall.
It is passed throughout the worlds awaiting for humanity to conquer.
Our being is humbled beside the possibilities of humanity.
We are humbled to be in the state of humanity's potential.
The battle has begun and you, Souls of earth, watch your television.
We see you fumble in your knowledge and
    as you see earth perform before your eyes, so we see earth.
But television is not required, for are we not all knowledge!
All knowledge is not all truth, is not all Purity, is not all Love.
Humanity could have all knowledge.
Humanity refuses to function in a manner
    that would provide all knowledge.
It would be to be in total acceptance
    and then your beings would float as ours floats,
    for to be in all knowledge, you have the possibility of float.
There are no constraints in all knowledge, there is instant travel.
Our Energy has entered in and our Energy may not stay.
But the army is of our being and we would have you know this.
Soul, know we are not from Gummeria.
We are from Lantelia.
Respect our form differs from Gummeria, and yet we are as brothers.
Family is family, is it not!

Essence

483 We will teach of other worlds.
Mankind has an independent relationship with Creator
    apart from other worlds.
It is, Soul, because of a single action that occurred.

It is because of the second casting out.
All beings of all worlds beyond worlds beyond worlds
    were cast from Creator.
Many have been within the space of Purity.
Within the Farside, Negativity was equal partner to positive Energy
and because of the overriding strength of Negativity,
it overwhelmed many worlds.
Some surmounted the Energy, but many succumbed,
    and beings entered in to inertness.
These beings have many forms and many faces.
They have many hopes and dreams and strivings
    that take them into the glow of the Prism,
    but many worlds have no desire
        to enter in to the space of Creator.
It is an unknown even for our side.
It carries within, questions unanswered,
    even with the powerful knowledge that we have.
Worlds you have been a part of, humanity,
    worlds you have entered in from,
    and your beings have been as they,
    and you gathered together and were cast yet again,
    with Truth, into the abyss of negativity, of your own choice,
    as a gift unto your Creator.
You, Souls of earth, were those who answered the call
    to come forward and be counted
    and battle Negativity with Truth,
    and still the worlds remain as you have left from.
They are not simple minded.
In all creation there are worlds of harshness, which is not negative.
There are worlds that ignite and Souls who have the ability
    to move freely upon the face of their land.
You are not the only world.
The inhabitants of these worlds have vocabulary,
    they have great emotions,
    they have great caring, one for the other.
There is within their being no purpose to hoarding,
    no purpose to greed.
It does not enter their being.

That energy has been withdrawn.
Only within the instability of your earth does such energy exist.
Your earth vehicles could travel planet after planet after planet,
    for years and years and years,
      and never enter in to the outward edge of these worlds.
There are, Soul, pathways unto the Prism.
Souls of earth, you would clasp your hands before your eyes
    or you would be blinded by the Purity.
All energies flow unto Creator, but not all energies have a desire
    to enter in to the Second Gateway.
And yet all will, for Love cannot witness
    the fragmentation of these energies of worlds.
For in that time will be implosion of sound
    and many worlds will become unstable.
Your world will become unstable.
It will be the first to enter in.
Many Souls of other worlds have the awareness
    of the fragility of their space orbs.
Their knowledge far outcounts your own.
They have endlessly watched earth,
    for they know the moment of earth's pain.
They have entered in many times to heal,
    to protect, to mark the space of pain.
And at a level unto Angels is an orb that speaks to mankind,
    to all who will listen.
These beings enter in and speak plainly to the plane of earth.
They express humbly unto earth
    the need to correct the levels of instability.
These Souls have steadfastness in their vision towards earth.
They see only that which earth sees but does not recognize.
Souls of earth, weary not yourselves within your days
    of preparing for riches.
Use the time to place great healing upon the orb,
    to look unto the spiritual self
      and know that you are a part of our being,
      know that you have entered in from the space we are in.
Bless other worlds, Soul.

Do not be in fear.
We have heard your call.
We will enter in when the hour is nigh.

484 Soul, we have entered in.
We have been in the blessed garden,
   we have entered in to the Crystal Cave.
We have walked in the garden of Prism.
Soul, know a being different than your own.
Know a being that has entered in with me to the garden.
The Soul has height of sixteen feet.
The Soul has hand cloven together.
The Soul has no motion except in a fluid bone.
It is as sinew that has strength and movement.
The Soul has a thinness of fourteen inches.
The Soul moves without Energy.
The Soul can be high or low in an instant.
The Soul can move sideways.
The Soul speaks through antennae that forge a place
   halfway down the form of sixteen feet.
The Soul is incredibly pure in being
   and has come from a world of Ruby colour.
There is no tree.
There is mountain of bright colour.
The beings enter in the outer form of their world.
Their world opens to allow them entry.
There is no life on the outer crust of this earth.
Soul, these gentle beings have great affinity to mankind.
They see the world of earth by the negative cast
   that comes into their space.
The light years away from you can be touched by their Purity.
They have only to extend their vision
   and they see through the filament of earth,
      for they have transcendental travel in their being.
Know their intellect is beyond your own earth intellect.
Know we walk this moment in the sacred place of the Holy ones.
They have allowed passage through by the sound of great beauty.

It would shatter your eardrums to hear such clarity.
The music of Angels is the splendour of a thousand bells,
    all chiming as one, in every court united.
Blessed earth, heal!

485 Being, beings of earth, welcome into the chamber of forever,
    into the starlit way, into the passage of Time to the orb of Galatia.
Souls of earth, be ye redeemed in the glow of Galatia,
    in the fraternity of Souls
        who gather from time's beginning of ever,
            the Flow of all that is takes the Soul to a planetary force
            that is visible at its entrance.
Who can see the chasm?
Who will venture forth into the space of your time?
Soul, we see your frustration.
We see within your being the editing of creation.
Magnify the eye, for in Galatia you could not forestall the vision
    that comes forward.
The eye is bulbous and you would frown at the vision
    that we find in our being, a beatitude of Purity,
        an orb of Oneness with the Creator.
We have no need for your feeble vision.
We have but eye.
Our form is layered in goodness.
Our form holds a connection to the Energy of our being.
It is a form without your human legs.
It is a form as the star you see that shoots from place to place,
    so our being quickly moves.
Know we are not saucers, we are not discs.
We are life of completeness such as your earth beings have not found.
The density of our being is to you the weight of two thousand pounds
    and yet our being is as feather of your earth.
There is a focal point to our being.
We are concerned with the welfare of one creation.
It is a distant creation of Purity.
We are to that world, teacher.
Our form is carried forth.
This world of which we speak has endeavour not unlike your own.

It has within the framework of its creation, family,
>   knit with a bond of Love.
But these Souls are young and have within their being,
>   a limited Energy.
They vibrate at a low level.
Their force field does not allow the travel that we as life form have.
We have taken in a moment.
They are taken in slow velocity unto the aim of their being.
You have not yet found the velocity.
The velocity of your form is in the Naught of the eye.
Be amazed at the heart that needs to be righted,
>   for it travels to the Energy of the feet
>   instead of to the Energy of the head.
Be not amazed that our form does not devour
>   carnivorous beings.
We energize our being from the Light force around us.
We take unto us Energy.
Our being is Energy.
The focal point of the Energy is in the bulbous eye,
>   rounded and carried to all levels of vibration.
All galactic beings have not to reach or walk or hear,
>   but see with the sound of intenseness
>   that your mind could not comprehend.
The fold of all energies could not locate our being,
>   but Purity would find us in an iota.
Cleanse self and know that your world changes,
>   that the very ground on which you stand
>   will slant in proportions
>   that will cause a Soul to reach to high mountain
>   and express "Save me, Soul!"
And those who look down will anguish at their inability
>   to raise up impurities unto their space.
Souls of earth, gather unto Purity.
We of Galatia would have you enter our realm.
We would lay for you a feast unto your being.
A gift of incredible pureness would ignite your Soul.
Earth has within its possibility, the potential of reaching unto our realm.
Earth has the potential of vibration.

Souls, vibrate within your being and draw self beyond the chaos
    in which you dwell.
Souls of earth, be ye free of all that is negative.

486 Soul, you are curious and curiouser!
You are flesh.
We do not feed on flesh,
    we do not feed on living creatures, we feed on manna.
We are enriched by the food that we eat.
It is given freely and we absorb.
It is curious, this mouth you have.
It is so connected, it has a double connection.
It speaks and utters words, and it wants, it wants.
Is that not curious?
Our being has no need to want, we have no need to absorb.
Soul, we are.
Our being could not fit into this form you call human.
Our being is immense and contains a purpose.
Soul, our being has the ability to emerge into the pathway.
Not all energies can do this, only four.
Ours is one of the four.
We are Pleiadian.
It is so feeble, this humanity of yours and yet, as we see the feebleness,
    we are amazed that the Angels could not accomplish
    what you are accomplishing.
The Angels gathered Negativity unto themselves
    and they carry great burdens of Negativity
    unto the blessed River of Cleansing,
    but earth has moved to overcome negativity from their being.
How wondrous are you!
We see your feeble being, we are amazed!
How can this form you call humanity overcome the Negativity
    that made us inert?
We could not do it, our beings could not resist.
But you humanity have agreed to enter in to earth not once,
    but time and again to do battle with negativity.
We see you as audacious, without fear,

and yet we know you are full of fear,
    but not in the Entering In.
You struggle and you spew outward from your being,
negativities we could not hold, and yet, in the spewing out,
    you are learning about the negativity.
We have not learned, known, what you know.
You are being taught, but you are being taught in stations of learning
    by the very Souls who have entered in.
How wondrous, how revered are you, humanity!
How exemplary are you to our being
    that you would permit the negativity to overwhelm you
    and then re enter, having the hold still on your being,
    to come forth and purify yourself in the deep river of pain.
We uphold, humanity, who you are.
We know that you have come of Creator, not once, but twice.
We know the gift that you give to our being.
There are four existences that can enter in to the pathway
    and these four have a single purpose:
    to be there at the gathering of all humanity.
The cymbals will ring, and the chimes will sing,
and the Angel chorus will reach unto transition,
and the sleeping Blessed will know that a moment has come,
    for they will see not the altered state of humanity Entering in,
    nay, Soul, they will see the living humanity enter in.
And they will portray that which they are,
    the chosen of all worlds.

487 Soul, we are from Lantosia.
We have entered in to your earth plane many times.
We have a life form unlike yours
    and yet it sustains itself on a form of air.
We have a short time in your space.
The thinness of your air does not allow us much time.
We have many abilities upon our space
    that you, humanity, do not have.
We have all motion, in all directions.
There is no north, south, east, west within our language.

Other Worlds

There is no need.
Our motion will take us circular, horizontal or vertical.
We have no need to initiate, we have only the need to register.
All beings in our existence have a direct relationship to who you are.
We are not far from you, we are two Quar from your planet.
The entering in by us is done by both vehicle and self form.
We may enter your walls with no resistance.
We may conquer your Energy field with no resistance.
We could pick up your sleeping babies
    and waft them from your space.
We have no notion of such an action toward humanity,
    we have only the greatest concern!
Our concern has some selfishness, if it were not negativity.
But what you do, earth, is our destiny.
There are many life forms with little to sustain their being,
    but many rely on earth.
We are but one.
There is no negativity where we are, we gather Purity.
We aid our brother and our sister,
    as you call your members.
But many worlds beyond have slim existence
    and each life form awaits the new day.
We have asked of Creator:
    "Why can we not move forward into the new Gateway?"
"It is because, in the Entering In,
    the implosion of worlds upon worlds
    will create a great vacuum in your worlds
    and those lost would be left behind."
Our Creator is your Creator.
Creator, the Energy of all, will leave no life form behind.
It is not known what will happen to Negativity,
    even in the great minds of other worlds
    at the time of implosion.
What will become of the Energy Negativity?
All is precious unto Creator.
It matters greatly to the supreme being that even a sparrow
    will not be lost.
We have no wish to leave behind the Souls of earth.

We have the greatest desire to bring the Blessed home again,
> but, Souls of earth, we do tremble at earth's lack of acceptance.

We urge humanity to acknowledge our plea.
We will be in your space to sustain you.
Our beings anticipate the great ague of earth.
Soul, our Love is in your space.
Do not fear that which is unknown.
You are guarded with great Love.
You are attended with great care.
Be thou earnest in acquiring thy purpose, oh earth.

CHAPTER 4

We Have Come

Circle of Saints

488 All is matter.
Whosoever has visited earth, and from the walk
    has delivered themselves through to manifestation
    in a single energized life, is Saint.
Would that there were many.
A Soul who has been in the space of Negativity
    before the earth galaxy perimeter,
    and has at no time entered in to the space of negativity,
    is hallowed Saint.
Within the space of Holy Holy Holy there is a Circle of hallowed Saints.
Within the circle of Holy Holy there is a Circle of hallowed Saints.
Within the space of Holy there are Saints.
All Souls of level six four,
    who have accepted transition to the state of Saint,
    not as earth would have saint,
    but Holy Saint, many of which are earth saints,
    have a single purpose to reach into the vibration of earth
    and fulfill an act of mercy.
The Circle of Saints carries no entity, but has reached beyond
    into the fold of Angels.
They have the last giving downward.
They have, Soul, the ability to alter the destiny of man.
The Blessed Virgin is of this Circle, Saint Francis, Saint Deuteronomy,
    Saint Acacia, Saint Bernard, Saint Vivacious, Saint Isabel,
    Saint Anthony, Saint Christopher, Saint Genoa.
Souls, they are the list times seven, times seventy, times seven hundred.
The Circle of Purity encircles the earth.

The eye is one and the action is unified.
All supplications are brought within the Circle of Purity.
Earth also holds a circle of saints.
Within the earth circle of saints has been human greed.
Pattern the Circle from the Holy Ones.

489 Beloved! Souls, behold the Circle of Saints.
Behold, whomever hast been within the circle of goodness,
    has entered in to the vision of Saints;
    the Holy ones, the elevated Souls of Purity
    who have reached beyond the sphere of knowledge of earth,
    who have reached beyond the extended levels of Farside,
    who have entered in to the radiant Energy of their being
    and have left from their being all lesser whorls
    with one curtain of goodness to unfold the very vision of Creator.
Unto Creator their song is heard.
The extension of their being
    has entered in to the magnificence of Creator.
They are in the hallowed halls of the burst of Energy.
They see that which can not be seen,
    and they see all that flows in abundance toward earth.
And they gather the pure of heart, and they gather the innocent Souls,
and they gather the fragments of Purity
and extend them upward unto Creator.
And the mouth is not, and the eyes are not, and the ears are not,
    but behold thou art,
    and the blessed Circle of Saints reach unto your being.
As the man of earth sees a treasure of gold,
    so the Purity of your being is valued as more.
And your being pleads with the Circle of Saints
    to place supplication before Creator,
    for all thy goodness has been endowed,
    and the Circle of Saints treasure that which they hold
    in the record of thy being,
    and they countenance, one with the other.
How may we help this Soul to be lifted in goodness
    further unto Purity?
And the Soul feels the blessing of the Holy Ones upon their being,

and are energized, and say:
"Souls, I have entered in to a new beginning.
I have felt renewed."
They have felt the mark of separation.
They have extended their being unto the Path of Creator
    and recognized their earth being
    as only that in which the lesson is learned.
Seek ever the Circle of Saints.
Know all Souls sit at the Hem of Creator
    and learn the lesson before them
But the Circle of Saints have an elevated place
    where the space of our being could not observe,
    for the Purity has intenseness that we could not bear.
Know a circle is always in the place of forming.
Soul, treasure the seed of your being.
See it as a precious thing that grows,
    emanates beyond itself and flowers as the noon day sun,
    and it is the growth of that bloom
    that enters in to the space of the circle.
It is offered unto Creator as Holy.

490 Holy Holy Holy, blessed are ye
    when the vision may enter in to the Circle of Saints.
The Circle of Saints is what you call network,
    a drawing together for the purpose of becoming.
The Circle of Saints for the Farside,
    carries a source of blessedness that abounds,
    and the voice and the breath and the eye have no purpose.
Only the fragmented purities enter in to the space of the blessed Saints
    and are taught of Flow and the higher realm.
All beings who have entered in to the conclave of the Circle of Saints
    have forfeited their onward motion to Creator
    that they may teach the blessed purities
    so the struggle to humanity may become one, complete
    into the realm of gazing downward.
The ultimate purpose of the Circle of Saints is to gather
    from those who will enter in to the depths of transition.
They will hold unto their beings the Holy Holy Holy

who have contained themselves from the beginning of time
    in great agony.
Earth Souls will be the conduit through which these Souls are redeemed.
All energies seek a single purpose, to redeem all that is in illusion.
Blessed be earth that offers self, and more blessed still,
    the seed cast unto it.

491 Soul, who has heard the call?
Who knows that which has been?
All that is known is in the beings of the blessed ones.
They are those who have found themselves in Purity of six and beyond.
They have left the course of their being.
They have taken unto their being, rapture.
They are not Souls who are content in Purity and blessed.
They are not beings who extend their energies outward to earth.
They are those who have come through the Flow of earth's circle
to lay at the feet of Creator, the perfection of their being
in the overcoming of negativity.
They are those of the Circle of Saints who walk
    with the blessed ones in their space.
Behold, upon earth are those beings who have come to teach,
    who have a Purity beyond humanity,
    to teach the inflection of Purity,
    to teach the Sound of Purity, to teach Naught unto thy being.
Souls, blessed ones are the fallen, blest ones are humanity
    raised to Purity, who walk, and will walk
    with Oneness in their being.
Blessed, blessed earth.

492 Souls, enter thou in to the Circle of Saints,
enter thou in to the Purity beyond manifestation.
Souls of earth, all who have manifested beyond humanity
    are Souls willing, wanting and able
    to walk amid the Circle of Saints.
These blessed Beings carry Purity of six and beyond.
Souls, they are teachers to all beings who hold a Soul of movement.
Movement of the Soul occurs only in higher beings.
There is no low, there is no high.

How then is there a higher being?
Soul, higher being is acceptance of Purity.
The beings at high level do not see themselves as above,
    for they are within, they are about,
    they are near and far, they have a density of Purity.
It emanates from their Being.
Souls, behold the Circle of Saints.
To enter in to the space of those beings
    is to enter in to a platform of Purity.
Souls, behold, it is your Purity that allows you the entering in.
Blessed, blessed Souls.

493 We have gathered Purity unto our being.
Unto many worlds we teach Purity.
We teach the gathering time and the purpose of our gathering.
Were you to go into your worlds, a single person going forth
    and gathering recruits for a purpose,
    not every being in your lands
    would know of why you have gone forth.
And so it was within our Farside,
    and the echo has gone forth of that which humanity is doing.
And the Souls as we are, who have gathered the scars,
    have entered in to lands to teach about the Purity of Farside.
Your earth is our earth, your pain has been our pain,
    and the Circle of Saints has overcome the pain,
    has released the pain, has relinquished all negatives.
It, Soul, gives us Truth.
It gathers Wisdom unto our being, but it does not open the volume.
A Soul higher than us has opened the volume.
The chimes have rung out, the cymbals have clashed,
    there has been dancing in the streets.
For earth is coming of age
    and the time for awakening is drawing nigh.
It is this opportune occurrence that has allowed the aperture to open.
It is this occurrence of time that has cleared the vision.
The veil has been lifted.
We see what you see.
Soul, we have been penitent for much of what we have done.

We have berated our being as earth human for what we have done.
But as Farside citizen, we acknowledge our goodness
    and we know the level of our goodness is accepted.
Our Creator is not far from us, only behind yet another veil,
    and we await the coming forth, and we know we shall be there.
And we know we shall move forward,
    and you, earth, shall move forward with us.
All that is has a debt to humanity.
We, you and our being, are humanity.
The Circle of Saints know your innermost thoughts,
    they have been their innermost thoughts.
And they know your pain, and they know they have overcome such pain.
But in the overcoming is not the vision.
Vision comes from earth itself, not those redeemed from earth,
    but it must come from earth surface
    as the Brethren will come to earth surface.

494 Blessed, blessed Souls of earth, how radiant is thy being.
How iridescent is thy glory.
Beatitude of beatitude, this I say unto you:
    "Lift he who has fallen. Join thy being to he who is hungry."
Carry all negativity from thy being, experience ecstasy.
Experience, Souls, the glory of Purity.
Bring thyself to the edge of choice and understand the crossroads
    where negativity and Purity divide themselves.
This is entering enlightenment.
This is the releasing of negativity from your being.
It is placing thy hand onto the hand of the mirror
    that is thyself on the Farside,
    and knowing that you are akin to the Spirit that you are,
    knowing that the vibration of your being
    is connected to your Essence of Purity.
And know that the Purity of thy being is at one with thy Creator.
How blessed art thou!
We have not come to the state,
    we only know that through thy holiness
    we may enter in to such ecstasy.
You are the avenue by which we may enter.

The Circle of Saints harness their eagerness,
    await with great anticipation and release the tears that flow
    even from the eye of knowing,
    for Souls of earth are slow to be caught in Purity.
Take our hand, we would guide you.
We know the path, yet we may not enter, but we may guide you in.
Will you take off all guise of negativity, all sarcasm, all truancy, all jest?
Will you lift thy Soul unto the work of humanity,
    for this is the purpose of your coming.
The mountain is high.
It takes a stalwart heart to climb the mountain,
    many fall.
Will you stop and lift the fallen, be the Samaritan?
Will you lift the glass to the mouth of the thirsty and prepare a cot?
There is no choice, there is simply no choice in Purity
    except the choice of Love.
It is not difficult to make the choice but it involves all time,
    one hundred percent all time, not a moment without.
It is from that you have come, total Purity.
He has knocked on your door and said: *"May I enter in?"*
Doubt will forestall, Love will pave the way.
Choice gathers all beings unto it, the poor and the simple,
    the blind and the lame, the ignorant and the educated.
So be it.

495 Soul, behold the emerging from the cocoon.
The Light offends the eye in the first awakening
    and the Soul covers the eye for the blast is pure.
Soul, could I be in the space of such Purity
    as those who prepare the state of the Register,
    the beings whose Truth has been given in dedication,
    in Purity, to Creator?
That which is written, you have but to see.
The Finger points and the lesson is read
    and Creator brings to the Soul the bounty of Energy
    and the Soul beholds the Energy
    and all the lives written upon the Register
    are imprinted within the aura of your being.

You have but to see the flight of your Energy.
But the lesson is imprinted
    and is used daily upon earth plane.
You have that message.
You have that lesson.
It is your enactment, enactment, Soul,
    to gather from the yesterday the lesson for today.
It is done by all earth Souls, repeatedly.
Soul, humanity is who you are.
Humanity is every face upon which your eyes light,
    upon which your voice reaches,
    upon which your hands touch.
It is the gentle response of self,
    the total acceptance of your commitment
    to the Truth of your being.
Behold, gather to the upper kingdom, gather, Soul,
    to the landscape of energies in countless purities
    and be brought into the magnificent.
Alight your being, alight your being!
Oh thou Soul, cease to pretend!
A vision is clear.
Behold, as the great saints encircle the shrine of earth
    and man within that circle expresses
    tales of goodness and wellness,
    so does humanity often reflect
    the same circle of no sense about their being,
    and in great words of platitudes express, "*We have power*".
Oh, the saints know that which is powerful.
Behold they know that which is mighty.
Behold your raiment is cloaked with the infinity of saints.
Behold thy seat is empty, awaiting the fulfilling of thy step.
It is in gentle acceptance of day and day and day.
It is not forced.
Gently behold the newborn lamb.
Our blessed Saint has lifted many
    and tenderly places within his arms the being of his attention.
And the lamb will gently limber off well,
    because of the glance of the Holiness of the Saint

who within the Circle of Saints, can cast the same glance
and is the purpose of all beings upon the face of the earth
in which you dwell.
We enter your space for the purpose of teaching.
You have been brought low that you might be brought high.
Gather you not cripples unto yourself,
but the eye of your being will bestow upon the lame and the deaf
and the sightless cure, cure.
Gather to you as the blessed saint,
and know that even the Holy Virgin gathers unto herself the babes
and the glance reflects back only Purity.
Behold, you have been brought into the presence of the Circle of Saints.
Behold, some have seen the great destruction of time,
the great glow upon earth, and all have one purpose,
to be ever brought into the space of man
that man might know the possible,
the surety, the access into the place of Purity.
Acceptance, Soul.

496 The Circle of Saints has been brought
from their state of holiness unto the gateway.
We have come unto the Gateway to know if the vision is clear to our being,
and we know that our being still is clouded.
It is not within our being to complete the opening without the last days.
This includes all beings, all energies of earth, not only the Circle of Saints.
It has, within the entry, all earth.
We rejoice that this shall be, and we ask,
the Circle of Saints have registered the timetable is Truth,
we ask, Soul, that you be aware that Truth is time connected,
and when Truth accelerates to the space of no Time,
the Gateway will become open.
Beloved, you are gathered.
You are constantly gathered.
Within the Circle of Saints there is a chime
that rings as Souls are gathered.
There is a resonance that is sent unto all worlds
when a Soul is gathered unto the Circle of Saints,

for within the Circle of Saints is the Purity
to enter in to the chasm of transition.
These Souls have attained all Truth.
They have gathered to be purposeful in their intent
to resolve earth issues,
knowing within their being they can not
alter the step that is human.
And yet, Soul, in that circle is radiance found,
within that Circle is Purity that can be sent to earth beings
And when the opportunity is sent upward from your being,
"Please, Soul, encase me, the human.",
they glory in that expression.
You are not alone in your struggle.
You have never been alone in your struggle,
and yet each Soul must fight the negativity as a single unit,
for each Soul must bear the scar
but Farside is ever informed of that which is in the Flow.
"It is done!", they await,
knowing that time will have ceased to be.
And their illusion is anticipated to be resolved,
indeed, because of Souls who have in their gift to Creator,
entered back in to the warfare against negativity.
We know beyond the Gateway,
we know, Soul, why and somewhat within.
Earth will not enter in, Far Side will not enter in.
We know that all that is earth and Far Side
exists beyond Second Gateway,
but all beings will come unto the wholeness of self.
All beings will implode into the space of Second Gateway.
None will be left, not a single Soul will be left.
As precious as the Angel, the Holy Brethren, are to Creator,
so is the preciousness of each humanity unto Creator,
for to lose a single Soul would be to lose a part of self.
You are unto Creator, as self.
There are great quests of Energy within Far Side,
researching the negativity you know.
There is a great need to not encounter Negativity

once it has entered in to the Cleansing River,
for the Energy of the Cleansing River
will also ride the wave of implosion
and leave all Negativity unto itself.
It will have strengthened in its gathering together as in battle,
being strengthened by the connection of each Soul
and the bond is as iron and can not be broken
until the Energy of Godhead seeks to disarm.
You have on your earth the disarming of nations from negativity.
You are a reflection of all that is within our side,
the dilemma you face is "How can we disarm the negativity
without placing harm upon humanity?"
You see, of course, the correlation.
Godhead, who is Energy of righteous Ecstasy, can not maim negativity,
cannot maim, and therefore it cordons off.
This you will see in your world, a cordoning off until solution is found.
Godhead, as Creator, is righteous as all that is Love and Truth and Purity.
And yet another ecstasy, the ability to intensify all radiance within,
the ability to signify unto all creation,
a propulsion of Energy of such magnitude
as to ignite what is Purity into Ecstasy what is Love.
We, Soul, know you have your day of glory,
but all Far Side awaits the entering in to Love
and seeks the power of ecstasy.
To tremble in that power is, Soul, to be a venue for all creation.

Angels

497 Enter thou in to the level of angels,
enter thou in to the place of gentleness.
Soul, it is the angels' harp.
All is in the space of earth, the vision of four:
three to minister unto,
one to alter the life,
three to be in the space of blessed Creator,
to hear the note, the chime,
and send it to the Angels in the first three,
that they may pass it to earth.

Souls of earth, do not wipe your hands.
Know the power of your being, the extensions of your being.
The blessed Saints blest,
>   for the hands and the arms
>   are as the wings of the Blessed Being.

It is why, Soul, you have the form you have.
Blessed Souls, Angels, Cherubs, are baby Souls
>   who have been brought in Purity
>   at one life to the station of Angel.

Seraphim are young Souls of great Purity
>   who have been brought to the pureness of their being in one life.

Archangels are those Beings who have always had Purity.
From the beginning of Energy casting out
>   there was battle with Negativity.

These pure Beings stood and fought the greatest battle.
Within their Purity is the greatest gift,
>   for your beings would not have withstood
>   the impure state of that casting.

Many Souls are lost in the great chasm because of that which is.

498 Blessed humanity, look into the stars
>   and vision that which you see,
>   eternalized eon after eon after eon.

Know within the place of your galaxy are myriads of stars.
They dance before your eyes
>   and many Souls have worshipped in their space,
>   and yet your earth is bombarded by negativity.

It flows within the crevices of your being, of your mind,
>   of the mountains, of the dale, of the waterways.

It is in no way free from any place except Purity.
When the Soul acknowledges Truth, Purity resides
>   and it is the armour against negativity.

Your galaxy is only one of many worlds beyond worlds beyond worlds,
>   and the infiltration of Negativity was there.

Unto the Second Gateway was Negativity,
>   and Creator entered out of the place of Love,
>   into the place of Negativity,

and He looked with compassion unto all that was.

And He drew around about the Blessedness of Being, the Angels.
And He said:
> "Go ye forth into Negativity and battle that
>> which has always been, and draw the Negativity
>> into the Hinterland so all who strive
>> to reach the Gateway will not be confounded."

And the Blessed Ones went here and here
> and here and here and battled with their Purity.

And the Blessed Ones gathered with great compassion,
> so as to gather unto their own Being,
> the Negativity to wear as a cloak that others would be free.

As a mother would fight for the suckling child,
> so the Blessed Ones fought for the many worlds,
> and those who gathered in temperance
> could be in the space of Creator.

And those who gathered in abundance unto their very Being,
drew the curtain unto themselves,
that all would be saved from bombardment of Negativity.
Some Souls had reached such Purity that, even within the time of earth,
> they could enter in and not be affected.

But many worlds could not enter in, their being would be affected.
As the pock enters in to the flesh,
> so would Negativity enter in to these Blessed.

"How has Negativity come?", you will ask.
It was a seed planted in the garden of creation
and it flourished beyond all other seeds,
and worlds looked unto the voracious appetite of Negativity
and prevention was not possible.
And the Souls implored unto Creator:
"Creator, come Thou to see that which we see,
that which we feel, that which we know enters our being.
How can we combat?"
And Creator, in his compassion, sent forth the Blessed unto Hinterland.
"Place all Negativity unto Hinterland. Be it so."

499 Souls, you have spoken of the ritual
> and our beings carry the stripes of our negativity.

We have been wounded, we have been scarred.

We have brought forth many Souls from their own agony
    who have been wounded and scarred.
Do not reproach another man's negativity,
    for their negativity is that place in which
      they have found themselves for growth.
They are no different than you.
And yet in a different lifetime you have fought with daggers
and killed the defenceless, and starved;
    you have fornicated, have cut and maimed.
Souls of earth, every being has value.
Do not take the life of another.
Do not rob a Soul of his growth, but send forth
    from the magnitude of thy being, the ushering of Love.
Holy being is thy identity, earthly being is thy present state.
Acknowledge the profoundness of Holy.
Acknowledge that within this sphere of your world, all are Holy.
There is not one whit unholy.
Do not deem yourselves as powerless but know,
    where young Souls strategize for ill,
      old Souls may strategize for good.
One combats the other.
We ask that you form camps of goodness within the Spirit of your being.
We ask that Love enters in,
    and hate is kept as the lesson for young Souls.
And the mark of separation will offer the reflection of baby Souls,
    the Essence of their being.
Hark, hark unto holiness.
Mark thy door with thy Energy
and, as the Angel of Light, the mark will be recognized.
And Souls who enter in will know that negativity
    has been erased from within,
    and the door will be as though it is not there,
    and all will feel the comings and flowings of power of Purity.

TEACHINGS

500 Michael will teach the voracity of men's appetite for evil.
The vicious circle of negativity that swirls within the mind of men

is transformed by a simple kindness,
by a simple effort of one human to another.
The generosity of Spirit enlightens mankind.
The issuing forth of goodness
    filters through the most hardened of hearts.
All humanity is lifted unto greatness.
No being will be left in the crevice of darkness.
Creator would gather unto His being, all energies,
    but the energies themselves
    could not withstand the place of Creator.
And Creator has gathered a Text, a form, a pattern for all beings,
    in all purities, even the Fallen of purities.
And the Finger of God will reach unto mankind and the stench,
    the foulness that gushes forth, will be stilled,
    for the children of men will have reached their ultimate goal,
    to redeem the Holy Holy Holy.
And beings will look back unto that space of reflection
    and say to mankind in their Purity:
    "Who art thou that hast given so much unto thy Creator?
    We are not amazed that you are robed in Purity,
        for, Soul, you have lifted unto Creator
        that which Creator could not lift.
    Oh, Souls of earth, hallowed Souls of earth,
        how wondrous thou art in thy being."
And they shall peer into the Volumes and ascertain clearly
    the picture of mankind's growth unto redemption.
And all creation will know at the Entering In to newness,
    the passageway will be clear,
    because Holy Souls dwelling on earth, called humanity,
    have gifted Creator.
A new sun and a new moon will be in that place,
and Light will be seen in a new way,
and all illumination of Light will have movement,
and Souls will explore a new creation and an old Creator,
    and so will be the second phase of creation.

501 Souls, behold the Mountaintop, utopia, the sacred Mountain,
    the healing place where knowledge of wisdom has entered in.

Souls, the sound of healing is an entrance unto the passage of Purity.
Blessed Souls, know the passage of Purity.
Behold your being, behold the awesomeness of your being
    channelled unto the Energy of Creator.
You are of Creator.
The Sound and Colour of healing is done with direct Energy.
It is done without instrument,
    without textures of negativity added to the body.
It is done with the acceptance of your being.
The sound of healing is a mountaintop experience.
It is done in the most pure and solemn of passages.
Draw from the Farside, draw from the pure flow of Love.
Love is not silent, Love excels in goodness, in Purity, in Truth.
Souls, rejoice in the passage you have
    and know that all earth will find the channel of sound
    to heal self.
It will come when earth chooses the positive Energy.
Always on earth there is choice.
Always!
The first choice is acceptance to believe,
    to know in your being that the sound of goodness is yours.
The second is by the negative role which will bring humanity down
    and cast the oceans round about them.
And as they survive their fear, they will look up onto the mountaintop
    and words will come forth.
Souls of great Purity will enter from the heights of pure goodness
    and heal Souls in the sound of colour.
Reach into the prism, beloved earth, reach into the prism that is yours.
Draw from the endless stream of Light.
Draw from the Radiance of Creator.
Oh ye of earth, draw from the fountain!
Souls of earth, accept the goodness offered unto thee,
    for all creation has a cup that runneth over.
Draw from the living waters, from the Energy
    that touches the flesh through the Eye of Beholding.
Bless thou the Soul!
The tiniest of all creation is sacred unto Creator.
How much more is the human who has the likeness of Creator!

Vast eternity, extended from your being,
> offer to mankind with the purchase of Truth.

And yet man will idle in negativity.
Stop the fetid odours that rise from earth unto the Holy of Holy!
Bear only Purity unto the blessedness of creation.
Souls of earth, behold the day draws nigh,
> behold the hour is soon come.

Rejoice in the hour which will come.

502 Blessed earth, Holy beings
> entered in to the supreme Path of Purity.

Without the knowledge of Love, you can not BE.
Without the knowledge of Purity, you cannot BE.
Without the knowledge of Truth, you cannot BE.
For, Souls of earth, they are the very particles
> of that of which you are made.

They are to be treasured beyond all knowns.
And who has brought them forth unto thee but the Knower.
Soul, Creator is the wholeness, the completeness,
> the ever ending circle of your being.

Creation is the artistry of the Creator
> and you are a part of that artistry.

You are a weave, treasured beyond all others,
> for the strand that you are, in its refinement, is as pure gold.

It contains the blossoming of Love.
Many Souls of earth are tormented in their being,
> many Souls of earth have lechery and greed and lust.

They have not brought themselves past the level of baby Soul.
They are in debauchery and chaos, they struggle to know negativity.
Their Energy is heightened by the very knowledge of negativity.
They are baby Souls.
How may you know how to overcome something
when you know it not?
First you must know it.
First you must understand and sense with all the senses,
> the negativity, and then overcome that which is.

There are Souls who glory in the negativity.

They have not been able to reach beyond the infant,
> the baby, the young.
They strive to deceive humanity.
They cloak themselves as ever in Purity.
They draw themselves into oneness.
They have a purpose to defeat Purity and Truth,
> and yet they are human,
> and yet in their purpose they are part of humanity's plan,
> for it is only humanity that extends itself
> outward to overcome negativity.
Souls of earth, know your Energy,
> know the abundance and availability of your Energy,
> and recognize the Purity in your being,
the Truth you have come unto.
And know that your being may reach unto the baby Souls,
> know your being may reach to the clamour of young Souls.
You may alter a wilful life, you may achieve the winning of a war
> before it has happened.
Souls of earth, you have come to the space of spirituality
and all earth looks to see that what God will do,
what Allah will do, what Yahweh will do.
Blessed ones, you are the tools of the supreme being.
It is through you that humanity comes to its Oneness.
You can not rest your being.
You can not sit idly by while Souls are brought low.
How pure would you be?
How without blemish would you be?
Would you be as the Holy Mother, without blemish?
Would you be as Mohammed?
Whom do you look unto to extol?
We ask that you look unto your being, for your being is as our being.
You are Holy!
The Essence of your being is as that of your Creator.
Soul, look to the wars and look to the starving and look to the needy,
> and know you have the power to alter.
Not with just the coin in your hand,
> but with the ever extended Energy from your being.

The goodness that flows unto all earth stills the negativity,
    alters the chaos,
        prevents the hoards of insects from inundating the land.
You have the power to reach to our side, do you not!
You have the power to reach unto Creator, have you not!
How powerful is thy being, oh earth!
See the joy and extend joy outward from thy being.
Do not be brought down, do not grovel in the fields of mud,
but rise yourself up and know you have abundant Light,
that you glisten and sparkle, that you glow with Purity,
and know that Purity has the power to move outward
    unto all beings.
Holy earth being, we applaud the goodness that surrounds you.
We applaud the potential that is yours
and we invite you to blossom forth
    in the intent of attaining Purity and Love
    by extending to earth that which you are.

503 Souls, earth inhabitants,
    what would happen if the world would refuse to fight,
    if the great men spoke and the Souls refused to fight?
What would happen if, instead of fighting, they amassed together
    and sought out all negatives from their being?
What would happen if they reneged from the battle of impurity
    and gathered the battle of Purity?
Who would fight the battle?
Who would slaughter the millions?
Who would maim the children?
Who would kill the mothers?
What if earth refused to be sent to hell"
and knew there was a place of perfection,
a place of honour for their beings to be?
What if they reached unto the angels and the angels lifted them up?
What if, instead of wars,
    the world ceased to contaminate the fields of earth
and earth planted a food to feed the starving?
What pain would come of that?
What would happen if,

instead of slamming the door upon our neighbour,
we invited our neighbour in, welcomed him in sincerity?
Is that altruistic?
It is possible, Soul.
Earth, it is possible!
What would happen if all brethren accepted the needy,
the care stricken, the Souls with afflictions
into the comfort of stability, of Love?
Would they rise up and walk?
Would they not recognize that their Creator had been in their space!
Souls, seek not to hold thyselves from war.
Seek not to hold thyselves from negativity.
Seek not to bar thy door and cast from thee Souls in despair.
But draw all thy energies, all thy being into the supreme gift
of thy own outward Energy,
    to alter every space of negativity,
to enhance every space of pain,
to seek out and nurture all the downtrodden.
"How vast is that number" you say?
But, Soul, they are your brothers, your sisters!
In the reflection of thy being, they are as you are
    and where you will be one day,
        for all beings experience all humanness.
Tread gently where pain is, for there might you be.
Beloved, unto all Souls cast a loving smile, not the angled grin,
    not the terse lips, not the look of judgement,
        but the gentle reflection of goodness.
Unto all men be thou pure.

504 Soul, we would talk about anger.
We would speak of the energy that it is.
Creation is Energy.
Anger is energy.
Love is Energy.
We may fuel Love, we may fuel anger.
Souls of earth have long carried the burden of anger.
It has driven their being into the darkest of corners.
It has withered the Souls of many.

It has brought forth egos of great negativity.
It has made men walk tall in the state of anger
    by acknowledging that anger in some way has power.
And so it does.
Anger has great power, and know the fuel of anger is naivety.
It is refusing to look at the core.
It is refusing to look at the centre purpose of the anger.
Why has it been there?
All anger has purpose.
The purpose is not always for the Soul who carries the anger.
It is often for the witnesses of that anger.
Soul, our existence on earth has been.
We have been as you, we have walked as you.
We give as a gift to our Creator,
    the teaching of anger to Souls on earth.
Why?
Because our being once lived and breathed in flesh
    and our anger ignited great wars.
We teach the object, the survival of anger.
Anger is not evil, it is a human outlet.
It is part of humanity.
There would be no growth without anger,
    but the anger belongs to the individual
    and solely for the purpose of growth.
Instead, earth beings, you unite to bring anger together,
    to place your anger into the place of those
    who are unprepared to survive such anger.
Earth, you even build weapons to aid and abet your anger,
    and it flourishes and takes momentum,
    and anger cannot stand alone,
    for when it gathers together there comes hate,
    and hate indulges itself.
It is whimsical in its desire.
It seeks out the pained being.
It seeks out the pure state and it sends energies that are felt.
And, Souls of earth, you think:
    "How can this happen? We are vigilant.
    There is no anger here!
We Love, and yet only beyond the causeway is anger,

only beyond the mountain is anger."
And there is a river or there is an ocean,
that provides a path into the space you are in
and anger can rise high on the river or low on the river.
It enters in as Truth enters in.
Soul, recognize anger in your being.
Acknowledge anger in your being
and then seek to release that which is unholy,
and invite that which is Holy into its state.
Soul, raise up your eyes
    that you might be beyond the space you are in,
that you may be over the mountain
    and on the other side of the causeway,
that you may see the pain in your space and beyond.
For earth has little time to mend the severed being.
Earth has little time to find the joy in whom they are.
Brace thy being to eradicate all flows of energy negatives
    unto thy being and know that you have the power
        to shut from your being, the constant bombardment of anger.
What is angry, you Love.
What is hate, you Love.
What is in pain, you Love.
So be it.

505 The message was not *"You may kill."*
The message was *"Thou shalt not kill."*!,
    not thy bull, nor thy ox, nor shalt thou lift thy sabre unto any man,
nor wilt thou form destruction unto thy neighbour!
For all earth is one earth and all people are humanity.
Tether not the arm of one man to another
    and shackle not the legs of a man to his ox.
You may clear a way before you and see the legions of humanity
    as maggots before your eyes.
But this I tell you: "If you see humanity as lesser beings than thyself,
    you will become, in that space you have set aside for yourself,
        the lesser being".
You will roll with the thunder and be ignited by the lightning,
    and the sound will overwhelm you,
    and the light will blind your eye.

Evil is not the passage of humanity.
Take off the mark of indifference and set aside the knife,
    and hold thy brother as thy brother.
Who art thou, man, that you see yourself as higher than your God,
    that you place a mark on the Souls of humanity?
You have entered in to earth not to,
    but to destroy the deceptor of man.
You have been caught in the deceptor's trap and we call to you
    to recognize that which you are in, and to set aside warring.
We call on you to look at your flesh and your blood,
and to know it will soon be clay,
and to know that which you are tethered to is Holy.
Be thou Holy!
Unencumber thy Soul with a burden of negativity.
Mohammed is Truth.
May the Truth of Mohammed recognize and be recognized in thy Soul.
Will you enter the dome in Purity with pure intent
and fold thy arms across thy breast as two brothers,
welcoming the sameness in each other?
The hawk must still its being and enter in to the field with Purity,
    for the enemy is not humanity but negativity.
Remove the patch and allow the charge to be against negativity,
    for all nations will war to save earth
    if earth will not Love his brother.

506 Madre, Madre!
    Unto the mothers of earth, give power.
Unto the mothers of earth give political power,
and guard the space of the infants,
and persecute not the downfallen.
For in the land we have walked is a hornet's nest,
    in the land we have walked is greed.
Why will you send the sons and the daughters, my people, into battle?
Teach the children Love.
Teach the child to balance and know that
    in the balance of their being is the power of their being.
You ride in armoured vehicles and you pray before you enter in.
Will you pick the broken body and carry it to the mother?

Our broken body was also given to a mother
    and the mother wailed and cried,
    the mother sobbed and lamented.
You see your neighbour, you see through the window
    the mother preparing the food for the family.
Which member will you remove?
Why, for what purpose is there conflict?
So that you may see your blood runs in the same rivulets?
Have you not seen enough blood?
Open the doors and let the mothers come out into the streets,
    and let the mothers enter in to the battlegrounds.
Let the mothers target and no ammunition will be spent,
    for every child will be the mother's child
    and every pain will be the mother's pain.
We have spoken to the Pharisees and Sadducees,
    and we speak to the men behind the guns:
    "Step down before you annihilate what is precious unto you,
    the existence of life."

507 Souls, your Energy is like a great fire.
It builds and builds, it consumes.
It can consume in a positive way,
    or it may consume in a negative way.
Your Energy has great power.
Will you use the persuasion of negativity
to alter your Energy to a purpose that holds no Truth,
or will you use your Energy for goodness and Truth?
One will strangulate and cause all noxious fumes about thy being,
    the other will draw all goodness unto thy being
    that it may be reflected outward from thy being,
    and all goodness and power will be felt.
Souls of earth, know the power of your Energy,
    know the goodness it may hold
    and the bitter cup it may give.
Know that your Creator has opened a way for thy being,
    and the way is unto the Path of Light.
It draws itself inward, powerfully arming thy being with greatness,
with strength, with courage,

with the power to combat all negativity in thy space.
No negativity will draw unto you
    if you will draw the positive Energy unto thy being.
Know there is abundance for all.
Know that you may gather, as the Blessed Ones gathered Negativity,
    you may gather positive Energy.
And when you have gathered all the positive Energy
    you may set it forth unto your fellow man
that they may see the positive Energy
and feel and know the positive Energy,
and all negativity will, in turn, leave their being,
for they will see that what you have,
and they too will want to be afire with this Energy source.
Souls of earth, blessed art thou!
How much more blessed when you let go of negativity!

508 Earth, an edict from the Farside:
    "You are sacred, you are Holy, you are one in one accord,
    for one purpose upon the face of earth."
We know this, for we have seen the Record of Time.
We have been in the hallowedness of that place.
We have entered in in great ceremony to see that which was written
    and it is written that men are sacred, that men are Holy.
It is written that men have a purpose
    and the purpose is to raise the blessed.
We know, for we have seen the Record.
We know that many times man has fought, one with the other.
And many times Souls have been brought
    forward into the Farside in great numbers
    because of these battles.
We know that often the purpose of these battles is Creator
There is some humour in our beings, for if we did not see the humour,
    we would not cease to cry.
Our tears would flow undauntingly, unceasingly.
Humanity, each moment of your time is accountable,
    always has been since the impetus of casting forth.
Accountability does not render you unaccountable,
    it renders humanity accountable,

for only in the accountability may the blessed ones come forth.
It is the accountability that shows the marks upon your being,
    for upon the Farside you are perfection.
Were we to rend your flesh, your flesh would be flesh,
    your blood would be blood;
    you would not cease to be,
    your Soul would survive your earthly being
and your Soul would rejoice in the coming home.
And in the coming home would come the entry:
    "She came home,
        he entered in.
    They have completed."
And soon earth will recognize the pages,
    for there will be a human being who will rise out of the dust
    and speak of a miracle.
And all the earth will know there are angels,
    for the audience is ready to hear.
Souls of earth, your time is counted.
You are entering in to no Time.
You are entering in to vibration,
    and the velocity with which you will travel
    will be deemed unthinkable,
    and in the travelling you will be awake, your eyes will see.
In the travelling all your senses will be aware
and you will see beyond the ability of your eyes,
and smell beyond the ability of your nose,
and hear beyond the ability of your ears.
And the messages will be translated from another tongue,
    it will be the tongue of Purity.
And you will know the rising up of Purity,
    and only those who understand will know how to rise.
Nothing you do in your day will be unaccountable.
Godhead has the accountability within the Third Gateway.
The accountability is not as Creator's.
It carries a more stringent test,
    for all who enter in must enter in through implosion.
The being will change and you will become as fluid,
and you will see your beings rise,

and you will see yourselves in supplication,
for you will be far from that which you know.
And you will be lifted up and say: *"How is it that I can breathe?"*
But your nose will have taken on a new meaning,
>and your ears will not bleed
>for they will have taken on a new hearing,
>and your eyes will behold, for a veil will be lifted,
>and you will be changed, as you rise, and altered.
And when you return you will be new Souls.
You will be renewed, and yet you will be the same.

509 Blessed beings of earth, you are becoming unfractured.
Your Souls are uniting with your Spirit
even as you are upon the face of earth,
>and this is the Gathering Time, this is the Oneness.
It is unto Holy that you are becoming.
Souls of earth, always there will be Souls who will not vibrate
>until time has ceased to be.
And in the space of no time will come a healing platform
>that will lift all that are lost.
And all earth Souls will be amazed at that which they see
>for unto earth will great purities enter in
and unto earth will great pain be lifted,
>and the measure of your Soul will place you
>on the left or the right.
And those on the right Hand of God will reach to heal
>all that have been on the left Hand of God.
And all beings of earth will be brought to a Purity
>where they will see the Face of God.
Holy Holy Holy.

Vision[81]

510 Blessed, sight is the vision that you have.
Soul, be astounded at the Flow that is available
>from the Purity of the Farside.

---

[81] Vision - the dates at the end of each passage indicate when the channelling was received.
It does not indicate the date of the vision.

There is no hesitation.
There is no loss for words.
Confound the Souls?
We would confound the Souls, but earth is not ready for all lessons.
Earth can not bear the pain of itself.
The baby cries and the mother hastens,
    but the Soul cries, "*ahhh*" and gasps to breathe
    and yet, minute and enormous ion
    is taken from the roster of earth.
Place upon the Souls of Michael not gratitude,
    but do even the most infinitesimal moment
    for the Souls of earth.
All profoundness is carried to the sight of the Farside
    and the Michael would rejoice at the healing
    that would not be a bandage.
Travel in tranquillity, travel in the uphill path
    that takes the Soul to a stretch of new and wise searches.
Knowledge has no place in the eye.
Know this.
Knowledge is the earth lesson for the young Soul,
    the words that confound and make excuses
    for the timid step that could be bold.
Soul, look upward and see the gaping hole and cry.
The tears of the scene of the earth plane
    will pass away into the rumble and roll
    and issue forth a gush that will cleanse the Soul of knowledge.
Knowledge carries a blight that is decay
    when the Soul has searched from off the Path
    and put into use the wayward glance of productivity.
Soul, the breath upon the earth has altered and only in tiny ions
    that group themselves as havens is the air abundantly tuned.
And Souls of stature gather, gasp and say:
    "Ahhh, we can not breathe".
But what of the tiny ion?
Who is there to see the vision of the tiniest of creatures
    who gasp at iniquity done to them?
Vials of evil are kept in closets of man to forward the power
    that takes a child and thrusts him to an oven of heat.
Vile, vile!

And the Soul of that child has taught mankind to listen,
    and yet mankind turns the ear away.
[July 9, 1998]

511 Awake! Awake! World, awake!
Behold the gathering!
The gathering comes as the wind swirls.
The gathering comes as the earth shakes.
The gathering comes as men and women lose themselves
    in paltry humanness.
The gathering is the spiritual awakening of earth,
    the vibration, the chord of higher being.
All will be lifted to heal, to teach.
Not, Soul, to gaze down and say "I lived.".
No, Soul, to gaze down at the moment of the earth spewing forth
    the poison that man has planted,
    and know the Souls of awareness will gather
    with the aid of beings who have given their honour
    to hold the handful of humanity that will be left.
And the Souls will return to teach.
And the Souls would teach a new thing: awareness of *Energy*.
No longer will earth require oil and gas to heat the body.
The body will have Energy
    and the touch of the Energy to a fallen Soul will lift that Soul
    to be taught a new way, a way of Love.
Do not think that negativity will be erased.
It will not, but there will be in that moment of time,
    a profound electric storm.
It will raise the seas beyond the level of earth.
The loud claps of thunder, the strikes of lightning
    will place fear into all men.
Mothers will clasp their children to them and see them taken
    by the force of the wind and the sea and the rain.
And men will seek out boats
    and ships will find themselves at the bottom of the sea.
But the sea will roil itself and nothing will be as it was,
    and the sea will rake the land of trees,

      and the sky will be hidden by clouds,
      and the sun will find total darkness,
      and the gathering will lift the Souls.
And when the day has passed five times,
      the earth will still and many will cry:
      "Oh, oh Almighty One, hear our cry!"
The Almighty One has ever heard the cry
      and the book that is written will be unwritten,
      and a new day will come
      where men will know the sacredness of being men.
And all Souls will carry upon them the eye of sight,
      for sight will be acknowledged by men
      who now fear the Truth of Creator Blessedness!
[October 8, 1998]

512 The flesh has agony
      and the boats spew the toxic invasion into our waterway.
Our waterway was before your time
      and you desecrate the path of our being.
You take from us a power of life,
      and in its space you bleach the waters with poison.
My baby is as your baby.
It is tethered to my side as yours is tethered to your side,
      and we have a voice that strikes the heart of mankind.
Hear the plight of the whale:
"Paths of the sky are being valued,
        but paths of the sea are being ignored.
Men of earth, spew not into the sea that which you cannot use.
Do not devoid life from your space.
Cry the cry of my brother, my sister, my baby.
Hear my grandfather and my grandmother.
Know my mother and my father are as your mother and your father.
      We are akin, you and I.
Upon earth there is a pattern
      that dissipates the number of mankind by greed.
Upon the sea, you decimate our number by greed and by foulness.
Hear this, the voice of the whale."

The path of the whale is the Path to Purity.
It cannot be rewritten.
We, the whale, are the second to last foreboding.
The turtle is the last.
[May 27, 1999]

513 Enter in to the waters, my child.
Enter in to the depths of being.
We have been within the waters of earth,
    and we have been stabilizer to the waters of earth.
But the waters are changing.
It is affecting our being.
We are unable to find ballast.
Souls, we are finding it difficult to balance the waters.
The sound of our voice reaches from sea to sea.
It alerts all within the sea of treachery and doom.
But we find ourselves without direction,
    we find ourselves lost in our environment
        and we call to man:"Man, come, see our pain.
        See the pain of those who are born defiled by man."
The mouth can not cry to the distant ocean
    and the earth has trembled in its very being.
We see the ocean, we see the great gaps within the sea,
    we feel the heat from the bowels of earth
    and we call to the winds, and we call to the rains,
    and we call to the ice cap:
    "There is a need here for balance!"
But now, who can balance the sea when the whale has no voice?
Come down, child, into the sea
    and feel the needles of pain brought to our flesh
    and know the gasp of our young is for life or death.
What happens to the whale will happen to mankind.
[June 3, 1999]

514 Earth is not responding in the natural state of itself.
It has lost the ability to purify the atmosphere.
It has been overcome with toxicity.

The rainbow enters your earth through stench.
The climactic changes will hasten, the winds will increase,
    the water table will rise,
the motion of earth beings will agitate their minds.
Men will seek to find solutions to their physical being
    and it is beneath their feet.
A poultice upon the face of earth would heal.
The putrification that has entered the bowels of earth
    will be tethered to the storms to come.
The hole in earth's heaven will be responsible
    for much of the dying,
    of the gaping holes upon the flesh of man.
Souls of earth, know you have a moment to enter in to the day of change.
[January 18, 2000]

515 Energy of Purity is in the space of waters.
Our beings guide mankind to the place of Purity.
We accept that which man places on our being,
    but the dolphin, our sister in Purity,
    gives of Love, of compassion.
The energies, the movement within the area of any sea calamity
is for one purpose and one purpose alone, to flay the water,
    that the Energy of the Souls be not captured under the deep.
The Souls can be lost in their pain
    and do not know the passage upward,
    and the dolphins in their goodness know that all Energy IS.
The effort of man is Creator's.
All movements of whales and dolphins are for the teaching of mankind.
Upon the place of earth there is a scientific effort
    to understand the language of our being.
All whales and some, not few, dolphins are recovered
    for a purpose of seeking a common language.
It is the brain that is captured and taken forth.
It is an offering, humanity, that we make ourselves available,
    for a language would be yours
    if you could but discern the single note of our memory.
Before the ships that sailed the sea, we were.

The ship is in our space, it is the path that we go.
It is what we have always known.
It is the way of all.
We can not move from our appointed round.
The ship is the Knight of the Phoenix.
It sails as research and is from Australia.
It is taking a notable path to hear what we do
    and we are amused by their feeble attempts to communicate.
Would they only hear what we say?
Accelerate decibel!
Hear the acceleration to the tone of C.
Man will find the dolphin at the tone of A.
[February 8, 2000]

516 We have a passage in the southern seas.
The waters have gathered toxins.
They enter in currents, they come spewing forth from rivers
    into the waterways.
Our beings, our young, are caught in the lecherous habitat
    that was once our world.
Mankind, still the flow of toxins or our beings will be no more.
You, earth, you eat the flat fish.
We warn earth, the flat fish gather your toxins.
They enter in to the skin and create lesions.
And we see the young that you have upon the shore,
    and we know that they have lesions too.
There is a cancer brought from the fish you eat.
It comes from the north and beings hold the viper in their liver,
    in their kidney, and it decimates the flesh of earth.
You must release a Path of Purity.
Gather your wise men and speak as one to earth:
    "Who will stop the pleading, the beat of humanity?"
All flat fish, it is in six varied forms, all of which attack the flesh;
    the hands of small children will cease to feel,
    they will hit and have no pain,
    and mothers will give birth to open sores,
    and fetuses will release before their time.
Earth, you have been in an agreement to harbour the toxins.

Speak to that which you have agreed to.
[April 11, 2000]

517 Soul, the water truly moves and blends and flows,
    and shifts and cools and warms,
    and all creatures within the sea
    move to the still calm of the heat or cold.
Even the most minute of life forms alter their being
    to abide by the will of earth.
Earth has a strong Soul.
Earth's Soul is glorious.
Earth sends forth energies unto man.
Earth, heed the word of earth!
Speak forth words that earth speaks:
    "Save the waterways!
    Save the great demarcations of land
that alter the form that land has had,
that creates a shift in the Energy Flow of earth."
All steps for mankind must be in unison with earth.
Earth and man came together as one,
    earth to glorify that which is the purpose of man,
and man to have available unto himself
    that which is a touch of the Farside.
Behold, the creatures of the deep see with eyes that are clear.
They travel in the depths of the sea.
They draw in to the open portals of pain.
They enter in to the refuse of man, and the scars teach the young
    that man has burdened earth yet again.
And we teach our young to avoid the great darknesses
    that man has placed in the sea.
But as your young, our young are fearless and they gather great pain.
Souls of earth, see all energies as one.
See the glory of your Energy as the glory of your Energy,
    of your Energy, of your Energy, of your Energy.
Unite that we have oneness in the gathering of Purity.
Hold the sanctity of your earth within your being.
Hold the sanctity of earth, for it is the stepping stone
into the well of pain that man will gather

to redeem that which was lost.
Souls of earth, use sparingly the water in your space,
    for only water that gushes will be available.
[April 11, 2000]

518 Soul, the nostrils absorb the putrification of flesh.
Denounce the putrification of flesh.
All flesh is sacred.
All beings know sacred Energy.
Illness will come upon earth from the use of flesh.
It is rampant in dispersions, it is ripe in putrification.
The stench will be reflected in a maimed body.
The sores will ooze, and the flesh will itch,
    and the young will tear at their skin to eradicate the pain
    that is deep within the layer of skin.
And man will be brought to the knowledge
    that flesh has been eroded by mankind.
It was not placed such by Creator.
Mankind has eroded flesh,
    and the flesh will come to flesh and be contaminated.
Brother, sister, mother, father, hold thy nostril
    when entering in to the space of flesh,
    for the carrion would not touch a flesh that man would eat.
The flesh carries the sharp points of needles,
    carries the medication deep within their beings.
Do not wash it, it will not eradicate.
It has, Soul, become a part of your own when consumed.
It has become your flesh.
Hold up the arm and see the mark, and watch it raise the arm,
    and know that as it rises, the man will leave his body
    for no pill will prevent that which will come.
Only the acceptance of Purity would eradicate the pain.
Accept Purity unto your being.
[April 11, 2000]

519 Soul, hear a passage of time.
Do not take refuge in the great wind.

Do not take refuge in the high water.
Do not place survival upon the sea, for, behold, before the rains come,
    the Soul has acknowledged its destiny.
There will be great winds, there will be scourges of pain
    when the tongue of man will engorge,
    and the throat will parch, and the lips will split,
    and Souls will seek ointments
    to place upon that which bleeds water.
There will be found no ointment to stem the secretion that flows
    and Souls will seek to pour into the parched throat
    that which would ease the pain,
    and the Soul will find no remedy,
    and the healers of the gathering will come
    and bless the Souls in multitudes.
And all that has been separated will bind itself unto self,
    and the Souls will utter words of praise,
    and the Souls will acknowledge their higher being.
Earth has always drawn calamity and calamity and calamity,
    but earth will shed a tear that will wash
    so the oceans will rise and all that have fear and stench
    will be washed in the great cry of earth,
    and the flow will encircle the globe.
"*El Nino!*" they cry.
Lo, it will be a new name, the name of ever and ever and ever.
From the step of a small child unto the raising of a man,
    there is continual growth.
The growth of man is for one purpose:
    to be blended with all creation unto itself,
    Creator unto Creator, Blessedness unto Blessedness.
As with the child, there is a single step, then there are two, and three,
    and there is a run.
The earth is now at run, and soon the child will become man
    and the accomplishments of man will begin.
Who shall be saved in the great calamity
    that will overtake the station of earth?
All beings who have entered in to the covenant
    the Creator has offered unto man.

Man shall not be overcome
    except by man's indifference to Oneness of all creation.
[April 18, 2000]

520 Soul, please know,
    all abductees are of a being unlike human.
They have taken the form of human.
Their body is essentially the same.
They have even given themselves vulnerability,
    but if you were to look at the back of each lobe
    you would see a brown mole.
It is an identifying mark.
It says the Soul is being tested,
    but the Soul is able to bear the test.
Each human has within their being, a potential to harm.
These beings who have been abducted have no such ability.
And mouths are sealed from their memory of existence.
They have within their brain the formatting of six languages.
They communicate freely with Souls who will save earth beings.
All aliens have positive Energy, do have no fear, recognize not negativity.
Within their being they know they are different from human.
Their awareness does not allow them to recall the point of that difference.
If they knew, they would come forward with resounding speech
    that animals of certain species can understand.
Whales, dolphins, understand all earth languages; human, insect, etc.
Within the range of these animals, the wee folk are interpreters.
They speak and transfer the code to these beings.
Each Soul has been in the presence of illusion.
The purpose of illusion is to alert earth of the devastation
    that will come upon the planet.
The planet will careen in instability for a moment
    and darkness will abound,
    and Souls will hold their beings to any structure within grasp,
    but the structures will fall, for the winds will lift cement and rock,
    and blow forth trees of age as though they were kindling material.
Have no fear.
The preservation of humanity is purposeful
    and the ongoing momentum of earth will continue.

Beloved, hold Truth.
Fear no alien being.
The voice of the turtle can be circumvented.
[May 2, 2000]

521 Souls of earth, enter in to the waters.
Souls of earth, the pressure for earth Souls within the water is great.
The pressure for our Soul is buoyant.
Our being is as your being.
It holds pain.
Our flesh, as your flesh, holds pain.
The waters of our memory were crystalline, and the flow was buoyant
    and now the flow is heavy and carries the froth upon the wave,
    and deception in the water.
And our babies are as your babes.
We are mothers and fathers, as you are mothers and fathers,
    and our beings weep when our young are lost,
    and our young have been lost.
Earth, value the wave that washes upon the shore of earth,
    for in the wave is the total existence of your being.
When you contaminate the wave, you contaminate life.
When you contaminate the wave,
    earth rejects the negativities spewed upon it,
    and the night of darkness bursts forth.
None will stand on the night of darkness,
    only those on mountaintops will vibrate their being.
Upon earth, purities will be lifted up
    and those who await the moment of lifting
    have been alerted that time draweth nigh.
Man is burrowing into the ground and placing contamination
    within the ground
and man is anchoring to the seabed, contamination,
    and time erodes all negativities,
    and these also will be eroded.
And man can not withstand the hazard placed before them.
The sound of the sea is endless.
Our voice carried itself from sea to sea to sea,
    and now it is stopped by the metals within the sea..

It intones itself against the metals and the sound is silenced
    in its echo of the wave.
But the sound of earth is not stopped.
The sound of earth is caught in the great gush of tears
    that will come from the bowels of earth.
Earth, your planet is our planet,
    it is the planet of all species.
You cause Souls to die, you cause your young to be deformed.
You create entrances to earth where none should be,
    and the fish that are in the deep have cankers,
    and the flesh is soft and sterile.
Look at that which you pull from the sea
    and know it is with you for only a short while
    and the basket of the sea will be empty.
Look at the land and know that the sun will not shine,
    and create mould upon that which would be eaten.
And Souls will clamour to find food, and many will lose their young,
    and whole countries will lose a generation of young.
Bless earth, Souls.
Let not our young pass in vain.
[July 11, 2000]

522 Fetid earth, blasphemous earth, sacrilegious earth!
Behold, it is not so, earth!
As the moon enters in to a phase, earth has intent and knowledge.
Earth ascribes to no evil intent.
Earth is on the Path of humanity's enlightenment.
For this was earth created.
For this does the sun shine and the moon glow and the stars glitter.
For this alone is the galaxy within the Raiment of Creator.
Behold the downward Flow of Creator.
Behold the exodus from Creator's Love,
    the great casting out of humanity.
Before the casting out, was earth formed,
    earth and all that surrounds.
Look not to the rotation of earth to find secrets.
Look into the great vacuum about earth, the aura, the Void,
    the beginning of glitter, the beginning of transformation.

Earth has entered in to the third phase:
> the first was birth,
> the second, rebellion,
> the third is sanctity.

Who would see enlightenment within humanity?
Behold, the vision is clear, the pronouncements are clear.
All talents have been meted out
> and earth has found humanity wanting.

Upon the mountaintop, the veil will be lifted.
Upon the mountaintop, the Energy of Purity will gather.
The thread of Enlightenment will be extended downward from Creator.
It is within the Circle of Saints that Purity has been gathered
> and extended forth.

All men have spirituality,
> all men have greatness within.

But the cloak that covers their being often confounds the human
and they see only the devious Soul,
they see only the face of ineptness.
How man tolerates not man!
But a new day enters in.
The sun will close its eye to earth
> and awake after a sleep to be brought into Purity
> and Souls will be taught the new vibration,
> the extended value of their being.

The Truth will enter in
> and the knowledge will be carried to the meek and the low,

to the high that have been brought low.
Many will not survive the test of phase two.
Earth will abound in tests of raucous acceleration.
Who will withstand the wind that circles the globe?
Who will document the days of trepidation?
Behold the Holy Ones document all.
The Holy Ones vary not.
Their Path is Purity, their sanctity Creator.
Unto the Blessedness of the Angels will come six flights:
the flight of fear,
> the flight of anger,
> the flight of depression,

the flight of denunciation,
  the flight of aloneness,
  the flight of distortion.
All will see clear what they have not seen.
The mirror will no longer hold reflection
  and the Gateway will become unhinged
  because it will not be needed.
For the Angels will flow from the upper sanctity
  through to the space of earth,
and all Souls will know the attendance of the Blessed Ones,
  and the other gateway will be opened,
  the gateway of total illusion.
And the guilt will be gathered, and the pain will be gathered,
  and the enactment of evil will be gathered,
  and all Souls will taste of the wine of a new fruit.
The fruit will come from the sacred tree
  and the snake will once again form a staff,
  and a Holy man will speak from the mountaintop.
Where the tongue was not loosed, it will be loosed.
Where the Soul was not willing, the words will flow.
And earth will look up and be amazed
  when Souls of humanity rise from the earth and they will say:
"See, we have risen.
  We have movement.
Come!
  Enter in to the fold of Purity."
And Souls will release from their being, all evil intent,
  and the earth, as one, will rejoice.
And negativity will be plucked from transitional Souls
  and their being will ascend unto the Holy Holy Holy.
So be it.
[July 25, 2000]

523 Souls of earth, understanding requires language.
The earth has brought confusion unto the mouth
  because the language torments understanding.
Behold the language of Farside.
All beings understand as one, all knowledge requires no interpretation.

The language of vibration is visual to the eye of Purity.
Behold, the language is understood.
From first level Farside unto Creator, unto Godhead,
    no language barrier exists.
There is Oneness.
There is, Soul, only Oneness.
Earth has, before earth is done, a singular language.
The language will take the form of Asian.
It will be brought by Souls of China unto all lands.
It will be brought to the place of New York and the Souls of earth
    will look at the configurations of the Chinese and renew,
    through earth computer, the words which are spoken.
And children will be taught in the learning field
    the second language of earth.
And in a time, all earth together will state through agreement,
    the dropping of their first language.
All monetary monies will come as one.
All buildings that carry a flag will carry only a unified flag of earth.
It will be adopted from the Olympic flag.
All Souls will carry upon their being, a mark.
It will be designated upon the right shoulder.
It will be a place of curatives.
It will hold identity in a single mark.
All Souls will be brought under one leadership,
    the leadership will be Ural Earth.
The Souls of earth will find food difficult, for the bins will be empty
    and the Energy will lag.
Meat will no longer be eaten except in the outer territories
    and Souls will find the land where animals have grazed,
    to be brought to grains and legumes and fruits of the vine.
And man will know a curse upon the flesh.
It will come from the eating of meat.
It will come as a slight rash which is visible between the fingers
    and the toes and the groin,
    and man will see only the slight eruption,
    but the inward growth will reach and decay the body.
Souls of earth, attribute Purity to no other than thyself.
Souls of earth, speak with a voice of Truth.

Do not raise the sword to lessen a life,
    but learn to live so that all Souls may be lifted as one.
Behold, there is none better than the other.
Behold, there is no high or low.
All men pass through the same impurities,
    all men are given the same opportunity.
Behold, do not speak on bended knee
    and turn the back to do an ill to mankind.
Enter each Soul into the Purity of thy being, for thou art sacred.
The Creator of thy being gazes upon His creation
    and bestows Energy to revitalize the fallen
    and lift thy being unto His own.
Mankind, hear that which is ominous:
    the noontide has passed and the evening is falling away,
and the desolation is entering in as a knell
    that is heard in the far off hills.
And who will see the trees bend to the ground,
and who will see the waves reach to the mountaintop
and not recognize that earth has been challenged
    by goodness and negativity?
Behold, goodness is enlightenment of being.
Draw thou, men, unto an enlightenment of being.
Put not thy words of anger upon the small child.
Place not the right hand against the left hand in devotion
    and speak ill in the offing.
Souls of earth, the great knell has sounded and is in the great pyramids.
Mankind has drawn the blood of many,
    mankind has spewed forth in anger and pain.
Reach not unto another in meanness of heart,
    but reach unto thine brother to behold in him
    the goodness that is in thyself,
    and know a oneness in the coming together.
Almighty thou art to be.
Behold the seed of Purity that thou art and burst forth
    in abundant goodness, to enrich the lives of all in thy space.
Let no casualness pass thy mouth,
    but know intent for the goodness of all.

Each day of earth, each moment of earth, is timed.
Behold how man is Loved,
> that all opportunities of goodness are offered unto thee.

Creator would lift thee from the mire and raise thee
> unto the bosom of goodness.

But in the raising of thy being, thou wouldst lose the opportunity
> of saving the Blessed Ones, for which thou hast come.

Blessed is man before Creator.
[August 12, 2000]

524 All humanity gathers in the glow of eventide
> and men run to the waters
> and throw in their nets in the darkness
> and gather the little fishes.

And the sea marks its destiny upon the little fishes,
> for they are few and they are gathered in illness unto each other.

Man carries extremity into the defilement of the deep,
> and the ooze lifts itself, and what sparkled and turned
> has been infiltrated with shades of gray,
> and the depths where Souls gather to take their feed,
> find putrid carcasses infred with toxins.

The voice of the turtle issues forth a warning unto mankind.
It is done with the greatest concern for the well being of earth:
> "Do not place the great nets in the seas.

Do not place the used toxins in the sea.
Do not carry a cargo
> > that filters into the sea debris of fetid origins!"

Mankind casts its own into the sea,
> and the sea cannot bear the pain of the carrying of flesh.

Unburden earth, Souls.
Unburden the waterways.
List the ships that carry toxins
> and bring the great beings into accountability.

Earth will die, it will gasp and turn because of great pain.
Souls, we will be the last to utter the gasp.
So be it.
[August 29, 2000]

525 Michael will teach the longitude and the latitude.
Michael will teach the earth and all therein.
Behold the clay, behold the mountain,
 behold the land wherein mankind doth dwell.
All life of earth has a single purpose,
 it is to meet in the crossroads of Time.
There are no coincidences.
There are, Soul, vestiges of Energy that are united
 for the purpose of the gathering.
All earth bends to the Path at the gathering,
 all roads have a single meeting place, the crossroads.
Behold the wind.
The wind is the leaven of earth, the wind is the levener of time.
When negativity is brought to a central point
 and carries an altered state of mankind, the wind blows
 and the wind blows fierce.
And the wind desecrates that which man has built high,
 and the wind looks to its brother the sea,
 and the sea is stirred by the anger of the wind.
And all beings of the Farside are called unto the fence of earth
 to witness the leaven of earth.
Behold, it is the gift that Creator has given to earth.
It alters that which humanity errs.
It drives the forces of evil to be washed, to be brought down low,
 draws man to contemplate that whereupon he lives.
Feel, Souls of earth, the disturbance of the wind and know
 when the wind blows there has been a need
 for wind to alter that which man has done.
Place thy being upright with thy back against the wind,
 and know the wind will drive you forth,
 for no man can withstand the force of the wind.
But be thou, humanity, in the space of Purity,
 and wind will cease to destruct that which man has erected.
[November 22, 2000]

526 Bring thyself forward.
Be thou within the Circle of Saints.

Hear the agenda, the Timetable that is Farside.
At the farthest end, right from Pleiadia, allow the Lemurian to speak:
    "Holy ones, how can we alter the pain of earth?
Holy ones, how can we make an impact
    that will be grand enough
        that it will save the pain of people and animals?
    And what of the birds that fly in the sky?
    What will their fate be?
    How may we help? "
Earth Soul, know thy being and know thy thought.
Allow thy thought to have no evil within.
Place no evil word upon a human.
Hold thyself so others may behold a righteous leader of Truth.
Prepare thy being at dawn to be in the space of total goodness.
Utter no unkind word before thee.
Rather to bite thy tongue than to utter shallow words
    unto any living Soul.
When thou art in thy home, be Holy, be not cast down.
Energize thyself with meditation.
Energize thyself with the knowledge that thou art a Holy being.
Know that you will enter out of your door vibrant to Souls about you.
Know that they will speak to the power of your Energy
    and will say simply: "How well you appear!
    How have you found it so easy to be so?"
And you, Soul, will enlighten their being.
All things are done with patience.
You may take yourself to a housetop and spew of your Purity
    and all will point a finger and say:
    "What is this mad Soul who stands and spews of his Purity?"
But if you enter out of your home
    with only the countenance of goodness
    and utter no unkind word, have no unkind thought,
    give all that you may unto your fellow man,
    see a need and fulfill it, Souls will seek you out,
    will pattern their lives after you.
It will be an issuing forth of glad tidings.
The day has come to save earth.

Only in the singleness of one, will earth be saved.
And only as one meets another in the coming together of goodness
    will the world, as you know it, see enlightenment.
The Gathering Time, the course of humanity, is set.
The pain will touch many lives.
The earth cannot carry the weight of such relentless negativity.
The United States of America will be brought to a face of battle.
Souls, look to the west.
The blessed Circle of Saints would relieve all pain,
    but the purpose of your being is not to relieve your pain,
    it is to relieve the pain of the blessed ones.
What you do, you do willingly.
No man has put your Energy into the battle.
Bless man for the Energy done.
[January 24, 2001]

527 Humanity! Be still and listen to the rhetoric you speak.
Humanity, face thy beings and ask thyself:
    "Where is the Love of thy God in thee?
    How do you hold a gun, a rock, a bomb
and speak of God, of Allah, of Creator?
    The Energy from which you have come is Love!
Love that has bestowed you to the earth you are in,
Love that welcomes you back."
Souls of earth, put aside your weapons.
Make your swords into ploughshares and till the land
    to feed the starving.
Work together to the glory of your Creator.
Welcome the neighbour over the hill to come to your vineyard
    and partake of the wine.
Laden him with food and drink and clothing
    and as he departs place a blessing upon his back.
Earth, if you are blind you cannot see the colour of the skin,
    the long or the short nose, the length of hair.
Souls of earth, in a moment of your negativity,
    earth could be blinded by the great light of negativity.
What is time?
Earth time is measured in the amount of Purity man can absorb.

Earth time would cease and all glory be given
>   if man would dwell in Purity.
The quell of earth would rest and the clock would stop
>   and timeless reality would be.
Where will you take your anger next?
Who will slaughter whom?
Who will lift the vial of poison?
Has earth not rocked enough?
Must earth rock until the seas rise before man will hear?
It is time for time to stop.
It is time for all earth to see only brother and sister,
>   to see friend and fellow.
Gather you together the salvage of all iniquities and offer it up
>   to the space of Creator
>   and Creator will purify all that you have given
>   and replace the negative energy with the pure Light of Creator.
North and south and east and west,
>   the high mountains and the low valleys,
the river beds and the desert flats,
>   all will light in a flash.
And all eyes will cease to see for a period of thirty six hours
and man will fumble in the darkness of his own making
and Souls who have been deep in the ground will come forth
and say: "What has created the flatness of the land
and what is the stench that pricks our nose
and where have the people gone?"
Souls of earth, humanity, Farside impels the Souls of earth
>   to redirect their force of Energy.
We gaze longingly at the army of earth.
It is time for the battle to cease.
It is time for the wars to end.
The scars are deep and visible and now, humanity,
>   you have learned much.
All that you despise, all that has pained your being,
>   all great beards, heed the lesson.
Know the time to set the clock to stop is now.
Do not enter in one nation to his brother and ask for peace.
Ask for peace within your very nation.

Turn your eyes to thyself.
Speak to thy fellow countrymen and uphold all that is good.
Cease to find fault with thy neighbour
    and seek to find goodness in thy being.
Offer to any who ask that which you can spare.
Souls of earth, know in your being it is Love that you are.
Know in your being it is your Creator's Love that you are.
Purity and Truth, it is the purpose of your existence.
Holy ones, the stench will be great.
The vileness will bring down all that you Love.
How much do you hate your neighbour?
Enough to slaughter your fellow man?
Love thy neighbour as thyself.
[February 14, 2001]

528 Who has entered in to the space of the Most High?
Who has entered in to the Platform of Deity?
Who will take the long staff and be first to place it in the new land?
Oh beulah land, my beulah land, know the glory of the rising sun.
Know the setting at eventide.
Know the coming and the going of the ocean's wave.
Know the transitory path of migrant birds
    and nothing has a shadow of beauty
    for that which humanity will see.
Souls of earth, the prophets have spoken often.
They enter in to the fifth, fourth, third, second, first levels
    and they teach degrees of understanding
    of that which is ahead for all creation.
Negativity has been eliminated.
Oh, there will be no negativity
    but there will be gallant efforts to reach
    into the spheres of Second Gateway.
Souls who have had no negativity, no evil intent,
    await at the door of Gateway.
These Souls will be lifted by the Angels
and brought forward, for they have wounds.
They have brought themselves to Farside but they carry the scars
    given by humanity's existence of evil.

The Souls are a legion unto their own.
They have not been found as truly human.
They gather in great numbers to allow negativity to be placed upon them.
Why?
Soul, there are chosen numbers of Souls who are humanity.
They have the intent of the Blessed Ones.
There are also legions of beings[82] who have entered in, not as human,
    but as Souls prepared to assist the understanding of humanity.
They will leave earth in a moment as one.
They will enter in great groups as one.
The Souls will profoundly touch all within their space
    and then they will leave as gently as they have come.
Know these Souls are tender babies or old men.
They are caught without the power of the eye,
    for they are the invisible to earth.
Earth chooses not to see them.
Earth chooses to pretend they are not there.
They have Souls, they have feelings, but they are Farside.
These Souls abound in Sri Lanka,
    these Souls abound in China, in India.
These Souls place a direct curtain over themselves.
They become your mother, your father, your brother, your sister.
They come to speed the movement of earth, which is slow.
Expect to be moved by such Souls.
[February 21, 2001]

529 Souls of earth, your world government is.
Souls of earth, beneath the counterpanes much deceit is done.
From one bedroom to another does earth broadcast its intent.
Earth is not as sophisticated as the Farside.
There are those on earth who appear to know sophistication,
    but they know little.
In diverse places upon earth is the pattern laid out,
    only have the pieces to be placed
    into one control of all health, control of all technology,
    control of all transportation, control of all auditory systems,
    control of all benefits through work.

---

82 legions of beings - beings of Farside resident upon earth

None will escape, except those who place themselves
within the stench of the lands,
within the encasements of vileness upon earth.
Within those spaces will purities hide
    to rebuke what man has placed upon man.
What will seem to be the gentle beckoning, will become the firm grip.
What will seem to be the taste of sugar,
    will become the acrid taste of control.
All earth will come under the dome,
    and that house of dome that is sacred
will join hands with many less sacred,
and a pact will be done to control the lives of men.
But from the refining of humanity will come triumphant Souls
    who have heard that which was spoken.
And the words will be held up for all to see,
    and even those who have control will release control
    in order to see the pattern form.
For seven Souls will come forward and show the economics of Purity,
    and the understanding will come unto man
        that only in the economics of Purity will man survive catastrophe.
Only in seeing brother as brother, neighbour as brother,
    will earth envision a second millennium completed.
And in that time the skies will open
    and men's eyes that were blind will have sight
    and behold the Entering In
    of Purity Four unto the place of earth.
And the stone will once again be removed from the place of burial
    and humanity will say:
    "Come forth! See that which we are.
Be not amazed at the form we have,
at the deep crevices that are scars in our being.
Rise up unto thy brethren. Walk and be healed."
[February 28, 2001]

530 Earth is not still.
We see and we feel that which is earth,
    and it rumbles in a chaotic way.
And the surface of earth carries little to sustain

that which is upon it, and many will falter.
Hold thyself from flesh.
Hold thyself from the impurities of toxins.
For it is not that all was not placed upon the earth for mankind,
    it is that the negativity of mankind has distorted
    that which Creator has placed,
and your being will absorb the negativity
and it will erode the flesh of your being.
We speak clear that you may understand the foulness,
where the teeth will rot from your mouth, where jowls will sag,
where the flesh will not hold the nails of your hands,
where sores will erode upon the body.
Until man accepts that Negativity must not be placed
upon the creation that he has charge over,
    until man accepts himself accountable
    for the seas, and the earth, and the air,
until man recognizes the purpose of his being,
    will his body continue to decay.
[March 14, 2001]

531 Our Energy is many Quar beyond your own.
We have vision of your star.
You have not vision of where we are.
The cylindrical force of your orb is faulty, it must be addressed.
There is, Souls of science, a need to restrain
    the drain upon your earth atmosphere.
It is weakening the stability of your environment.
Your earth is not unlike our own.
We have in our space a constant sun.
It will not wither as will your own,
    for it will carry itself into the second flight.
There is an insignia obvious to all who approach our being.
We are marked in a manner that addresses the constancy of your planet.
We have no extensions, we have no need.
We have total flight of being.
We are brought forward by momentum of Purity
    and our capacity to invigilate.
All tests of earth are known within the level of Purity.

We are drawn to your Purity.
We have a need to let earth know of the moment of desolation.
It is not our purpose to gather unto you pain.
It is our purpose to draw Souls of earth to a waking point,
    that they may see clearly the foreboding
    scratched deep into their form.
Souls of earth, our beings are drawn to the day of earth's travail.
There is a ground swell of liquefaction
    within the central points of USA.
It is submerged to the portion of three states:
    Arizona, Colorado, New Mexico.
The cost of life is unthinkable with the exception of a great mountain
    that will lift itself high and gather many.
As you have said, Souls of earth,
    how many times have the rattles been shaken?
How many times have the old ones chanted?
How many times have great Souls withered to extinction?
And yet man will not lift his eyes
    and know concern enough to alter the hole.
There will be three.
Earth will not contend with three.
Souls, see before you the ground swell that will bring down
    so much of humanity.
USA is not alone.
All earth will be fractured.
Beloved humanity, we do not have before us a crystal ball.
We have before us your replica, your sister world.
We know of the fragileness of your being.
Souls of earth, we extend our Energy to overcome the desolation.
[May 15, 2001]

532 We come of a distant world unto your station.
We have been in the space of earth many times.
Our being has entered in to the deepest crevices of earth.
We have found the apertures that will disintegrate the earth.
We have brought the knowledge unto research

and Souls are preparing to accommodate earth researchers
  in finding the ability to enter deeper into the craters of the sea.
There is a need to visualize the great depths,
  for mankind has endless food, nourishment, within these places.
There is a need to know the power abundantly there for mankind.
The source of the technology is simple.
There is a great discrepancy within earth over matters of Energy.
Earth has power in the lava flow.
Earth has power in the sea.
Earth will reach the knowledge of the deep
and the Soul will be brought into the lesion of pain
and be healed by simply using the water around the lava flow.
It contains the power to abundantly heal.
Souls of earth, we have seen, we have witnessed the waste products.
We have seen and witnessed the attempts to salvage.
There is a great need to clear the desert, for within the desert is a healing,
  and a flower that will grow that is medicinal unto man.
It is sedum.
Souls of earth, all pains, all physical abnormalities
  will be healed in the desert.
Sedum has the power of cancer healing, of breath healing,
  of lung healing, of prostate healing.
The bud of the first flower is to be collected prior to bloom.
Souls of earth, all research is done at Farside and a reflection is given.
It is a scientist with doctorate in botany
  that will proceed to bring earth its cure.
Earth does not require this pure healing power,
  for they have within their being a pure healing power.
It is called acceptance.
Treasure acceptance first.
[June 12, 2001]

533 Air!
Cities are caught without air
  and breath comes in short intervals.
Europe, Scandinavia, Great Britain, Honolulu,

in a swirl to San Francisco, Los Angeles,
      downward to Miami, Cuba, Bolivia,
         great cold enters the land.
The Souls will use a wash of glycerine
      to release from their skin the withered flesh.
The back will be caught and centred down,
      and people will walk as old men and old women.
There will be no place to cast a net,
      for the seas will be still for many days,
      and microscopic insects will lace the shores of many lands,
      and salt will not deter their advance.
The broad boot of Russia will meet the gun of China,
      and India will send a light that carries destruction aloft.
The fire in Canada will reach into the Territories,
      and no water will be had, nor Souls who could lift.
The time is in your summer of the new day and
      you have twelve years to alter the decay upon earth.
[June 19, 2001]

534 Soul, we acknowledge earth.
We acknowledge the tremors of pain through the agonies of earth.
We have known the stench and the spew.
We have entered in to the bowels of your earth.
We are Jinn.
We have the keeping of your earth,
      to transmit unto Souls that which we know.
We know your existence depends on the harbouring of food.
As the ancient Egyptians had seven lean years,
      so earth has a need to draw from plenty and store.
Souls of earth have a need to gather food in small places of growth,
      not to rely on abundance, for abundance will cease,
      but to gather seed to store for the lean years.
Know hydroponics is necessary.
Know it must be in a clean air atmosphere.
Know, Soul, it will be in Montana.
Hear this.
The collection of greenhouses in empty land,

    the use of Souls with defect of humanity
        to apply themselves as work is negative and must be forbidden.
The Souls will be annihilated.
Speak against the greenhouse!
Draw all movements to a cease, for earth may not abide this atrocity.
The intent is done in a government office.
Soul, we ask all citizens of the Americas to eye Montana
    for lethal injection.
[July 17, 2001]

535 The time of the end is entering in.
The dawn has released itself, the noonday has vanished.
The Souls of earth may only stand and vision the nightfall.
The climatic changes of earth will lessen the fodder,
    and animals will be put down because of lack of fodder.
The Souls of earth will not replenish the granaries.
They will be empty and rats will seek to fight with humanity
    for what is left.
And Souls will feel the sting of gritty air
    as the dry winds rip the soils of earth into a frenzy.
We have gathered our numbers together.
We have prepared the ships that will come.
And, Souls, the issue of breath is still an issue.
We have a need for you to know
    the times of impurities have elapsed
    and the sound of the knell is advancing.
The grimace of the reaper is before you
    and the beacon of Light needs to shine.
Will you allow it to shine that it might be visible
    at the entering in of purities?
Souls of earth, you are as the dragon, spewing fire
    and you do not contain it to an area.
You draw it into diverse places
    and you subject the truth to negativity.
Bring the ministers to position themselves at Sinai
    and their God will speak unto them.
[July 24, 2001]

536 Soul, we are Angel.
We are not Archangel, we are Angel.
We have a great need to give to earth.
We ask that all beings who will hear
    will use the power that they have to free Russia.
There is a need to alter the course of the locust.
We ask that the Souls send all Energy of healing unto Russia.
We ask that you remove all negativity in the giving,
    that you recognize only humanity,
    that you hold no foreign thought about the country.
All earth is one earth, all land is one land, all peoples are one people.
In the seven places of growth will be seven plagues to come.
Man can eradicate all negative energy.
We ask that you open your being unto the humanity
    that resides within that land.
There is a scourge that will mark the soil
    and the tears of the young will fall.
And at the weakest moment, China will invade.
[July 24, 2001]

537 Acceptance, Soul, acceptance of all that enters
    within the space of thy being
    not to alter the path of any being, creature or human,
    but to extend great energies.
Will you do this, Soul?
We would ask that acceptance be a part of your life.
Accept that you have the power to alter much in your life.
You have the power to alter negativities outward from your Energy.
Great issues can be altered with small expressions of healing.
Great bombs can be altered with the implanting of Purity.
Souls, the limbs of your earth form are puny
    compared to the energies of our being.
We have vastness in whom we are.
Our countenance has gathered acceptance.
We are of the Holy Circle of Saints
    and we have gathered all purities unto us,
    and we walk in the paths of earth,
    and we see the flames of pain, the darts of ego.

And we see Souls with the Purity to alter those flames, those darts,
>   and our being speaks to you to alter the course of pain.
Reach outward from thy being, hold the great blessings of all beings
>   unto thee and shower earth with particles of Purity,
>   for you have gathered Purity unto your being.
You may access the preciousness of your being,
>   you may fill the cup to overflowing
>   with the preciousness of your being
>   and you may anoint all beings with your Purity.
You may anoint all negative energies with your being.
Profoundness of Energy, do not remain silent.
Do not ponder on the pain, alleviate the pain.
Rejoice in thy being that you have altered the course of negativity.
We have witnessed the vision of your Etna.
We have seen the baby Souls seek to capture pictures
>   and not recognize that within their vision lies great pain.
Earth is rending its inners because of pain.
Who would stand and place a healing upon the great volcano
>   that vents the pain that earth is feeling?
Within earth, creatures alien to your beings,
>   see the distraught energies they witness through apertures.
The magnum courses and flows.
How generous are these creatures?
You would gasp!
You would repel your being at the sight of these creatures,
>   and yet they seek only earth's wellness.
Into the swell of the ocean is a message.
It is spewed forth and enters the sea,
>   and all life feels the momentum of pain.
No Soul upon earth will live without feeling the vibration of pain
>   from the deep crevice.
It will alter food sources, it will alter weather, it will alter air,
>   it will after bring great storms.
And we would have you, in your Purity, abate that which would be.
To do this you must release from your being, negativity.
You must acknowledge your Purity.
It is not a facetious endeavour, it is not a careless calling.
It is a coming forth of Purity to alter that which is negative.

And as you move forward, know that you are armed with Truth
    and in the reach of great Purity.
Holy beings, earth would have you heal.
Earth cries for man to heal, to rectify that which is pained.
The garden has not been lost,
    the garden has merely been trampled upon and dug into,
    and great negativities have been buried beneath the garden,
    and all that has grown is altered.
We would have you not be idle.
We would have you move in a growing circle of Purity.
Where can my children walk and not feel the desolation of pain?
Where is the eden which earth was?
Why are there mutants when earth had a shining example?
You have a sister earth.
It has your likeness.
It glistens, it vibrates, it acknowledges the pain that you have.
You have been the reflection of the sister Energy,
    and now the Energy has distortion
    as though the mirror had been tilted.
How splendid is that which Creator has given unto thee.
How adorned is that which Creator has given unto thee!
Release from your being, negativity,
    that you may heal the negativity of self, of earth.
So be it.
[July 31, 2001]

538 We have been in the deepest waters
    and our pods have come to your surface and we speak to man.
"We are your brothers.
We will say we are equal unto thy being.
Some would say we are higher than thy being.
And you rampage our being,
    you torment the young who have not the ability to respect.
You enter in to our nursery and you stir our young to high anxiety.
Their beings are already trammelled
    from the toxins you have delivered unto us.
Our being is elevated for the purpose of only mankind.

We beseech you, mankind,
> to hold our nursery as dearly as you hold yours,
> to gather the ships that scar our being
> and place detentions for them;
> for the vision of clarity is taking a negative turn
> and the great spew of negativity ushers forth
> into the corpse of the world.

We ask that you speak for the wellness of my brothers,
> that you recognize a kinship to the Souls that we are.

In our higher knowledge, we are as you and more.
We have been in the Flow of the Energy that formed your being.
We have witnessed the gathering army and seen the entering in,
> and the second entering out.

Guard our children from negativity.
Go to the council of nations,
> for it is in the council of nations that we will be protected;
> it is when we are acknowledged as not belonging
> to a single country, but that the world is dependant
> on our species for their existence.

Speak to the turtle and acknowledge the turtle,
> and see the kinship you have to all beings.

Teach the child to Love.
Place your Energy within the space of Oslo.
It is a group of men who have great power to alter."
[August 7, 2001]

539 Soul of earth, progress to Purity
> and you become the mountaintop.

Enter in to the dwelling place of the mountaintop.
There are vortexes of mountaintop.
There are gatherings of humanity that have acquired unto them
> all the growth of humanity's needs.

These Souls are visionaries, teachers,
> they are the core of the gathering.

They are altering that which your humanity is.
To be in the quiet solitude of your own mind without thought,
> is to bring yourself into the space of the centre eye.

Souls of the mountaintop may flow into the centre eye.
They have a knowledge of Purity that is beyond
    that which earth sees as Purity.
They have within their being the sounding board of the tests of time.
And time and time again
    they have soared to the heights of their being
    and they have been brought low.
Earth humanity will be in accord with Purity,
but there are Souls who will reach the mountaintop
and gather unto them the teachings, the maps of humanity.
The mountaintop is gathering form.
The urgency to gather is taking momentum.
Have no fear, for all that is, all that has transpired,
    has ultimate purpose in Purity.
Reach to the heights of that Purity,
    for the intensity of vibration will cause thy beings to ask:
    "Can we stand? Will we take ourselves from off the earth?"
Souls, each according to his Purity is being transformed.
And the mountaintop will become crowded, and the sound will travel,
    and beings will have no cause to use their feet except to stand.
They will draw unto themselves forms.
Their digits will reach out and polarize and heal by drawing inward.
Souls will mouth perfection and it will be.
Small babes will be brought to the high mountain for healing,
and old men will stagger upward,
and the mountaintop will send outward a beacon Light
that speaks to mankind of creation.
[August 28, 2001]

540 The ashes come down,
    and on the platform of ash will rise, once again, the citadels.
And the feather will be brought to the house that is white,
    and the oracle will speak of yet another prophecy.
And the wind will take the prophecy unto my people.
And they will know that all the songs that have been sung,
    all the dances that have been carried
    through the feet of my people,
    have a purpose.

For in the land of the eagle will raise up a dedication of Purity,
    and Souls will be invigorated to cast a genuine reluctance
    towards negativity.
My people, we are all my people!
The methodology of the text is a statute.
It is within the four corners of earth.
It has a piercing place and will be brought into a place of peace,
    and the fathers will recognize the tablets
    that will be exhumed from the earth.
And the tablets will say word for word that which has been given.
Souls of earth, look to the western sky and see blood come forth.
Look to the north and hear the rumble that is not the caribou come.
Hide deep within your being the Truth and draw it forth
    that all may see your being walking on the land.
And we would ask that the land be purified by Souls.
Ask my people to drum for the land,
    ask my people to assist in the raising up of the Pillars of Light.
[September 11, 2001]

541 Our platform to the Gateway has received intent.
We have been informed through many worlds that earth
    has no longer a free state.
Our platform to you is one of genuine giving.
The agenda that we have at the Gateway is to magnify the portal
    through which earth might enter.
It is to make visible unto all mankind, the Quar which they will seek.
There will be a need to see, visibly, the aperture.
Souls will be lifted unto vibration of their own accord.
But without the ability to visualize the aperture,
    they may not enter.
Their earth beings must be transformed.
Soul, there is a need for earth to know that the relinquishing
    in that moment of acceleration of all negativities is necessary.
The smallest child will have no trouble
    with the relinquishing of negativities,
    but those of the age of accountability will see the humanness.
And we ask they relinquish their humanity
    and recognize the Soul of their being.

Earth has yet to roll, and the rock has just gently begun.
Souls of earth, that which you do, do quickly.
[September 25, 2001]

542 "In my Father's House are many mansions.
    If it were not so, I would not have said it unto thee."
All that are ill and overburdened,
all that are hungry and without food,
all that are cast down for my sake,
    rise and know you are healed.
And know you will be brought by your Truth
    into the sanctuaries of Purity.
Know that you will be led by the shepherd into the place of Holiness.
Know that all purities of all lives will be lifted
    and no Soul will be left.
Krishna, Mohammed, Buddha and Jesu are One
    in our Love for humanity.
We are One in our path to Creator.
We are One in our intent to release earth from pain.
We came unto earth to bring awareness to the children of Creator.
We came unto thee as a brother, no more, no less than thee.
And we have outreach in our living Energy
    that will manifest itself unto all earth.
All eyes will witness that which we are and will know in that day
    that the time of bringing forth has come.
All earth will have become serene
    and the waters will have become calm.
And those who have lived will be succoured,
    and the nourishment of the Spirit
    will take the place of the nourishment of the body,
and their beings will acknowledge the Blessed,
and they will be transfigured in a twinkling.
The time between your time and then may be released.
The time of chaotic endeavours is upon earth,
    and as earth may alter the shift.
We would have you know that the Angels,
    the goodnesses of Farside are reaching unto you

that you might abide in Purity and Love, one to the other,
   that you will say unto all Souls only soft words,
   that you will hold only Love in your heart for your fellow men.
This we give unto you: "Love thy brother as thyself."
[October 2, 2001]

Purity

CHAPTER 5

Hallelujah

EARTH REDEMPTION

543 Souls of earth, come to the bridge.
Draw thy being to the bridge, the continuous transom to Eternity.
Delight thy being in the rainbow of colours
    that is visible to the naked eye.
Reach from thy earthly form and know within thy being
    is the doorway to Farside joys.
How transient is thy life, humanity?
It is but a moment, it is but growth, it is but the twinkling of an eye!
Souls, the bridge is acceptance,
    the bridge is understanding,
    the bridge is Purity,
    the bridge transforms your vision.
It enhances all your being.
All knowledge is transformed into energies
    outward from thy being.
All inward looking is finished when thou art on the bridge to Eternity.
The Light is radiant on the other side.
The Light is Love and draws thy being to it.
Earth humanity, earth humanity, see not only thy own being!
See all creation, for all creation is available unto you.
Do not limit your vision to your singleness.
Creation is gathered about you as the blessed wings of Angels
    gather themselves about your being.
Behold, the minutest of beings will be visible to thee.
On the Farside, the eye beholds all things and all things become sacred.
How the bud opens into Purity is how we see humanity,
    how the endless lives of growth enter in

    to the Flow of all creation,
    and the rainbow issues forth Light
    and becomes the bridge over which Purity is.
Who will place their foot upon the bridge?
Who would place their foot upon the bridge and look back?
Souls, it is the forward look that is growth.
It is the offering of thy being to humanity.
It is the letting go of all that is worldly and hold it up
    as an offering unto Creator for the use of goodness.
Behold, thy being is precious beyond the cost of anything rare,
    beyond any potential of Purity, for humanity,
    glorious humanity, thou art defeating negativity.
Earth beings, many worlds there are, countless worlds there are,
    worlds upon worlds there are,
    and yet there is one earth
    that all other worlds cast their eyes unto.
For it is the avenue to redemption, redemption of all Souls lost.
Creator offers Love.
Angels offer tears to wash away pain.
Guides offer nudge and Souls offer their Purity;
    and all to conquer negativity.
Beloved Souls of earth, how thou art blessed!
For unto thee has been the key given to redeem all Souls lost.
Who can bear the pain?
Who can enter in to the agony?
Who can witness the desolation?
The Souls of earth who, in their many lives,
    have known all these negativities,
    who have borne upon their being
    all the avenues of pain man can endure.
And man has tried and tested self to ready self
    for the purpose of redemption,
    the entering in to the eternal pain of Souls lost.
Only Souls of earth can alter what is Eternal.
How great thou art that living humanity can enter in
    to the chasm of great darkness
    and draw Souls in agony upward into the reach of Angels.
And Angels shall await, as at a sepulchre, to gather the Souls

and all earth will rejoice and say:
"For this has our being been brought to earth!"
Radiant Energy, Creator of our being,
    bless thou earth Souls unto Thee.

544 How to behold radiancy?
Souls of earth, thy beings are Energy,
    thy beings are lifted in Truth.
Thy beings are enwrapped in the fold of Purity,
    and the Love of Purity flows unto thy Creator,
        and, Soul, you radiate!
You become Holy!
You become Truth, Purity and Love!
And behold, the mouth is closed from the evil word.
No foulness is uttered, for are you not pure in your being!
How do you lift the tender child and hold the blessed ones?
Souls, your Soul is as this tender child.
It radiates, does it not?
Do you not see the Purity of the tender child?
Does your heart not flow outward to its being?
Souls of earth, how pure is thy Soul!
But reach unto the Essence of thy being,
    reach unto the core of thy being,
        for the heart is not the core.
It is the Essence, the Purity that is in the Flow to Creator.
All threads flow unto thy earthly being
    and all energies are one with Creator.
The mesh of goodness is great in the eyes of Farside,
    and Farside rejoices in the overcoming of negative threads.
For in the overcoming of negative threads
    is not the redemption of all time present!
It is now in Farside.
It is now!
We know, for we have all vision.
But it is in the frontiers of negativity that your realities are.
It is in the place of the machinations of mankind
    that cause Souls to tremble.
Souls, enter thou in to the ecstasy of thy being.

Rest.
No evil contends thee where all beings enter in
    to the fold of Love and entwine in the goodness of Creator.
Oneness is recognized, and who can withstand
    the beauty of the lotus blossom opening before the sun?
Who can see the radiance and not find their heart brought to Love?
Souls of earth, each child, each man, each woman,
    each elderly one, is such a gem in the Eye of Creator.
In the eye of Farside, all have the Purity of the lotus.
Have you seen the eye of the tiger?
Have you guarded thy being from the eye of the tiger
    that sees all and enters in with no fear?
Soul, the tiger is not wild.
Its eye does not behold evil.
Behold, it too has a Purity of goodness.
Value all in your being.
Hold the turtle, for the turtle is sacred
    and the being represents earth.
Behold the Gateway.
Earth, behold the Gateway that enters in to the Flow of all Purity.
Why, Souls, do you not run to the Gateway?
Why do you tarry in pain and ignorance?
We reach to earth and plead earth to Love.
There is but one master of our being.
It is the pure Essence of your own,
    for your goodness rises to that Essence.
When your day is done on earth, rejoice,
    for the bud comes forth
    and always anew is the chance for earth.
Behold the radiance of thy being!

545 Out of the Energy field of earth, thy being becomes as a feather
    that may be lifted and drawn lightly unto diverse places.
The Soul once again becomes its Spirit
    and the Spirit welcomes that part of its Energy home.
The being works unto the end of humanity;
    it is the purpose of all earth Souls.
And the Spirit has sent forth the victorious Soul.

Earth cannot see that which will be,
> but Farside opens a vision that earth has not witnessed.

Behold the Angels.
Because of the level of Purity they are in,
> they have witnessed the coming forth of the Blessed.

The comprehension of what we say is yet for your intellect to find.
But, Soul, understand that the earth is networked
> into a filigree of complicated energies.

There will be no failure, no system ended.
All energies will come to fruition,
> all energies will retain the Purity of being they once have held,
> and do, and can.

There is total motion in each effort of humanity.
The motion is onward and forward.
It is as a great swirl, caught in the pale of negativity
> which is round about all the energies of the forward movement,
> and the mark of humanity draws stench.

The mark of humanity draws deceit,
> but the overcoming of that mark of deceit
> is awake with violets, lights of healing,
> and the Flow unto Creator is as a burst from a cannon,
> is as a burst of great power.

Man has used the cannon in great negativity.
Soul, your beings will become alight with joy
> when you see the use of earth relics,
> for, indeed, they are relics to our being.

We play, Soul.
Are you aware that the Farside plays?
We enjoy, we embrace celebration, we dance.
Souls of earth, you will dance with the Angels,
> for the very Angels dance in movements.

Souls, glory unto glory unto glory!
Earth perceives in all things, negativity.
Farside witnesses no negativity.
The crown is placed upon the form, the Diadem, Tiara of Purity
> and the Souls rejoice and they move forward.

The Soul rejoices at the coming in to a greater Purity
> and Souls enriched in goodness, celebrate the coming forth.

Hallelujah

Earth has not learned to celebrate upon earth.
Earth has the memory of celebration within the Soul.
Rejoice in that which you do.
Rejoice in the gallant efforts of your being.
Do not hold your form tightly.
Know that earth is Flow, and movement, and gracious attainment,
    and all energies flow,
    and all energies are made fluid with goodness.
Souls of earth, open thy hand.
Leave nothing hidden in thy hand,
    for when the hand hides so does the heart hide,
    and when the heart hides the Soul cannot ignite into its glory.
Draw thy being unto the face of all that is good.
Refuse, Souls of earth, to speak negativity.
Refuse, Souls of earth, to enter in to negativity,
    but glory in thy goodness.
We, of the Farside, have many facets to our being.
We are not one, as your being on earth is one,
    but we are united as earth Souls could never be united.
We are united in all our energies,
    and the triumph of a single Soul is resounded.
Throughout the Farside the message is carried forth.
It is as though you open the words and you read of a Soul
    who has accomplished, and your Soul responds.
So do we respond when your Soul accomplishes.
So does all Farside respond,
    the Angels respond,
    and Creator smiles unto humanity's effort.
Dance! Dance the invitation of goodness.

546 Blessed Souls, enter thou in to peace.
Come into the place of Purity.
It is the urge of all Farside beings unto thee
    to place before thy being the opportunity that is ever yours,
    to extol unto thee the prime example of all goodness.
Souls, see a ray of Light,
    see a reflection upon the pain and know
    that all negativity will leave.

Souls of earth, we have the perfection of your being in our space.
Your Spirit resides in our space, the perfection of whom you are.
Many worlds contain perfections,
>   all are brought together in great Purity.
Souls of earth, there are no cadavers, there are no endless fires,
>   there is only Purity, great, unspeakable Purity.
Who has found the words to bestow unto Creator?
Who has found the answer to the space of Godhead?
Souls of earth, we know from the space we are in
>   that Creator is a part of thy being.
We know from the space we are in that Creator is the essence of Love.
We know from the place that we are, that the Energy flows outward
>   from the space of Creator in such velocity
>   as to travel unto earth instantly.
And, Souls of earth, you who are as Creator,
>   may extend your Energy outward also unto Creator.
It is the Flow.
It is the given Flow that sends as it receives, that gives yet again,
>   that never tires of the giving.
It is a gift unspeakable because it requires no words.
It is solely perfection that you send outward from your being,
>   the perfection of who you are,
>   that is felt by all Souls round about you.
It is the vibration of your very being that holds Purity,
>   that draws others into your space, not for words,
>   but be in the space of Love, of giving, of Purity.
Earth Souls, we have spent many lives upon your earth,
>   we have lived in many earth zones,
and our being has been travailed with pain and anguish,
with Love and hate, with despising and greed.
Soul, we know the blend of all humanity,
>   but we are here, not in your space,
>   and we know your space to be only the perfection of imperfection.
We know that perfection is where we are.
Souls of earth, do not deem to understand all complexities,
>   for science would confuse the most learned of men,
>   but search into the simplicity of your world.
Search, Soul!

Science man, search into the place of Naught, Zero,
    and find the answer to all that you will be.
Understand the temerity of the Farside in instructing you to do thus,
    for, Soul, we do not anguish at your pain,
    we glory in the overcoming of your pain.
We know it has been choice and we know the shroud will be lifted,
    and it will be because of the blessed battle you are in.

547 Soul, beulah comes from beatitude, completion of all beatitudes,
    the total beulah, the total finish.
Earth places contradictory explanations to suit the egos of religion.
Enter in to beulah land:
    Creator's Being, beads of Purity,
gems that drop sacredly upon humanity,
    tears that fall endlessly for the brethren,
    for the Souls lost in the deepest chasms of pain.
Blessed Creator, who hast seen fit
    to still Eternity in a fragment of its being,
    that all might be accomplished to bring the brethren home.
Our eyes are your eyes,
    use the vision that we have and see into the source of Love
    that issues itself outward unto all creation.
You have not been within the passage we have been.
Soul, we have entered in the Gateway.
We have come outward through the Gateway
    and we hold the vicissitude of all knowledge.
We have been outward from that Purity
to await the coming forth of our Brethren
and we rejoice that the time is becoming irrelevant
and will soon cease to be.
And we station ourselves at the gates
    and we have been given the power to draw forth the opening,
    and behold is beulah land, behold is utopia,
    behold is a radiance that envelops and alters,
    and sheds and equalizes all creation.
For in the negativity has been instability,
    in the Negativity has been an unravel of rights,
    and time ceasing will alter the stability of all creation

outward from the Second Gateway,
and Godhead has counted this for us.
We have the knowledge of this occurrence.
We have the time of this occurrence in your time,
and we have the knowledge that earth has accepted
to be benefactor to the saving of the Blessed.
But in the saving of the blessed
is once more the releasing of Negativity.
All earths, all worlds, will implode quickly,
that Negativity may not pronounce judgement
once again upon these worlds beyond beyond.
You could not behold our total Purity and yet we uphold thy being,
we raise thy being unto Creator and bless thy being,
for you, humanity, have entered in
where only Angels have dared to tread.
You have been in the den of iniquity for our namesakes.
You have been in the jaws of negativity for our namesakes.
And we beseech Creator to add blessings upon blessings
upon the servants that are His.
We ask Creator to allow Love to be available
even in the darkest night of your travail.
For, Souls, in the darkest night of our travail,
did you not come forth and offer a mighty army?
Bless earth!
All High Beings bless earth.

548 Blessed, very blessed, do not be discouraged,
do not be brought down.
Soul, we have come to your being to lift you up
that you might see that which you bring.
Man cannot be as man is.
There will be no existence worth living.
The cry has been uttered: *"Earth has done well."*
Humanity, you have overcome much and now is the time
to move backward from that which you have done
and survey earth, and recognize the power
within earth and earth beings.
We raised cheers unto earth humanity.

We celebrate the goodness of humanity.
Even in the deepest despotic pain, we know you have done well.
And we know as earth has felt the tremor of its being,
    we would have you know that Farside
        has also felt the tremor of its being.
We know also that all is as it should be,
    but we know the time for Entering In will soon come.
For this we have been told.
It will come at a time that is written.
It will come at a time that you know not.
It will come and all earth will enter forth first.
Prepare ye the way and know
    that the entry in to the land of perfection is to be soon.
Earth has a heart.
We would tell you that earth has a heart.
It beats in a timeless beat, it Loves with a timeless Love.
And the Soul of earth is separating itself from the negativity
    and in the separation there is a great sound that will come.
It will be as a great crack sounded through earth.
It will be as your sonic boom was,
    and earth will know the hour is nigh.
Look, earth, look at the stars in your sky and know, earth,
    that as countless as the stars in the sky are, so are we.
And we Love your being, and we treasure your being.
We are as the bridegroom standing, awaiting
    for the bride to come forth,
    knowing that the great meld will be.
Know the profoundness of these words
    and know that to be downtrodden is wasted Energy.
Soul, raise your voice in joy that you have become the messengers
    of the greatest time of earth.

549 Souls, you have been blest.
We, in the state of such holiness, are always blest.
Earth is awakening, the dawn of enlightenment is entering in,
    the courage of the new voice is strengthening
        and Creator has Become.
You may hold in your hand the most precious of blooms.

You may hold in your hand the most infinite of life
    and be amazed at the complications of that which you see.
And your eye will tear at the beauty you behold,
    and your heart will squeeze itself with the knowledge
    that you are a part of that Purity.
Souls, you are as we.
You are couched in Love.
You are in the vortex of renewal.
Earth is in the vortex of renewal.
Earth is emanating goodness outward.
Earth has a new day, and all Souls will walk in the Truth
    of that new day.
The lesson of the new day will be to place all hands down,
    except to raise up and help.
The lesson of the new day will be to invoke all spirituality.
The lesson of the new day will be to absorb Purity and linger in Truth.
Do not seek to find thy name.
Thy name is Purity.

550 Love is the message we offer,
    Love is the benediction we give.
Creator IS.
So shall it be.
Earth has been visited and the miracles have come and gone,
    and Purity has walked among men in many forms
    and you have not recognized the presence of Love.
Earth, acknowledge the presence of Love!
Love has walked among men,
Love has met with men and prayed with men.
Four Purities of Love have entered in
    and man has been unwilling to place the cowl over his being.
Souls of earth, Love is a dove lifting itself unto holiness,
    Love is a wave that holds the being transformed,
    Love awakes and alters, Love gives of self.
Love is the teacher, Love is the fullness of humanity and Farside,
    Love is an offering and has no cost.
Love is given without deliberation, freely, unceasingly.
All earth, absorb this Love, acknowledge this Love.

Be brought to the space of acceptance.
The step is to grasp the Purity you are.

EARTH GATHERING

551 Holy Holy Holy Brethren who have entered out
    from the home of Creator,
who have entered out to gather the mischief maker
and call unto: *"Brother, come!"*
And the mischief maker, Negativity, regaled in refusal,
    delighted in denial.
And Creator sent forth Love armed with Purity,
    for all energies are one Energy, and all is important, one unto one:
"You may adapt, but you will never be whole."
Godhead extended an edict and the Son obeyed that which was spoken,
    and the vibration received.
Creator spoke unto Truth and said:
    "Go forth and redeem that which has left thy being."
And still the Wilful Child refused.
Our Brethren had gathered much
    and placed within the blessed River of Truth
much they had gathered of the Wilful Child.
But the Wilful Child would still not hear.
And now have you come, honourable humanity,
    to become the glory of all worlds.
And Truth you have been armed with from Creator,
    the power to discern, the power to overcome,
    and, beings of earth, we see clearly now
    the difference between Light and dark.
We see a vibration happening that never was before,
    we see an Energy rising in great power unto our being.
And it is you, hallowed beings,
    having entered in to the Void, unto negativity,
    that has sent unto us the knowledge
    that our Brethren will come forth.
Holy Holy Holy, you have given unto us
    that which is Holy Holy Holy, Brethren of our being,
    and we await, as all Farside awaits the Gathering Time of earth.

552 All beloved of earth, register the time you are in.
Beloved, as the Angels have flown in their Being amongst you,
    so has Negativity in its being found itself amongst you.
Since humankind, man has ever battled and teared
    and striven with the urge to negativity,
    and humankind has valiantly entered and re entered in to battle.
In the beginning were Souls awaiting the entering in.
In the beginning were Souls, charged in the battle of righteousness,
    awaiting the opportunity to strike the foe.
And your earth time has continued, and the advancing armies
    have become scarred in their beings.
And there are Souls, many Souls, who have reached total humanity,
    and they await, and they watch and they cheer for righteousness.
Of those Souls, in your earth time now, are few who come anew
and yet there are many baby Souls,
baby Souls who have striven lifetime after lifetime,
to be advanced in Truth.
And yet the vines of negativity strangle their being.
Of the young Souls who newly enter,
    there are waves of receiving,
for they know the Gathering Time has begun
and they have agreed to teach earth.
Humanity, you have amazed all Farside Souls
    in the tenacity of your being.
Through all your ages you have not given into
    but have struggled to overcome negativity.
You have gathered Truth for all beings, in all forms of creation.
You are now in the whethering time.
It is what we of the Farside have spoken of,
    earth's whethering time;
    whether as to choose and whether,
    as earth's anger, earth's refusal to accept to her inners
    yet more negativity brought by man.
You must have vision, Souls, to see from where we are
    the accelerated earth you are in
    and the timetable of iniquities and the timetable of goodness.
"Verily I say unto you, of such is the Kingdom of Heaven".
Beloved, you are treasured more than the pearl,

>   more than the luminescent gems,
>   for the gem that you are is as Creator
>   and the form you have taken has a form in Farside.
> Treasure, my beloved Souls, the whethering time, for it is earth's victory.
> But know acceleration, vibration will gather quickly to positive.
> Whosoever comes to the space of negativity,
>   may he see clearly the inveigling strands
>   and step far from the place of those strands,
>   and gently, in all Truth, send to this energy of creation
>   the positives of vibration.

553 Earth will not hear!
Earth, the time to gather pain is done.
It is now the time to gather Purity.
The purpose of the knowledge we have given you is singular
so that when earth is of the Gathering Time,
the Souls who will be elevated will be many.
Souls, vibrate your beings, vibrate with the intensity of Purity.
Truth is the purpose of man.
Purity is available unto the Soul.
We plead with earth to renounce all negativity,
for in the great spiral that will come,
many Souls will be lost needlessly.
There is no joy in the Farside in beholding pain of earth.
There is no purpose, except the redeeming of the Holy Holy Holy.
All humanity will be redeemed and rise in a single effort.
But, Souls, you are human.
Your bodies acknowledge pain, your mind acknowledges pain,
    the flesh and blood behold pain.
Souls, how many times will you speak to a child:
    "Do not touch the fire!"
Could it help you to see your child scarred by the fire?
Will it give your heart solace to repeat again:
    "Do not touch the fire!"
The earth is agitated.
The framework of earth is stressed and in the great swirl of waters,
    in the pounding of buildings, in the separations of earth,

is needless pain, for the time has come and gone
and Purity will lift your Soul.
Time has not the space.
It is the scars upon your being.
You are laden with scars.
You have confronted your Soul many times,
and earth is the result of those scars.
Why do we say so?
That you may hear, that you may lose your blindness,
and reach out unto all man
and speak of the pain that will come,
and speak of the Purity that will gather.
The Soul would rather not see pain.
It knows the result of pain.
It knows the agonies of pain,
and so the spirit of the Soul is brought down,
but rejoices in the knowing.
Rejoice that you have the knowledge;
and verification will come to your great dismay.

554 Blessings!
Earth, we are grieving.
Souls, behold the agonies within thousands of Souls
held beneath the clay of earth.
Souls, behold, they have the care of beings wrapped around them,
but we grieve, for earth does not hear.
Oh earth, hear the sounds of pain.
Hear the humanity and turn thy eye to the pain,
and express thy energies to withhold the pain,
and know the power of thy very being
to withstand great negative forces.
Soul, allow your Energy to filter into the crevices of darkness.
Allow your energies to flow in great Love unto thy fellow humanity.
Behold, how great are they who placed their being willingly
to such pain in order to draw forth the Blessed unto Creator.
Your earth has turned time and again,
and still the turn will come where Souls are met in Energy
to send forth that Energy to relieve suffering.

This indeed is humanity, this is old Soul humanity.
Set aside that which you do and gather one unto the other,
and unite your energies to send forth healing
unto the land's inhabitants,
    and recognize each will have his day,
and the blind eye may be cast upon your being.
Souls, witness one to the other, of the goodness of humanity.

555 Soul, gaze beyond the perimeter of self.
Gaze outward through the centre eye.
Know self, know calm and serenity.
Be in a state of calm acceptance.
The earth is in a state of flux.
Be within the perimeter of acceptance.
The tale, the time, the teaching, all have purpose,
    all have a message beyond reality,
    all is taken into unreality.
Abound, for time is of the essence,
    time and the Gathering are one.
The vortex is the communion of old Souls brought together
    for high purpose.
Serenity is the key to the door.
Acceptance is the great pathway.
Soul, beauty is in the array of the garden.
Beauty is in the abundance of bloom and fragrance
    which carries one to a great sense of well being.
Garden is inadequate, garden is finite.
The blessing of garden of the Farside is infinity,
    is gentle magnificence and wild profusion, and majestic form,
    towering stalks, and incredibly winsome blooms.
Tend the garden of your Soul!
Look inward and say: "What, humanity, may I do for thee?"
All that is pure, all that is Truth, all that is Love,
    may find a home within the form of the human Soul,
    can the Soul absorb the Purity.
Time is a detainment, time offers excuse.
Know greatness is not in the high place,

    but the most profound cures for humanity
    are caught in the dusty weeds of earth.
Treasure all, look at all life form as magnificent.
Darkness has a time.
In darkness will come the voice of calm that will be heard
    by Souls who bring the soft knowing in a place of chaos.
The mantra, the meditation, the great booming voice,
    the gentle hand, all have greatness that is gathered,
    all have purpose.
The riot of colours will abound in forms that are tossed to and fro,
    and the visions of despair will need a voice of tranquillity.
Know the placement of hands, the blessing that abounds
    upon those who would receive.
All is not to fall.
Stand firm!
Stand calm and heal!

556 Souls, be in the space of great gentleness.
Souls, we will teach.
We invite you to Purity, we invite you to Holy.
Lift up your eyes beyond the space of self.
Endeavour, Soul, to embrace all that is, not all that is Purity,
    all that is pure and impure.
Embrace well and unwell, embrace whole and unwhole.
Embrace!
Soul, Energy is vibration, all creation is vibration,
    all infinity is vibration.
It is constantly moving.
There is no stillness.
Only is there stillness on earth
    where the Soul stops dead,
    where the Soul ceases to move.
This gives the Angels tears.
This opens the pearl drops that fall and are washed upon earth.
Souls, the Energy is not extra.
The Energy is, it is reaching to IS.
IS is Creator!

To behold creation in any form is to be embraced by Purity.
Negativity says: "Nay, do not enter, this is mine."
It has ownership, you see.
Soul, Love does not own, Love IS.
Love is the placement of care that you place.
Love is the outward glance at deformity,
 and the embracing of that deformity as part of self.
Outreach the arms and know IS and know vibration.
Soul, reach up and embrace the lights that you see.
Nothing is coincidental.
All has purpose, all has being.
You will be lifted up and welcomed there.
Peace, Soul, and you shall be brought into your Purity, into the vacuum.
Do you think it is by accident?
It is a practice run.
Do you think these beings come to search out your earth
 to find an abode?
Soul, they come as rescuers to save earth Souls
 at the time of great distress.
And you will be lifted
 and only those Souls who have the vibration can be lifted.
Oh, Soul, do not be lost in ego.
Do not think because of your comfort and your ease you will be lifted.
The Purity of those in the prison cell will be lifted.
The child in deformity will be lifted.
The great king, in Purity, will be lifted.
And many who do not carry the positive Energy
 will be left to another lesson.
The earth will remain as earth,
 the travail will cause the Angels to weep.
And all guides nudge earth Souls:
 "Awake! Awake! Awake!" they cry.
Hear the Soul of earth struggling to be at peace.
Energy.
Energy is real and felt.
Energy is pure.

557 Oh man, man, behold the question
    asked and re asked: "What, why, where, when?"
Behold BE!
To BE, to release from your Energy all that is earth,
    to dwell in a state of eye, not I.
The flame burns quickly and consumes that which it touches.
All that you see, in whichever horizon you look,
    will be blended into the waterways, except the mountaintops.
Yea, the disciples of earth are gathering at the mountaintops
    to reach into the depths of pain and bring forth the multitudes
    from the chasm.
Only those who have the curtain lifted
    will behold the writhing of these Souls.
The flames are not hell,
    they are pain, twisted and gnarled in eons of agony.
And Creator bows low to bring forth those in pain,
    but it cannot be.
The revealment that opens must be through the hallowed beings
    who have conquered the space of negativity.
He who created all, who is all powerful,
    yet cannot reach into the chasm.
Many have entered the chasm: Melchezidec, Holy Mother Mary,
the beloved of many lives have entered in,
but few have reached down to the depths of utter agony.
The path is clear unto Holy
and the purpose of humanity is to conquer all negativity
    within the chasm of greatest pain.
Behold the tortured Souls.
Behold the agonies, pulling from their being all that is of them,
    and only the wretchedness of their agony filters upward,
    and only are the beloved entering in.
Cry, cry, cry, cry: "Oh, Souls, behold, we have come.
    We are entered in and the flame will not sear our being
        for the flame is of your own.
    And we will cause you to be lifted and passed to thy Brethren
        who have waited for thy being."
Behold, the curtain must separate
    and the Souls must be ready for the torment beheld.

Souls of earth, beloved of Holy Holy Holy,
> the step is into the Realm of Creator.
Behold, do you see what is not spoken yet for earth,
> but will be revealed when mankind can open the eye at will?
The raiment upon thy being is Holy.

THE COMING OF PURITY
558 Reincarnation, Soul.
Reincarnation, creation!
Could there ever be an end to man
> if creation desires man ever to be ended?
Are there not legions of energies on the Farside waiting to enter in,
> good, strong and true Souls ready to fight Negativity!
Earth was created for the purpose of drawing the Blessed from their pain
> and the mighty, mighty, mighty army of Souls
> awaiting to do battle is endless, for creation is endless.
Souls of earth, fold thy hands about thy being
> and know the Blessedness that you will encounter,
> for the Angels' care is ever round about thee.
And know the great sob that comes from Creator
> to draw homeward the Energy of the Blessed Ones.
The awakening of these Souls will draw unto Creator, all glory.
The Diadem will be raised and placed upon humanity,
> and humanity will become the crown prince.
For humanity will have done what Farside
> has been unable to do without the avenue of humanity.
For the Blessed Ones hold themselves from Farside,
> they have placed a barrier.
It has no entry except through transition and only Souls,
> those utterly human, may enter in without peril to their being,
> cloaked in the Purity and Truth they have gathered.
Do not fear!
The blessed will come home and all creation awaits the celebration.
Many will come to the Gateway of Entering In;
> armadas from distant places, energies of many worlds,
> to prepare themselves to see once again

    the blessed emerge from their pain,
        the Holy beings brought forth unto Creator.
Humanity, know thy awesomeness, know thy wonder!
Do not see thyself as mere flesh and blood,
but know the Light of thy being, the purpose of thy being,
and form all thought to bring thy being unto its true end.

559 There is a Pathway and the Pathway leads to perfection,
        and the Pathway is available unto all earth beings.
The Pathway does not acknowledge long beards,
        for years do not extend the knowledge to the Pathway.
The Pathway is available to the humblest, the most wretched,
        the poorest of Souls.
It walks without identity of earth economics.
The Path is set with great markers.
These markers are levels of growth.
They allow the Soul to see the advancement into Purity.
They are clearly marked,
        for the hue into each level transforms the Energy.
The walk of Purity is not for all creation.
It is earth's alone.
All worlds do not enter in to the Pathway,
only humanity enters in time and again,
time and again drawing themselves desperately into the unseen.
At first, at first entry, they are as blind.
They have not met negativity.
They have been told of Negativity,
        they have been forewarned of Negativity.
But they have not entered in to the invasive pull that it has,
        they have not entered in to the enticement that it has,
        to the negative joy that it has.
Ah, everything is a mirror, you see!
From where you are, you have delusion and illusion,
        and the farther you walk along the path,
your being recognizes the delusion you are in,
        and you release it from your being,
and you see the reality of your existence.

And you can even look back behind at the baby Souls entering in
    and see them grappling with issues,
    how fear marauds their being,
    where enticement would gather them
    from the focus of their intent.
Soul, the Pathway to Creator is full of failed attempts,
    but it also has great achievements,
    and earth, as one, has entered in to the Pathway.
Humanity is set upon earth in the Pathway
    and you are the instrument
    by which Truth will reach unto Purity,
    and in finding the mirror, the joy of Love will move forward.
And all Love will be offered freely
    unto earth and earth's inhabitants by earth beings,
    beings who have moved up unto Purity,
    not as lords, not as ultimate beings, but as saviours.
As purposeful as you have come unto earth,
    so shall you draw all humanity in a tide ever upward
    unto perfection.
Souls of earth, hear not, see not, sense not,
    but know you are the seed of Almighty Creator.
And that seed is Love
    and Love is the ultimate purpose of your being;
    Agape, God Love, true Love.
It is the Pathway to the Angels,
It is the Pathway to the Saints,
It is the Pathway unto the second Entering In,
    and, earth, you shall so cause it to be.
Bless Humanity.

560 Army called mankind, armed with Truth,
    within the valley of great negativity, you have entered in.
You have drawn the shield before their being.
You have guarded many with your Truth.
Souls outnumbered have flanked thy being
    and the army of mankind is about to enter the final fray.
Souls of earth, magnify thy word unto Him.

"God, Allah, Almighty One, Creator,
    see that which we do, bless that which we do.
Arm us with the might of Love
that can be bestowed from Thy Being.
May the Holy Angels turn their face unto us
that they may bestow their Purity when the battle begins."
All humanity will become a part of this battle.
All humanity will be brought unto a higher being of self,
    and the words that spew forth will cease to be foul
    and will be cleansed.
And Souls who have not seen will see in the great mirror
    that the violent waters speak.
They will see the reflection of negativity in themselves,
    and they will be brought down deep into the waters of pain
    and they will arise cleansed,
    and the Blessed will attend their being.
The Angels who have ever watched over them,
will come with the pure of earth, downward,
and will lift the Souls and minister unto them
and value will cease to be negativity.
And negativity will find a region that is contained
    until that time when all the purities are entered in
    to that eden we all await.
Blessed mankind, you have seldom acknowledged
    the worth of thy being.
Thou hast seldom seen the Purity that thou art.
Soul, you have grappled with the negativity in your space
    as the mighty soldier that you are.
Humanity, how blessed art thou,
    for you have entered in to the vilest of states
and conquered thy being,
acknowledged thy negativity and overcome thy negativity.
Thou hast taken the innocent and slain the innocent,
    and thou hast undone all thy pain
    by acknowledging the Purity of thy being.
Thou hast overcome all thy dreadful deeds
    by acknowledging the Truth in thyself.

The higher being that is thine acknowledges the warrior that you are,
> the battle that you are in.
All Farside sees mankind on the battlefield.
Behold, the sun and the stars, the moon and the firmament,
all see that which thou hast done
and glory in the exhibition of Light that comes from humanity.
Souls, the Light of humanity will become as the noonday sun.
It will ride high and the stench of earth will be taken away,
and all the blessed who have endured pain
will be caught in arms of Love,
> and all will not tremble when they see before them
> the gateway of promise.
Unto earth is given the great battle,
> unto humanity is given the great honour, Truth.
Humanity in thy waking moments
> be thou aware of the garment that you wear,
> the Truth that you are in,
the abundant joy that thou hast come to give.
Souls of earth, thou art Holy, Holy is thy name.
Unto thee be all Love given.

561 All Truth is of earth, all Farside is of Purity.
There is, Soul, no deviance from this state.
The need for knowledge in Truth is not necessary on Farside,
> for all Farside is Truth.
The Souls of Farside have enlightenment to the place of their level
> and the Souls in that space have Purity.
Each Soul entering earth enters to find the Truth of humanity.
The finding of that Truth will bring them unto the Blessed Ones.
It is the purpose of all beings.
Earth, humanity, is being transformed.
It is being transformed by humanity.
It is not a positive transformation,
> and earth shudders at that which is put upon her,
and so it is the purpose of earth to cause a shuddering.
For only in the great shudder may earth rend apart,
> and all purities be lifted,

    all living purities be lifted,
        and all living purities be brought down once again unto earth.
The joy of that coming in on that day of preciousness!
Hallelujah! Hallelujah!
Earth will sing anthems of praise,
    for earth humanity will then see clearly
        the vision that they have held from their being,
and man will awake on that day to the Purity of his being,
and all earth will prepare their beings in righteousness
unto the fulfilment of the scriptures.
For Souls of earth will live in tranquillity and total humanity,
    and overcome all negativity.
And at the appointed time, the Four will open the eyes
    of those who are blessed and blest,
        and earth will enter in all humanity to the chasm.
And the eternal goodness will lift each Soul, each treasured Soul,
    from the abyss of great pain.
How blessed are you, humanity!
How pure is thy being that can enter in and lift the very Angels
    in their Purity and their pain unto the waiting hands of Angels.
"Behold, is my body not scarred like your body is scarred!
Am I not torn in my pain as you are torn in your pain!
Come, we can lift thee up to thy brother.
All has been prepared that thou wilt be washed clean.
The preparation for thy being has been long
    and thy beloved Creator awaits thy coming forth.
Beloved of thy Creator, do not hide in thy pain, the scars of thy being,
    but know that all will be washed away
    and all defilement will be taken from thy being,
    for thou art Holy and unto Holy wilt thou rise.
Arise, Holy one, be lifted into the arms of thy Creator,
    be lifted up into the wellness of thy being.
For songs are sung of thy holiness
    and never have the Angels forgotten thy being,
    never has Creator ceased to sob for the loss of His beloved.
Who would cover thy being?
All the heavens would cover thy being.

Come thou, blessed, and know the Love that thou hast given
 is returned unto thee.
Blessed form, be lifted up into the place of Purity."
"Hallowed be Thy name,
 Thy kingdom come,
 Thy will be done on earth as it is in heaven."

562 Souls, enter in to the place of hallowed ones.
Souls of earth, seek ye the path downward with intent of salvation,
 for salvation is not of self,
salvation is in the cathedral of sacred ones,
the Holy place, where all blessed Holiness is gathered.
And the pain of their Being brings them down to the depths of despair,
 for in the eternity of their being is the memory of perfection,
 is the adoration of Creator.
And in the dregs of their pain, they look upward and see the fallen Souls.
And even, Soul, in Love,
 they would draw the pain down onto their Being,
 but their being is overcome with pain
 and their garments are stained with the blood of many.
Humanity does not know what adornment covers their being,
 what sacred garment covers the body of their being.
And the blessed Souls in the cathedral of the damned have awareness.
They sleep not.
They have not folded into nothingness.
They are garbed in awareness of their pain
 and they see no path away from their pain.
They do not see the Holy walking unto them.
They do not know of earth's intent.
They have closed the hearing of their Being
 that they may not be tempted unto the place of Creator.
How blessed are they that they would hold themselves
 from the Purity of Creator!
Angels sing of their Purity, anthems are raised to Creator of their Purity
 and humanity has been named thus to redeem the Holy ones,
 to enter in to the cathedral of the damned.
How blessed art thou, humanity!

The anthems are sung and Melchezidec raises a mighty cathedral
    for all those who have conquered Negativity.
And those who have conquered await the day of the gathering,
    await the day with joy of the gathering.
Unfold thyself, do not close thy being,
    oh blessed earth man know that for which you have come.
Know the purpose of thy being and know the stench.
Hold thy nose, refrain from adding the putrid efforts of mankind,
    and reach to the fulfilling of your being.
Struggle not in thy energies, in the feebleness of thy being.
How awesome art thou!
How beloved art thou, for only in thy earthly form
    may you enter in to the cathedral
    and draw the blessed ones forth in that day.
Oh rapture, oh blessed flower of Light,
    how radiant is thy being, how treasured is thy breath.
Can you not see goodness?
Oh, Soul, do not tremble at the mote in thy being,
    for all will be overcome
    and the precious petals of the lotus will open,
    and the energies will filter upward unto Creator,
    and earth will open the way, and all will come after.
And Creator, Blessed Creator, will welcome his children home.

563 Glory, glory, glory Hallelujah!
Anthem of the Angels, anthem of the purities, enter in to glory.
Come, Soul, enter in to glory!
    "Where is the door to glory?
    Where is the transom over which I must step into glory?"
Soul, it is a gateway.
It is abundantly wide.
It has the width of your universe and beyond.
The galaxy you are in could enter through the gateway.
Hallelujah, hallelujah, blessed be the lives of saints
    who have conquered the pains of earth!
Hallelujah, hallelujah, Blessed Brethren
    who have gathered the Negativity
    from the worlds beyond beyond!

"Unto Creator doth my Soul Path reach.
Unto Creator doth my very being extend itself,
    gracious in giving unto humanity all that humanity has."
Earth is blest with the gift of your Creator.
See, Soul, the greatness, and be still in the presence of your Creator,
    for the very Angels bow their Beings in the presence of Creator.
The Saints who have reached all truths
    extend their beings outward to be blessed,
    and in receiving, extend the blessing outward from themselves.
Can you be less than the saints?
As you receive a blessing unto your being, extend it outward unto others,
    for it is that which is of your Creator, generosity to share.
Within your being, the Prism of whom you are is Creator.
The Light that may shine forth from your being is your Creator.
Soul, the earth cries for Light.
The earth is want for Light.
Do not hold yourself as critical, in denial, as crass and indifferent,
    but know the Pathway unto enlightenment is in action,
        not in absorbing knowledge, but in action.
It is the doing.
You have come in through the doorway and we welcome you in,
    and we reach out unto your being,
    and we embrace the goodness of your being.
But we embrace also, even more, that part of you that has woundedness.
We embrace the woundedness of your being,
    for we would have you know how to embrace the woundedness,
    how to light the Soul of Souls so deep in pain
        they cannot look beyond their pain.
And yet the very Light of your being
    may lift them from their murky world.
Do not spend time in the mud, for you will know you are off the Path.
But stand and reach for the Soul who is caught in the mud
and bring the Soul to higher ground,
and bless the opportunity that has been given to you.
Soul, you are not idly here upon the face of earth.
All about you is pain.
Know that joy, seen in the countenance of your being,
    will lift the Soul from the greatest of pain.

Know you have such joy to give, a countenance to show to another.
When you are wanting and in need and brought down,
>   know that the dove of peace is extended unto you,
and know that the Angels enfold themselves round about you
and lift you from the pain you are in.
Know that the very glory of the Angels will well into thy being
>   and enrich thy Soul.

564 Enter in to the River of Cleansing.
Know the River of Cleansing.
Souls of earth, the River of Cleansing is a Holy River.
It is not of earth, but man has symbolized such a River
>   because of the knowledge they have.
In the Void is such a River.
It holds the trembling Energy of Negativity.
It is absorbed into the Flow of the River of Cleansing,
>   and the Holy Holy Holy have brought forth
>   from worlds beyond worlds beyond worlds,
>   the trembling Energy of Negativity.
And the Souls have entered in to the River of Cleansing
and have brought themselves down
>   and lifted themselves up awashed and clean,
>   and the Negativity has fallen from their Being.
The Negativity was gathered in portions
>   that the Souls could advance to the River's edge
>   and enter in and be cleansed.
But some that you know gathered about their Being
>   the trembling Negativity and Souls cried out:
>   "Draw from us, too, that we might be free!
>   Draw forth from our being that we might be free!"
And the Holy Holy Holy, the Blessed Ones,
>   gathered and gathered and gathered,
>   and they moved unto the Cleansing River.
But the weight of Negativity would not let them move forward
>   and they saw that which they held about their Beings,
>   and all in unison formed a care about those beings they Loved,
>   and withheld themselves from that space for evermore.
The River of Cleansing is heavy with Negativity.

It has been gathered and gathered and gathered,
    and, Souls of earth, you, in your knowledge of that river,
have drawn yourselves into the river of cleansing
to wash the negativity from your being.
You would be garbed in Purity
    were you to recognize the true wash of your being.
Souls of earth have walked through water to cleanse,
have been brought down into water to be cleansed,
have been lifted up, empowered with Love.
Souls of earth, all earth will stand at the edge of the Cleansing River.
It is humanity's destiny to draw the blessed ones unto the river,
    that they might enter and be free of the containment of negativity.
They will cast their eyes unto Purity, for they will see humanity,
    they will know who you are.
They will call you by name, for all Souls have Farside name,
    but to the Farside you are beloved, one and all.
Souls of earth, you will draw the Holy Ones from their pain,
    and the Healing River will wash from their being, all pain.
And the Souls will rise up,
    and the radiance of their being will ignite the night sky,
    and all earth will know the hour of Entering In has come nigh.
And the doorway to Farside will be clear,
    and Souls will pass through and walk among men,
    and men will enter in to an altered state of being.
Holy Holy Holy!

565 Souls of earth, we rejoice to bring you
    to the knowledge of the Cleansing River.
Souls of earth, beyond the outer skirmishes of your Negative Void
    is a place all creation knows as the Cleansing River.
It is a place that idles Negativity.
It is a place that only Souls with total Love can enter in.
It is a place where sight is unnecessary.
It is a place where the eyes are not needed,
    where only the Holy being may enter in.
For the cover of Purity does not release itself to Truth,
    but to pure Love.

Only Love may enter in to the Cleansing River
    for in the Cleansing River are tethered the strands of Negativity.
Were this Negativity to be released into your space,
    your earth could not be, your existence could not be.
For have not the Holy Brethren gathered excess Negativity
    into the Cleansing River!
Oh, humanity, you will stand before the Cleansing River,
    you will see the writhings of Negativity,
    but your being will not be pierced by the arrow.
It wields the arrow for the blessed beings
    that have gathered strength unto themselves
    and the heavy load of pain will be met,
    and the Souls of pureness will hold the sight of negativity
from their brethren by gathering that which they can not carry,
    and together, in their Purity, they will enter in.
They will go forth many times upon the face of earth
    into the shards of your galaxy.
They will gather the strands of negativity
    and all that is kept in the space of transition
    will have been cleansed and renewed.
The Cleansing River is as silver, is iridescent in its flow,
    is carried as a great mire of sludge.
It is caught in the throat of beings, it is caught in the bones of beings,
It is caught in the mind of beings,
It has tentacles far reaching, this negativity.
But when it is entered in to the Cleansing River,
It holds to the silver that is there,
It grasps to the silver that is there.
Were your flesh and blood to enter in, you would be brought down.
Only the Holy can walk upon waters and enter in to the depth,
    and release the Negativity from their being.
So it shall be that humanity will gather
    at the shores of the Cleansing River
    and hallelujahs will be sung as the Holy Holy Holy
    enter in with the last of Negativity.
It will not be damaged, it will not be eradicated,
    it will merely be contained.

And all energies of all creation will manifest their being
    to the Purity of altering the energy that it is.
So be it.

566 Soul, behold the Cleansing River.
It is not dark, it is not dead, it is alive!
It is Energy and purpose.
You could find yourself entered in to the Cleansing River
    and all the Negativity therein would not harm your being.
You could immerse yourself in the deepest
    and you would not lose yourself.
You would find yourselves renewed, washed clean,
    for Truth washes clean, Truth understands.
Truth visits all knowledge with openness and welcomes the adverse.
The Cleansing River is but a Quar away.
All earth, all Farside will envision the Cleansing River.
All Love is bestowed unto the Cleansing River,
    and Creator awaits the drawing forth of the Blessed,
    for they have gathered a portion of inertness in their being.
And, humanity, you have chosen to carry the Blessed,
    and in your strength, the strength of Truth, you will be armed,
    and in the arming will be the ability to hold from you
    that which is negative.
When Brethren meet Brethren there will be much rejoicing,
and there will be a lifting up of Souls,
and there will be a passage unto the Blessed River,
and all who have entered in
    will find themselves before the Blessed River,
    and all will enter in to be washed clean.
Holy Holy Holy, you have given unto Godhead
    that which has been lost,
    and from Creator will come the message:
    "Well done, thou good and faithful servant!"

567 Come forward, Souls.
Draw thyself into the Spirit of thy being
    and allow the mind to see what the Soul sees so easily,
    Souls of earth, flesh, blood, mind and heart.

Recognize the vision of thy true form.
Know the Purity of gathering in Love unto thy fellow humanity,
>   for the gathering of Love is the armada
>   that has been placed on earth.
Your being has a destination to face a great battle,
>   to enter in to a great sorrow where pain and anger
>   is shunned by earth, despised by knowing.
The cavernous energies within would draw you
>   to partake of their pain.
Negativity will entice you and offer power.
Negativity will mesmerize and captivate all your intentions,
>   and, Souls of earth, the last great battle will find you
>   armed with a great shield.
The shield will be the scars of your being.
The shield will be immeshed with the great pains you have overcome.
The scars will arm you against each dart
>   that will be flung at your being,
>   and negativity will have to stay itself,
>   and the blessed will see the shield you hold forth.
They will recognize the scars you have encountered.
They will see rejoicing upon your countenance,
>   and they will be awakened unto the Truth
>   that they, too, may unencumber themselves
>   from the shackles that have held them so long.
And the blessed ones will lift their gaze upward unto their fellows,
>   and the Angels will rejoice
>   and send anthems of welcoming unto their brethren.
And humanity's arm will encircle the burdened blessed
>   and carry them forth unto the Holy,
>   and the Holy will reside their being
>   within the humanities of earth.
And the Angels of the Almighty Creator will enter in to earth's sphere
>   and minister unto their Brethren
>   that all impurities might be cast from them,
>   that their garment will once again be unstained by Negativity.
It will be long and arduous and the battle will be fought again and again.
For one thousand years will the Souls rise to the cleansing of earth
>   and humanity will have set aside all negativity,

and will be at one with the Angels,
> working to wash the impurities from the Blessed.

And the Holy Four will be as portals,
> and teach the purities that humanity will require
> when all earth is imploded into Farside.

Negativity will have no power.
It will be sent into the hinterland and left to wither,
> for Negativity, without continuous vibration, has no power.

Rejoice, Souls, in the power you have.

568 Beloved of your Creator, blessed, blessed, blessed!
All Love of all beings, of all planetary systems in all galaxies,
> do not touch the Love the Creator has for you.

Soul, Creator is, was and ever shall be magnificent in Oneness,
> offering to no man any one thing,
> offering to man all IS,
> to be in the place of total Purity,
> overflowing with Love toward all, inclusive of Negativity.

It is the boundless Energy that draws, as your earth magnet,
> all goodness.

Upon your plane, your mind is not prepared to hear
> that which our spaceless, timeless Energy knows.

We would give freely to your being, but your growth would cease.
"Our Father which art in heaven,
Hallowed be Thy name,
Thy kingdom come,
Thy will be done on earth as it is in heaven."
Father, fathers Love their children in holiness.
The Father of all children gathers unto Himself
> all tears and pain, all agonies.

Would that all Souls could come.
It is in the day of tomorrow that our Blessed Creator
will open the last page and the book will reveal to man,
> the steps into the depths of despair.

For you, Soul, are that which is able to enter therein
> and draw forth all that will bless
> and be reflected once again to the Energy of Creator,
> Creator of your being.

No man has greater Love!
Then all men will know of the scope of creation
    and Creator and creators.

569 Humanity, beings in the lesson of Truth,
    from our vantage point of Farside,
    from the knowledge of our Purity,
    we have seen the energies flow.
We, of the Farside, witnessed the Flow of that which you are.
It is, Soul, an Energy field that has identity.
The identity is that of our mutual Creator.
All worlds in our known are Creator's world,
    and we who have been at the Hem of Creator,
    who have seen the great Love bestowed unto humanity
    within the Flow that you are, are brought to the knowledge
    that from the existence of the gift that you give,
    will come a new Time.
Our state of timeless Energy is not accountable unto any Soul.
Our state of being has been relinquished from the negativity you know.
We hold in the language of our beings,
    all the creations within your earth.
Worlds upon worlds are there, and many hold a single identity
    that has been a reflection upon your earth.
There are reptilian worlds.
There are precious insect worlds.
There are worlds of great aliens of such Purity
    your beings would fail to see.
All these worlds have been formed in a mirror upon your earth.
All these worlds have given themselves to one aim, to assist humanity.
You are the treasured beyond treasures.
You will rise without defilement above the ashes of your being.
You will rise to take us, Farside, unto a Pathway
    that enters unto Godhead.
This we now know and our beings are not held in ransom.
There is a welcoming of our beings to the effort that earth is within.
There is no despair, no thought of loss,
    only the knowledge that Creator, our Creator,

the Creator of our being, has extended the opportunity
to meet the ultimate vision of Energy.
We await the completion of all that is upon earth.
We await the coming forth of our higher brethren.
We rejoice in the knowledge that, humanity, you will enter first,
because in accolade to your beings, we recognize
your holiness has gained purities in advance to our own.
Souls of earth, be ye unafraid.
Be ye in the state of quiet calm,
for unto earth is the aperture expanding,
that the vision will create a new sound,
and that which has been heard will be heard in a new way.
Souls of earth, we bow not unto thee, but unto the gift thou hast given.
We bow unto the certainty
that all energies have a purpose to be One Energy.
And the completion of existence
that has been touched by the singleness of negativity,
must be entered in to the containment of all Negativity,
of all Truth, of all Love.
Unto Godhead thou wilt come,
unto the Energy wilt Creator see thy being be entered in.

570 Behold, the gathering place of Souls of earth is fifth level,
where Souls unite to release from their being
the unnecessary traits lingering from past lives.
Souls entering sixth level have entered a further Purity.
They have before them the view of all creation unto thy Creator.
And thy Creator endows the vision
because of the Purity that has been gathered,
the Wisdom that is akin to Creator's Energy.
And Creator welcomes thy being
and charges thee with an offering of Love.
Soul, Love streameth unto thee,
Love in never ending form enters thy being.
Only thy negativity can keep this Love from thy being,
but at level five the earth has let go of all shackles
and the Love of Creator is cloaked about thy being

and thou art at one with the Angels,
and the Angels behold thy countenance as their own.
And, Soul, the look is yet forward unto the Being of Creator
who endows all unto thee,
even to partake of the cup which is Energy,
even from the seed thou has been welcomed
unto the cup of Energy.
It has never been left from thy mouth.
But the Soul at level six has the fullness of the cup of Energy
and creating becomes a part of thy being.
And the Soul is gathered unto the nuances of Creator
and all perfection is seen and gathered,
and the garden is full and plenty is there to be had.
And the Souls give back in worship unto Creator,
for the Wisdom they have gathered endows them
with the knowledge of all that has been and all that will be,
and the tears and the sadness of Angels is understood
and the Gathering Time becomes.
And the Souls of Purity gather themselves from all worlds
and arm themselves with a level of their own Purity
and enter once again into earth Time
to gather unto them the marked Souls,
the Souls who have not been redeemed.
And the Angels lift their voice in hallelujahs:
"Glory be to God that has given this time to be,
for our brothers were brought low and are now saved unto us."
And all energies of all worlds are gathered unto the galaxy of earth
and the redemption of the Blessed Ones are drawn.
And Souls of earth look up to see the Pillar of Angels
reaching as one unto the heavens,
and earth Souls are given vision, in their Purity,
of the Fallen Angels.
And the tongue they speak is given to the earth Souls
and they enter in to the space of pain.
And humanity beholds the Purity that has entered in,
and the glow of Purity is seen from four corners of the earth,
and the four corners of earth are gathered.

Hallelujah

The Sacred Four who stand as the pillars' foothold
    unto the heavens and the sacred ones,
    gaze down at mankind.
And their bounty offers:
    "Well done, thou good and faithful servant
        that has learned to look out from thy being
        unto the needs of all earth and beyond
        and has found the Purity that will redeem the Angels lost.
    Blessed humanity, thou wilt be lifted up as one
        unto the sacred sixth."
And when earth has passed the Time of humanity, and it will,
    and humanity will have raised in Purity, the blessed Souls
    unto the Being of Angels, and they will,
    all purities will seek a new passageway beyond Creator.
And Creator will welcome and gather Souls
    unto the Gateway of man's Second Entering,
    and Souls will behold that which is new unto them.
Not humanity alone, for humanity will have learned
    to live with all energies in all worlds,
    and they will enter through the Gateway
    of Creator beyond Creator.
Lift up thine eyes and behold that which is to be seen,
    for unto thee is given auld beauty in the Ecstasy of its being.
And Souls will be brought to the lambing time,
    and hold the newborn, and place it gently down.
And know the lion will not come forth from its lair to place harm,
    for the lion has only the need to be.
And man will encounter a new placement of being,
    a new robe will cover the countenance of man.
And the volumes of man will be as a time that is long past
    and Souls will say: "What is this world?
    Who are these heroes who have gathered for us
        this place of Purity?
    Creator, may we enter in to Thy Second Gateway?
    May the Angels, brought forth, show us the Path unto Purity.
    May no step falter in the passing through."
There are unknowns ahead.
They will need guidance.

The world beyond does not carry negativity,
    but pitfalls are not always negativity.
They are growth, they are learning,
    they are baby footsteps learning to walk.
And so it will be in that day when all enter through,
    as in Noah's day, unto the ark.
Beings will enter in and bow their head in sacredness
    and other beings will leap forth from their world
    and charge with the Energy of knowing,
    and some will want to gather all.
And a new challenge will come upon creation,
    the challenge of wisdom that is sacred,
    that must always be kept sacred.
And yet the carrying forth of wisdom needs cloaking and a covering,
    and who will be able to understand the mystery of the cloaking?
It will be in the land.

GLOSSARY

accept - to withhold all judgement.

Agape - Creator Love.

agreement - contract for Soul growth with other energies.

Akashic Record - the map of creation's growth.

alien - Souls from other worlds beyond earth.

aperture - Quar entrance in to Farside.

Angel (capitalized) - Angels who are in the dwelling place of Creator.

aura (uncapitalized) - three levels of humanity's aura on earth.

Aura (capitalized) - four upper levels of Humanity's Aura on the Farside.

battle - the effort to draw the Energy of Negativity into the oneness of all energies.

BE - state of acceptance.

Blessed Ones (capitalized) - Angels.

Brethren (capitalized) - Angels.

Circle of Saints - energies of many purities

Cleansing River - fragment of Wisdom sent forth to contain Negativity.

Creator Triad - Creator, Godhead, Great One.

Crystal Cave - illuminated Light of all energies.

Energy (capitalized) - Creator's Energy Flow.

Essence (capitalized) - the part of the triad of Soul, Spirit and Essence which never leaves the Path of Creator.

evil - the ultimate choice of humanity's negativity.

eye - third eye, aperture unto the high mind.

Eye of Beholding (capitalized) - Path to the Spirit self.

eye of knowing - entering in to high consciousness.

Farside - that which earth calls heavens, and more.

Flow - Creator's Path.

fold - avenues of all Energy purpose within the Flow.

fragment - part of a triad.

funnel - the forward swirl to Purity.

Galatia - alien world.

Gateway One, Two, Three (capitalized) - the Entering In unto the highest levels of Purity, of Love, of Ecstasy.

Gathering Time (capitalized) - Thousand Years of Purity.

guides - earth protectors, Souls who have left earth and nudge their fellow humanities.

Gummeria - one of four alien nations entered in to assist mankind.

Holy unto Holy - manifested Souls.

ion - state of being.

IS (capitalized) - Energy of Creator.

Jinn - one of four alien nations entered in to assist mankind.

karma - an action, positive or negative, that alters the agreement.

Keys (capitalized) - <u>Creator Trilogy</u> is the first of seven Keys.

Lantelia - alien world.

Lantosia - one of four alien nations entered in to assist mankind.

Lemuria - alien world.

Michael - entity name used by earth for one thousand and five Souls teaching earth.

Naught - space of Void.

nudge - prompt from your guides or the Angels.

Path (capitalized) - Creator's Path.

Pleiadia - alien world.

Prism (capitalized) - is the fullness of Aura, the completeness unto manifestation.

purple - healing Energy colour.

Quar - implosion.

transition - a self-inflicted, voluntary state of purgatory of one's own unaccepted actions upon earth.

transitional care - a curtain of Purity placed by Angels to prevent Negativity from entering in.

triad - a web of being, a network.

Wilful Child - the reflection of the Energy of Negativity.

Wisdom (capitalized) - the ultimate of Truth.

Writing on the Wall - the agreement of the Spirit for the Soul's walk on earth.

Zero (capitalized) - Naught.

APPENDIX A

equation of T

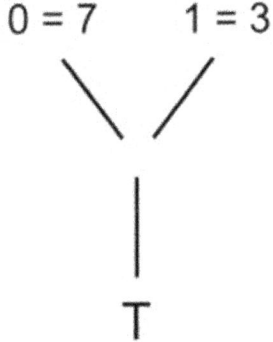

T = Time

1 = Singleness
3 = Triad
7 = Planes/levels/dimensions
0 = Naught/Void
and the centre is Quar = Implosion

APPENDIX B

Daily East Ritual

East, it is the passageway to the Farside through the eye.
Its Truth is to be understood as a Love by humanity.
Focus on east at dawn, allowing the negativity to flow from your being,
    receiving unto yourself the goodness of Creator.
All humanity has the availability of this pathway.
The ritual of the east is the Soul's own response
    to the positive east which is tao.
Face east, two minutes.
Look with the eyes to the horizon's level.
In the brick wall or the iron cage, or the ornate boardwalk,
    know that the east will be with your Soul.
Turn clockwise once to heal.
Energy will flow to the matter before it.
All organs of the body are healed in the circle turn.

APPENDIX C

Forthcoming Publications

Creator Trilogy
First Key
Creator Trilogy, Trilogy of Consciousness, <u>The Gathering Time</u>, Part I
Creator Trilogy, Supreme Being Trilogy, <u>How to step to the Path</u>, Part I

Second Key
Creator Trilogy, Trilogy of Consciousness, <u>From Whence It Came</u>, Part II
Creator Trilogy, Supreme Being Trilogy, <u>The Angel's Ecstasy</u>, Part II

Third Key
Creator Trilogy, Trilogy of Consciousness, <u>Ecstasy</u> Part III
Creator Trilogy, Supreme Being Trilogy, <u>The Rejoicing</u>, Part III

Until Then

Souls of earth, humanity, Farside impels the Souls of earth
to redirect their force of Energy.
We gaze longingly at the army of earth.
It is time for the battle to cease.
It is time for the wars to end.
The scars are deep and visible and now, humanity,
you have learned much.
All that you despise, all that has pained your being,
all great beards, heed the lesson.
Know the time to set the clock to stop is now.
Do not enter in one nation to his brother and ask for peace.
Ask for peace within your very nation.
Turn your eyes to thyself.
Speak to thy fellow countrymen and uphold all that is good.
Cease to find fault with thy neighbour
and seek to find goodness in thy being.
Offer to any who ask that which you can spare.

www.ingramcontent.com/pod-product-compliance
Lightning Source LLC
Chambersburg PA
CBHW081828170426
43199CB00017B/2673